*Second Edition*

*Pocket Guide to*

# DIAGNOSTIC

# TESTS

**Diana Nicoll, MD, PhD**
Clinical Professor and Vice Chair
Department of Laboratory Medicine
University of California, San Francisco
Associate Dean
University of California, San Francisco
Chief of Staff and Chief, Laboratory Medicine Service
Veterans Affairs Medical Center, San Francisco

**Stephen J. McPhee, MD**
Professor of Medicine
Division of General Internal Medicine
University of California, San Francisco

**Tony M. Chou, MD**
Assistant Professor of Medicine
University of California, San Francisco
Associate Director
Adult Cardiac Catheterization Laboratories
Moffitt Hospital, San Francisco

**William M. Detmer, MD, MS**
Assistant Clinical Professor of Medicine
University of California, San Francisco

With Associate Authors

APPLETON & LANGE
Stamford, Connecticut

Copyright © 1997 by Appleton & Lange, © 1992 by Appleton & Lange
A Simon & Schuster Company

98 99 00 01 / 10 9 8 7 6 5 4 3

Prentice Hall International (UK) Limited, *London*
Prentice Hall of Australia Pty. Limited, *Sydney*
Prentice Hall Canada, Inc., *Toronto*
Prentice Hall Hispanoamericana, S.A., *Mexico*
Prentice Hall of India Private Limited, *New Delhi*
Prentice Hall of Japan, Inc., *Tokyo*
Simon & Schuster Asia Pte. Ltd., *Singapore*
Editora Prentice Hall do Brasil Ltda., *Rio de Janeiro*
Prentice Hall, *Upper Saddle River, New Jersey*

ISSN: 1061-3463

ISBN 0-8385-8100-5

90000

9 780838 581001

Acquisitions Editor: Shelley Reinhardt
Production Editor: Chris Langan
Designer: Mary Skudlarek
Senior Art Manager: Eve Siegel

PRINTED IN THE UNITED STATES OF AMERICA

# Table of Contents

# Associate Authors

**Dan Berrios, MD, MPH**
Postdoctoral Fellow
Section of Medical Informatics
Stanford University School of Medicine
Stanford, California
*Common Laboratory Tests: Selection and Interpretation*

**G. Thomas Evans, Jr., MD**
Assistant Clinical Professor of Medicine
University of California, San Francisco
Director of Electrocardiography
Moffit–Long Hospitals, San Francisco
*Basic Electrocardiography*

**Stuart J. Hutchison, MD**
Clinical Instructor
Division of Cardiology
Department of Medicine
University of California, San Francisco
*Basic Electrocardiography*

**Lynn Pulliam, PhD**
Associate Professor of Laboratory Medicine
University of California, San Francisco
Chief, Microbiology Section
Laboratory Medicine Service
Veterans Affairs Medical Center, San Francisco
*Microbiology: Test Selection*

**Susan D. Wall, MD**
Professor of Radiology
University of California, San Francisco
Veterans Affairs Medical Center, San Francisco
*Diagnostic Imaging: Test Selection and Interpretation*

# *Preface*

## Purpose

This book is intended to serve as a pocket reference manual for medical and other health professional students, house officers, and practicing physicians. It is a quick reference guide to the selection and interpretation of commonly used diagnostic tests, including laboratory procedures in the clinical setting, laboratory tests (chemistry, hematology, and immunology), microbiology tests (bacteriology, virology, and serology), diagnostic imaging tests (plain radiography, CT, MRI, and ultrasonography), and electrocardiography.

This book will enable readers to understand commonly used diagnostic tests and diagnostic approaches to common disease states.

## Outstanding Features

- Over 350 tests are presented in a concise, consistent, and readable format.
- Fields covered include internal medicine, pediatrics, general surgery, neurology, and gynecology.
- Costs and risks of various procedures and tests are emphasized.
- Literature references are included for most diagnostic tests.
- An index for quick reference is included on the back cover.

## Organization

This pocket reference manual is not intended to include all diagnostic tests or disease states. Rather, the authors have selected those tests and diseases that are most common and relevant to the general practice of medicine.

The *Guide* is divided into 8 sections:

1. Basic Principles of Diagnostic Test Use and Interpretation
2. Laboratory Procedures in the Clinical Setting
3. Common Laboratory Tests: Selection and Interpretation
4. Therapeutic Drug Monitoring: Principles and Test Interpretation
5. Microbiology: Test Selection
6. Diagnostic Imaging: Test Selection and Interpretation
7. Basic Electrocardiography
8. Diagnostic Testing: Algorithms, Nomograms, and Tables

## Intended Audience

In this era of rapidly changing medical technology, many new diagnostic tests are being introduced every year and are replacing older tests as they are shown to be more sensitive, specific, or cost-effective. In this environment, students, house officers, and practicing physicians are looking for a pocket reference on diagnostic tests.

Medical students will find the concise summary of diagnostic laboratory, microbiologic, and imaging studies, and of electrocardiography in this pocket-sized book of great help during clinical ward rotations.

Busy house officers will find the clear organization and citations to the current literature useful in devising proper patient management.

Practitioners (internists, family physicians, pediatricians, surgeons, and other specialists who provide generalist care) may use the *Guide* as a refresher manual to update their understanding of laboratory tests and diagnostic approaches.

Nurses and other health practitioners will find the format and scope of the *Guide* valuable for understanding the use of laboratory tests in patient management.

Portions of this book can now be found on the Internet at the following address: http://dgim--www.ucsf.edu/TestSearch.html. In 1997, the contents of this book will be integrated with the contents of *Pocket Guide to Commonly Prescribed Drugs*, 2nd ed. by Glenn N. Levine, MD in a new CD-ROM, *Current Medical Diagnosis & Treatment 1997 CD-ROM.*

## Acknowledgments

We wish to thank our associate authors, Dan Berrios, MD, MPH, G. Thomas Evans, Jr., MD, Stuart J. Hutchison, MD, Lynn Pulliam, PhD, and Susan D. Wall, MD for their contributions to this book. In addition, we are grateful to the many physicians, residents, and students who contributed useful suggestions and to Jim Ransom for his careful editing of the manuscript.

We welcome comments and recommendations from our readers for future editions.

Diana Nicoll, MD, PhD
Stephen J. McPhee, MD
Tony M. Chou, MD
William M. Detmer, MD

San Francisco
September 1996

# 1

# Basic Principles of Diagnostic Test Use and Interpretation*

*Diana Nicoll, MD, PhD, and William M. Detmer, MD*

The clinician's main task is to make reasoned decisions about patient care despite imperfect clinical information and uncertainty about clinical outcomes. While data elicited from the history and physical examination are often sufficient for making a diagnosis or as a guide to therapy, more information may be required. In these situations, clinicians often turn to diagnostic tests for help.

## 1. BENEFITS; COSTS AND RISKS

When used appropriately, diagnostic tests can be of great assistance to the clinician. Tests can be helpful for **screening,** ie, to identify risk factors for disease and to detect occult disease in asymptomatic persons. Identification of risk factors may allow early intervention to prevent disease occurrence, and early detection of occult disease may reduce disease morbidity and mortality through early treatment. Optimal screening tests meet the criteria listed in Table 1–1.

Tests can also be helpful for **diagnosis,** ie, to help establish or exclude the presence of disease in symptomatic persons. Some tests assist in early diagnosis after onset of symptoms and signs; others assist in differential diagnosis of various possible diseases. Still others help determine the stage or activity of disease.

Finally, tests can be helpful in **patient management.** Tests can help to: (1) evaluate the severity of disease, (2) estimate prognosis, (3) monitor the course of disease (progression, stability, or resolution), (4) detect disease recurrence, (5) select drugs and adjust dosages, and (6) select and adjust therapy.

*Chapter modified, with permission, from Tierney LM Jr, McPhee SJ, Papadakis MA (editors): *Current Medical Diagnosis & Treatment 1997.* Appleton & Lange, 1997.

**TABLE 1–1. CRITERIA FOR USE OF SCREENING PROCEDURES.**

Characteristics of population
1. Sufficiently high prevalence of disease.
2. Likely to be compliant with subsequent tests and treatments.

Characteristics of disease
1. Significant morbidity and mortality.
2. Effective and acceptable treatment available.
3. Presymptomatic period detectable.
4. Improved outcome from early treatment.

Characteristics of test
1. Good sensitivity and specificity.
2. Low cost and risk.
3. Confirmatory test available and practical.

Diagnostic tests are not without disadvantages, however. First, diagnostic tests can be expensive. An individual test such as MRI of the head can cost more than $1400.00. Diagnostic tests as a whole account for approximately one-fifth of health-care expenditures in the USA. Second, some tests carry a risk of morbidity or mortality. For instance, intravenous contrast material used in some CT scans leads to death from anaphylaxis in approximately one in 30,000 examinations. Third, some diagnostic tests cause discomfort to patients. The discomfort from tests such as sigmoidoscopy or barium enema, for example, will deter some patients from completing a diagnostic workup. Fourth, the result of a diagnostic test often has implications for further care in that a test result may mandate further testing or frequent follow-up. For instance, a patient with a falsely positive fecal occult blood test may incur significant cost, risk, and discomfort during follow-up sigmoidoscopy, barium enema, or colonoscopy. Last, classifying a healthy patient as diseased based on a falsely positive diagnostic test can cause psychologic distress and may lead to risks from unnecessary therapy.

Therefore, when ordering diagnostic tests, clinicians should weigh these potential costs and disadvantages against the potential benefits.

## 2. PREPARATION FOR DIAGNOSTIC TESTS

Factors affecting both the patient and the specimen are important.

### Patient Preparation

The preparation of the patient is important for certain tests. For example, a fasting state is needed for optimal glucose and triglyceride measurements. Controlled conditions are frequently needed for endocrinology testing. For instance, posture and sodium intake must be strictly controlled when measuring renin and aldosterone levels. Strenuous exercise should be avoided before obtaining some tests such as creatine kinase, since vigorous muscle activity can lead to falsely abnormal results.

## Specimen Collection

Careful attention must be paid to patient identification and specimen labeling. Knowing when the specimen was collected may be important. For instance, aminoglycoside levels cannot be interpreted appropriately without knowing whether the specimen was drawn just before ("trough" level) or just after ("peak level") drug administration. Drug levels cannot be interpreted if they are drawn during the drug's distribution phase (eg, digoxin levels drawn during the first 6 hours after an oral dose). Substances that have a circadian variation (eg, cortisol) can be properly interpreted only with knowledge of the time of day the sample was drawn.

During specimen collection, other principles should be remembered. Specimens should not be drawn above an intravenous line, as this may contaminate the sample with intravenous fluid. Excessive tourniquet time will lead to hemoconcentration and increased concentration of protein-bound substances such as calcium. Lysis of cells during collection of a blood specimen will result in spuriously increased serum levels of substances concentrated in cells (eg, lactate dehydrogenase and potassium). Certain test specimens may require special handling or storage (eg, blood gas specimens). Delay in delivery of specimens to the laboratory can result in ongoing cellular metabolism and therefore spurious results for some studies (eg, low blood glucose).

## 3. TEST CHARACTERISTICS

Table 1–2 lists the characteristics of all useful diagnostic tests. Most of the principles detailed below can be applied not only to diagnostic tests but also to historical facts and physical examination findings.

## Accuracy

The accuracy of a laboratory test is its correspondence with the true value. An inaccurate test is one that differs from the true value even though the results may be reproducible (Figures 1–1A and 1–1B). In

**TABLE 1–2. PROPERTIES OF USEFUL DIAGNOSTIC TESTS.**

1. Test methodology has been described in detail so that it can be accurately and reliably reproduced.
2. Test accuracy and precision have been determined.
3. The reference range has been established appropriately.
4. Sensitivity and specificity have been reliably established by comparison with a gold standard. The evaluation has used a range of patients, including those who have different but commonly confused disorders and those with a spectrum of mild and severe, treated and untreated disease. The patient selection process has been adequately described so that results will not be generalized inappropriately.
5. Independent contribution to overall performance of a test panel has been confirmed if a test is advocated as part of a panel of tests.

the clinical laboratory, accuracy of tests is maximized by calibrating laboratory equipment with reference material and by participation in external quality control programs.

## Precision

Test precision is a measure of a test's reproducibility when repeated on the same sample. An imprecise test is one that yields widely varying results on repeated measurements (Figure 1–1B). The precision of diagnostic tests, which is monitored in clinical laboratories by using control material, must be good enough to distinguish clinically relevant changes in a patient's status from the analytic variability of the test. For instance, the manual white blood cell differential count is not precise enough to detect important changes in the distribution of cell

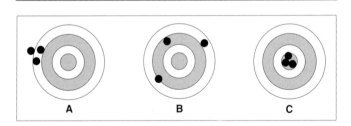

**Figure 1–1.** Relationship between accuracy and precision in diagnostic tests. The center of the target represents the true test result. Figure (**A**) represents a diagnostic test which is precise but inaccurate; on repeated measurement, the test yields very similar results, but all results are far from the true value. Figure (**B**) shows a test which is imprecise and inaccurate; repeated measurement yields widely different results, and the results are far from the true value. Figure (**C**) shows an ideal test, one that is both precise and accurate.

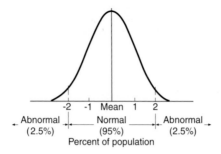

**Figure 1–2.** The reference range is usually defined as within 2 standard deviations (SD) of the mean test result (shown as –2 and 2) in a small population of healthy volunteers. Note that in this example, test results are normally distributed; however, many biologic substances will have distributions that are skewed.

___

types, because it is calculated by subjective evaluation of a small sample (100 cells). Repeated measurements by different technicians on the same sample result in widely different results. Automated differential counts are more precise because they are obtained from machines that use objective physical characteristics to differentiate a much larger sample (10,000 cells).

## Reference Range

Patient test results are interpreted by comparing them with published reference ranges. These ranges are method- and laboratory-specific. In practice, reference ranges often represent test results found in 95% of a small population presumed to be healthy; by definition, 5% of healthy patients will have a positive (abnormal) test (Figure 1–2). As a result, slightly abnormal results should be interpreted in a critical fashion: they may be either truly abnormal or falsely abnormal. The practitioner should be aware also that the more tests ordered, the greater the chance for obtaining a falsely abnormal result. For instance, a healthy person subjected to 20 independent tests has a 64% probability of having at least one abnormal test result (Table 1–3).

It is important to consider also whether published reference ranges are appropriate for the patient being evaluated, since some ranges depend on age, sex, weight, diet, time of day, activity status, or posture. For instance, the reference ranges for hemoglobin concentration are age- and sex-dependent.

**TABLE 1–3. RELATIONSHIP BETWEEN THE NUMBER OF TESTS AND THE PROBABILITY THAT A HEALTHY PERSON WILL HAVE ONE OR MORE ABNORMAL RESULTS.**

| Number of Tests | Probability That One or More Tests Will Be Abnormal |
|---|---|
| 1 | 5% |
| 6 | 26% |
| 12 | 46% |
| 20 | 64% |

## Interfering Factors

The results of diagnostic tests can be altered by external factors, such as ingestion of drugs; and internal factors, such as abnormal physiologic states. External interferences can affect test results in vivo or in vitro. In vivo, alcohol increases γ-glutamyl transpeptidase, and diuretics can affect sodium and potassium concentrations. Cigarette smoking can induce hepatic enzymes and thus reduce levels of substances such as theophylline that are metabolized by the liver. In vitro, cephalosporins may produce spurious serum creatinine levels due to interference with a common laboratory method of creatinine measurement. Internal interferences result when an abnormal physiologic state interferes with the measurement of a test. As an example, patients with gross lipemia may have spuriously low serum sodium levels if the test methodology used includes a step where serum is diluted before sodium is measured. Because of the potential for test interference, clinicians should be wary of unexpected test results and should investigate reasons other than disease that may explain abnormal results, including laboratory error.

## Sensitivity and Specificity

Clinicians should use measures of test performance such as sensitivity and specificity to judge the quality of a diagnostic test for a particular disease. Test **sensitivity** is the likelihood that a diseased patient has a positive test. If all patients with a given disease have a positive test (ie, no diseased patients have negative tests), then the test sensitivity is 100%. A test with high sensitivity is useful to exclude a diagnosis because a highly sensitive test will render few results that are falsely negative. To exclude infection with the AIDS virus, for instance, a clinician might choose a highly sensitive test such as the HIV antibody test.

A test's **specificity** is the likelihood that a healthy patient has a negative test. If all patients who do not have a given disease have negative tests (ie, no healthy patients have positive tests), then the test specificity is 100%. A test with high specificity is useful to confirm a diagnosis, because a highly specific test will have few results that are falsely positive. For instance, to make the diagnosis of gouty arthritis, a clinician might choose a highly specific test, such as the presence of negatively birefringent needle-shaped crystals within leukocytes on microscopic evaluation of joint fluid (Figure 2–7).

To determine test sensitivity and specificity for a particular disease, the test must be compared against a "gold standard," a procedure that defines the true disease state of the patient. For instance, the sensitivity and specificity of the ventilation/perfusion scan for pulmonary embolus is obtained by comparing the results of scans with the gold standard, pulmonary arteriography. However, for many disease states (eg, pancreatitis), such a gold standard either does not exist or is very difficult or expensive to perform. Therefore, reliable estimates of test sensitivity and specificity are sometimes difficult to obtain.

Test sensitivity and specificity depend on the reference range used, ie, the cutoff point above which a test is interpreted as abnormal (Figure 1–3). If the cutoff is modified, sensitivity will be enhanced at the expense of specificity or vice versa.

Sensitivity and specificity values can also be affected by the population from which these values are derived. For instance, many

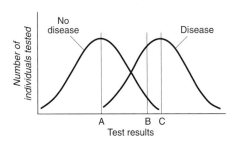

**Figure 1–3.** Hypothetical distribution of test results for healthy and diseased individuals. The position of the "cutoff point" between "normal" and "abnormal" (or "negative" and "positive") test results determines the test's sensitivity and specificity. If point (**A**) is the cutoff point, the test would have 100% sensitivity but low specificity. If point (**C**) is the cutoff point, the test would have 100% specificity but low sensitivity. For most tests, the cutoff point (point **B**) is determined by the reference range, ie, the range of test results that are within 2 SD of the mean (point (**B**)). In some situations, the cutoff is altered to enhance either sensitivity or specificity.

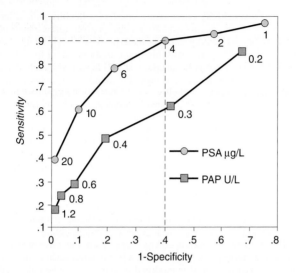

**Figure 1–4.** Receiver operator characteristic (ROC) curves for prostate-specific antigen (PSA) and prostatic acid phosphatase (PAP) in the diagnosis of prostate cancer. For all cutoff values, PSA has higher sensitivity and specificity; therefore, it is a better test based on these performance characteristics. (Modified and reproduced, with permission, from Nicoll D et al: Routine acid phosphatase testing for screening and monitoring prostate cancer no longer justified. Clin Chem 1993;39:2540.)

diagnostic tests are evaluated first using patients who have severe disease and control groups who are young and well. Compared with the general population, this study group will have more results that are truly positive (because patients have more advanced disease) and more results that are truly negative (because the control group is healthy). Thus, test sensitivity and specificity will be higher than would be expected in the general population, where more of a spectrum of health and disease is found. Clinicians should be aware of this **spectrum bias** when generalizing test results to their own practice.

The performance of two tests can be compared by plotting the sensitivity and (1 minus the specificity) of each test at various reference range cutoff values. The resulting receiver operator characteristic (ROC) curve will often show which test is better; a clearly superior test will have an ROC curve that always lies above and to the left of the inferior test curve. For instance, Figure 1–4 shows the ROC curves for prostate-specific antigen (PSA) and prostatic acid phosphatase

(PAP) in the diagnosis of prostate cancer. PSA is a superior test because it has higher sensitivity and specificity for all cutoff values.

## 4. USE OF TESTS IN DIAGNOSIS AND MANAGEMENT

The value of a test in a particular clinical situation depends not only on the test's sensitivity and specificity but also on the probability that the patient has the disease before the test result is known (**pretest probability**). The results of a valuable test will substantially change the probability that the patient has the disease (**posttest probability**). Figure 1–5 shows how sensitivity, specificity, and posttest probability can be calculated from test results on patients also evaluated using the gold standard by first filling in a $2 \times 2$ table using the definitions of true-positive, true-negative, false-positive, and false-negative tests.

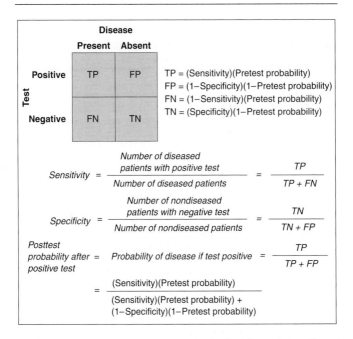

**Figure 1–5.** Calculation of sensitivity, specificity, and probability of disease after a positive test (posttest probability). (TP, true positive; FP, false positive; FN, false negative; TN, true negative.)

TABLE 1–4. INFLUENCE OF PRETEST PROBABILITY ON THE POSTTEST PROBABILITY OF DISEASE WHEN A TEST WITH 90% SENSITIVITY AND 90% SPECIFICITY IS USED.

| Pretest Probability | Posttest Probability |
|---|---|
| 0.01 | 0.08 |
| 0.50 | 0.90 |
| 0.99 | 0.999 |

The posttest probability can be calculated directly from the known sensitivity and specificity and the estimated pretest probability (or disease prevalence).

The pretest probability of disease has a profound effect on the posttest probability. As demonstrated in Table 1–4, when a test with 90% sensitivity and specificity is used, the posttest probability can vary from 1% to 99% depending on the pretest probability of disease. Furthermore, as the pretest probability of disease decreases, it becomes less likely that someone with a positive test actually has the disease and more likely that the result represents a false positive.

As an example, suppose the clinician wishes to calculate the posttest probability of prostate cancer using the PSA test with a cutoff of 4 ng/mL. Using the data shown in Figure 1–4, sensitivity is 90% and specificity 60%. The clinician estimates the pretest probability of disease given all evidence and then calculates the posttest probability using the approach shown in Figure 1–5. The pretest probability that an otherwise healthy 50-year-old man has prostate cancer is equal to the prevalence of prostate cancer in that age group (probability = 10%) and the posttest probability is only 20%—ie, even though the test is positive, there is still an 80% chance that the patient does not have prostate cancer (Figure 1–6A). If the clinician finds a prostate nodule on rectal examination, the pretest probability of prostate cancer is 50% and the posttest probability using the same test is 69% (Figure 1–6B). Finally, if the clinician estimates the pretest probability to be 98% based on a prostate nodule, bone pain, and lytic lesions on spine x-rays, the posttest probability using PSA is 99% (Figure 1–6C). This example illustrates that pretest probability has a profound effect on posttest probability and that tests provide more information when the diagnosis is truly uncertain (pretest probability about 50%) than when the diagnosis is either unlikely or nearly certain.

## 5. ODDS-LIKELIHOOD RATIOS

Another way to calculate the posttest probability of disease is to use the odds-likelihood approach. This method may be easier for clinicians to

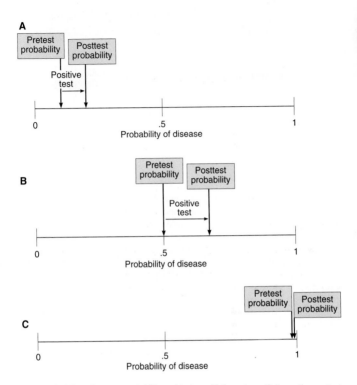

**Figure 1–6.** Effect of pretest probability and test sensitivity and specificity on the posttest probability of disease. (See text for explanation.)

use. Sensitivity and specificity are combined into an entity called the likelihood ratio (LR).

$$LR = \frac{\text{Probability of result in diseased persons}}{\text{Probability of result in nondiseased persons}}$$

Every test has two likelihood ratios, one corresponding to a positive test ($LR^+$) and one corresponding to a negative test ($LR^-$):

$$LR^+ = \frac{\text{Probability that test is positive in diseased persons}}{\text{Probability that test is positive in nondiseased persons}}$$

$$= \frac{\text{Sensitivity}}{1 - \text{specificity}}$$

$$LR^- = \frac{\text{Probability that test is negative in diseased persons}}{\text{Probability that test is negative in nondiseased persons}}$$

$$= \frac{1 - \text{sensitivity}}{\text{Specificity}}$$

Lists of likelihood ratios can be found in some textbooks, journal articles, and computer programs (see Table 1–5 for sample values). Likelihood ratios can be used to make quick estimates of the usefulness of a contemplated diagnostic test in a particular situation. The simplest method for calculating posttest probability from pretest probability and likelihood ratio is to use a nomogram (Figure 1–7). The clinician places a straightedge through the points that represent the pretest probability and the likelihood ratio and then notes where the straightedge crosses the posttest probability line.

A more formal way of calculating posttest probabilities uses the likelihood ratio as follows:

Pretest odds × Likelihood ratio = Posttest odds

To use this formulation, probabilities must be converted to odds, where the odds of having a disease are expressed as the chance of having the disease divided by the chance of not having the disease. For instance, a probability of 0.75 is the same as 3:1 odds (Figure 1–8).

To estimate the potential benefit of a diagnostic test, the clinician first estimates the pretest odds of disease given all available clinical information and then multiplies the pretest odds by the positive and negative likelihood ratios. The results are the **posttest odds,** or the odds that the patient has the disease if the test is positive or negative. To obtain the posttest probability, the odds are converted to a probability (Figure 1–8).

For example, if the clinician believes that the patient has a 60% chance of having a myocardial infarction (pretest odds of 3:2) and the

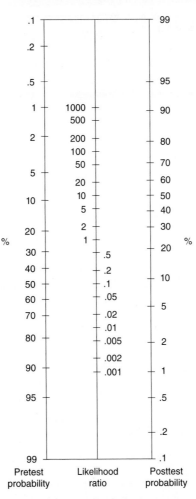

**Figure 1–7.** Nomogram for determining posttest probability from pretest probability and likelihood ratios. To figure the posttest probability, place a straightedge between the pretest probability and the likelihood ratio for the particular test. The posttest probability will be where the straightedge crosses the posttest probability line. (Adapted and reproduced, with permission, from Fagan TJ: Nomogram for Bayes's theorem. N Engl J Med 1975;293:257.)

**TABLE 1–5. LIKELIHOOD RATIOS FOR A SAMPLE OF DIAGNOSTIC TESTS.**

| Test | Disease | LR$^+$ | LR$^-$ |
|---|---|---|---|
| Carcinoembryonic antigen | Dukes A colon cancer | 1.6 | 0.87 |
| Creatine kinase MB | Myocardial infarction | 32 | 0.05 |
| Free thyroxine index | Hyperthyroidism | 6.8 | 0.06 |
| Ferritin | Iron deficiency anemia | 85 | 0.15 |
| Antinuclear antibody | SLE | 4.5 | 0.13 |

creatine kinase MB test is positive (LR$^+$ = 32), then the posttest odds of having a myocardial infarction are

$$\frac{3}{2} \times 32 = \frac{96}{2} \quad \text{or} \quad 48:1 \text{ odds} \left( \frac{48/1}{48/1+1} = \frac{48}{48+1} = 98\% \text{ probability} \right)$$

If the CKMB test is negative (LR$^-$ = 0.05), then the posttest odds of having a myocardial infarction are

$$\frac{3}{2} \times 0.05 = \frac{0.15}{2} \text{ odds} \left( \frac{0.15/2}{0.15/2+1} = \frac{0.15}{0.15+2} = 7\% \text{ probability} \right)$$

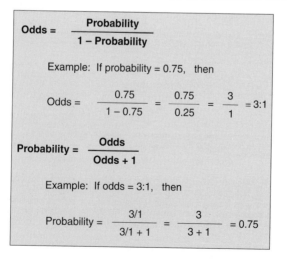

**Odds** = $\dfrac{\text{Probability}}{1 - \text{Probability}}$

Example: If probability = 0.75, then

$$\text{Odds} = \frac{0.75}{1 - 0.75} = \frac{0.75}{0.25} = \frac{3}{1} = 3:1$$

**Probability** = $\dfrac{\text{Odds}}{\text{Odds} + 1}$

Example: If odds = 3:1, then

$$\text{Probability} = \frac{3/1}{3/1+1} = \frac{3}{3+1} = 0.75$$

**Figure 1–8.** Formulas for converting between probability and odds.

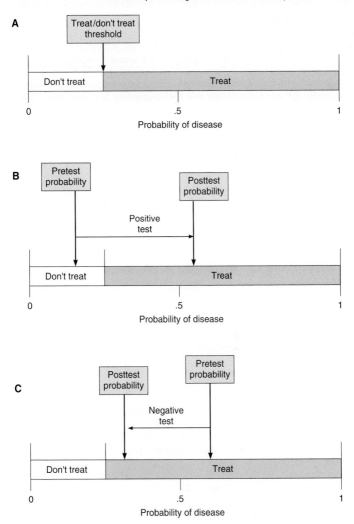

**Figure 1–9.** Threshold approach applied to test ordering. If the contemplated test will not change patient management, the test should not be ordered. (See text for explanation.)

## Sequential Testing

To this point, the impact of only one test on the probability of disease has been discussed, whereas during most diagnostic experiences, clinicians obtain clinical information in a sequential fashion. To calculate the posttest odds after three tests, for example, the clinician might estimate the pretest odds and use the appropriate likelihood ratio for each test:

$$\text{Pretest odds} \times LR_1 \times LR_2 \times LR_3 = \text{Posttest odds}$$

When using this approach, however, the clinician should be aware of a major assumption: the chosen tests or findings must be conditionally independent. (For instance, with liver cell damage, the aspartate aminotransferase [AST] and alanine aminotransferase [ALT] enzymes may be released by the same process and are thus not conditionally independent.) If conditionally dependent tests are used in this sequential approach, an overestimation of posttest probability will result.

## Threshold Approach to Decision Making

When contemplating the use of a test in a management decision, the clinician should first decide on the treatment threshold and then assess whether the test result would shift the probability of disease across this treatment threshold. For example, a clinician might decide to treat with antibiotics if the probability of streptococcal pharyngitis in a patient with a sore throat is greater than 25% (Figure 1–9A). If, after reviewing evidence from the history and physical examination, the clinician estimates the pretest probability of strep throat to be 15%, then a diagnostic test such as throat culture ($LR^+ = 7$) would be useful only if a positive test would shift the probability of disease above 25%. Use of the nomogram shown in Figure 1–7 indicates that the posttest probability would be 55% (Figure 1–9B), and ordering the test is thus justified as it affects patient management. On the other hand, if the history and physical examination had suggested that the pretest probability of strep throat were 60%, the throat culture ($LR^- = 0.33$) would be indicated only if a negative test would lower the disease probability below 25%. In this case, using the nomogram shown in Figure 1–7, the posttest probability after a negative test would be 33% (Figure 1–9C). Therefore, ordering the throat culture would not be justified.

  In summary, tests should be ordered only if they will affect patient management.

# 2

# Laboratory Procedures in the Clinical Setting*

*Stephen J. McPhee, MD*

This chapter presents information on how to perform common bedside laboratory procedures. Information on interpretation of results of body fluid analysis is included in some of the sections. Test results can be used for patient care only if the tests have been performed according to strict federal guidelines.

**Contents**                                                                   **Page**

*Portions of this chapter modified, with permission, from Krupp MA et al: Physician's Handbook, 21st ed. Lange, 1985.

# 1. OBTAINING AND PROCESSING BODY FLUIDS

## A. Safety Considerations

### General Safety Considerations

Because all patient specimens are potentially infectious, the following precautions should be observed:

a. Universal body fluid and needle stick precautions must be observed at all times.

b. Disposable gloves, gown, mask, and goggles should be worn when collecting specimens.

c. Gloves should be changed and hands washed after contact with each patient. Dispose of gloves in an appropriate bio-hazard waste container.

d. Any spills should be cleaned up with 10% bleach solution.

### Handling and Disposing of Needles and Gloves

a. Do not resheath needles.

b. Discard needles and gloves only into designated containers.

c. Do not remove a used needle from a syringe by hand. The needle may be removed using a specially designed waste collection system, or the entire assembly may (if disposable) be discarded as a unit into a designated container.

d. When obtaining blood cultures, it is hazardous and unnecessary to change needles.

e. Do not place phlebotomy or other equipment on the patient's bed.

## B. Specimen Handling

### Identification of Specimens

a. Identify the patient before obtaining the specimen. (If the patient is not known to you, ask for the name and check the wristband.)

b. Label each specimen container with the patient's name and identification number.

**Specimen Tubes:** Standard specimen tubes are now widely available and are easily identified by the color of the stopper (see also p 35):

a. Red-top tubes contain no anticoagulants or preservatives and are used for chemistry tests.

b. Marbled-top tubes contain material that allows ready separation of serum and clot by centrifugation.

c. Lavender-top tubes contain EDTA and are used for hematology tests (eg, blood or cell counts, differentials).

d. Green-top tubes contain heparin and are used for tests that require plasma or anticoagulation.

e. Blue-top tubes contain citrate and are used for coagulation tests.

f. Gray-top tubes contain fluoride and are used for some chemistry tests (eg, glucose) if the specimen cannot be analyzed immediately.

**Procedure**

a. When collecting multiple specimens, fill sterile tubes used for bacteriologic tests, then tubes without additives (ie, red-top tubes) before filling those with additives to avoid the potential for bacterial contamination, transfer of anti-coagulants, etc. However, be certain to fill tubes containing anticoagulants before the blood specimen clots.

b. The recommended order of filling tubes is (by type and color): (1) blood culture, (2) red top, (3) blue top, (4) green top, (5) lavender top.

c. Fill each stoppered tube completely. Tilt each tube containing anticoagulant or preservative to mix thoroughly. Place any specimens on ice as required (eg, arterial blood). Deliver specimens to the laboratory promptly.

d. For each of the major body fluids, Table 2–1 summarizes commonly requested tests and requirements for specimen handling and provides cross-references to tables and figures elsewhere in this book for help in interpretation of the results.

# 2. BASIC STAINING METHODS

## A. Gram's Stain

### Preparation of Smear

a. Obtain a fresh specimen of the material to be stained (eg, sputum) and smear a small amount on a glass slide. Thin smears give the best results (eg, press a sputum sample between two glass slides).

b. Let the smear air-dry before heat-fixing, because heating a wet smear will usually distort cells and organisms.

c. Heat-fix the smear by passing the clean side of the slide quickly through a Bunsen burner or other flame source (no more than three or four times). The slide should be warm, not hot.

d. Let the slide cool before staining.

### Staining Technique

a. Put on gloves.

b. Stain with crystal violet (10 seconds).

c. Rinse with gently running water (5 seconds).

d. Flood with Gram's iodine solution (10–30 seconds).

e. Rinse with gently running water (5 seconds).

f. Decolorize with acetone-alcohol solution until no more blue color leaches from the slide (5 seconds).

**TABLE 2–1. BODY FLUID TESTS, HANDLING, AND INTERPRETATION.**

| Body Fluid | Commonly Requested Tests | Specimen Tube and Handling | Interpretation Guide |
|---|---|---|---|
| Arterial blood | pH, $Po_2$, $Pco_2$ | Glass syringe. Evacuate air bubbles; remove needle; position rubber cap; place sample on ice; deliver immediately. | See acid-base nomogram, p 309. |
| Ascitic fluid | Cell count, differential<br>Protein, amylase<br>Gram stain, culture<br>Cytology (if neoplasm suspected) | Lavender top<br>Red top<br>Sterile<br>Cytology | See ascitic fluid profiles, p 314. |
| Cerebrospinal fluid | Cell count, differential<br>Gram stain, culture<br>Protein, glucose<br>VDRL or other studies (oligoclonal bands)<br>Cytology (if neoplasm suspected) | Tube #1<br>Tube #2<br>Tube #3<br>Tube #4<br><br>Cytology | See cerebrospinal fluid profiles, p 318. |
| Pleural fluid | Cell count, differential<br>Protein, glucose, amylase<br>Gram stain, culture<br>Cytology (if neoplasm suspected) | Lavender top<br>Red top<br>Sterile<br>Cytology | See pleural fluid profiles, p 346. |
| Synovial fluid | Cell count, differential<br>Protein, glucose<br>Gram stain, culture<br>Microscopic examination for crystals<br>Cytology (if neoplasm [villonodular synovitis, metastatic disease] suspected) | Lavender top<br>Red top<br>Sterile<br>Green top<br><br>Cytology | See synovial fluid profiles, p 357, and Figure 2–7. |
| Urine | Urinalysis<br>Dipstick<br>Microscopic examination<br>Gram stain, culture<br>Cytology (if neoplasm suspected) | Clean tube<br>Centrifuge tube<br>Sterile<br>Cytology | See Table 8–24, p 364.<br>See Table 2–2, p 27.<br><br>See Figure 2–4, p 29. |

    g. Rinse immediately with water (5 seconds).

    h. Counterstain with safranin O (10 seconds).

    i. Rinse with water (5 seconds).

    j. Let the slide air-dry (or carefully blot with filter paper), then examine it under the microscope.

### Microscopic Examination

    a. Examine the smear first using the low-power lens for leukocytes and fungi. Screen for the number and color of polymorphonuclear cells (cell nuclei should be pink, not blue).

    b. Examine using the high-power oil-immersion lens for microbial forms. Screen for intracellular organisms. Review the slide systematically for (1) fungi (mycelia, then yeast), (2) small gram-negative rods (*Bacteroides, Haemophilus,* etc) (3) gram-negative cocci (*Neisseria,* etc), (4) gram-positive rods (*Listeria,* etc), and (5) gram-positive cocci (*Streptococcus, Staphylococcus,* etc).

    c. Label positive slides with the patient's name and identification number and save them for later review.

    d. Figure 2–1 illustrates typical findings on a Gram-stained smear of sputum.

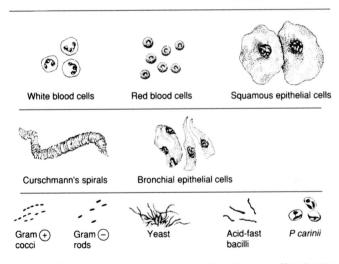

White blood cells    Red blood cells    Squamous epithelial cells

Curschmann's spirals    Bronchial epithelial cells

Gram (+) cocci    Gram (−) rods    Yeast    Acid-fast bacilli    *P carinii*

**Figure 2–1.** Common findings on microscopic examination of the sputum. Most elements can be seen on Gram-stained smears except for acid-fast bacilli (Kinyoun stain) and *Pneumocystis carinii* (Giemsa stain). (Modified and reproduced, with permission from Krupp MA et al: *Physician's Handbook,* 21st ed. Lange, 1985.)

**B. Acid-Fast (Kinyoun) Stain**

**Preparation of Smear and Staining Technique**

    a. Prepare the slide as above for Gram's stain: fix the air-dried thin smear by passing it quickly through a flame (three or four times). Let the smear cool before staining.

    b. Put on gloves.

    c. Stain with Kinyoun stain (5 minutes).

    d. Rinse with gently running water (5 seconds).

    e. Decolorize with acid-alcohol solution until no more color leaches from the slide (3–4 minutes).

    f. Rinse well with water (5 seconds).

    g. Counterstain with methylene blue (2 minutes).

    h. Rinse thoroughly with water (5 seconds).

    i. Let the slide air-dry (do not blot), then examine it under the microscope.

**Microscopic Examination**

    a. Examine the smear first using the low-power lens for leukocytes (cell nuclei should be blue, not pink).

    b. Examine using the high-power oil-immersion lens for acid-fast bacilli (AFB appear as bright pink against the blue background).

    c. Review the slide systematically for 5 minutes or longer.

    d. Label positive slides with the patient's name and save them for later review.

**C. Wright's Stain of Peripheral Blood Smear**

**Preparation of Smear**

    a. Obtain a fresh specimen of blood by pricking the patient's finger with a lancet. If alcohol is used to clean the fingertip, wipe it off first with a gauze pad.

    b. Place a single drop of blood on a glass slide. Lay a second glass slide over the first one and rapidly pull it away lengthwise to leave a thin smear.

    c. Let the smear air-dry. Do not heat-fix.

**Staining Technique**

    a. Stain with fresh Wright stain (1 minute).

    b. Gently add an equal amount of water and gently blow on the smear to mix the stain and water. Repeat by adding more water and blowing to mix. Look for formation of a shiny surface scum. Then allow the stain to set (3–4 minutes).

    c. Rinse with gently running water (5 seconds).

    d. Clean the back of the slide with an alcohol pad if necessary.

**Microscopic Examination**

    a. Examine the smear first using the low-power lens to select a good area for study (red and white cells separated from one another).

    b. Then move to the high-power oil-immersion lens. Review the slide systematically for (1) platelet morphology, (2) white cells (differential types, morphology, toxic granulations and vacuoles, etc), and (3) red cells (size, shape, color, stippling, nucleation, etc).

    c. Label slides with the patient's name and identification number and save them for later review.

    d. See Figure 2–2 for examples of common peripheral blood smear abnormalities.

**D. Methylene Blue Stain for Fecal Leukocytes**
**Preparation of Smear and Staining Technique**

    a. Place a small amount of fecal mucus (or stool if no mucus is present) on a glass slide. *Note:* This technique is unreliable if the sample is taken from a rectal swab, a dried stool smear, or the center of formed stool.

    b. Add 2 drops of methylene blue solution. Mix thoroughly.

    c. Place a coverslip over the area to be examined.

    d. Wait 2–3 minutes for cell nuclei to take up the stain.

    e. Alternatively, one may prepare a Wright-stained smear of dried mucus, using the same technique as for the peripheral blood smear.

**Microscopic Examination**

    a. Examine under the microscope, using the high-dry, then oil-immersion lenses.

    b. Look for leukocytes and bacteria.

    c. Screen for both polymorphonuclear and mononuclear cells (cell nuclei should be blue). The presence of any fecal leukocytes is abnormal and indicates inflammation or disruption of colonic mucosal lining (infectious diarrheal disorders—eg, shigellosis, salmonellosis, invasive *E coli* colitis, amebic colitis, pseudomembranous colitis—ulcerative colitis, Crohn's disease, diverticulitis, or necrotic neoplasm).

    d. Normally, there are many types of bacteria. In children with diarrhea, examine using the high-power oil-immersion lens to exclude staphylococcal enterocolitis (single bacterial coccal form present).

    e. Label positive slides with the patient's name and identification number and save them for later review.

**RED BLOOD CELLS**

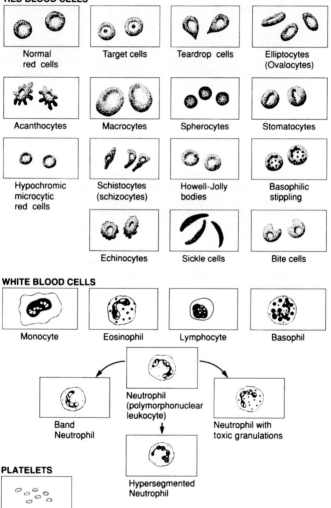

Normal
red cells

Target cells

Teardrop cells

Elliptocytes
(Ovalocytes)

Acanthocytes

Macrocytes

Spherocytes

Stomatocytes

Hypochromic
microcytic
red cells

Schistocytes
(schizocytes)

Howell-Jolly
bodies

Basophilic
stippling

Echinocytes

Sickle cells

Bite cells

**WHITE BLOOD CELLS**

Monocyte

Eosinophil

Lymphocyte

Basophil

Neutrophil
(polymorphonuclear
leukocyte)

Band
Neutrophil

Neutrophil with
toxic granulations

Hypersegmented
Neutrophil

**PLATELETS**

**Figure 2–2.** Common peripheral blood smear findings.

**E. Tzanck Smear**

**Preparation of Smear**

a. Use an alcohol pad to gently clean the skin. Wipe the alcohol off with a gauze pad, or let the skin air-dry.

b. Obtain a specimen by removing the top of a blister with a No. 15 scalpel blade, being careful not to disturb its base.

c. Then gently scrape the edge of the blade across the exposed floor of the blister. Smear the material adhering to the forward edge of the blade on a glass slide.

d. Let the smear air-dry, or heat-fix.

**Staining Technique**

a. Stain with fresh Wright stain (using the same technique as for peripheral blood smear) or fresh Giemsa stain. If Giemsa stain is used, the specimen must first be fixed to the slide with methyl alcohol for 10–15 minutes.

b. Clean the back of the slide with an alcohol pad if necessary.

**Microscopic Examination**

a. Examine the smear first using the low-power lens to select a good area for study.

b. Then move to the high-power oil-immersion lens. Review the slide for multinucleated giant cells (Figure 2–3) from viral infection of epidermal cells (eg, herpes simplex, varicella-zoster viruses).

c. Label positive slides with the patient's name and identification number and save them for later review.

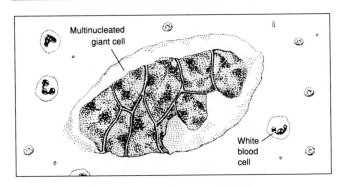

**Figure 2–3.** Tzanck smear showing a multinucleated giant cell.

## 3. OTHER BEDSIDE LABORATORY PROCEDURES

### A. Urinalysis

#### Collection and Preparation of Specimen

a. Obtain a midstream urine specimen from the patient. The sample must be free of skin epithelium or bacteria, secretions, hair, lint, etc.

b. Examine the specimen while fresh (still warm). Otherwise, bacteria may proliferate, casts and crystals may dissolve, and particulate matter may settle out. (Occasionally, amorphous crystals precipitate out, obscuring formed elements. In cold urine, they are amorphous urate crystals; these may be dissolved by gently rewarming the urine. In alkaline urine, they are amorphous phosphate crystals; these may be dissolved by adding 1 mL of acetic acid.)

c. Place 10 mL in a tube and centrifuge at 2000–3000 rpm for 3–5 minutes.

d. Discard the supernatant. Resuspend the sediment in the few drops that remain by gently tilting the tube.

e. Place a drop on a glass slide, cover it with a coverslip, and examine under the microscope; no stain is needed. If bacterial infection is present, a single drop of methylene blue applied to the edge of the coverslip, or a Gram-stained smear of an air-dried, heat-fixed specimen, can assist in distinguishing gram-negative rods (eg, *E coli, Proteus, Klebsiella*) from gram-positive cocci (eg, *Enterococcus, Staphylococcus saprophyticus*).

#### Procedural Technique

a. While the urine is being centrifuged, examine the remainder of the specimen by inspection and reagent strip ("dipstick") testing.

b. Inspect the specimen for color and clarity. Normally, urine is yellow or light orange. Dark orange urine is caused by ingestion of the urinary tract analgesic phenazopyridine (Pyridium, others); red urine, by hemoglobinuria, myoglobinuria, beets, senna, or rifampin therapy; green urine, by *Pseudomonas* infection or iodochlorhydroxyquin or amitriptyline therapy; brown urine, by bilirubinuria or fecal contamination; black urine, by intravascular hemolysis, alkaptonuria, melanoma, or methyldopa therapy; purplish urine, by porphyria; and milky white urine, by pus, chyluria, or amorphous crystals (urates or phosphates). Turbidity of urine is caused by pus, red blood cells, or crystals.

c. Reagent strips provide information about specific gravity, pH, protein, glucose, ketones, bilirubin, heme, nitrite, and esterase (Table 2–2). Dip a reagent strip in the urine and

**TABLE 2–2. COMPONENTS OF THE URINE DIPSTICK.[1]**

| Test | Values | Lowest Detectable Range | Comments |
|------|--------|------------------------|----------|
| Specific gravity | 1.001–1.035 | 1.000–1.030 | Highly buffered alkaline urine may yield low specific gravity readings. Moderate proteinuria (100–750 mg/dL) may yield high readings. Loss of concentrating or diluting capacity indicates renal dysfunction. |
| pH | 5–9 units | 5–8.5 units | Excessive urine on strip may cause protein reagent to run over onto pH area, yielding falsely low pH reading. |
| Protein | 0 | 15–30 mg/dL albumin | False-positive readings can be caused by highly buffered alkaline urine. Reagent more sensitive to albumin than other proteins. A negative result does not rule out the presence of globulins, hemoglobin, Bence Jones proteins, or mucoprotein.<br>1+ = 30 mg/dL    3+ = 300 mg/dL<br>2+ = 100 mg/dL    4+ = ≥ 2000 mg/dL |
| Glucose | 0 | 75–125 mg/dL | Test is specific for glucose. False-negative results occur with urinary ascorbic acid concentrations ≥ 50 mg/dL and with ketone body levels ≥ 50 mg/dL. Test reagent reactivity also varies with specific gravity and temperature.<br>Trace = 100 mg/dL    1 = 1000 mg/dL<br>1/4 = 250 mg/dL    2 = ≥ 2000 mg/dL<br>1/2 = 500 mg/dL |
| Ketone | 0 | 5–10 mg/dL acetoacetate | Test does not react with acetone or β-hydroxybutyric acid. (Trace) false-positive results may occur with highly pigmented urines or those containing levodopa metabolites or sulfhydryl-containing compounds (eg, mesna).<br>Trace = 5 mg/dL    Moderate = 40 mg/dL<br>Small = 15 mg/dL    Large = 80–160 mg/dL |
| Bilirubin | 0 | 0.4–0.8 mg/dL | Indicates hepatitis (conjugated bilirubin). False-negative readings can be caused by ascorbic acid concentrations ≥ 25 mg/dL. False-positive readings can be caused by etodolac metabolites. Test is less sensitive than Ictotest Reagent tablets. |
| Blood | 0[2] | 0.015–0.062 mg/dL hemoglobin | Test equally sensitive to myoglobin and hemoglobin (including both intact erythrocytes and free hemoglobin). False-positive results can be caused by oxidizing contaminants (hypochlorite) and microbial peroxidase (urinary tract infection). Test sensitivity is reduced in urines with high specific gravity, captopril, or heavy proteinuria. |
| Nitrite | 0 | 0.06–0.1 mg/dL | Test depends on the conversion of nitrate (derived from the diet) to nitrite by gram-negative bacteria in urine. Test specific for nitrite. False-negative readings can be caused by ascorbic acid. Test sensitivity is reduced in urines with high specific gravity. |

*(continued)*

**TABLE 2–2 (CONT'D). COMPONENTS OF THE URINE DIPSTICK.[1]**

| Test | Values | Lowest Detectable Range | Comments |
|------|--------|-------------------------|----------|
| Leuko-cytes (este-rase) | 0[3] | 5–15 WBCs/hpf | Indicator of urinary tract infection. Test detects esterases contained in granulocytic leukocytes. Test sensitivity is reduced in urines with high specific gravity, elevated glucose concentrations ($\geq 4$ g/dL), or presence of cephalexin, cephalothin, tetracycline, or high concentrations of oxalate. |

[1]Package insert, revised 4/94. Ames Reagent Strip for N-Multistix SG, Ames Division, Miles Laboratory.
[2]Except in menstruating females.
[3]Except in females with vaginitis.

compare it with the chart on the bottle. Follow the timing instructions carefully. *Note:* Reagent strips cannot be relied on to detect some proteins (eg, globulins, light chains) or sugars (other than glucose).

    d. Record the results.

**Microscopic Examination**

    a. Examine the area under the coverslip under the low-power and high-dry lenses for cells, casts, crystals, and bacteria. (If a Gram stain is done, examine under the oil immersion lens.)

    b. Cells may be red cells, white cells, squamous cells, transitional (bladder) epithelial cells, or atypical (tumor) cells. Red cells suggest upper or lower urinary tract infections (cystitis, prostatitis, pyelonephritis), glomerulonephritis, collagen vascular disease, trauma, renal calculi, tumors, drug reactions, and structural abnormalities (polycystic kidneys). White cells suggest inflammatory processes such as urinary tract infection (most common), collagen vascular disease, or interstitial nephritis. Red cell casts are considered pathognomonic of glomerulonephritis; white cell casts, of pyelonephritis; and fatty (lipid) casts, of nephrotic syndrome.

    c. The finding on a Gram-stained smear of unspun, clean, fresh urine of even one bacterium per field under the oil-immersion lens correlates fairly well with bacterial culture colony counts of greater than 100,000 organisms per μL.

    d. See Table 8–24, p 364, for a guide to interpretation of urinalysis; and Figure 2–4 for a guide to microscopic findings in urine.

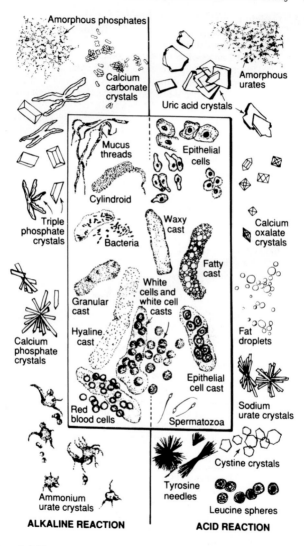

**Figure 2–4.** Microscopic findings on examination of the urine. (Modified and reproduced, with permission from Krupp MA et al: *Physician's Handbook,* 21st ed. Lange, 1985.)

### B. Vaginal Fluid Wet Preparation
#### Preparation of Smear and Staining Technique
    a. Place a small amount of vaginal discharge on a glass slide.
    b. Add 2 drops of sterile saline solution.
    c. Place a coverslip over the area to be examined.
#### Microscopic Examination
    a. Examine under the microscope, using the high-dry lens and a low light source.
    b. Look for motile trichomonads (undulating protozoa propelled by four flagella). Look for clue cells (vaginal epithelial cells with large numbers of organisms attached to them, obscuring cell borders), pathognomonic of *Gardnerella vaginalis*-associated vaginosis.
    c. See Figure 2–5 for an example of a positive wet prep (trichomonads, clue cells) and Table 8–25, p 365, for the differential diagnosis of vaginal discharge.

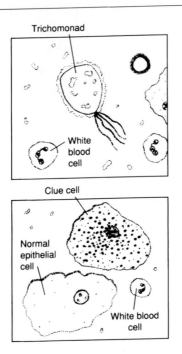

**Figure 2–5.** Wet preparation showing trichomonads, white blood cells, and "clue" cells.

**C. Skin or Vaginal Fluid KOH Preparation**
   **Preparation of Smear and Staining Technique**
   a. Obtain a skin specimen by using a No. 15 scalpel blade to scrape scales from the skin lesion onto a glass slide or to remove the top of a vesicle onto the slide. Or place a single drop of vaginal discharge on the slide.
   b. Place 1–2 drops of potassium hydroxide (10–20%) on top of the specimen on the slide. Lay a coverslip over the area to be examined.
   c. Heat the slide from beneath with a match or Bunsen burner flame until the slide contents begin to bubble.
   d. Clean carbon off the back side of the slide with an alcohol pad if necessary.
   *Note:* A fishy amine odor upon addition of KOH to a vaginal discharge is typical of bacterial vaginosis caused by *Gardnerella vaginalis.*

   **Microscopic Examination**
   a. Examine the smear under the high-dry lens for mycelial forms. Branched, septate hyphae are typical of dermatophytosis (eg, *Trichophyton, Epidermophyton, Microsporum* spp); branched, septate pseudohyphae with or without budding yeast forms are seen with candidiasis (*Candida* spp); and short, curved hyphae plus clumps of spores ("spaghetti and meatballs") are seen with tinea versicolor (*Malassezia furfur*).
   b. See Figure 2–6 for an example of a positive KOH prep.

**D. Synovial Fluid Examination for Crystals**
   **Preparation of Smear**
   a. No stain is necessary.
   b. Place a small amount of synovial fluid on a glass slide.
   c. Place a coverslip over the area to be examined.

   **Microscopic Examination**
   a. Examine under a polarized light microscope with a red compensator, using the high-dry lens and a moderately bright light source.
   b. Look for needle-shaped, negatively birefringent urate crystals (crystals parallel to the axis of the compensator appear yellow) in gout or rhomboidal, positively birefringent calcium pyrophosphate crystals (crystals parallel to the axis of the compensator appear blue) in pseudogout.

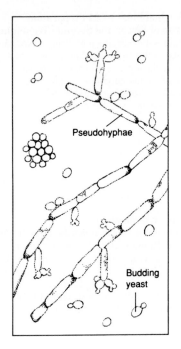

**Figure 2–6.** KOH preparation showing mycelial forms (pseudohyphae) and budding yeast typical of *Candida albicans*.

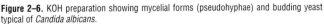

    c. See Figure 2–7 for examples of positive synovial fluid examinations for these two types of crystals.

## E. Pulse Oximetry
### Indications
To measure oxygen saturation in a noninvasive and often continuous fashion.
### Contraindications
a. Hypotension, hypothermia, and severe anemia (hemoglobin < 5 g/dL) cause inaccurate readings.

b. Hyperbilirubinemia, methemoglobinemia, fetal hemoglobinemia, and carboxyhemoglobinemia can falsely elevate oxygen saturation measurements.

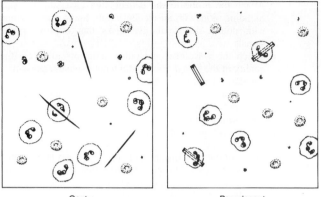

Gout                                    Pseudogout

**Figure 2–7.** Examination of synovial fluid for crystals, using a compensated, polarized microscope. In gout, crystals are needle-shaped, negatively birefringent, and composed of monosodium urate. In pseudogout, crystals are rhomboidal, positively birefringent, and composed of calcium pyrophosphate dihydrate. In both diseases, crystals can be found free-floating or within polymorphonuclear cells.

c. Excessive ambient light, simultaneous use of a blood pressure cuff, the presence of intravascular dyes (eg, methylene blue), and electrical interference (eg, MRI scanners, electrosurgery) can also cause erroneous readings.

**Approach to the Patient**

The patient should be positioned close to the pulse oximeter and should hold the probe site still. The sampling area should have good circulation and be free of skin irritation.

**Procedural Technique**

a. Plug the pulse oximeter into a grounded AC power outlet or make sure that sufficient battery power is available. Turn the oximeter on and wait until self-calibration is complete.

b. Select the probe to be used and connect it to the pulse oximeter. The probe consists of a light source (a red light-emitting device [LED] in most cases) and a photodetector. Probes are available for the ear, finger, and, in neonates, the foot, ankle, palm, calf, and forearm.

c. Attach the probe to the patient after cleansing the surrounding skin with an alcohol swab. Some probes come with double-sided adhesive disks that improve probe signal.

d. Watch the waveform and pulse indicators to assess the quality of the signal. Readjust if a poor signal is present.

e. Set alarm warnings on the device.

f. Check the probe site at least every 4 hours. Care should be taken not to apply tension to the probe cables.

**Possible Complications**

Allergic reaction to adhesives.

**Comments**

Because of the curvilinear nature of the oxygen-hemoglobin dissociation curve, oxygen saturation ($SaO_2$) is not directly proportional to oxygen partial pressure ($PaO_2$). Therefore, a relatively small change in oxygen saturation (eg, from 94% to 83%) can represent a large change in $PaO_2$ (eg, from 80 mm Hg to 50 mm Hg). In addition, the dissociation curve varies markedly from patient to patient and with pH, temperature, and altitude. To ensure accurate assessment of oxygenation, one should correlate pulse oximetry with arterial blood gas analysis.

# 3

# Common Laboratory Tests: Selection and Interpretation

*Diana Nicoll, MD, PhD, Stephen J. McPhee, MD,*
*Tony M. Chou, MD, Dan Berrios, MD, MPH,*
*and William M. Detmer, MD*

## HOW TO USE THIS SECTION

This section contains information about commonly used laboratory tests. It includes most of the blood, urine, and cerebrospinal fluid tests found in this book, with the exception of drug levels (Chapter 4). Entries are in tabular format and are arranged alphabetically.

### Test/Reference Range/Collection

This first column begins with the common test name, the specimen analyzed, and any test name abbreviation (in parentheses).

Below this in the first column is the reference range for each test. The first entry is in conventional units, and the second entry (in [brackets]) is in SI units (*Système International d'Unités*). Any panic values for a particular test are placed here after the word "Panic." The reference ranges provided are from several large medical centers; consult your own clinical laboratory for those used in your institution.

This column also shows which tube to use for collecting blood and other body fluids, how much the test costs (in relative symbolism; see below), and how to collect the specimen. Listed below are the common collection tubes and their contents:

| Tube Color | Tube Contents | Typically Used In |
|---|---|---|
| Lavender | EDTA | Complete blood count |
| Marbled | Serum separator | Serum chemistry tests |
| Red | None | Blood banking (serum) |

*(continued)*

| Tube Color | Tube Contents | Typically Used In |
|------------|---------------|-------------------|
| Blue | Citrate | Coagulation studies |
| Green | Heparin | Plasma studies |
| Yellow | Acid citrate | HLA typing |
| Navy | Trace metal free | Trace metals (eg, lead) |

The scale used for the cost of each test is:

| Approximate Cost | Symbol Used in Tables |
|------------------|-----------------------|
| $1–20 | $ |
| $21–50 | $$ |
| $51–100 | $$$ |
| > $100 | $$$$ |

## Physiologic Basis

This column contains physiologic information about the substance being tested. Information on classification and biologic importance, as well as interactions with other biologic substances and processes, is included.

## Interpretation

This column lists clinical conditions that affect the substance being tested. Generally, conditions with higher prevalence will be listed first. When the sensitivity of the test for a particular disease is known, it will follow the disease name in parentheses, eg, "rheumatoid arthritis (83%)." Some of the common drugs that can affect the test substance in vivo will also be included in this column.

## Comments

This column sets forth general information pertinent to the use and interpretation of the test and important in vitro interferences with the test procedure. Appropriate general references are also listed.

## Test Name

In the last column, the test name is placed perpendicularly to the rest of the table to allow for quick referencing.

| | ABO grouping | | |
|---|---|---|---|
| Test/Range/Collection | Physiologic Basis | Interpretation | Comments |
| **ABO grouping**, serum and red cells (ABO)<br><br>Red<br>$<br><br>Properly identified and labeled blood specimens are critical. | The four blood groups A, B, O, and AB are determined by the presence of antigens A and B or their absence (O) on a patient's red blood cells. Antibodies are present in serum in which red cells lack antigen. | In the US white population, 45% are type O, 40% A, 11% B, 4% AB.<br>In the African-American population, 49% are type O, 27% A, 20% B, 4% AB.<br>In the US Asian population, 40% are type O, 28% A, 27% B, 5% AB.<br>In the Native American population, 79% are type O, 16% A, 4% B, < 1% AB. | For both blood donors and recipients, routine ABO grouping includes both red cell and serum testing, as checks on each other.<br>Tube testing is as follows: patient's red cells are tested with anti-A and anti-B for the presence or absence of agglutination (forward or cell grouping), and patient's serum is tested against known A and B cells (reverse or serum grouping).<br>Ref: *Technical Manual of the American Association of Blood Banks*, 11th ed. American Association of Blood Banks, 1993. |

| | Acetaminophen | | |
|---|---|---|---|
| **Test/Range/Collection** | **Physiologic Basis** | **Interpretation** | **Comments** |
| **Acetaminophen,** serum (Tylenol; others)<br><br>10–20 mg/L<br>[66–132 μmol/L]<br>***Panic:*** > 50 mg/L<br><br>Marbled<br>$$<br>For suspected overdose, draw two samples at least 4 hours apart, at least 4 hours after ingestion. Note time of ingestion, if known. Order test stat. | In overdose, liver and renal toxicity are produced by the hydroxylated metabolite if it is not conjugated with glutathione in the liver. | **Increased in:** Acetaminophen overdose. Interpretation of serum acetaminophen level depends on time since ingestion. Levels drawn < 4 hours after ingestion cannot be interpreted since the drug is still in the absorption and distribution phase. Use nomogram (Figure 8–1, p 307) to evaluate possible toxicity. Levels > 150 mg/dL at 4 hours or > 50 mg/dL at 12 hours after ingestion suggest toxicity. | Do not delay acetylcysteine (Mucomyst) treatment (140 mg/kg orally) if stat levels are unavailable.<br>Ref: Lancet 1971;1:519.<br>Ref: Pediatrics 1975;55:871.<br>Ref: Lancet 1976;2:109. |

| Test / Specimen | Description | Present/Positive in | Comments |
|---|---|---|---|
| **Acetoacetate,** serum or urine<br><br>0 mg/dL [μmol/L]<br><br>Marbled or urine container<br><br>$<br><br>Urine sample should be fresh. | Acetoacetate, acetone, and β-hydroxybutyrate contribute to ketoacidosis when oxidative hepatic metabolism of fatty acids is impaired. Proportions in serum vary but are generally 20% acetoacetate, 78% β-hydroxybutyrate, and 2% acetone. | **Present in:** Diabetic ketoacidosis, alcoholic ketoacidosis, prolonged fasting, severe carbohydrate restriction with normal fat intake. | Nitroprusside test is semiquantitative; it detects acetoacetate and is sensitive down to 5–10 mg/dL.<br>Trace = 5 mg/dL, small = 15 mg/dL, moderate = 40 mg/dL, large = 80 mg/dL [1 mg/dL = 100 μmol/L].<br>β-Hydroxybutyrate is not a ketone and is not detected by the nitroprusside test. Acetone is also not reliably detected by this method.<br>Failure of test to detect β-hydroxybutyrate in ketoacidosis may produce a seemingly paradoxical increase in ketones with clinical improvement as nondetectable β-hydroxybutyrate is replaced by detectable acetoacetate.<br>Ref: Br Med J 1972;2:565. |
| **Acetylcholine receptor antibody,** serum<br><br>Negative<br><br>Marbled<br><br>$$ | Acetylcholine receptor antibodies are involved in the pathogenesis of myasthenia gravis. Sensitive radioassay or ELISA is available based on inhibition of binding of $^{125}I$ alpha-bungarotoxin to the acetylcholine receptor. | **Positive in:** Myasthenia gravis. | Titer has been found to correlate with clinical severity.<br>Ref: J Neurol Neurosurg Psychiatry 1993;56:496.<br>Ref: Clin Chem 1993;39:2053. |

| Test/Range/Collection | Physiologic Basis | Interpretation | Comments |
|---|---|---|---|
| **Acid phosphatase (prostatic)**, serum<br><br>0.1–0.9 IU/L<br>[< 15 nkat/L]<br>(method-dependent)<br><br>Marbled<br>$$<br>Rapid loss of enzyme activity unless kept at pH 5–6 and analyzed promptly. | Acid phosphatases are present in high concentration in the prostate gland, erythrocytes, platelets, liver, and spleen. | **Increased in:** Carcinoma of prostate (91% stage D, 18% stage A), prostate palpation or surgery, benign prostatic hypertrophy, Gaucher's disease. | Test has been largely replaced by prostate-specific antigen, which is much more sensitive (see p 150).<br>Only use is in monitoring of therapeutic responses or disease progression in prostate cancer patients on hormone therapy. It is not a good screening test.<br>Ref: Am J Clin Pathol 1985;84:334.<br>Ref: Curr Prob Cancer 1991;15:299.<br>Ref: Arch Surg 1991;126:1404. |

| | Adrenocorticotropic hormone | | Alanine aminotransferase |
|---|---|---|---|
| **Adrenocorticotropic hormone,** plasma (ACTH)

20–100 pg/mL
[4–22 pmol/L]

Heparinized plastic container
$$$$
Send promptly to laboratory on ice. ACTH is unstable in plasma, is inactivated at room temperature, and adheres strongly to glass. Avoid all contact with glass. | Pituitary ACTH (release stimulated by hypothalamic corticotropin-releasing factor) stimulates cortisol release from the adrenal gland. There is feedback regulation of the system by cortisol.
ACTH is secreted episodically and shows circadian variation, with highest levels at 6:00–8:00 AM; lowest levels at 9:00–10:00 PM. | **Increased in:** Pituitary (40–200 pg/mL) and ectopic (200–71,000 pg/mL) Cushing's syndrome, primary adrenal insufficiency (> 250 pg/mL), adrenogenital syndrome with impaired cortisol production.
**Decreased in:** Adrenal Cushing's syndrome (< 20 pg/mL), pituitary ACTH (secondary adrenal) insufficiency (< 50 pg/mL). | ACTH levels (RIA) can only be interpreted when measured with cortisol after standardized stimulation or suppression tests (see Adrenocortical insufficiency algorithm, p 310, and Cushing's syndrome algorithm, p 322).
Ref: Br Med J 1971;1:374. |
| **Alanine aminotransferase,** serum (ALT, SGPT, GPT)

0–35 U/L
[0–0.58 μkat/L]
(laboratory-specific)

Marbled
$ | Intracellular enzyme involved in amino acid metabolism. Present in large concentrations in liver, kidney; in smaller amounts, in skeletal muscle and heart. Released with tissue damage, particularly liver injury. | **Increased in:** Acute viral hepatitis (ALT > AST), biliary tract obstruction (cholangitis, choledocholithiasis), alcoholic hepatitis and cirrhosis (AST > ALT), liver abscess, metastatic or primary liver cancer; right heart failure, ischemia or hypoxia, injury to liver ("shock liver"), extensive trauma. Drugs that cause cholestasis or hepatotoxicity.
**Decreased in:** Pyridoxine (vitamin $B_6$) deficiency. | ALT is the preferred enzyme for evaluation of liver injury.
Ref: Compr Ther 1994;20:50.
Ref: Hosp Pract (Off Ed) Nov 1994;29:32. |

| Test/Range/Collection | Physiologic Basis | Interpretation | Comments |
|---|---|---|---|
| **Albumin,** serum<br><br>3.4–4.7 g/dL<br>[34–47 g/L]<br><br>Marbled<br><br>$ | Major component of plasma proteins; influenced by nutritional state, hepatic function, renal function, and various diseases. Major binding protein. While there are > 50 different genetic variants (alloalbumins), only occasionally does a mutation cause abnormal binding (eg, in familial dysalbuminemic hyperthyroxinemia). | **Increased in:** Dehydration, shock, hemoconcentration.<br>**Decreased in:** Decreased hepatic synthesis (chronic liver disease, malnutrition, malabsorption, malignancy, congenital analbuminemia [rare]). Increased losses (nephrotic syndrome, burns, trauma, hemorrhage with fluid replacement, fistulas, enteropathy, acute or chronic glomerulonephritis). Hemodilution (pregnancy, CHF). Drugs: estrogens. | Serum albumin gives an indication of severity in chronic liver disease. Useful in nutritional assessment if there is no impairment in production or increased loss of albumin and is an independent risk factor for all-cause mortality in the elderly (age > 70). There is a 10% reduction in serum albumin level in late pregnancy (related to hemodilution).<br>Ref: J Med Genet 1994;31:355.<br>Ref: Proc Natl Acad Sci U S A 1994;91:6476.<br>Ref: JAMA 1994;272:1036. |

| Aldosterone, plasma | | | |
|---|---|---|---|
| **Aldosterone,** plasma<br><br>*Salt-loaded* (120 meq Na+/d):<br>Supine: 3–10<br>Upright: 5–30 ng/dL<br><br>*Salt-depleted* (10 meq Na+/d):<br>Supine: 12–36<br>Upright: 17–137 ng/dL<br>[1 ng/dL = 27.7 pmol/L]<br><br>Lavender or green<br>$$$$<br>Early AM fasting specimen. Separate immediately and freeze. | Aldosterone is the major mineralocorticoid hormone and is a major regulator of extracellular volume and serum potassium concentration.<br>For evaluation of hyperaldosteronism (associated with hypertension and hypokalemia), patients should be salt-loaded and recumbent when specimen is drawn.<br>For evaluation of hypoaldosteronism (associated with hyperkalemia), patients should be salt-depleted and upright when specimen is drawn. | **Increased in:** Primary hyperaldosteronism (72%).<br>**Decreased in:** Primary or secondary hypoaldosteronism. | Testing for hyperaldosteronism and hypoaldosteronism must be done using specific protocols, and results must be interpreted based on reference values from the laboratory performing the test.<br>24-hour urinary excretion of aldosterone is the most sensitive test for hyperaldosteronism. (See Aldosterone, urine, below.)<br>The significance of an elevated plasma aldosterone level is difficult to interpret without simultaneous determination of plasma renin activity (PRA). In primary aldosteronism, plasma aldosterone is usually elevated while PRA is low; in secondary hyperaldosteronism, both plasma aldosterone and PRA are usually elevated.<br>Ref: Am J Med 1983;74:641.<br>Ref: Med Clin North Am 1988;72:1117.<br>Ref: Mayo Clin Proc 1990;65:96. |

| Test/Range/Collection | Physiologic Basis | Interpretation | Comments |
|---|---|---|---|
| **Aldosterone, urine**<br><br>*Salt-loaded* (120 meq Na+/d for 3–4 days):<br>1.5–12.5 μg/24 h<br><br>*Salt-depleted* (20 meq Na+/d for 3–4 days):<br>18–85 μg/24 h<br>[1 μg/ 24 h = 2.77 nmol/d]<br><br>Bottle containing boric acid<br>$$$$<br><br>To evaluate hyperaldosteronism, patient is salt-loaded and recumbent. Obtain 24-hour urine for aldosterone (and sodium to check that sodium excretion is > 250 meq/day). To evaluate hypoaldosteronism, patient is salt-depleted and upright; check patient for hypotension before 24-hour urine collected. | Secretion of aldosterone is controlled by the renin-angiotensin system. Renin (synthesized and stored in juxtaglomerular cells of kidney) is released in response to both decreased perfusion pressure at the juxtaglomerular apparatus and negative sodium balance. Renin then hydrolyses angiotensinogen to angiotensin I, which is converted to angiotensin II, which then stimulates the adrenal gland to produce aldosterone. | **Increased in:** Primary and secondary hyperaldosteronism, some patients with essential hypertension.<br><br>**Decreased in:** Primary hypoaldosteronism (eg, 18-hydroxylase deficiency), secondary hypoaldosteronism (hyporeninemic hypoaldosteronism). | Urinary aldosterone is the most sensitive test for primary hyperaldosteronism. Levels > 14 μg/ 24 h after 3 days of salt-loading have a 96% sensitivity and 93% specificity for primary hyperaldosteronism. Only 7% of patients with essential hypertension have urinary aldosterone levels > 14 μg/24 h after salt-loading.<br>Neither serum potassium nor plasma renin activity (PRA) is a satisfactory screening test for hyperaldosteronism. Hypokalemia is present in only 73% of patients with hyperaldosteronism on a normal sodium diet, and in 86% after salt loading. Suppressed PRA has only a 64% sensitivity and 83% specificity for hyperaldosteronism.<br>Ref: Am J Med 1983:74:641.<br>Ref: Med Clin North Am 1988:72: 1117.<br>Ref: Mayo Clin Proc 1990:65:96.<br>Ref: Endocrinol Metab Clin North Am 1994:23:271. |

|  | Alkaline phosphatase | Amebic serology |
|---|---|---|
| **Alkaline phosphatase,** serum<br><br>41–133 IU/L<br>[0.7–2.2 μkat/L]<br>(method- and age-dependent)<br><br>Marbled<br>$ | Alkaline phosphatases are found in liver, bone, intestine, and placenta. | **Increased in:** Obstructive hepatobiliary disease, bone disease (physiologic bone growth, Paget's disease, osteomalacia, osteogenic sarcoma, bone metastases), hyperparathyroidism, rickets, benign familial hyperphosphatasemia, pregnancy (third trimester), GI disease (perforated ulcer or bowel infarct), hepatotoxic drugs. **Decreased in:** Hypophosphatasia. |
| | | Normal in osteoporosis. Alkaline phosphatase isoenzyme separation by electrophoresis or differential heat inactivation is unreliable. Use $\gamma$-glutamyl transpeptidase (GGT), which increases in hepatobiliary disease but not in bone disease, to infer origin of increased alkaline phosphatase (ie, liver or bone).<br>Ref: Arch Pathol Lab Med 1978;102:509.<br>Ref: Endocrinol Metab Clin North Am 1990;19:1. |
| **Amebic serology,** serum<br><br>< 1:64 titer<br><br>Marbled<br>$$ | Test for presence of *Entamoeba histolytica* by detection of antibodies which develop 2–4 weeks after infection.<br>Tissue invasion by the organism may be necessary for antibody production. | **Increased in:** Current or past infection with *E histolytica*. Amebic abscess (91%), amebic dysentery (84%), asymptomatic cyst carriers (9%), patients with other diseases and healthy people (2%). |
| | | In some endemic areas, as many as 44% of those tested have positive serologies. Precipitin or indirect hemagglutination (IHA) and recombinant antigen-based ELISA tests are available.<br>Ref: N Engl J Med 1978;298:262.<br>Ref: Ann Trop Parasitol 1993;87:31. |

| | **Ammonia** | | |
|---|---|---|---|
| **Test/Range/Collection** | **Physiologic Basis** | **Interpretation** | **Comments** |
| **Ammonia,** plasma (NH$_3$)<br><br>18–60 µg/dL<br>[11–35 µmol/L]<br><br>Green<br>$$<br>Separate plasma from cells immediately. Avoid hemolysis. Analyze immediately. Place on ice. | Ammonia is liberated by bacteria in the large intestine or by protein metabolism and is rapidly converted to urea in liver.<br>In liver disease or portal-systemic shunting, the blood ammonia concentration increases.<br>In acute liver failure, elevation of blood ammonia may cause brain edema; in chronic liver failure, it may be responsible for hepatic encephalopathy. | **Increased in:** Liver failure, hepatic encephalopathy (especially if protein consumption is high or if there is GI bleeding), fulminant hepatic failure, Reye's syndrome, portacaval shunting, cirrhosis, urea cycle metabolic defects, urea-splitting urinary tract infection with urinary diversion, and organic acidemias. Drugs: diuretics, acetazolamide, asparaginase, fluorouracil (5-FU) (transient), others.<br>Spuriously increased by any ammonia-containing detergent on laboratory glassware.<br>**Decreased in:** Decreased production by gut bacteria (kanamycin, neomycin). Decreased gut absorption (lactulose). | Correlates poorly with degree of hepatic encephalopathy. Test not useful in adults with known liver disease. Test is not as useful as CSF glutamine (see p 97).<br>Ref: Klin Wochenschr 1990;68:175.<br>Ref: Baillieres Clin Gastroenterol 1992;6:609.<br>Ref: Proc Soc Exp Biol Med 1994;206:329. |

| | Amylase | Angiotensin-converting enzyme |
|---|---|---|
| **Amylase,** serum<br><br>20–110 U/L<br>[0.33–1.83 µkat/L]<br>(laboratory-specific)<br><br>Marbled<br>$ | Amylase hydrolyzes complex carbohydrates.<br>Serum amylase is derived primarily from pancreas and salivary glands and is increased with inflammation or obstruction of these glands.<br>Other tissues have some amylase activity, including ovaries, small and large intestine, and skeletal muscle. | **Increased in:** Acute pancreatitis (70–95%), pancreatic pseudocyst, pancreatic duct obstruction (cholecystitis, choledocholithiasis, pancreatic carcinoma, stone, stricture, duct sphincter spasm), bowel obstruction and infarction, mumps, parotitis, diabetic ketoacidosis, penetrating peptic ulcer, peritonitis, ruptured ectopic pregnancy, macroamylasemia. Drugs: azathioprine, hydrochlorothiazide.<br>**Decreased in:** Pancreatic insufficiency, cystic fibrosis. Usually normal or low in chronic pancreatitis. | Macroamylasemia is indicated by high serum but low urine amylase.<br>Serum lipase is an alternative test for acute pancreatitis.<br>Amylase isoenzymes are not of practical use because of technical problems.<br>Ref: Gastroenterol Clin North Am 1990;19:793.<br>Ref: J Gastroenterol 1994;29:189.<br>Ref: Gastroenterologist 1994;2:119. |
| **Angiotensin-converting enzyme,** serum (ACE)<br><br>12–35 U/L<br>[< 590 nkat/L]<br>(method-dependent)<br><br>Marbled<br>$$ | ACE is a dipeptidyl carboxypeptidase that converts angiotensin I to the vasopressor, angiotensin II.<br>ACE is normally present in the kidneys and other peripheral tissues. In granulomatous disease, ACE levels increase, derived from epithelioid cells within granulomas. | **Increased in:** Sarcoidosis (65%), hyperthyroidism, acute hepatitis, primary biliary cirrhosis, diabetes mellitus, multiple myeloma, osteoarthritis, amyloidosis, Gaucher's disease, pneumoconiosis, histoplasmosis, miliary tuberculosis. Drugs: dexamethasone.<br>**Decreased in:** Renal disease, obstructive pulmonary disease, hypothyroidism. | Test is not useful as a screening test for sarcoidosis (low sensitivity).<br>Specificity is compromised by positive tests in diseases more common than sarcoidosis.<br>Some advocate measurement of ACE to follow disease activity in sarcoidosis.<br>Ref: JAMA 1979;242:439.<br>Ref: J Clin Pathol 1983;36:938. |

| | **Antibody screen** | |
|---|---|---|
| Test/Range/Collection | Physiologic Basis | Interpretation | Comments |
| **Antibody screen,** serum<br><br>Red<br><br>$<br><br>Properly identified and labeled blood specimens are critical. | Detects antibodies to non-ABO red blood cell antigens in recipient's serum, using reagent red cells selected to possess antigens against which common antibodies can be produced.<br>Further identification of the specificity of any antibody detected (using panels of red cells of known antigenicity) makes it possible to test donor blood for the absence of the corresponding antigen. | **Positive in:** Presence of alloantibody, autoantibody. | In practice, a type and screen (ABO and Rh grouping and antibody screen) is adequate workup for patients undergoing operative procedures unlikely to require transfusion.<br>A negative antibody screen implies that a recipient can receive type-specific (ABO-Rh identical) blood with minimal risk.<br>Ref: *Technical Manual of the American Association of Blood Banks*, 11th ed. American Association of Blood Banks, 1993. |

| Antidiuretic hormone | | |
|---|---|---|
| **Antidiuretic hormone,** plasma (ADH)<br><br>If serum osmolality > 290 mosm/kg $H_2O$: 2–12 pg/mL<br>If serum osmolality < 290 mosm/kg $H_2O$: < 2 pg/mL<br><br>Lavender<br>$$$$<br>Draw in two chilled tubes and deliver to lab on ice. Specimen for serum osmolality must be drawn at same time. | Antidiuretic hormone (vasopressin) is a hormone secreted from the posterior pituitary that acts on the distal nephron to conserve water and regulate the tonicity of body fluids.<br>Water deprivation provides both an osmotic and a volume stimulus for ADH release by increasing plasma osmolality and decreasing plasma volume.<br>Water administration lowers plasma osmolality and expands blood volume, inhibiting the release of ADH by the osmoreceptor and the atrial volume receptor mechanisms. | **Increased in:** Nephrogenic diabetes insipidus, syndrome of inappropriate antidiuretic hormone (SIADH). Drugs: nicotine, morphine, chlorpropamide, clofibrate, cyclophosphamide.<br>**Normal relative to plasma osmolality in:** Primary polydipsia.<br>**Decreased in:** Central (neurogenic) diabetes insipidus. Drugs: ethanol, phenytoin. | Test very rarely indicated. Measurement of serum and urine osmolality usually suffices.<br>Test not indicated in diagnosis of SIADH.<br>Patients with SIADH show decreased plasma sodium and decreased plasma osmolality, usually with high urine osmolality relative to plasma. These findings in a normovolemic patient with normal thyroid and adrenal function are sufficient to make the diagnosis of SIADH without measuring ADH itself.<br>Ref: N Engl J Med 1981;305:1539. |

| | Antiglobulin test, direct | | |
|---|---|---|---|
| **Test/Range/Collection** | **Physiologic Basis** | **Interpretation** | **Comments** |
| **Antiglobulin test, direct**, red cells (Direct Coombs, DAT)<br><br>Negative<br><br>Lavender or red<br><br>$<br><br>Blood anticoagulated with EDTA is used to prevent in vitro uptake of complement components. A red top tube may be used, if necessary. | Direct antiglobulin test demonstrates in vivo coating of washed red cells with globulins, in particular IgG and C3d.<br><br>Washed red cells are tested directly with antihuman globulin reagent. DAT is positive (shows agglutination) immediately when IgG coats red cells. Complement or IgA coating may only be demonstrated after incubation at room temperature. | **Positive in:** Autoimmune hemolytic anemia, hemolytic disease of the newborn, alloimmune reactions to recently transfused cells, and drug-induced hemolysis. Drugs: cephalosporins, levodopa, methadone, methyldopa, penicillin, quinidine, phenacetin. | A positive DAT implies in vivo red cell coating by immunoglobulins or complement. Such red cell coating may or may not be associated with immune hemolytic anemia. Polyspecific and anti-IgG reagents detect approximately 500 molecules of IgG per red cell, but autoimmune hemolytic anemia has been reported with IgG coating below this level.<br><br>10% of hospital patients have a positive DAT without clinical manifestations of immune-mediated hemolysis. A false-positive DAT is often seen in patients with hypergammaglobulinemia, eg, in some HIV-positive patients.<br><br>Ref: *Technical Manual of the American Association of Blood Banks,* 11th ed. American Association of Blood Banks, 1993. |

| Test | Physiologic Basis | Interpretation | Comments |
|---|---|---|---|
| **Antiglobulin test, indirect**, serum (Indirect Coombs)<br><br>Negative<br><br>Red<br><br>$ | Demonstrates presence in patient's serum of unexpected antibody to ABO and Rh-compatible red blood cells.<br><br>First, the patient's serum is incubated in vitro with reagent red cells and washed to remove unbound globulins. Then antihuman globulin (AHG, Coombs) reagent is added. Agglutination of red cells indicates that serum contains antibodies to antigens present on the reagent red cells. | **Positive in:** Presence of alloantibody or autoantibody. Drugs: methyldopa. | The technique is used in antibody detection and identification and in the major cross-match prior to transfusion (see Type and Cross-Match, p 180).<br>Ref: *Technical Manual of the American Association of Blood Banks*, 11th ed. American Association of Blood Banks, 1993. |
| **$\alpha_1$-Antiprotease ($\alpha_1$-antitrypsin)**, serum<br><br>110–270 mg/dL<br>[1.1–2.7 g/L]<br><br>Marbled<br><br>$$ | $\alpha_1$-Antiprotease is an $\alpha_1$ globulin glycoprotein serine protease inhibitor (Pi) whose deficiency leads to excessive protease activity and panacinar emphysema in adults or liver disease in children (seen as ZZ and SZ phenotypes). Cirrhosis of the liver and liver cancer in adults are also associated with the Pi Z phenotype. | **Increased in:** Inflammation, infection, rheumatic disease, malignancy, and pregnancy because it is an acute phase reactant.<br>**Decreased in:** Congenital $\alpha_1$-antiprotease deficiency, nephrotic syndrome. | Smoking is a much more common cause of chronic obstructive pulmonary disease in adults than is $\alpha_1$-antiprotease deficiency.<br>Ref: N Engl J Med 1978;299:1045.<br>Ref: N Engl J Med 1978;299:1099. |

| Test/Range/Collection | Physiologic Basis | Interpretation | Comments |
|---|---|---|---|
| **Antistreptolysin O titer,** serum (ASO)<br><br>Children < 5 years: < 85<br>5–19 years: < 170<br>Adults: < 85 Todd units (laboratory-specific)<br><br>Marbled<br>$$ | Detects the presence of antibody to the antigen streptolysin O produced by group A streptococci.<br>Streptococcal antibodies appear about 2 weeks after infection. Titer rises to a peak at 4–6 weeks and may remain elevated for 6 months to 1 year.<br>Test is based on the neutralization of hemolytic activity of streptolysin O toxin by antistreptolysin O antibodies in serum. | **Increased in:** Recent infection with group A beta-hemolytic streptococci: scarlet fever, erysipelas, streptococcal pharyngitis/tonsillitis (40–50%), rheumatic fever (80–85%), poststreptococcal glomerulonephritis. Some collagen-vascular diseases.<br>Certain serum lipoproteins, bacterial growth products, or oxidized streptolysin O may result in inhibition of hemolysis and thus cause false-positive results. | Standardization of (Todd) units may vary significantly from laboratory to laboratory.<br>ASO titers are not useful in management of acute streptococcal pharyngitis.<br>In patients with rheumatic fever, test may be a more reliable indicator of recent streptococcal infection than throat culture.<br>An increasing titer is more suggestive of acute streptococcal infection than a single elevated level. Even with severe infection, ASO titers will rise in only 70–80% of patients.<br>Ref: N Engl J Med 1970;282:23,78.<br>Ref: J Clin Epidemiol 1993;46:1181. |

**Antistreptolysin O titer**

| Antithrombin III | | | |
|---|---|---|---|
| **Antithrombin III (AT III), plasma**<br><br>84–123% (qualitative)<br>22–39 mg/dL (quantitative)<br><br>Blue<br>$$<br>Transport to lab on ice. Plasma must be separated and frozen in a polypropylene tube within 2 hours. | Antithrombin III is a serine protease inhibitor that protects against thrombus formation by inhibiting thrombin and factors IXa, Xa, XIa, XIIa, plasmin, and kallikrein. It accounts for 70–90% of the anticoagulant activity of human plasma. Its activity is enhanced 100-fold by heparin.<br>There are two types of assay: functional (qualitative) and immunologic (quantitative). Since the immunologic assay cannot rule out functional AT III deficiency, a functional assay should be ordered first. Functional assays test AT III activity in inhibiting thrombin or factor Xa. Given an abnormal functional assay, the quantitative immunologic test indicates whether there is decreased synthesis of AT III or intact synthesis of a dysfunctional protein. | **Increased by:** Oral anticoagulants.<br>**Decreased in:** Congenital and acquired AT III deficiency (renal disease, chronic liver disease), oral contraceptive use, chronic disseminated intravascular coagulation, acute venous thrombosis (consumption), and heparin therapy. | Congenital and acquired AT III deficiency results in a hypercoagulable state, venous thromboembolism, and heparin resistance.<br>Congenital AT III deficiency is present in 1:2000–1:5000 people and is autosomal codominant. Heterozygotes have AT III levels 20–60% of normal.<br>Ref: Semin Thromb Hemost 1982;8:276.<br>Ref: Thromb Haemost 1993;69:231. |

| Test/Range/Collection | Physiologic Basis | Interpretation | Comments |
|---|---|---|---|
| **Aspartate amino-transferase,** serum (AST, SGOT, GOT)<br><br>0–35 IU/L<br>[0–0.58 µkat/L]<br>(laboratory-specific)<br><br>Marbled<br>$ | Intracellular enzyme involved in amino acid metabolism. Present in large concentrations in liver, skeletal muscle, brain, red cells, and heart. Released into the bloodstream when tissue is damaged, especially in liver injury. | **Increased in:** Acute viral hepatitis (ALT > AST), biliary tract obstruction (cholangitis, choledocholithiasis), alcoholic hepatitis and cirrhosis (AST > ALT), liver abscess, metastatic or primary liver cancer; right heart failure, ischemia or hypoxia, injury to liver ("shock liver"), extensive trauma. Drugs that cause cholestasis or hepatotoxicity.<br>**Decreased in:** Pyridoxine (vitamin $B_6$) deficiency. | Test is not indicated for diagnosis of myocardial infarction.<br>Ref: Compr Ther 1994;20:50.<br>Ref: Hosp Pract (Off Ed) Nov 1994;29:32. |
| **B cell immunoglobu-lin heavy chain gene rearrangement**<br>Whole blood, bone marrow, or frozen tissue<br><br>Lavender<br>$$$$ | In general, the percentage of B lymphocytes with identical immunoglobulin heavy chain gene rearrangements is very low; in malignancies, however, the clonal expansion of one population leads to a large number of cells with identical B cell immunoglobulin heavy chain gene rearrangements. Southern blot is used to identify a monoclonal population. | **Positive in:** B cell neoplasms such as lymphoma. | Samples with > 10% of cells showing a given B cell rearrangement are considered positive. However, a large monoclonal population is consistent with—but not diagnostic of—malignancy.<br>Ref: Arch Path Lab Med 1988;112:117. |

| | | | |
|---|---|---|---|
| **bcr/abl translocation**<br>Blood<br>Lavender<br>$$$$ | Approximately 95% of chronic myelogenous leukemia (CML) is associated with the "Philadelphia chromosome," a translocation that moves the c-abl proto-oncogene from chromosome 9 to the breakpoint cluster (bcr) region of chromosome 22. Southern blot is used to identify the translocation. | **Positive in:** Chronic myelogenous leukemia (sensitivity 95%) and acute lymphocytic leukemia (sensitivity 10–15%). | This assay will detect the 9:22 translocation if it has taken place in > 10% of the cells. CML patients with bone marrow transplants can be monitored for recurrence of disease with this test.<br>Ref: N Engl J Med 1988;319:990. |
| **Bilirubin,** serum<br>0.1–1.2 mg/dL<br>[2–21 μmol/L]<br>Direct (conjugated to glucuronide) bilirubin: 0.1–0.4 mg/dL [< 7 μmol/L];<br>Indirect (unconjugated) bilirubin: 0.2–0.7 mg/dL [< 12 μmol/L]<br>Marbled<br>$$ | Bilirubin, a product of hemoglobin metabolism, is conjugated in the liver to mono- and diglucuronides and excreted in bile.<br>Some conjugated bilirubin is bound to serum albumin, so-called D (delta) bilirubin.<br>Elevated serum bilirubin occurs in liver disease, biliary obstruction, or hemolysis. | **Increased in:** Acute or chronic hepatitis, cirrhosis, biliary tract obstruction, toxic hepatitis, neonatal jaundice, congenital liver enzyme abnormalities (Dubin-Johnson, Rotor's, Gilbert's, Crigler-Najjar syndromes), fasting, hemolytic disorders. Hepatotoxic drugs. | Assay of total bilirubin includes conjugated (direct) and unconjugated (indirect) bilirubin plus delta bilirubin (conjugated bilirubin bound to albumin).<br>It is usually clinically unnecessary to fractionate total bilirubin. The fractionation is unreliable by the diazo reaction and may underestimate unconjugated bilirubin. Only conjugated bilirubin appears in the urine, and it is indicative of liver disease; hemolysis is associated with increased unconjugated bilirubin.<br>Persistence of delta bilirubin in serum in resolving liver disease means that total bilirubin does not effectively indicate the time course of resolution.<br>Ref: Pediatrics 1992;89:80.<br>Ref: Br J Hosp Med 1994;51:181.<br>Ref: Pediatr Rev 1994;15:233. |

| | Test/Range/Collection | Physiologic Basis | Interpretation | Comments |
|---|---|---|---|---|
| **Bleeding time** | **Bleeding time**<br><br>2–10 minutes<br><br>$$<br><br>Test done by laboratory personnel. Simplate (presterilized device with spring-loaded blade) is used to make single cut 1 mm deep and 6 mm long on dorsal aspect of forearm after inflation of sphygmomanometer to 40 mm Hg. Filter paper is used to absorb blood from wound margins every 30 seconds, and time to cessation of bleeding is noted. | This is a test of platelet function, not a test of coagulation factors. | **Increased in:** Platelet disorders, thrombocytopenia, Bernard-Soulier syndrome, thrombasthenia. Also elevated in some forms of von Willebrand's disease, which is a disorder of factor VIII coagulant activity and not primarily a platelet disorder. Drugs: aspirin and other preparations containing aspirin. | Test is useful as a screening test (with aspirin challenge) for diagnosis of von Willebrand's disease and platelet disorders.<br><br>Test adds no clinically useful information to the prediction of clinically significant bleeding beyond that obtained from the history, physical examination, and other laboratory tests—platelet count, blood urea nitrogen (BUN), prothrombin time (PT), and partial thromboplastin time (PTT).<br><br>In patients with no history of bleeding and no intake of nonsteroidal anti-inflammatory drugs, an increased bleeding time does not correlate with actual surgical bleeding.<br><br>Ref: Semin Thromb Hemost 1990; 16:1.<br><br>Ref: Blood 1994;84:3363.<br><br>Ref: Med Clin North Am 1994;78:577. |

| Test / Specimen / Range | | Increased/Decreased | Comments |
|---|---|---|---|
| **Blood urea nitrogen, serum (BUN)**<br><br>8–20 mg/dL<br>[2.9–7.1 mmol/L]<br><br>Marbled<br><br>$ | Urea, an end product of protein metabolism, is excreted by the kidney. BUN is directly related to protein intake and nitrogen metabolism and inversely related to the rate of excretion of urea. Urea concentration in glomerular filtrate is the same as in plasma, but its tubular reabsorption is inversely related to the rate of urine formation. Thus, the BUN is a less useful measure of glomerular filtration rate than the serum creatinine (Cr). | **Increased in:** Renal failure (acute or chronic), urinary tract obstruction, dehydration, shock, burns, CHF, GI bleeding. Nephrotoxic drugs (eg, gentamicin).<br>**Decreased in:** Hepatic failure, nephrotic syndrome, cachexia (low-protein and high-carbohydrate diets). | Urease assay method commonly used. BUN/Cr ratio (normally 12:1–20:1) is decreased in acute tubular necrosis, advanced liver disease, low protein intake, and following hemodialysis. BUN/Cr ratio is increased in dehydration, GI bleeding, and increased catabolism.<br>Ref: N Engl J Med 1971;285:385.<br>Ref: Nursing 1994;24:88. |
| ***Brucella* antibody, serum**<br><br>< 1:80 titer<br><br>Marbled<br><br>$ | Patients with acute brucellosis generally develop an agglutinating antibody titer of ≥ 1:160 within 3 weeks. The titer may rise during the acute infection, with relapses, brucellergin skin testing, or use of certain vaccines (see Interpretation). The agglutinin titer usually declines after 3 months or after successful therapy. Low titers may persist for years. | **Increased in:** *Brucella* infection (except *B canis*) (97% within 3 weeks of illness); recent brucellergin skin test; infections with *Francisella tularensis, Yersinia enterocolitica, Salmonella,* Rocky mountain spotted fever; vaccinations for cholera and tularemia.<br>**Normal in:** *B canis* infection. | This test will detect antibodies against all of the *Brucella* species except *B canis*.<br>A fourfold or greater rise in titer in separate specimens drawn 1–4 weeks apart is indicative of recent exposure. Final diagnosis depends on isolation of organism by culture.<br>Ref: J Clin Microbiol 1980;11:691.<br>Ref: J Infect Dis 1989;159:219.<br>Ref: Rev Infect Dis 1991;13:359. |

| | C1 esterase inhibitor | | |
|---|---|---|---|
| **Test/Range/Collection** | **Physiologic Basis** | **Interpretation** | **Comments** |
| **C1 esterase inhibitor (C1 INH),** serum<br><br>Method-dependent<br><br>Marbled<br>$$ | C1 esterase inhibitor (C1 INH) is an alpha-globulin, which controls the first stage of the classic complement pathway and inhibits thrombin, plasmin, and kallikrein. Deficiency results in spontaneous activation of C1, leading to consumption of C2 and C4. The functional assay involves the measurement of C1 INH as it inhibits the hydrolysis of a substrate ester by C1 esterase. Immunoassay of C1 INH is also available. | **Decreased in:** Hereditary angioedema (HAE) (85%) (15% of patients with HAE will have normal levels by immunoassay, but the protein is nonfunctional and levels determined by the functional assay will be low). | C1 esterase inhibitor deficiency is an uncommon cause of angioedema. There are two subtypes of hereditary angioedema. In one, the protein is absent; in the other, it is nonfunctional. Acquired angioedema has been attributed to massive consumption of C1 INH (presumably by tumor or lymphoma-related immune complexes) or to anti-C1 INH autoantibody. When clinical suspicion exists, a serum C4 level screens for HAE. Low levels of C4 are present in all cases during an attack. C1 esterase inhibitor levels are not indicated unless either the C4 level is low or there is a very high clinical suspicion of HAE in a patient with normal C4 during an asymptomatic phase between attacks. In acquired C1 INH deficiency, the C1 level is also significantly decreased (often 10% of normal), whereas in HAE the C1 level is normal or only slightly decreased.<br>Ref: Am J Med 1990;88:656.<br>Ref: Ann Allergy 1991;67(2 Part 1): 107.<br>Ref: Med Clin North Am 1992;76:805.<br>Ref: South Med J 1992;85:1084. |

|  | C-peptide | Calcitonin |
|---|---|---|
| | C-peptide is an inactive by-product of the cleavage of proinsulin to active insulin. Its presence indicates endogenous release of insulin.<br>C-peptide is largely excreted by the kidney. | Calcitonin is a 32-amino-acid polypeptide hormone secreted by the parafollicular C cells of the thyroid. It decreases osteoclastic bone resorption and lowers serum calcium levels. |
| | **Increased in:** Renal failure, ingestion of oral hypoglycemic drugs, insulinomas, B cell transplants.<br>**Decreased in:** Factitious hypoglycemia due to insulin administration, pancreatectomy, type I diabetes mellitus (decreased or undetectable). | **Increased in:** Medullary thyroid carcinoma (> 500 pg/mL on two occasions), Zollinger-Ellison syndrome, pernicious anemia, pregnancy (at term), newborns, carcinoma (breast, lung, pancreas), chronic renal failure. |
| | Test is most useful to detect factitious insulin injection (increased insulin, decreased C-peptide) or to detect endogenous insulin production in diabetic patients receiving insulin (C-peptide present).<br>A molar ratio of insulin to C-peptide in peripheral venous blood > 1.0 in a hypoglycemic patient is consistent with surreptitious or inadvertent insulin administration but not insulinoma.<br>Ref: Arch Intern Med 1977;137:625.<br>Ref: Am J Med 1989;86:335.<br>Ref: Arch Intern Med 1993;153:650. | Test is useful to diagnose and monitor medullary thyroid carcinoma, although stimulation tests may be necessary (eg, pentagastrin test). Genetic testing is now available for the diagnosis of multiple endocrine neoplasia type II. (MEN II is the most common familial form of medullary thyroid carcinoma.)<br>Ref: Mayo Clin Proc 1975;50:53.<br>Ref: Ann Intern Med 1995;122:118. |

**C-peptide,** serum

0.8–4.0 ng/mL [μg/L]

Marbled

$$$

Fasting sample preferred.

**Calcitonin,** plasma

Male: < 90 pg/mL [ng/L]

Female: < 70 pg/mL [ng/L]

Green

$$$

Fasting sample required. Place on ice.

| | Calcium, serum | | |
|---|---|---|---|
| **Test/Range/Collection** | **Physiologic Basis** | **Interpretation** | **Comments** |
| **Calcium**, serum ($Ca^{2+}$)<br><br>8.5–10.5 mg/dL<br>[2.1–2.6 mmol/L]<br>*Panic:* < 6.5 or > 13.5 mg/dL<br><br>Marbled<br>$<br><br>Prolonged venous stasis during collection causes false increase in serum calcium. | Serum calcium is the sum of ionized calcium plus complexed calcium and calcium bound to proteins (mostly albumin).<br><br>Level of ionized calcium is regulated by parathyroid hormone and vitamin D. | **Increased in:** Hyperparathyroidism, malignancies secreting parathyroid hormone–related protein (PTHrP) (especially squamous cell carcinoma of lung and renal cell carcinoma), vitamin D excess, milk-alkali syndrome, multiple myeloma, Paget's disease of bone with immobilization, sarcoidosis, other granulomatous disorders, familial hypocalciuria, vitamin A intoxication, thyrotoxicosis, Addison's disease.<br>Drugs: antacids (some), calcium salts, chronic diuretic use (eg, thiazides), lithium, others.<br>**Decreased in:** Hypoparathyroidism, vitamin D deficiency, renal insufficiency, pseudohypoparathyroidism, magnesium deficiency, hyperphosphatemia, massive transfusion, hypoalbuminemia. | Need to know serum albumin to interpret calcium level. For every decrease in albumin by 1 mg/dL, calcium should be corrected upward by 0.8 mg/dL. In 10% of patients with malignancies, hypercalcemia is attributable to coexistent hyperparathyroidism, suggesting that serum PTH levels should be measured at initial presentation of all hypercalcemic patients (see pp. 334 and 344).<br>Ref: Ann Intern Med 1990;112:499.<br>Ref: Nursing 1993;23:69.<br>Ref: Clin Endocrinol 1994;41:407. |

| Calcium, ionized | | |
|---|---|---|
| **Calcium, ionized,** serum<br><br>4.4–5.4 mg/dL (at pH 7.4)<br>[1.1–1.3 mmol/L]<br><br>Whole blood specimen must be collected anaerobically and anticoagulated with standardized amounts of heparin. Tourniquet application must be brief. Specimen should be analyzed promptly.<br><br>Marbled<br>$$ | Calcium circulates in three forms: as free $Ca^{2+}$ (47%), protein-bound to albumin and globulins (43%), and as calcium–ligand complexes (10%) (with citrate, bicarbonate, lactate, phosphate, and sulfate). Protein binding is highly pH-dependent, and acidosis results in an increased free calcium fraction. Ionized $Ca^{2+}$ is the form that is physiologically active. Ionized calcium is a more accurate reflection of physiologic status than total calcium in patients with altered serum proteins (renal failure, nephrotic syndrome, multiple myeloma, etc), altered concentrations of calcium-binding ligands, and acid-base disturbances. Measurement of ionized calcium is by ion-selective electrodes. | **Increased in:** ↓ blood pH.<br>**Decreased in:** ↑ blood pH, citrate, heparin, EDTA. | Ionized calcium measurements are not needed except in special circumstances. eg, massive blood transfusion, liver transplantation, neonatal hypocalcemia, and cardiac surgery. Validity of test depends on sample integrity.<br>Ref: Ann Clin Lab Sci 1991;21:297. |

| Test/Range/Collection | Physiologic Basis | Interpretation | Comments |
|---|---|---|---|
| **Calcium, urine** ($U_{Ca}$)<br><br>100–300 mg/24 h<br>[2.5–7.5 mmol/24 h or 2.3–3.3 mmol/12 h]<br><br>Urine bottle containing hydrochloric acid<br>$$$<br><br>Collect 24-hour urine or 12-hour overnight urine. | Ordinarily there is moderate urinary calcium excretion, the amount depending on dietary calcium, parathyroid hormone (PTH) level, and protein intake.<br><br>Renal calculi occur much more often in hyperparathyroidism than in other hypercalcemic states. | **Increased in:** Hyperparathyroidism, osteolytic bone metastases, myeloma, osteoporosis, vitamin D intoxication, distal RTA, idiopathic hypercalciuria, thyrotoxicosis, Paget's disease, Fanconi's syndrome, hepatolenticular degeneration, schistosomiasis, sarcoidosis, malignancy (breast, bladder), osteitis deformans, immobilization. Drugs: acetazolamide, calcium salts, cholestyramine, corticosteroids, dihydrotachysterol, initial diuretic use (eg, furosemide), others.<br><br>**Decreased in:** Hypoparathyroidism, pseudohypoparathyroidism, rickets, osteomalacia, nephrotic syndrome, acute glomerulonephritis, osteoblastic bone metastases, hypothyroidism, celiac disease, steatorrhea, hypocalciuric hypercalcemia, other causes of hypocalcemia. Drugs: aspirin, bicarbonate, chronic diuretic use (eg, thiazides, chlorthalidone), estrogens, indomethacin, lithium, neomycin, oral contraceptives. | Approximately one-third of patients with hyperparathyroidism have normal urine calcium excretion.<br><br>The extent of calcium excretion can be expressed as a urine calcium ($U_{Ca}$)/ urine creatinine ($U_{Cr}$) ratio. Normally,<br><br>$$\frac{U_{Ca}\,(mg/dL)}{U_{Cr}\,(mg/dL)} < 0.14$$<br><br>and<br><br>$$\frac{U_{Ca}\,(mmol/L)}{U_{Cr}\,(mmol/L)} < 0.40$$<br><br>Hypercalciuria is defined as a ratio > 0.20 or > 0.57, respectively.<br><br>Test is useful in the evaluation of renal stones but is not usually needed for the diagnosis of hyperparathyroidism, which can be made using serum calcium (see pp. 334 and 344) and PTH measurements (see pp. 334 and 344). It may be useful in hypercalcemic patients to rule out familial hypocalciuric hypercalcemia.<br><br>In the diagnosis of hypercalciuria, $U_{Ca}/U_{Cr}$ ratios in random single-voided urine specimens correlate well with 24-hour calcium excretions.<br>Ref: Arch Intern Med 1991;151:1587.<br>Ref: Miner Electrolyte Metab 1993;19:385. |

| | **Carbon dioxide** | **Carboxyhemoglobin** |
|---|---|---|
| **Carbon dioxide (CO$_2$), total,** serum (bicarbonate) <br><br> 22–28 meq/L [mmol/L] <br> **Panic:** < 15 or > 40 meq/L [mmol/L] <br><br> Marbled <br> $ <br> Do not leave exposed to air since this will cause falsely low CO$_2$ levels. | Bicarbonate-carbonic acid buffer is one of the most important buffer systems in maintaining normal body fluid pH. <br> Total CO$_2$ is measured as the sum of bicarbonate concentration plus carbonic acid concentration plus dissolved CO$_2$. <br> Since bicarbonate makes up 90–95% of the total CO$_2$ content, total CO$_2$ is a useful surrogate for bicarbonate concentration. | **Increased in:** Primary metabolic alkalosis, compensated respiratory acidosis, volume contraction, mineralocorticoid excess, congenital chloridorrhea. Drugs: diuretics (eg, thiazide, furosemide). <br> **Decreased in:** Metabolic acidosis, compensated respiratory alkalosis. Fanconi's syndrome, volume overload. Drugs: acetazolamide, outdated tetracycline. | Total CO$_2$ determination is indicated for all seriously ill patients on admission. <br> If arterial blood gas studies are done, total CO$_2$ test is redundant. <br> Simultaneous measurement of pH and PCO$_2$ is required to fully characterize a patient's acid-base status. |
| **Carboxyhemoglobin,** whole blood (HbCO) <br><br> < 9% [< 0.09] <br><br> Lavender <br> $$ <br> Do not remove stopper. | Carbon monoxide (CO) combines irreversibly with hemoglobin at the sites that normally bind oxygen. This produces a decrease in oxygen saturation and a shift in the oxyhemoglobin dissociation curve, resulting in decreased release of oxygen to the tissues. | **Increased in:** Carbon monoxide poisoning. Exposure to automobile exhaust or smoke from fires. Cigarette smokers can have up to 9% carboxyhemoglobin, nonsmokers have < 2%. | Test (if available within minutes, together with O$_2$ saturation by oximeter) is useful in evaluation of CO poisoning. <br> PO$_2$ is usually normal in CO poisoning. Test measures carboxyhemoglobin spectrophotometrically. <br> Ref: N Engl J Med 1989;321:1474. |

| | Carcinoembryonic antigen | | |
|---|---|---|---|
| Test/Range/Collection | Physiologic Basis | Interpretation | Comments |
| **Carcinoembryonic antigen**, serum (CEA)<br><br>0–2.5 ng/mL [μg/L]<br><br>Marbled<br>$$ | CEA is an oncofetal antigen, a glyco-protein associated with certain malig-nancies, particularly epithelial tumors. | **Increased in:** Colon cancer (72%), lung cancer (76%), pancreatic cancer (91%), stomach cancer (61%), cigarette smok-ers, benign liver disease (acute 50% and chronic 90%), benign GI disease (peptic ulcer, pancreatitis, colitis). Elevations > 20 ng/mL are generally associated with malignancy. | **Screening:** Test is not sensitive or spe-cific enough to be useful in cancer screening.<br>**Monitoring after surgery:** Test is used to follow progression of colon cancer after surgery (elevated CEA levels suggest recurrence 3–6 months before other clinical indicators), although such monitoring has not yet been shown to improve survival rates. If monitoring is done, the same assay method must be used consistently in order to eliminate any method-depen-dent variability.<br>Ref: Ann Intern Med 1986;104:66.<br>Ref: Ann Intern Med 1991;115:623. |

| CD4/CD8 ratio | | |
|---|---|---|
| **CD4/CD8 ratio,** whole blood<br><br>Ratio: 0.8–2.9<br>CD4: 359–1725 cells/µL (29–61%)<br>CD8: 177–1106 cells/µL (18–42%)<br><br>Lavender<br>$$$<br>If an absolute CD4 count is required, also request a CBC and differential. | Lymphocyte identification depends on specific cell surface antigens (clusters of differentiation, CD), which can be detected with monoclonal antibodies using flow cytometry. CD4 cells are predominantly helper-inducer cells of the immunologic system. They react with peptide class II major histocompatibility complex antigens and augment B cell responses and T cell lymphokine secretion. CD4 cells are the major target of HIV-1.<br>CD8 cells can be divided into suppressor cells, which decrease B cell responses, and cytotoxic T cells. | **Increased in:** Rheumatoid arthritis, type I diabetes mellitus, SLE without renal disease, primary biliary cirrhosis, atopic dermatitis, Sézary syndrome, psoriasis, chronic autoimmune hepatitis.<br>**Decreased in:** AIDS/HIV infection, SLE with renal disease, acute CMV infection, burns, graft-versus-host disease, sunburn, myelodysplasia syndromes, acute lymphocytic leukemia in remission, recovery from bone marrow transplantation, herpes infection, infectious mononucleosis, measles, ataxia-telangiectasia, vigorous exercise. | Progressive decline in the number and function of CD4 lymphocytes seems to be the most characteristic immunologic defect in AIDS. Absolute CD4 measurement is particularly useful (more useful than the CD4/CD8 ratio) in determining eligibility for therapy (usually when CD4 < 500 cells/µL) and in monitoring the progress of the disease.<br>Most AIDS-defining infections occur when the CD4 count drops below 200 cells/µL.<br>Absolute CD4 count depends, analytically, on the reliability of the white blood cell differential count, as well as on the percentage of CD4 cells identified using the appropriate monoclonal antibody.<br>Ref: Hematol Oncol Clin North Am 1991;5:215.<br>Ref: Arch Intern Med 1994;154:1561. |

| Test/Range/Collection | Physiologic Basis | Interpretation | Comments |
|---|---|---|---|
| | **Centromere antibody** | | **Ceruloplasmin** |
| **Centromere antibody, serum (ACA)**<br><br>Negative<br><br>Marbled<br>$$ | Anticentromere antibodies are antibodies to nuclear proteins of the kinetochore plate. | **Positive in:** CREST (70–90%), scleroderma (10–15%), Raynaud's disease (10–30%). | In patients with connective tissue disease, the predictive value of a positive test is > 95% for scleroderma or related disease (CREST, Raynaud's disease). Diagnosis of CREST is made clinically (calcinosis, Raynaud's disease, esophageal dysmotility, sclerodactyly, and telangiectasia).<br>In the absence of clinical findings, the test has low predictive value.<br>(See also Autoantibodies table, p 316.)<br>Ref: Rheum Dis Clin North Am 1992; 18:483.<br>Ref: Ann Rheum Dis 1993;52:586.<br>Ref: Clin Rheumatol 1994;13:427.<br>Ref: Ann Rheum Dis 1995;54:148. |
| **Ceruloplasmin, serum**<br><br>20–35 mg/dL<br>[200–350 mg/L]<br><br>Marbled<br>$$ | Ceruloplasmin, a 120,000–160,000 MW $\alpha_2$-glycoprotein synthesized by the liver, is the main (95%) copper-carrying protein in human serum. | **Increased in:** Acute and chronic inflammation, pregnancy. Drugs: oral contraceptives, phenytoin.<br>**Decreased in:** Wilson's disease (hepatolenticular degeneration) (95%), CNS disease other than Wilson's (15%), liver disease other than Wilson's (23%), malabsorption, malnutrition, primary biliary cirrhosis, nephrotic syndrome, severe copper deficiency, Menkes' disease (X-linked inherited copper deficiency). | Slitlamp examination for Kayser-Fleischer rings and serum ceruloplasmin level recommended for diagnosis of Wilson's disease.<br>Serum copper level is very rarely indicated.<br>5% of patients with Wilson's disease have low-normal levels of ceruloplasmin.<br>Ref: Q J Med 1979;48:447.<br>Ref: Q J Med 1987;65:959. |

| | Chloride |
|---|---|

| **Chloride,** serum (Cl⁻) 98–107 meq/L [mmol/L] Marbled $ | Chloride, the principal inorganic anion of extracellular fluid, is important in maintaining normal acid-base balance and normal osmolality. If chloride is lost (as HCl or $NH_4Cl$), alkalosis ensues; if chloride is ingested or retained, acidosis ensues. | **Increased in:** Renal failure, nephrotic syndrome, renal tubular acidosis, dehydration, overtreatment with saline, hyperparathyroidism, diabetes insipidus, metabolic acidosis from diarrhea (loss of $HCO_3^-$), respiratory alkalosis, hyperadrenocorticism. Drugs: acetazolamide (hyperchloremic acidosis), androgens, hydrochlorothiazide, salicylates (intoxication). **Decreased in:** Vomiting, diarrhea, gastrointestinal suction, renal failure combined with salt deprivation, overtreatment with diuretics, chronic respiratory acidosis, diabetic ketoacidosis, excessive sweating, SIADH, salt-losing nephropathy, acute intermittent porphyria, water intoxication, expansion of extracellular fluid volume, adrenal insufficiency, hyperaldosteronism, metabolic alkalosis. Drugs: chronic laxative or bicarbonate ingestion, corticosteroids, diuretics. | Test is helpful in assessing normal and increased anion gap metabolic acidosis and in distinguishing hypercalcemia due to primary hyperparathyroidism (high serum chloride) from that due to malignancy (normal serum chloride). Ref: Exp Clin Endocrinol 1991;98:179. Ref: Crit Care Med 1992;20:227. |

| | Cholesterol | |
|---|---|---|
| **Test/Range/Collection** | **Physiologic Basis** | **Interpretation** | **Comments** |
|---|---|---|---|
| **Cholesterol,** serum<br><br>Desirable < 200<br>Borderline 200–239<br>High risk > 240 mg/dL<br>[Desirable < 5.2<br>Borderline 5.2–6.1<br>High risk > 6.2<br>mmol/L]<br><br>Marbled<br>$<br><br>Fasting preferred. | Cholesterol level is determined by lipid metabolism, which is in turn influenced by heredity, diet, and other liver, kidney, thyroid, and endocrine organ functions.<br>Total cholesterol (TC) = low density lipoprotein (LDL) cholesterol + high density lipoprotein (HDL), cholesterol + (triglycerides [TG] / 5) (valid only if TG < 400).<br>Since LDL cholesterol is the clinically important entity, it is calculated as<br><br>$$LDL = TC - HDL - \frac{TG}{5}$$<br><br>This calculation is valid only if specimen is obtained fasting (in order to obtain relevant triglyceride and HDL levels). | **Increased in:** Primary disorders: polygenic hypercholesterolemia, familial hypercholesterolemia (deficiency of LDL receptor), familial combined hyperlipidemia, familial dysbetalipoproteinemia. Secondary disorders: hypothyroidism, uncontrolled diabetes mellitus, nephrotic syndrome, biliary obstruction, anorexia nervosa, hepatoma, Cushing's syndrome, acute intermittent porphyria. Drugs: corticosteroids.<br>**Decreased in:** Severe liver disease (acute hepatitis, cirrhosis, malignancy), hyperthyroidism, severe acute or chronic illness, malnutrition, malabsorption (eg, HIV), extensive burns, familial (Gaucher's disease, Tangier disease), abetalipoproteinemia, intestinal lymphangiectasia. | It is important to treat the cause of secondary hypercholesterolemia (eg, hypothyroidism).<br>National Cholesterol Education Program Expert Panel has published clinical recommendations for cholesterol management (see JAMA reference).<br>Ref: Arch Intern Med 1988;148:36.<br>Ref: JAMA 1993;260:3015.<br>Ref: Med Clin North Am 1994;78:117.<br>Ref: Circulation 1995;91:908. |

## Chorionic gonadotropin, β-subunit, quantitative

| | | |
|---|---|---|
| **Chorionic gonadotropin, β-subunit, quantitative,** serum (β-hCG)<br><br>Males and nonpregnant females: undetectable or < 2 mIU/mL [IU/L]<br><br>Marbled<br><br>$$ | Human chorionic gonadotropin is a glycoprotein made up of two subunits (α and β). Human glycoproteins such as LH, FSH, and TSH share the α subunit of hCG, but the β subunit is specific for hCG. hCG is produced by trophoblastic tissue, and its detection in serum or urine is the basis for pregnancy testing. Serum hCG can be detected as early as 24 hours after implantation at a concentration of 5 mIU/mL.<br><br>During normal pregnancy, serum levels double every 2–3 days and are 50–100 mIU/mL at the time of the first missed menstrual period. Peak levels are reached 60–80 days after the last menstrual period (LMP) (30,000–100,000 mIU/mL), and levels then decrease to a plateau of 5,000–10,000 mIU/mL at about 120 days after LMP and persist until delivery. | **Increased in:** Pregnancy, hyperemesis gravidarum, trophoblastic tumors (hydatidiform mole, choriocarcinoma of uterus), some germ cell tumors (teratomas of ovary or testicle, seminoma), ectopic hCG production by other malignancies (stomach, pancreas, lung, colon, liver). Failure of elevated serum levels to decrease after surgical resection of trophoblastic tumor indicates metastatic tumor; levels rising from normal indicate tumor recurrence.<br>**Decreasing over time:** Threatened abortion. | Routine pregnancy testing is done by *qualitative* serum or urine hCG test. Test will be positive (> 50 mIU/mL) in most pregnant women at the time of or shortly after the first missed menstrual period.<br>*Quantitative* hCG testing is indicated for (1) the evaluation of suspected ectopic pregnancy (where levels are lower than in normal pregnancy at the same gestational age) if the routine pregnancy test is negative; (2) the evaluation of threatened abortion. In both situations, hCG levels fail to demonstrate the normal early pregnancy increase.<br>Test is also indicated for following the course of trophoblastic and germ cell tumors.<br><br>Ref: Hum Reprod 1992;7:701.<br>Ref: West J Med 1993;159:195.<br>Ref: Urology 1994;44:392. |

| | *Clostridium difficile* enterotoxin | |
|---|---|---|
| **Test/Range/Collection** | **Physiologic Basis** | **Interpretation** | **Comments** |

| Test/Range/Collection | Physiologic Basis | Interpretation | Comments |
|---|---|---|---|
| ***Clostridium difficile* enterotoxin,** stool<br><br>Negative (≤ 1:10 titer)<br><br>Urine or stool container<br>$$$<br><br>Must be tested within 12 hours of collection as toxin (B) is labile. | *Clostridium difficile,* a motile, gram-positive rod, is the major recognized agent of antibiotic-associated diarrhea, which is toxigenic in origin (see Antibiotic-associated colitis, p 225). There are two toxins (A and B) produced by *C difficile.* Cell culture is used to detect the cytopathic effect of the toxins, whose identity is confirmed by neutralization with specific antitoxins.<br>Toxin A (more weakly cytopathic in cell culture) is enterotoxic and produces enteric disease.<br>Toxin B (more easily detected in standard cell culture assays) fails to produce intestinal disease. | **Positive in:** Antibiotic-associated diarrhea (15–25%), antibiotic-associated colitis (50–75%), and pseudomembranous colitis (90–100%). About 3% of healthy adults and 10–20% of hospitalized patients have *C difficile* in their colonic flora. There is also a high carrier rate of *C difficile* and its toxin in healthy neonates. | Definitive diagnosis of disease caused by *C difficile* toxin is by endoscopic detection of pseudomembranous colitis.<br>Direct examination of stool for leukocytes, gram-positive rods, or blood is not helpful.<br>Culture of *C difficile* is not routinely performed, as it would isolate numerous nontoxigenic *C difficile* strains.<br>Ref: CRC Crit Rev Clin Lab Sci 1986;24:235.<br>Ref: Rev Infect Dis 1990;12:S243. |

| | Clotting time, activated | | *Coccidioides* antibodies | |
|---|---|---|---|---|
| **Clotting time, activated,** whole blood (ACT)<br><br>114–186 seconds<br><br>Special black tube<br>$$<br><br>Performed at patient bedside. Avoid traumatic venipuncture, which may cause contamination with tissue juices and decrease clotting time.<br><br>A bedside or operating room test that assesses heparinization by measuring time taken for whole blood to clot. | **Prolonged in:** Heparin therapy, severe deficiency of clotting factors (except factors VII and XIII), functional platelet disorders, afibrinogenemia, circulating anticoagulants.<br><br>**Normal in:** Thrombocytopenia, factor VII deficiency, von Willebrand's disease. | | Many consider this test unreliable. Reproducibility of prolonged ACTs is poor.<br><br>Increasingly, the ACT has been used in the operating room, critical care centers and during interventional cardiology/radiology procedures to monitor anticoagulation and titrate heparin dosages.<br><br>At centers without experience, should not be used to regulate therapeutic heparin dosage adjustments; use partial thromboplastin time (PTT) instead.<br>Ref: Am J Crit Care 1993;2(1):81.<br>Ref: Clin Cardiol 1994;17(7):357. | |
| ***Coccidioides* antibodies,** serum or CSF<br><br>Negative<br><br>Marbled<br>$$<br><br>Screens for presence of antibodies to *Coccidioides immitis.* Some centers use the mycelial-phase antigen, coccidioidin, to detect antibody.<br><br>IgM antibodies appear early in disease in 75% of patients, begin to decrease after week 3, and are rarely seen after 5 months. They may persist in disseminated cases, usually in the immunocompromised.<br><br>IgG antibodies appear later in the course of the disease.<br><br>Meningeal disease may have negative serum IgG and require CSF IgG antibody titers. | **Positive in:** Infection by *Coccidioides* (90%).<br><br>**Negative in:** Coccidioidin skin testing; many patients with chronic cavitary *Coccidioides;* 5% of meningeal *Coccidioides* is negative by CSF complement fixation (CF) test. | | Diagnosis is based upon culture and serologic testing. Precipitin and CF tests detect 90% of primary symptomatic cases.<br><br>Precipitin test is most effective in detecting early primary infection or an exacerbation of existing disease. Test is diagnostic but not prognostic.<br><br>CF test becomes positive later than precipitin test, and titers can be used to assess severity of infection. Titers rise as the disease progresses and decline as the patient improves.<br>Ref: Clin Microbiol Rev 1990;3:247.<br>Ref: N Engl J Med 1995;332:1077. | |

| Test/Range/Collection | Physiologic Basis | Interpretation | Comments |
|---|---|---|---|
| **Cold agglutinins, plasma**<br><br>< 1:20 titer<br><br>Lavender or blue<br>$$<br>Specimen should be kept at 37 °C. | Detects antibodies that agglutinate red blood cells in the cold (strongly at 4 °C, weakly at 24 °C, and weakly or not at all at 37 °C).<br><br>These antibodies are present in primary atypical pneumonias due to *Mycoplasma pneumoniae*, in certain autoimmune hemolytic anemias, and in normal persons (not clinically significant). | **Increased in:** Chronic cold agglutinin disease, lymphoproliferative disorders (eg, Waldenström's macroglobulinemia), autoimmune hemolytic anemia, collagen-vascular diseases, *M pneumoniae* pneumonia, infectious mononucleosis, mumps orchitis, cytomegalovirus, tropical diseases (eg, trypanosomiasis). | In *Mycoplasma* pneumonia, titers rise early, are maximal at 3–4 weeks after onset, and then disappear rapidly. These antibodies are usually IgM anti-I antibodies distinct from antibodies to *M pneumoniae*.<br>A rise in cold agglutinin antibody titer is suggestive of recent *Mycoplasma* infection but is found in other diseases.<br>Ref: N Engl J Med 1977;297:583. |
| **Complement C3, serum**<br><br>64–166 mg/dL<br>[640–1660 mg/L]<br><br>Marbled<br>$$ | The classic and alternative complement pathways converge at the C3 step in the complement cascade. Low levels indicate activation by one or both pathways.<br><br>Most patients with immune complexes will show decreased C3 levels.<br><br>Test is usually performed as an immunoassay (by radial immunodiffusion or nephelometry). | **Increased in:** Many inflammatory conditions as an acute phase reactant, active phase of rheumatic diseases (eg, rheumatoid arthritis, SLE), acute viral hepatitis, myocardial infarction, cancer, diabetes mellitus, pregnancy, sarcoidosis, amyloidosis, thyroiditis.<br>**Decreased by:** Decreased synthesis (protein malnutrition, congenital deficiency, severe liver disease), increased catabolism (immune complex disease, membranoproliferative glomerulonephritis [75%], SLE, Sjögren's syndrome, rheumatoid arthritis, disseminated intravascular coagulation, paroxysmal nocturnal hemoglobinuria, autoimmune hemolytic anemia, gram-negative bacteremia), increased loss (burns, gastroenteropathies). | Complement C3 levels may be useful in following the activity of immune complex diseases.<br>The best test to detect inherited deficiencies is CH50.<br>Ref: N Engl J Med 1987;316:1525. |

|  | | | |
|---|---|---|---|
| **Complement C4,** serum<br><br>15–45 mg/dL<br>[150–450 mg/L]<br><br>Marbled<br>$$ | C4 is a component of the classic complement pathway. Depressed levels usually indicate classic complement pathway activation.<br>Test is usually performed as an immunoassay and not a functional assay. | **Increased in:** Various malignancies (not clinically useful).<br>**Decreased by:** Decreased synthesis (congenital deficiency), increased catabolism (SLE, rheumatoid arthritis, proliferative glomerulonephritis, hereditary angioedema), and increased loss (burns, protein-losing enteropathies). | Low C4 accompanies acute attacks of hereditary angioedema, and C4 is used as a first-line test for the disease. C1 esterase inhibitor levels are not indicated for the evaluation of hereditary angioedema unless C4 is low. Congenital C4 deficiency occurs with an SLE-like syndrome.<br>Ref: N Engl J Med 1987;316:1525.<br>Ref: Am J Med 1990;88:656. |
| **Complement CH50,** plasma or serum (CH50)<br><br>22–40 U/mL (laboratory-specific)<br><br>Marbled<br>$$$ | The quantitative assay of hemolytic complement activity depends on the ability of the classic complement pathway to induce hemolysis of red cells sensitized with optimal amounts of anti-red cell antibodies.<br>For precise titrations of hemolytic complement, the dilution of serum that will lyse 50% of the indicator red cells is determined as the CH50.<br>This arbitrary unit depends on the conditions of the assay and is therefore laboratory-specific. | **Decreased with:** > 50–80% deficiency of classic pathway complement components (congenital or acquired deficiencies).<br>**Normal in:** Deficiencies of the alternative pathway complement components. | This is a functional assay of biologic activity. Sensitivity to decreased levels of complement components depends on exactly how the test is performed.<br>It is used to detect congenital and acquired severe deficiency disorders of the classic complement pathway.<br>Ref: N Engl J Med 1987;316:1525. |

| | | Cortisol | | Cortisol (urinary free) |
|---|---|---|---|---|
| **Test/Range/Collection** | **Physiologic Basis** | **Interpretation** | **Comments** | |
| **Cortisol,** plasma or serum<br><br>8:00 AM: 5–20 µg/dL [140–550 nmol/L]<br><br>Marbled, lavender, or green<br>$$ | Release of corticotropin-releasing factor (CRF) from the hypothalamus stimulates release of ACTH from the pituitary, which in turn stimulates release of cortisol from the adrenal. Cortisol provides negative feedback to this system.<br>Test measures both free cortisol and cortisol bound to cortisol-binding globulin (CBG).<br>Morning levels are higher than evening levels. | **Increased in:** Cushing's syndrome, acute illness, surgery, trauma, septic shock, depression, anxiety, alcoholism, starvation, chronic renal failure, increased CBG (congenital, pregnancy, estrogen therapy).<br>**Decreased in:** Addison's disease; decreased CBG (congenital, liver disease, nephrotic syndrome). | Cortisol levels are useful only in the context of standardized suppression or stimulation tests. (See Cosyntropin stimulation test, p 310, and Dexamethasone suppression tests, p 322).<br>Circadian fluctuations in cortisol levels limit usefulness of single measurements.<br>Analysis of diurnal variation of cortisol is not useful diagnostically.<br>Ref: Crit Care Clin 1991;7:23.<br>Ref: Endocrinol Metab Clin North Am 1994;23:511. | |
| **Cortisol (urinary free),** urine<br><br>10–110 µg/24 h [30–300 nmol/d]<br><br>Urine bottle containing boric acid.<br>$$$<br>Collect 24-hour urine. | Urinary free cortisol measurement is useful in the initial evaluation of suspected Cushing's syndrome (see Cushing's syndrome algorithm, p 322). | **Increased in:** Cushing's syndrome, acute illness, stress.<br>**Not increased in:** Obesity. | This test replaces both the assessment of 17-hydroxycorticosteroids and the 17-ketogenic steroids in the initial diagnosis of Cushing's syndrome.<br>Not useful for the diagnosis of adrenal insufficiency.<br>Ref: Ann Intern Med 1992;116:211. | |

| | Cosyntropin stimulation test | Creatine kinase |
|---|---|---|
| **Cosyntropin stimulation test,** serum or plasma<br><br>Marbled, green, or lavender<br><br>$$$ | Cosyntropin (synthetic ACTH preparation) stimulates the adrenal to release cortisol.<br>A normal response is a doubling of basal levels or an increment of 7µg/dL (200 nmol/L) to a level above 18 µg/dL (>504 nmol/L).<br>A poor cortisol response to cosyntropin indicates adrenal insufficiency (see Adrenocortical insufficiency algorithm, p 310). | **Decreased in:** Adrenal insufficiency, pituitary insufficiency. AIDS. |
| First draw a cortisol level. Then administer cosyntropin (0.25 mg IV). Draw another cortisol level in 30 minutes. | | Test does not distinguish primary from secondary (pituitary) adrenal insufficiency. In secondary adrenal insufficiency the atrophic adrenal may be unresponsive to cosyntropin. Test may not reliably detect pituitary insufficiency.<br>Metyrapone test (see p 310) may be useful to assess the pituitary-adrenal axis.<br>Ref: Crit Care Clin 1991;7:23.<br>Ref: Resp Med 1991;85:511. |
| **Creatine kinase,** serum (CK)<br><br>32–267 IU/L [0.53–4.45 µkat/L] (method-dependent)<br><br>Marbled<br>$ | Creatine kinase splits creatine phosphate in the presence of ADP to yield creatine and ATP.<br>Skeletal muscle, myocardium, and brain are rich in the enzyme.<br>CK is released by tissue damage. | **Increased in:** Myocardial infarction, myocarditis, muscle trauma, rhabdomyolysis, muscular dystrophy, polymyositis. severe muscular exertion, malignant hyperthermia, hypothyroidism, cerebral infarction, surgery, Reye's syndrome, tetanus, generalized convulsions, alcoholism, IM injections. DC countershock. Drugs: clofibrate. |
| | | CK is as sensitive a test as aldolase for muscle damage, so aldolase is not needed.<br>During a myocardial infarction (MI), serum CK level rises rapidly (within 3–5 hours); elevation persists for 2–3 days post-myocardial infarction.<br>Total CK is not specific enough for use in diagnosis of MI, but a normal total CK has a high negative predictive value. A more specific test is needed for diagnosis of MI (eg, CK-MB or cardiac troponin I).<br>Ref: Br Heart J 1994;72:112. |

| Test/Range/Collection | Physiologic Basis | Interpretation | Comments | |
|---|---|---|---|---|
| | | | **Creatine kinase MB** | **Creatinine** |
| **Creatine kinase (CKMB) enzyme activity**<br><br>< 16 IU/L<br>[< 0.27 μkat/L]<br>or < 4% of total CK or < 7 μg/L mass units (laboratory specific)<br><br>Marbled<br>$$ | CK consists of 3 isoenzymes, made up of 2 subunits, M and B. The fraction with the greatest electrophoretic mobility is CK1 (BB); CK2 (MB) is intermediate and CK3 (MM) moves slowest towards the anode.<br>Skeletal muscle is characterized by isoenzyme MM and brain by isoenzyme BB.<br>Myocardium has approximately 40% MB isoenzyme.<br>Assay techniques include isoenzyme separation by electrophoresis (isoenzyme activity units) or immunoassay using antibody specific for MB fraction (mass units). | **Increased in:** Myocardial infarction, cardiac trauma, certain muscular dystrophies, and polymyositis. Slight persistent elevation reported in a few patients on hemodialysis. | CKMB is a relatively specific test for MI. It appears in serum approximately 4 hours after infarction, peaks at 12–24 hours, and declines over 48–72 hours. CKMB mass concentration is a more sensitive marker of MI than CKMB isoenzymes or total CK within 4–12 hours after infarction. Cardiac troponin I levels are useful in the late (after 48 hours) diagnosis of MI since, unlike CKMB, levels remain elevated for 5–7 days. Within 48 hours, sensitivity and specificity of troponin I are similar to CKMB. Specificity of troponin I is higher than CKMB in patients with skeletal muscle injury or renal failure, or postoperatively. Cardiac troponin I is therefore the preferred test.<br>Estimation of CKMM and CKBB is not clinically useful. Use total CK.<br>Ref: Br Heart J 1994;72:112.<br>Ref: Clin Chem 1994;40(7 Pt1):1291.<br>Ref: N Engl J Med 1994;330:670.<br>Ref: N Engl J Med 1994;331:561. | |
| **Creatinine, serum (Cr)**<br><br>0.6–1.2 mg/dL<br>[50–100 μmol/L]<br><br>Marbled<br>$ | Endogenous creatinine is excreted by filtration through the glomerulus and by tubular secretion. Creatinine clearance is an acceptable clinical measure of glomerular filtration rate (GFR), though it sometimes overestimates GFR (eg, in cirrhosis).<br>For each 50% reduction in GFR, serum creatinine approximately doubles. | **Increased in:** Acute or chronic renal failure, urinary tract obstruction, nephrotoxic drugs, hypothyroidism.<br>**Decreased in:** Reduced muscle mass. | | In alkaline picrate method, substances other than Cr (eg, acetoacetate, acetone, β-hydroxybutyrate, α-ketoglutarate, pyruvate, glucose) may give falsely high results. Therefore, patients with diabetic ketoacidosis may have spuriously elevated Cr.<br>Cephalosporins may spuriously increase or decrease Cr measurement.<br>Increased bilirubin may spuriously decrease Cr.<br>Ref: Clin Chem 1990;36:1951.<br>Ref: Ann Pharmacother 1993;27:622. |

| Creatinine clearance | | | |
|---|---|---|---|
| **Creatinine clearance, (Cl$_{Cr}$)**<br><br>Adults: 90–130 mL/min/1.73 m$^2$ BSA<br><br>$$<br><br>Collect carefully timed 24-hour urine and simultaneous serum/plasma creatinine sample. Record patient's weight and height. | Widely used test of glomerular filtration rate (GFR). Theoretically reliable, but often compromised by incomplete urine collection.<br>Creatinine clearance is calculated from measurement of urine creatinine (U$_{Cr}$ [mg/dL]), plasma/serum creatinine (P$_{Cr}$ [mg/dL]), and urine flow rate (V [mL/min]) according to the formula:<br><br>$$Cl_{Cr}\,(mL/min) = \frac{U_{Cr} \times V}{P_{Cr}}$$<br><br>where<br><br>$$V\,(mL/min) = \frac{24\ hour\ urine\ volume\ (mL)}{1440}$$<br><br>Creatinine clearance is often "corrected" for body surface area (BSA [m$^2$]) according to the formula:<br><br>$$Cl_{Cr}\ (corrected) = Cl_{Cr}\ (uncorrected) \times \frac{1.73}{BSA}$$ | **Increased in:** High cardiac output, exercise, acromegaly, diabetes mellitus (early stage), infections, hypothyroidism.<br>**Decreased in:** Acute or chronic renal failure, decreased renal blood flow (shock, hemorrhage, dehydration, CHF). Drugs: nephrotoxic drugs. | Serum Cr may, in practice, be a more reliable indicator of renal function than 24-hour Cl$_{Cr}$ unless urine collection is carefully monitored. An 8-hour collection provides results similar to those obtained by a 24-hour collection.<br>Cl$_{Cr}$ will overestimate GFR to the extent that Cr is secreted by the renal tubules (eg, in cirrhosis).<br>Cl$_{Cr}$ can be estimated from the serum creatinine using the following formula:<br><br>$$Cl_{Cr}\ (mL/min) = \frac{(140 - Age) \times Wt(Kg)}{72 \times P_{Cr}}$$<br><br>Ref: Crit Care Med 1993;21:1487.<br>Ref: Pharmacotherapy 1993;13:135.<br>Ref: Arch Intern Med 1994;154:201. |

| | | | Cryoglobulins | Cryptococcal antigen |
|---|---|---|---|---|
| | **Test/Range/Collection** | **Physiologic Basis** | **Interpretation** | **Comments** |
| | **Cryoglobulins,** serum<br><br>< 0.12 mg/mL<br><br>Marbled<br>$<br><br>Must be immediately transported to lab at 37 °C | Cryoglobulins are immunoglobulins (IgG, IgM, IgA, or light chains) which precipitate on exposure to the cold.<br><br>Type I cryoglobulins (25%) are monoclonal proteins, most commonly IgM, occasionally IgG, and rarely IgA or Bence Jones protein, seen in multiple myeloma and Waldenström's macroglobulinemia.<br><br>Type II (25%) are mixed cryoglobulins with a monoclonal component (usually IgM but occasionally IgG or IgA) that complexes with autologous normal IgG in the cryoprecipitate.<br><br>Type III (50%) are mixed polyclonal cryoglobulins (IgM and IgG). | **Increased in:** Immunoproliferative disorders (multiple myeloma, Waldenström's macroglobulinemia, chronic lymphocytic leukemia, lymphoma), collagen-vascular disease (SLE, polyarteritis nodosa, rheumatoid arthritis), hemolytic anemia, essential mixed cryoglobulinemia, hepatitis B and C infection. | All types of cryoglobulins may cause cold-induced symptoms, including Raynaud's phenomenon, vascular purpura, and urticaria.<br><br>Patients with type II and III cryoglobulinemia often have immune complex disease, with vascular purpura, arthritis, and nephritis.<br><br>Typing of cryoglobulins by electrophoresis is not necessary for diagnosis or clinical management.<br><br>About 50% of essential mixed cryoglobulinemia patients have evidence of hepatitis C infection.<br>Ref: Am J Med 1980;68:757.<br>Ref: JAMA 1982;248:2670.<br>Ref: Am J Med 1994;96:124. |
| | **Cryptococcal antigen,** serum or CSF<br><br>Negative<br><br>Marbled (serum) or glass or plastic tube (CSF)<br>$$ | The capsular polysaccharide of *Cryptococcus neoformans* potentiates opportunistic infections by the yeast. The cryptococcal antigen test used is often a latex agglutination test. | **Increased in:** Cryptococcal infection. | False-positive and false-negative results have been reported. False-positives due to rheumatoid factor can be reduced by pretreatment of serum using pronase before testing.<br>96% of cryptococcal infections occur in AIDS patients.<br>Ref: Infect Immun 1994;62:1507.<br>Ref: J Clin Microbiol 1994;32:2158. |

| Test / Range / Specimen / Cost | Physiologic Basis | Interpretation | Comments |
|---|---|---|---|
| **Cytomegalovirus antibody**, serum (CMV) <br><br> Negative <br><br> Marbled <br><br> $$$ | Detects the presence of antibody to CMV, either IgG or IgM. CMV infection is usually acquired during childhood or early adulthood. By age 20–40 years, 40–90% of the population has CMV antibodies. | **Increased in:** Previous or active CMV infection. False-positive CMV IgM tests occur when rheumatoid factor or infectious mononucleosis is present. | Serial specimens exhibiting a greater than fourfold titer rise suggest a recent infection. Active CMV infection must be documented by viral isolation. Useful for screening of potential organ donors and recipients. Detection of CMV IgM antibody in the serum of a newborn usually indicates congenital infection. Detection of CMV IgG antibody is not diagnostic, since maternal CMV IgG antibody passed via the placenta can persist in newborn's serum for 6 months. Ref: Rev Infect Dis 1988;10:S468. |
| **Dexamethasone suppression test (single low-dose, overnight)**, serum <br><br> 8:00 AM serum cortisol level: < 5 µg/dL [< 140 nmol/L] <br><br> $$ <br><br> Give 1 mg dexamethasone at 11:00 PM. At 8:00 AM, draw serum cortisol level. | In normal patients, dexamethasone suppresses the 8:00 AM serum cortisol level to below 5 µg/dL. Patients with Cushing's syndrome have 8:00 AM levels > 10 µg/dL (> 276 nmol/L). | **Positive in:** Cushing's syndrome (98% sensitivity, 98% specificity in lean outpatients), obese patients (13%), hospitalized or chronically ill patients (23%). | Good screening test for Cushing's syndrome. If this test is abnormal, use high-dose test (see below) to determine etiology. (See also Cushing's syndrome algorithm, p 322.) Patients taking phenytoin may fail to suppress because of enhanced dexamethasone metabolism. Depressed patients may also fail to suppress morning cortisol level. Ref: Metabolism 1979;28:955. |

| | Dexamethasone suppression test (high-dose) | | |
|---|---|---|---|
| **Test/Range/Collection** | **Physiologic Basis** | **Interpretation** | **Comments** |
| **Dexamethasone suppression test (high-dose, overnight),** serum<br><br>8:00 AM serum cortisol level: < 5 μg/dL [< 140 nmol/L]<br><br>$$<br><br>Give 8 mg dexamethasone dose at 11:00 PM. At 8:00 AM, draw cortisol level. | Suppression of plasma cortisol levels to < 50% of baseline with dexamethasone indicates Cushing's disease (pituitary-dependent ACTH hypersecretion) and differentiates this from adrenal and ectopic Cushing's syndrome (see Cushing's syndrome algorithm, p 322). | **Positive in:** Cushing's disease (88–92% sensitivity; specificity 57–100%). | Test indicated only after a positive low-dose dexamethasone suppression test.<br>Sensitivity and specificity depend on sampling time and diagnostic criteria.<br>The ovine corticotropin-releasing hormone (CRH) stimulation test and bilateral sampling of the inferior petrosal sinuses combined with CRH administration are being evaluated for the definitive diagnosis of Cushing's disease.<br>Measurement of urinary 17-hydroxycorticosteroids has been replaced in this test by measurement of serum cortisol.<br>Ref: Ann Intern Med 1986;104:180.<br>Ref: Ann Intern Med 1990;112:434.<br>Ref: J Clin Endocrinol Metab 1994;78:418.<br>Ref: N Engl J Med 1994;331:629.<br>Ref: Medicine 1995;74:74. |

| | Double-stranded | Epstein-Barr virus antibodies |
|---|---|---|
| **Double-stranded-DNA antibody (ds-DNA)**, serum (ds-DNA)<br><br>< 1:10 titer<br><br>Marbled<br>$$ | IgG or IgM antibodies directed against host double-stranded DNA. | **Increased in:** Systemic lupus erythematosus (60–70% sensitivity, 95% specificity).<br>**Not increased in:** Drug-induced lupus. | High titers are seen only in SLE. Titers of ds-DNA antibody correlate well with disease activity and with occurrence of glomerulonephritis. (See also Autoantibodies table, p 316.)<br>Ref: West J Med 1987;147:210.<br>Ref: Clin Immunol Immunopathol 1988;47:121. |
| **Epstein-Barr virus antibodies**, serum (EBV)<br><br>Negative<br><br>Marbled<br>$$ | Antiviral capsid antibodies (anti-VCA) (IgM) often reach their peak at clinical presentation and last up to 3 months; anti-VCA IgG antibodies last for life. Early antigen antibodies (anti-EA) are next to develop, are most often positive at 1 month after presentation, typically last for 2–3 months, and may last up to 6 months in low titers. Anti-EA may also be found in some patients with Hodgkin's disease, chronic lymphocytic leukemia, and some other malignancies.<br>Anti-EB nuclear antigen (anti-EBNA) antibody begins to appear in a minority of patients in the third or fourth week but is uniformly present by 6 months. | **Increased in:** EB virus infection, infectious mononucleosis.<br>Antibodies to the diffuse (D) form of antigen (detected in the cytoplasm and nucleus of infected cells) are greatly elevated in nasopharyngeal carcinoma. Antibodies to the restricted (R) form of antigen (detected only in the cytoplasm of infected cells) are greatly elevated in Burkitt's lymphoma. | Most useful in diagnosing infectious mononucleosis in patients who have the clinical and hematologic criteria for the disease but who fail to develop the heterophile agglutinins (10%) (see Heterophile agglutination, p 109). EBV antibodies cannot be used to diagnose "chronic" mononucleosis. Chronic fatigue syndrome is not caused by EBV.<br>The best indicator of primary infection is a positive anti-VCA IgM (check for false-positives caused by rheumatoid factor).<br>Ref: Rose NR et al (editors): *Manual of Clinical Laboratory Immunology*, 4th ed. American Society for Microbiology, 1992. |

| Test/Range/Collection | Physiologic Basis | Interpretation | Comments |
|---|---|---|---|
| **Erythrocyte count,** whole blood (RBC count)<br><br>$4.2-5.6 \times 10^6/\mu L$ [$\times 10^{12}$/L]<br><br>Lavender<br>$ | Erythrocytes are counted by auto-mated instruments using electrical impedance or light scattering. | **Increased in:** Secondary polycythemia (hemoconcentration), polycythemia vera. Spurious increase with increased white blood cells.<br>**Decreased in:** Anemia. Spurious decrease with autoagglutination. | Ref: Lab Med 1983;14:509. |
| **Erythrocyte sedimentation rate,** whole blood (ESR)<br><br>Male: < 10<br>Female: < 15 mm/h<br>(laboratory-specific)<br><br>Lavender<br>$<br>Test must be run within 2 hours after sample collection. | In plasma, erythrocytes (red blood cells [RBCs]) usually settle slowly. However, if they aggregate for any reason (usually because of plasma proteins called acute phase reactants, eg, fibrinogen) they settle rapidly. Sedimentation of RBCs occurs because their density is greater than plasma.<br>ESR measures the distance in mm that erythrocytes fall during 1 hour. | **Increased in:** Infections (osteomyelitis, pelvic inflammatory disease [75%]), inflammatory disease (temporal arteritis, polymyalgia rheumatica, rheumatic fever), malignant neoplasms, paraproteinemias, anemia, pregnancy, chronic renal failure, GI disease (ulcerative colitis, regional ileitis).<br>**Decreased in:** Polycythemia, sickle cell anemia, spherocytosis, anisocytosis, hypofibrinogenemia, hypogammaglobulinemia, congestive heart failure, microcytosis. Drugs: high-dose corticosteroids. | There is a good correlation between ESR and C-reactive protein, but ESR is less expensive.<br>Test is useful and indicated only for diagnosis and monitoring of temporal arteritis and polymyalgia rheumatica. The test is not sensitive or specific for other conditions.<br>ESR is higher in women, blacks, and older persons.<br>Low value is of no diagnostic significance.<br>Ref: Am J Med 1985;78:1001.<br>Ref: Ann Intern Med 1986;104:515. |

| | Erythropoietin | Ethanol |
|---|---|---|
| **Erythropoietin, serum** (EPO)<br><br>5–20 mIU/mL<br>[4–26 IU/L]<br><br>Marbled<br>$$$ | Erythropoietin is a glycoprotein hormone produced in the kidney that induces red blood cell production by stimulating proliferation, differentiation, and maturation of erythroid precursors.<br>Hypoxia is the usual stimulus for production of EPO.<br>In conditions of bone marrow hyporesponsiveness, EPO levels are elevated.<br>In chronic renal failure, EPO production is decreased. | **Increased in:** Anemias associated with bone marrow hyporesponsiveness (aplastic anemia, iron deficiency anemia), secondary polycythemia (high-altitude hypoxia, COPD, pulmonary fibrosis), erythropoietin-producing tumors (cerebellar hemangioblastomas, pheochromocytomas, renal tumors), pregnancy, polycystic kidney disease. **Decreased in:** Anemia of chronic disease, renal failure, inflammatory states, primary polycythemia (polycythemia vera) (39%). | Test is not very useful in differentiating polycythemia vera from secondary polycythemia.<br>Since virtually all patients with severe anemia due to chronic renal failure respond to EPO therapy, pretherapy EPO levels are not indicated.<br>Patient receiving EPO as chronic therapy should have iron deficiency screening routinely.<br>Ref: N Engl J Med 1986;315:283.<br>Ref: Transfusion 1989;29:46.<br>Ref: Curr Opin Nephrol Hypertens 1994;3:620. |
| **Ethanol, serum** (EtOH)<br><br>0 mg/dL [mmol/L]<br><br>Marbled<br>$$<br>Do not use alcohol swab. Do not remove stopper. | Measures serum level of ethyl alcohol (ethanol). | **Present in:** Ethanol ingestion. | Whole blood alcohol concentrations are about 15% lower than serum concentrations.<br>Each 0.1 mg/dL of ethanol contributes about 22 mosm/kg to serum osmolality.<br>Legal intoxication in many states is defined as > 80 mg/dL (> 17 mmol/L).<br>Ref: N Engl J Med 1976;294:757. |

| Test/Range/Collection | Physiologic Basis | Interpretation | Comments |
|---|---|---|---|
| **Factor V (Leiden) mutation**<br>Blood<br><br>Lavender or blue<br>$$$$ | The Leiden mutation is a single nucleotide base substitution leading to an amino acid substitution (glutamine replaces arginine) at one of the sites where coagulation factor V is cleaved by activated protein C. The mutation causes factor V to be partially resistant to protein C, which is involved in inhibiting coagulation. Factor V mutations may be present in up to half of the cases of unexplained venous thrombosis and are seen in 95% of patients with activated protein C resistance. | **Positive in:** Hypercoagulability secondary to factor V mutation (specificity approaches 100%). | The presence of mutation is only a risk factor for thrombosis, not an absolute marker for disease. Homozygotes have a 50- to 100-fold increase in risk of thrombosis (relative to the general population) and heterozygotes have a 7-fold increase in risk. The current PCR and reverse dot blot assay only detects the Leiden mutation of factor V; other mutations may yet be discovered.<br>Ref: N Engl J Med 1995;332:912.<br>Ref: Nature 1994;369:64. |
| **Factor VIII assay,** plasma<br>40–150% of normal, (varies with age)<br><br>Blue<br>$$$<br>Deliver immediately to laboratory on ice. Stable for 2 hours. | Measures activity of factor VIII (antihemophilic factor), a key factor of the intrinsic clotting cascade. | **Increased in:** Inflammatory states (acute phase reactant), last trimester of pregnancy, oral contraceptives. **Decreased in:** Hemophilia A, von Willebrand's disease, disseminated intravascular coagulation, acquired factor VIII antibodies. | Normal hemostasis requires at least 25% of factor VIII activity. Symptomatic hemophiliacs usually have levels ≤ 5%. Disease levels are defined as severe (< 1%), moderate (1–5%), and mild (> 5%).<br>Factor VIII assays are used to guide replacement therapy in patients with hemophilia.<br>Ref: Semin Hematol 1967;4:93. |

| **Fecal fat** | | |
|---|---|---|
| **Fecal fat,** stool<br><br>Random: < 60 droplets of fat/ high power field<br>72 hour: < 7 g/d<br><br>$$$<br>Qualitative: random stool sample is adequate.<br>Quantitative: dietary fat should be at least 50–150 g/d for 2 days before collection. Then all stools should be collected for 72 hours and refrigerated. | In healthy people, most dietary fat is completely absorbed in the small intestine. Normal small intestinal lining, bile acids, and pancreatic enzymes are required for normal fat absorption. | **Increased in:** Malabsorption from small bowel disease (regional enteritis, celiac disease, tropical sprue), pancreatic insufficiency, diarrhea with or without fat malabsorption. | A random, qualitative fecal fat (so-called Sudan stain) is only useful if positive. Furthermore, it does not correlate well with quantitative measurements. Sudan stain appears to detect triglycerides and lipolytic by-products, whereas 72-hour fecal fat measures fatty acids from a variety of sources, including phospholipids, cholesteryl esters, and triglycerides.<br>The quantitative method can be used to measure the degree of fat malabsorption initially and then after a therapeutic intervention.<br>A normal quantitative stool fat reliably rules out pancreatic insufficiency and most forms of generalized small intestine disease.<br>Ref: Gastroenterol Clin North Am 1989;18:467.<br>Ref: Gastroenterology 1992;102:1936. |

| | Fecal occult blood | |
|---|---|---|
| **Test/Range/Collection** | **Physiologic Basis** | **Interpretation** | **Comments** |

| Test/Range/Collection | Physiologic Basis | Interpretation | Comments |
|---|---|---|---|
| **Fecal occult blood, stool**<br><br>Negative<br><br>$<br><br>Patient should be on a special diet free of exogenous peroxidase activity (meat, fish, turnips, horseradish), GI irritants (aspirin, non-steroidal anti-inflammatory drugs), and iron. To avoid false-negatives, patients should avoid taking vitamin C. | Measures blood in the stool using gum guaiac as an indicator reagent. In the Hemoccult test, gum guaiac is impregnated in a test paper that is smeared with stool using an applicator. Hydrogen peroxide is used as a developer solution. The resultant phenolic oxidation of guaiac in the presence of blood in the stool yields a blue color. | **Positive in:** Upper GI disease (peptic ulcer, gastritis, variceal bleeding, esophageal and gastric cancer), lower GI disease (diverticulosis, colonic polyps, colon carcinoma, inflammatory bowel disease, vascular ectasias, hemorrhoids). | Although fecal occult blood testing is an accepted screening test for colon carcinoma, the sensitivity and specificity of the test are low.<br>An asymptomatic patient > 45 years old with a positive Hemoccult II test has about a 10% chance of having colorectal cancer, and a high percentage of existing lesions (50–60%) will not be detected.<br>Reduction in mortality rates as a result of fecal occult blood screening is controversial.<br>HemoQuant is a quantitative test for fecal occult blood that is specific for heme and measures both intact and metabolized hemoglobin. It is not used routinely.<br>Ref: JAMA 1989;261:586.<br>Ref: Ann Intern Med 1990;112:328.<br>Ref: JAMA 1993;269:1262.<br>Ref: JAMA 1994;271:1011. |

| Ferritin | | | |
|---|---|---|---|
| **Ferritin,** serum<br><br>Males 16–300 ng/mL [μg/L]<br>Females 4–161 ng/mL [μg/L]<br><br>Marbled<br><br>$$ | Ferritin is the body's major iron storage protein.<br>The serum ferritin level correlates with total body iron stores.<br>The test is used to detect iron deficiency, to monitor response to iron therapy, and, in iron overload states, to monitor iron removal therapy. It is also used to predict homozygosity for hemochromatosis in relatives of affected patients.<br>In the absence of liver disease, it is a more sensitive test for iron deficiency than serum iron and iron-binding capacity (transferrin saturation). | **Increased in:** Iron overload (hemochromatosis, hemosiderosis), acute or chronic liver disease, alcoholism, various malignancies (eg, leukemia, Hodgkin's disease), chronic inflammatory disorders (eg, rheumatoid arthritis, adult Still's disease), thalassemia minor, hyperthyroidism, HIV infection, non-insulin-dependent diabetes mellitus, and postpartum state.<br>**Decreased in:** Iron deficiency (60–75%). | Serum ferritin is clinically useful in distinguishing between iron deficiency anemia (serum ferritin levels diminished) and anemia of chronic disease or thalassemia (levels usually normal or elevated).<br>Liver disease will increase serum ferritin levels and mask the diagnosis of iron deficiency.<br>Ref: Am J Hematol 1993;42:177.<br>Ref: Br J Haematol 1993;85:787.<br>Ref: J Intern Med 1994;236:315. |

| Test/Range/Collection | Physiologic Basis | Interpretation | Comments |
|---|---|---|---|
| **α-Fetoprotein,** serum (AFP)<br><br>0–15 ng/mL [μg/L]<br><br>Marbled<br>$$<br>Avoid hemolysis. | α-Fetoprotein is a glycoprotein produced both early in fetal life and by some tumors. | **Increased in:** Hepatocellular carcinoma (72%), massive hepatic necrosis (74%), viral hepatitis (34%), chronic active hepatitis (29%), cirrhosis (11%), regional enteritis (5%), benign gynecologic diseases (22%), testicular carcinoma (embryonal) (70%), teratocarcinoma (64%), teratoma (37%), ovarian carcinoma (57%), endometrial cancer (50%), cervical cancer (53%), pancreatic cancer (23%), gastric cancer (18%), colon cancer (5%).<br>**Negative in:** Seminoma. | The test is not sensitive or specific enough to be used as a general screening test for hepatocellular carcinoma. However, screening may be justified in populations at very high risk for hepatocellular cancer.<br>In hepatocellular cancer or germ cell tumors associated with elevated AFP, the test may be helpful in detecting recurrence after therapy.<br>AFP is also used to screen pregnant women at 15–20 weeks gestation for possible fetal neural tube defects. AFP level in maternal serum or amniotic fluid is compared with levels expected at a given gestational age.<br>Ref: N Engl J Med 1987;317:342.<br>Ref: Clin Chem 1992;38(8B Part 2):1523.<br>Ref: West J Med 1993;159:312. |

| | | Fibrin D-dimers | Fibrinogen (functional) |
|---|---|---|---|
| **Fibrin D-dimers,** plasma<br><br>Negative<br><br>Blue<br>$$ | Plasmin acts on fibrin to form various fibrin degradation products. The D-dimer level can be used as a measure of activation of the fibrinolytic system. | **Increased in:** Disseminated intravascular coagulation (DIC), other thrombotic disorders, pulmonary embolism, venous or arterial thrombosis. | Fibrin D-dimer assay has replaced the Fibrin(ogen) Split Products test as a screen for DIC, because the D-dimer assay can distinguish fibrin degradation products (in DIC) from fibrinogen degradation products (in primary fibrinogenolysis). Since the presence of fibrin D-dimer is not specific for DIC, the definitive diagnosis of DIC must depend on other tests, including the platelet count and serum fibrinogen level. Ref: Am J Clin Pathol 1986;85:360. |
| **Fibrinogen (functional),** plasma<br><br>175–433 mg/dL [1.75–4.3 g/L]<br>*Panic:* < 75 mg/dL<br><br>Blue<br>$$ | Fibrinogen is synthesized in the liver and has a half-life of about 4 days. Thrombin cleaves fibrinogen to form insoluble fibrin monomers, which polymerize to form a clot. | **Increased in:** Inflammatory states (acute phase reactant), use of oral contraceptives, pregnancy. **Decreased in:** Decreased hepatic synthesis, increased consumption (disseminated intravascular coagulation [DIC], thrombolysis). Hereditary: Afibrinogenemia (rare), hypofibrinogenemia, dysfibrinogenemia. | Hypofibrinogenemia is an important diagnostic laboratory feature of DIC. Diagnosis of dysfibrinogenemia depends upon the discrepancy between measurable antigenic and low functional (clottable) fibrinogen levels. Ref: Blood 1982;60:284. Ref: Am Intern Med 1993;118:956. |

| | Fluorescent treponemal antibody-absorbed | |
|---|---|---|
| **Test/Range/Collection** | **Physiologic Basis** | **Interpretation** | **Comments** |
| **Fluorescent trepone-mal antibody-absorbed,** serum (FTA-ABS)<br><br>Nonreactive<br><br>Marbled<br><br>$$ | Detects specific antibodies against *Treponema pallidum.* Patient's serum is first diluted with nonpathogenic treponemal antigens (to bind nonspecific antibodies). The absorbed serum is placed on a slide that contains fixed *T pallidum.* Fluorescein-labeled antihuman gamma globulin is then added to bind to and visualize (under a fluorescence microscope) the patient's antibody on treponemes. | **Reactive in:** Syphilis: primary (95%), secondary (100%), late (96%), late latent (100%); also rarely positive in collagen-vascular diseases in the presence of antinuclear antibody. | Used to confirm a reactive nontreponemal screening serologic test for syphilis such as RPR or VDRL (see pp 156 and 182, respectively).<br>Once positive, the FTA-ABS may remain positive for life. However, one study found that at 36 months after treatment, 24% of patients had nonreactive FTA-ABS tests.<br>In a study of HIV-infected men with a prior history of syphilis, 38% of patients with AIDS or ARC had loss of reactivity to treponemal tests, compared with 7% of HIV-seropositive asymptomatic men and 0% of HIV-seronegative men.<br>Ref: Ann Intern Med 1986;104:368.<br>Ref: J Infect Dis 1990;162:862.<br>Ref: Ann Intern Med 1991;114:1005. |

| Folic acid (RBC) | | |
|---|---|---|
| **Folic acid (RBC),** whole blood<br><br>165–760 ng/mL [370–1720 nmol/L]<br><br>Lavender<br><br>$$$ | Folate is a vitamin necessary for methyl group transfer in thymidine formation, and hence DNA synthesis. Deficiency can result in megaloblastic anemia. | **Decreased in:** Tissue folate deficiency (from dietary folate deficiency), $B_{12}$ deficiency (50–60%, since cellular uptake of folate depends on $B_{12}$). | Red cell folate level correlates better than serum folate level with tissue folate deficiency.<br>A low red cell folate level may indicate either folate or $B_{12}$ deficiency.<br>A therapeutic trial of folate (and not red cell or serum folate testing) is indicated when the clinical and dietary history is strongly suggestive of folate deficiency and the peripheral smear shows hypersegmented polymorphonuclear leukocytes. However, the possibility of vitamin $B_{12}$ deficiency must always be considered in the setting of megaloblastic anemia, since folate therapy will treat the hematologic, but not the neurologic, sequelae of vitamin $B_{12}$ deficiency.<br>Ref: Blood 1983;61:624. |

| Test/Range/Collection | Physiologic Basis | Interpretation | Comments |
|---|---|---|---|
| **Follicle-stimulating hormone** | | | **Follicle-stimulating hormone** |
| **Follicle-stimulating hormone**, serum (FSH)<br><br>Male: 1–10 mIU/mL<br>Female: (mIU/mL)<br>Follicular 4–13<br>Luteal 2–13<br>Midcycle 5–22<br>Postmenopausal 20–138<br>(laboratory-specific)<br><br>Marbled<br>$$ | FSH is stimulated by the hypothalamic hormone GnRH and is then secreted from the anterior pituitary in a pulsatile fashion. Levels rise during the prevovulatory phase of the menstrual cycle and then decline. Elevation of FSH is the most sensitive indicator of onset of menopause. | **Increased in:** Primary (ovarian) gonadal failure, ovarian or testicular agenesis, castration, postmenopause, Klinefelter's syndrome, drugs.<br>**Decreased in:** Hypothalamic disorders, pituitary disorders, pregnancy, anorexia nervosa. Drugs: corticosteroids, oral contraceptives. | Test indicated in the workup of amenorrhea in women (see Amenorrhea algorithm, p 311), delayed puberty, impotence, and infertility in men. Impotence workup should begin with serum testosterone measurement. Basal FSH levels in premenopausal women depend on age, smoking history, and menstrual cycle length and regularity.<br>Ref: Br Med J 1987;294:815.<br>Ref: Endocrinol Metab Clin North Am 1992;21:921.<br>Ref: JAMA 1993;270:83.<br>Ref: J Clin Endocrinol Metab 1994; 79:1105. |
| **Free erythrocyte protoporphyrin**, whole blood (FEP)<br><br>< 35 µg/dL (method-dependent)<br><br>Lavender<br>$$$ | Protoporphyrin is produced in the next to last step of heme synthesis. In the last step, iron is incorporated into protoporphyrin to produce heme. Enzyme deficiencies, lack of iron, or presence of interfering substances (lead) can disrupt this process and cause elevated FEP. | **Increased in:** Decreased iron incorporation into heme (iron deficiency, infection, and lead poisoning), erythropoietic protoporphyria. | FEP can be used to screen for lead poisoning in children provided that iron deficiency has been ruled out. Test does not discriminate between uroporphyrin, coproporphyrin, and protoporphyrin, but protoporphyrin is the predominant porphyrin measured.<br>Ref: Clin Pediatr 1991;30:74.<br>Ref: Am J Dis Child 1993;147:66. |

| Gamma-glutamyl transpeptidase | | | Gastrin | |
|---|---|---|---|---|

**Gamma-glutamyl transpeptidase, serum (GGT)**

9–85 U/L
[0.15–1.42 µkat/L]
(laboratory-specific)

Marbled
$

GGT is an enzyme present in liver, kidney, and pancreas.
It is induced by alcohol intake and is an extremely sensitive indicator of liver disease, particularly alcoholic liver disease.

**Increased in:** Liver disease: acute viral or toxic hepatitis, chronic or subacute hepatitis, alcoholic hepatitis, cirrhosis, biliary tract obstruction (intrahepatic or extrahepatic), primary or metastatic liver neoplasm, mononucleosis. Drugs (by enzyme induction): phenytoin, carbamazepine, barbiturates, alcohol.

GGT is useful in follow-up of alcoholics undergoing treatment since the test is sensitive to modest alcohol intake.
GGT is elevated in 90% of patients with liver disease.
GGT is used to confirm hepatic origin of elevated serum alkaline phosphatase.
Ref: Alcohol Clin Exp Res 1990;14:250.
Ref: Am J Gastroenterol 1992;87:991.

**Gastrin, serum**

< 300 pg/mL [ng/L]

Marbled
$$
Overnight fasting required.

Gastrin is secreted from G cells in the stomach antrum and stimulates acid secretion from the gastric parietal cells.
Values fluctuate throughout the day but are lowest in the early morning.

**Increased in:** Gastrinoma (Zollinger-Ellison syndrome) (93%), antral G cell hyperplasia, hypochlorhydria, achlorhydria, chronic atrophic gastritis, pernicious anemia. Drugs: antacids, cimetidine, and other $H_2$ blockers; omeprazole and other proton pump inhibitors.
**Decreased in:** Antrectomy with vagotomy.

Gastrin is the first-line test for determining whether a patient with active ulcer disease has a gastrinoma. Gastric analysis is not indicated.
Before interpreting an elevated level, be sure that the patient is not taking antacids, $H_2$ blockers, or proton pump inhibitors.
Both fasting and post-secretin infusion levels may be required for diagnosis.
Ref: Mayo Clin Proc 1982;57:211.
Ref: Ann Intern Med 1983;98:59.
Ref: Endocrinol Metab Clin North Am 1993;22:823.

| | Glucose | |
|---|---|---|
| **Test/Range/Collection** | **Physiologic Basis** | **Interpretation** | **Comments** |
|---|---|---|---|
| **Glucose**, serum<br><br>60–115 mg/dL<br>[3.3–6.3 mmol/L]<br>*Panic:* < 40 or > 500 mg/dL<br><br>Marbled<br>$<br><br>Overnight fasting usually required. | Normally, the glucose concentration in extracellular fluid is closely regulated so that a source of energy is readily available to tissues and so that no glucose is excreted in the urine. | **Increased in:** Diabetes mellitus, Cushing's syndrome (10–15%), chronic pancreatitis (30%). Drugs: corticosteroids, phenytoin, estrogen, thiazides.<br>**Decreased in:** Pancreatic islet cell disease with increased insulin, insulinoma, adrenocortical insufficiency, hypopituitarism, diffuse liver disease, malignancy (adrenocortical, stomach, fibrosarcoma), infant of a diabetic mother, enzyme deficiency diseases (eg, galactosemia). Drugs: insulin, ethanol, propranolol; sulfonylureas, tolbutamide, and other oral hypoglycemic agents. | Diagnosis of diabetes mellitus requires a fasting plasma glucose of > 140 mg/dL on more than one occasion.<br>Hypoglycemia is defined as a glucose of < 50 mg/dL in men and < 40 mg/dL in women.<br>While random serum glucose levels correlate with home glucose monitoring results (weekly mean capillary glucose values), there is wide fluctuation within individuals. Thus, glycosylated hemoglobin levels are favored to monitor glycemic control.<br>Ref: N Engl J Med 1976;294:766.<br>Ref: Arch Intern Med 1991;151:1133. |

| **Glucose tolerance test** | | |
|---|---|---|
| **Glucose tolerance test,** serum<br><br>Fasting : < 115<br>1-hour: < 200<br>2-hour: < 140 mg/dL<br>[Fasting: < 6.4<br>1-hour: < 11.0<br>2-hour: < 7.7 mmol/L]<br><br>Marbled<br>$$<br>Subjects should receive a 150- to 200-g/d carbohydrate diet for at least 3 days prior to test. A 75-g glucose dose is dissolved in 300 mL of water for adults (1.75 g/kg for children) and given after an overnight fast. Serial determinations of plasma or serum venous blood glucoses are obtained at baseline, at 1 hour, and at 2 hours. | The test determines the ability of a patient to respond appropriately to a glucose load. | **Increased glucose rise (decreased glucose tolerance) in:** Diabetes mellitus, impaired glucose tolerance, gestational diabetes, severe liver disease, hyperthyroidism, stress (infection), increased absorption of glucose from GI tract (hyperthyroidism, gastrectomy, gastroenterostomy, vagotomy, excess glucose intake), Cushing's syndrome, pheochromocytoma. Drugs: diuretics, oral contraceptives, glucocorticoids, nicotinic acid, phenytoin.<br>**Decreased glucose rise (flat glucose curve) in:** Intestinal disease (celiac sprue, Whipple's disease), adrenal insufficiency (Addison's disease), hypopituitarism), pancreatic islet cell tumors or hyperplasia. | Test is not generally required for diagnosis of diabetes mellitus; diagnosis is made by finding fasting plasma glucose levels of > 140 mg/dL on more than one occasion.<br>In screening for gestational diabetes, the glucose tolerance test is performed between 24 and 28 weeks of gestation. After a 50-g oral glucose load, a 2-hour postprandial blood glucose is measured as a screen. If the result is > 140 mg/dL, then the full test with 100-g glucose load is done using the following reference ranges:<br><br>Fasting: < 105<br>1-hour: < 190<br>2-hour: < 165<br>3-hour: < 145 mg/dL<br><br>Routine screening for gestational diabetes has not been found to be cost-effective, and is not recommended by the Canadian Task Force on the Periodic Health Examination.<br>Ref: Annu Rev Med 1983;34:295.<br>Ref: J Fam Pract 1993;37:27. |

| | Glucose-6-phosphate dehydrogenase | | |
|---|---|---|---|
| Test/Range/Collection | Physiologic Basis | Interpretation | Comments |
| Glucose-6-phosphate dehydrogenase screen, whole blood (G6PD)<br><br>4–8 units/g Hb [0.07–0.14 μkat/L]<br><br>Green or blue<br><br>$$ | G6PD is an enzyme in the hexose monophosphate shunt that is essential in generating reduced glutathione and NADPH, which protect hemoglobin from oxidative denaturation. Numerous G6PD isoenzymes have been identified.<br><br>Most African-Americans have G6PD-A(+) isoenzyme. 10–15% have G6PD-A(−), which has only 15% of normal enzyme activity. It is transmitted in an X-linked recessive manner.<br><br>Some Mediterranean people have the B− variant that has extremely low enzyme activity (1% of normal). | **Increased in:** Young erythrocytes (reticulocytosis).<br>**Decreased in:** G6PD deficiency. | In deficient patients, hemolytic anemia can be triggered by oxidant agents; antimalarial drugs (eg, chloroquine), nalidixic acid, nitrofurantoin, dapsone, phenacetin, vitamin C, and some sulfonamides. Any African-American about to be given an oxidant drug should be screened for G6PD deficiency. (Also screen people from certain Mediterranean areas: Greece, Italy, etc.)<br>Hemolytic episodes can also occur in deficient patients who eat fava beans, in patients with diabetic acidosis, and in infections.<br>G6PD deficiency may be the cause of hemolytic disease of newborns in Asians and Mediterraneans.<br>Ref: Br J Haematol 1979;43:465.<br>Ref: Ann Intern Med 1985;103:245. |

|  | Glutamine | Glycohemoglobin |
|---|---|---|
| **Interpretation** | Test is not indicated if albumin, alanine aminotransferase (ALT), bilirubin, and alkaline phosphatase are normal or if there is no clinical evidence of liver disease.<br>Hepatic encephalopathy is essentially ruled out if the CSF glutamine is normal.<br>Ref: Arch Intern Med 1971;127:1033.<br>Ref: Science 1974;183:81. | Test is not indicated for diagnosis of diabetes mellitus. It is used to monitor long-term control of blood glucose level.<br>Reference ranges are method-specific.<br>Development and progression of chronic complications of diabetes are related to the degree of altered glycemia. Measurement of HbA$_{1c}$ can improve metabolic control by leading to changes in diabetes treatment.<br>Ref: N Engl J Med 1993;329:979.<br>Ref: Clin Chem 1994;40:1637.<br>Ref: Diabetes Care 1994;17:938. |
| | **Increased in:** Hepatic encephalopathy. | **Increased in:** Diabetes mellitus, splenectomy. Falsely high results can occur depending on the method used and may be due to presence of hemoglobin F or uremia.<br>**Decreased in:** Any condition that shortens red cell life span (hemolytic anemias, congenital spherocytosis, acute or chronic blood loss, sickle cell disease, hemoglobinopathies). |
| | Glutamine is synthesized in the brain from ammonia and glutamic acid.<br>Elevated CSF glutamine is associated with hepatic encephalopathy. | During the life span of each red blood cell, glucose combines with hemoglobin to produce a stable glycated hemoglobin.<br>The level of glycated hemoglobin is related to the mean plasma glucose level during the prior 1–3 months.<br>There are three glycated A hemoglobins, HbA$_{1a}$, HbA$_{1b}$, and HbA$_{1c}$.<br>Some assays quantitate HbA$_{1c}$; some quantitate total HbA$_1$; and some quantitate all glycated hemoglobins, not just A. |
| | **Glutamine, CSF**<br>Glass or plastic tube<br>6–15 mg/dL<br>*Panic:* > 40 mg/dL<br>$$$ | **Glycohemoglobin; glycated (glycosylated) hemoglobin,** serum (HbA$_{1c}$)<br>3.9–6.9% (method-dependent)<br>Lavender<br>$$ |

| Test/Range/Collection | Physiologic Basis | Interpretation | Comments |
|---|---|---|---|
| | | | **Growth hormone** |
| **Growth hormone, serum (GH)**<br><br>0–5 ng/mL [μg/L]<br><br>Marbled<br>$$$ | Growth hormone is a single-chain polypeptide of 191 amino acids that induces the generation of somatomedins, which directly stimulate collagen and protein synthesis.<br>GH levels are subject to wide fluctuations during the day. | **Increased in:** Acromegaly (80% have GH levels > 10 ng/mL), Laron dwarfism (defective GH receptor), starvation. Drugs: dopamine, levodopa.<br>**Decreased in:** Pituitary dwarfism, hypopituitarism. | Nonsuppressibility of GH levels to < 2 ng/mL after 100 g oral glucose and elevation of somatomedin C levels are the two most sensitive tests for acromegaly. Random determinations of GH are rarely useful in the diagnosis of acromegaly.<br>For the diagnosis of hypopituitarism or growth hormone deficiency in children, an insulin hypoglycemia test has been used. Failure to increase GH levels to > 5 ng/mL after insulin (0.1 unit/kg) is consistent with GH deficiency.<br>Ref: Hosp Pract (Off Ed) Aug 1978; 13:57.<br>Ref: N Engl J Med 1991;324:826.<br>Ref: Endocrinol Metab Clin North Am 1992;21:649. |

| Haptoglobin | | |
|---|---|---|
| **Haptoglobin,** serum<br><br>46–316 mg/dL<br>[0.5–2.2 g/L]<br><br>Marbled<br>$$ | Haptoglobin is a glycoprotein synthesized in the liver that binds free hemoglobin. | **Increased in:** Acute and chronic infection (acute phase reactant), malignancy, biliary obstruction, ulcerative colitis, myocardial infarction, and diabetes mellitus.<br>**Decreased in:** Newborns and children, posttransfusion intravascular hemolysis, autoimmune hemolytic anemia, liver disease (10%). May be decreased following uneventful transfusion (10%) for unknown reasons. | Low haptoglobin is considered an indicator of hemolysis, but it is of uncertain clinical predictive value because of the greater prevalence of other conditions associated with low levels and because of occasional normal individuals who have very low levels. It thus has low specificity.<br>High-normal levels probably rule out significant intravascular hemolysis.<br>Ref: JAMA 1980;243:1909.<br>Ref: Clin Chem 1987;33:1265. |

| Test/Range/Collection | Physiologic Basis | Interpretation | Comments |
|---|---|---|---|
| | | ***Helicobacter pylori* antibody** | |
| ***Helicobacter pylori* antibody,** serum<br><br>Negative<br><br>Marbled<br>$$ | *Helicobacter pylori* is a gram-negative spiral bacterium that is found on gastric mucosa. It induces acute and chronic inflammation in the gastric mucosa and a positive serologic antibody response. Serologic testing for *H pylori* antibody (IgG) is by ELISA. | **Increased (positive) in:** Histologic (chronic or chronic active) gastritis due to *H pylori* infection (with or without peptic ulcer disease). Sensitivity: 88–99%; specificity: 86–95%; asymptomatic adults: 15–50%. | 95% of patients with duodenal ulcers and > 70% of patients with gastric ulcers have chronic infection with *H pylori* along with associated histologic gastritis. All patients with peptic ulcer disease and positive *H pylori* serology should be treated to eradicate *H pylori* infection.<br>The prevalence of *H pylori*-positive serologic tests in asymptomatic adults is approximately 35% overall but is > 50% in patients over age 60. Fewer than one in six adults with *H pylori* antibody develop peptic ulcer disease. Treatment of asymptomatic adults is not currently recommended. The role of *H pylori* in patients with chronic dyspepsia is controversial. There is currently no role for treatment of such patients except in clinical trials.<br>After successful eradication, serologic titers fall over a 3- to 6-month period but remain positive in up to 50% of patients at 1 year.<br>Ref: Gastroenterol Clin North Am 1993;22:105.<br>Ref: Gut 1994;35:19.<br>Ref: Ann Intern Med 1994;120:977.<br>Ref: JAMA 1994;272:65. |

| Hematocrit | | | |
|---|---|---|---|
| **Hematocrit,** whole blood (Hct)<br><br>Male: 39–49%<br>Female: 35–45% (age-dependent)<br><br>Lavender<br>$ | The hematocrit represents the percentage of whole blood volume composed of erythrocytes.<br>Laboratory instruments calculate the Hct from the erythrocyte count (RBC) and the mean corpuscular volume (MCV) by the formula:<br><br>$$Hct = RBC \times MCV.$$ | **Increased in:** Hemoconcentration (as in dehydration, burns, vomiting), polycythemia, extreme physical exercise.<br>**Decreased in:** Macrocytic anemia (liver disease, hypothyroidism, vitamin $B_{12}$ deficiency, folate deficiency), normocytic anemia (early iron deficiency, anemia of chronic disease, hemolytic anemia, acute hemorrhage) and microcytic anemia (iron deficiency, thalassemia). | Conversion from hemoglobin (Hb) to hematocrit is roughly Hb × 3 = Hct. Hematocrit reported by clinical laboratories is not a spun hematocrit. The spun hematocrit may be spuriously high if the centrifuge is not calibrated, if the specimen is not spun to constant volume, or if there is "trapped plasma."<br>In determining transfusion need, the clinical picture must be considered in addition to the hematocrit.<br>Point-of-care instruments may not measure hematocrit accurately in all patients.<br>Ref: JAMA 1988;259:2433.<br>Ref: Arch Pathol Lab Med 1994;118:429.<br>Ref: Clin Chem 1995;41:306. |

| Test/Range/Collection | Physiologic Basis | Interpretation | Comments |
|---|---|---|---|
| **Hemoglobin A₂, whole blood (HbA₂)**<br><br>1.5–3.5% of total hemoglobin (Hb)<br><br>Lavender<br><br>$$ | HbA₂ is a minor component of normal adult hemoglobin ($< 3.5\%$ of total Hb). | **Increased in:** β-Thalassemia major (HbA₂ levels 4–10% of total Hb), β-thalassemia minor (HbA₂ levels 4–8% of total Hb).<br><br>**Decreased in:** Untreated iron deficiency, hemoglobin H disease. | Test is useful in the diagnosis of β-thalassemia minor (in absence of iron deficiency, which decreases HbA₂ and can mask the diagnosis).<br><br>Quantitated by column chromatographic or automated HPLC techniques.<br><br>Normal HbA₂ levels are seen in delta β-thalassemia or very mild β-thalassemias.<br><br>Ref: Blood 1988;72:1107.<br>Ref: J Clin Pathol 1993;46:852.<br>Ref: Hematol Pathol 1994;8:25. |
| **Hemoglobin electrophoresis, whole blood**<br><br>HbA: $> 95$<br>HbA₂: 1.5–3.5%<br><br>Lavender, blue, or green<br><br>$$ | Hemoglobin electrophoresis is used as a screening test. It is used to detect and differentiate hemoglobin variants.<br><br>Separation of hemoglobins by electrophoresis is based on different rates of migration of charged hemoglobin molecules in an electric field. | ↑HbS: HbA > HbS = Sickle cell trait (HbAS) or sickle α-thalassemia; HbS and F, no HbA = Sickle cell anemia (HbSS) or sickle β-thalassemia; HbS > HbA and F: Sickle β+-thalassemia.<br>↑HbC: HbA > HbC = HbC trait (HbAC); HbC and F, no HbA = HbC disease; HbC > HbA = HbC β+-thalassemia.<br>↑HbH: HbH disease.<br>↑HbA₂, F: See HbA₂, above, and HbF, below. | Evaluation of a suspected hemoglobinopathy should include electrophoresis of a hemolysate to detect an abnormal hemoglobin and quantitation of hemoglobins A₂ and F.<br><br>Automated HPLC instruments are proving to be useful alternative methods for hemoglobinopathy screening. Molecular diagnosis aids in genetic counseling of patients with thalassemia and combined hemoglobinopathies.<br><br>Ref: Semin Perinatol 1990;14:483.<br>Ref: Clin Chem 1990;36:903. |

|  | **Hemoglobin A₂** | **Hemoglobin electrophoresis** |

## Hemoglobin, fetal

| Hemoglobin, fetal, whole blood (HbF)<br><br>Adult: < 2% (varies with age)<br><br>Lavender, blue, or green<br><br>$$ | Fetal hemoglobin constitutes about 75% of total hemoglobin at birth and declines to 50% at 6 weeks, 5% at 6 months, and < 1.5% by 1 year. During the first year, adult hemoglobin (HbA) becomes the predominant hemoglobin. | **Increased in:** Hereditary disorders: eg, β-thalassemia major (60–100% of total Hb is HbF), β-thalassemia minor (2–5% HbF), sickle cell anemia (1–3% HbF), hereditary persistence of fetal hemoglobin (10–40% HbF). Acquired disorders (< 10% HbF): aplastic anemia, megaloblastic anemia, leukemia.<br>**Decreased in:** Hemolytic anemia of the newborn. | Semiquantitative acid elution test provides an estimate of fetal hemoglobin only and varies widely between laboratories. It is useful in distinguishing hereditary persistence of fetal hemoglobin (all RBCs show an increase in fetal hemoglobin) from β-thalassemia minor (only a portion of RBCs are affected).<br>Enzyme-linked antiglobulin test is used to detect fetal red cells in the Rh(−) maternal circulation in suspected cases of Rh sensitization and to determine the amount of RhoGAM to administer (1 vial/15 mL fetal RBC). Prenatal diagnosis of hemoglobinopathies may be accomplished by quantitative hemoglobin levels by HPLC or molecular diagnostic techniques.<br>Ref: J Clin Pathol 1972;25:738.<br>Ref: Clin Chem 1992;38:1906. |

| Test/Range/Collection | Physiologic Basis | Interpretation | Comments |
|---|---|---|---|
| **Hemoglobin, total**, whole blood (Hb)<br><br>Male: 13.6–17.5<br>Female: 12.0–15.5 g/dL (age-dependent)<br>[Male: 136–175<br>Female: 120–155 g/L]<br>***Panic:*** $\leq 7$ g/dL<br><br>Lavender<br>$ | Hemoglobin is the major protein of erythrocytes and transports oxygen from the lungs to peripheral tissues. It is measured by spectrophotometry on automated instruments after hemolysis of red cells and conversion of all hemoglobin to cyanmethemoglobin. | **Increased in:** Hemoconcentration (as in dehydration, burns, vomiting), polycythemia, extreme physical exercise.<br>**Decreased in:** Macrocytic anemia (liver disease, hypothyroidism, vitamin $B_{12}$ deficiency, folate deficiency), normocytic anemia (early iron deficiency, anemia of chronic disease, hemolytic anemia, acute hemorrhage), and microcytic anemia (iron deficiency, thalassemia). | Hypertriglyceridemia and very high white blood cell counts can cause false elevations of Hb.<br>Ref: JAMA 1988;259:2433. |
| **Hemosiderin,** urine<br><br>Negative<br><br>Urine container<br>$$<br>Fresh, random sample. | Hemosiderin is a protein produced by the digestion of hemoglobin. Its presence in the urine indicates acute or chronic release of free hemoglobin into the circulation with accompanying depletion of the scavenging proteins, hemopexin and haptoglobin. Presence of hemosiderin usually indicates intravascular hemolysis or recent transfusion. | **Increased in:** Intravascular hemolysis: hemolytic transfusion reactions, paroxysmal nocturnal hemoglobinuria, microangiopathic hemolytic anemia, mechanical destruction of erythrocytes (heart valve hemolysis), sickle cell anemia, thalassemia major, oxidant drugs with G6PD deficiency (eg, dapsone). Hemochromatosis. | Hemosiderin can be qualitatively detected in urinary sediment using Prussian blue stain.<br>Ref: J Lab Clin Med 1951;38:3.<br>Ref: Med Clin North Am 1992;76:649. |

| | Hepatitis A antibody | Hepatitis B surface antigen |
|---|---|---|
| **Test / Specimen / Range / Cost** | **Hepatitis A antibody,** serum (Anti-HAV) <br><br> Negative <br><br> Marbled <br><br> $$ | **Hepatitis B surface antigen,** serum (HBsAg) <br><br> Negative <br><br> Marbled <br><br> $$ |
| **Physiologic Basis** | Hepatitis A is caused by a nonenveloped 27 nm RNA virus of the enterovirus-picornavirus group and is usually acquired by the fecal-oral route. IgM antibody is detectable within a week after symptoms develop and persists for 6 months. IgG appears 4 weeks later than IgM and persists for years (see Figure 8–7, p 330, for time course of serologic changes). | In hepatitis B virus infection, surface antigen is detectable 2–5 weeks before onset of symptoms, rises in titer, and peaks at about the time of onset of clinical illness. Generally it persists for 1–5 months, declining in titer and disappearing with resolution of clinical symptoms (see Figure 8–8, p 331, for time course of serologic changes). |
| **Interpretation** | **Positive in:** Acute hepatitis A (IgM), convalescence from hepatitis A (IgG). | **Increased in:** Acute hepatitis B, chronic hepatitis B (persistence of HBsAg for > 6 months, positive HBcAb [total]), HBsAg-positive carriers. May be undetectable in acute hepatitis B infection. If clinical suspicion is high, HBcAb (IgM) test is then indicated. |
| **Comments** | The most commonly used test for hepatitis A antibody is an immunoassay that detects total IgG and IgM antibodies. This test can be used to establish immune status. Specific IgM testing is necessary to diagnose acute hepatitis A. IgG antibody positivity is found in 40–50% of adults in USA and Europe (higher rates in developing nations). Testing for anti-HAV (IgG) may reduce cost of HAV vaccination programs. Ref: Arch Intern Med 1994;154:663. | First-line test for the diagnosis of acute or chronic hepatitis B. If positive, no other test is needed. HBeAg is a marker of extensive viral replication found only in HBsAg-positive sera. Persistently HBeAg-positive patients are more infectious than HBeAg-negative patients and more likely to develop chronic liver disease. Ref: Annu Rev Med 1981;32:1. |

| Test/Range/Collection | Physiologic Basis | Interpretation | Comments |
|---|---|---|---|
| | | | **Hepatitis B surface antibody** |
| | | | **Hepatitis B core antibody** |
| **Hepatitis B surface antibody,** serum (HBsAb, anti-HBs)<br><br>Negative<br><br>Marbled<br>$$ | Test detects antibodies to hepatitis B virus (HBV) which are thought to confer immunity to hepatitis B. Since several subtypes of hepatitis B exist, there is a possibility of subsequent infection with a second subtype. | **Increased in:** Hepatitis B immunity due to HBV infection or hepatitis B vaccination.<br>**Absent in:** Hepatitis B carrier state, non-exposure. | Test indicates immune status.<br>It is not useful for the evaluation of acute or chronic hepatitis.<br>(See Figure 8–8, p 331, for time course of serologic changes.)<br>Ref: Ann Intern Med 1985;103:201.<br>Ref: Dig Dis Sci 1986;31:620. |
| **Hepatitis B core antibody, total,** serum (HBcAb, anti-HBc)<br><br>Negative<br><br>Marbled<br>$$ | HBcAb (IgG and IgM) will be positive (as IgM) about 2 months after exposure to hepatitis B. Its persistent positivity may reflect chronic hepatitis (IgM) or recovery (IgG). (See Figure 8–8, p 331, for time course of serologic changes.) | **Positive in:** Hepatitis B (acute and chronic), hepatitis B carriers (high levels), prior hepatitis B (immune) when IgG present in low titer with or without HBsAb.<br>**Negative:** After hepatitis B vaccination. | HBcAb (total) is useful in evaluation of acute or chronic hepatitis only if HBsAg is negative. An HBcAb (IgM) test is then indicated only if the HBcAb (total) is positive.<br>HBcAb (IgM) may be the only serologic indication of acute HBV infection.<br>Ref: Dig Dis Sci 1985;30:1022.<br>Ref: Mayo Clin Proc 1988;63:201. |

| Hepatitis Be antigen/antibody | | |
|---|---|---|
| **Hepatitis Be antigen/ antibody (HBeAg/ Ab), serum**<br><br>Negative<br><br>Marbled<br>$$ | HBeAg is a soluble protein secreted by hepatitis B virus, related to HBcAg, indicating viral replication and infectivity. Two distinct serologic types of hepatitis B have been described, one with a positive HBeAg and the other with a negative HBeAg and a positive anti-HBe antibody. | **Increased (positive) in:** HBV (acute, chronic) hepatitis. | The assumption has been that loss of HBeAg and accumulation of HBeAb are associated with decreased infectivity. Testing has proved unreliable, and tests are not routinely needed as indicators of infectivity. All patients positive for HBsAg must be considered infectious.<br>Anti-HBeAb is used to select patients for clinical trials of interferon therapy or liver transplantation.<br>Ref: Proc Natl Acad Sci U S A 1991;88:4186.<br>Ref: J Med Microbiol 1994;41:374. |

| Test/Range/Collection | Physiologic Basis | Interpretation | Comments |
|---|---|---|---|
| | **Hepatitis C antibody** | | |
| **Hepatitis C antibody,** serum (HCAb)<br><br>Negative<br><br>Marbled<br><br>$$ | Detects antibody to hepatitis C virus. Current screening test (ELISA) detects antibodies to proteins expressed by putative structural (HC34) and nonstructural (HC31, C100-3) regions of the HCV genome. The presence of these antibodies indicates that the patient has been infected with HCV, may harbor infectious HCV, and may be capable of transmitting HCV.<br><br>A recombinant immunoblot assay (RIBA) is available as a confirmatory test. | **Increased in:** Acute hepatitis C (only 20–50%; seroconversion may take 6 months or more), posttransfusion chronic non-A, non-B hepatitis (70–90%), sporadic chronic non-A, non-B hepatitis (30–80%), blood donors (0.5–1%), non-blood-donating general public (2–3%), hemophiliacs (75%), intravenous drug abusers (40–80%), hemodialysis patients (1–30%), male homosexuals (4%). | Sensitivity of current assays is 86%, specificity 99.5%.<br>Hepatitis C remains a clinical diagnosis of exclusion.<br>Seropositivity for hepatitis C documents previous exposure, not necessarily acute infection.<br>Seronegativity in acute hepatitis does not exclude the diagnosis of hepatitis C, especially in immunosuppressed patients.<br>Testing of donor blood for hepatitis C has significantly reduced the incidence of posttransfusion hepatitis.<br>Ref: N Engl J Med 1989;321:1538.<br>Ref: Hepatology 1993;18:497.<br>Ref: Dis Mon 1994;40(3):117. |
| | **Hepatitis D antibody** | | |
| **Hepatitis D antibody,** serum (Anti-HDV)<br><br>Negative<br><br>Marbled<br><br>$$ | This antibody is a marker for acute or persisting infection with the delta agent, a defective RNA virus that can only infect HBsAg-positive patients. Hepatitis B virus (HBV) plus hepatitis D virus (HDV) infection may be more severe than HBV infection alone. Antibody to HDV ordinarily persists for about 6 months following acute infection. Further persistence indicates carrier status. | **Positive in:** Hepatitis D. | Test only indicated in HBsAg-positive patients.<br>Chronic HDV hepatitis occurs in 80–90% of HBsAg carriers who are superinfected with delta, but in less than 5% of those who are coinfected with both viruses simultaneously.<br>Ref: Hepatology 1985;5:188.<br>Ref: Ann Intern Med 1989;110:779. |

| Heterophile agglutination | | |
|---|---|---|
| **Heterophile aggluti-nation**, serum (Monospot, Paul-Bunnell test)<br><br>Negative<br><br>Marbled<br>$ | Infectious mononucleosis is an acute saliva-transmitted infectious disease due to the Epstein-Barr virus (EBV). Heterophile (Paul-Bunnell) antibodies (IgM) appear in 60% of mononucleosis patients within 1–2 weeks and in 80–90% within the first month. They are not specific for EBV but are found only rarely in other disorders. Titers are substantially diminished by 3 months after primary infection and are not detectable by 6 months. | **Positive in:** Infectious mononucleosis (90–95%).<br>**Negative in:** Heterophile-negative mononucleosis: CMV, heterophile-negative EBV, toxoplasmosis, hepatitis viruses, HIV-1 seroconversion, listeriosis, tularemia, brucellosis, cat scratch disease, Lyme disease, syphilis, rickettsial infections, medications (phenytoin, sulfasalazine, dapsone), collagen-vascular diseases (especially lupus), subacute infective endocarditis. | The three classic signs of infectious mononucleosis are lymphocytosis, a "significant number" (> 10–20%) of atypical lymphocytes on Wright-stained peripheral blood smear, and positive heterophile test.<br>If heterophile test is negative in the setting of hematologic and clinical evidence of illness, a repeat test in 1–2 weeks may be positive. EBV serology (anti-VCA and anti-EBNA) may also be indicated, especially in children and teenage patients who may have negative heterophile tests (see EBV antibodies, p 81).<br>Ref: Hum Pathol 1974;5:551.<br>Ref: Pediatrics 1985;75:1011.<br>Ref: Clin Microbiol Rev 1988;1:300. |

| | *Histoplasma capsulatum* antigen | | | |
|---|---|---|---|---|
| **Test/Range/Collection** | **Physiologic Basis** | **Interpretation** | **Comments** | |
| ***Histoplasma capsulatum* antigen,** urine, serum, CSF (HPA)<br><br>Negative<br><br>Marbled (serum)<br><br>$$<br><br>Deliver urine, CSF in a clean plastic or glass container tube. | Heat-stable *H capsulatum* polysaccharide is detected by radioimmunoassay or ELISA using alkaline phosphatase or horseradish peroxidase-conjugated antibodies. | **Increased in:** Disseminated histoplasmosis (90–97% in urine, 50–78% in blood, and approximately 42% in CSF), localized disease (16% in urine), blastomycosis (urine and serum), coccidioidomycosis (CSF). | RIA for *H capsulatum* var *capsulatum* polysaccharide antigen in urine is a useful test in diagnosis of disseminated histoplasmosis and in assessing efficacy of treatment or in detecting relapse, especially in AIDS patients and when serologic tests for antibodies may be negative. Because the test has low sensitivity in localized pulmonary disease, it is not useful for ruling out localized pulmonary histoplasmosis. HPA in bronchoalveolar lavage fluid has 70% sensitivity for the diagnosis of pulmonary histoplasmosis.<br>Ref: N Engl J Med 1986;314:83.<br>Ref: Am J Med 1989;87:396.<br>Ref: Arch Intern Med 1989;149:302.<br>Ref: Am Rev Respir Dis 1992;145:1421. | |

| *Histoplasma capsulatum* **precipitins** | | |
|---|---|---|
| *Histoplasma capsulatum* precipitins, serum<br><br>Negative<br><br>Marbled<br><br>$$ | Histoplasmosis is the most common systemic fungal infection and typically starts as a pulmonary infection with influenza-like symptoms. This may heal, progress, or lie dormant with reinfection occurring at a later time.<br>This test screens for presence of *Histoplasma* antibody by detecting precipitin "H" and "M" bands.<br>Positive H band indicates active infection, M band indicates acute or chronic infection or prior skin testing. Presence of both suggests active histoplasmosis. | **Positive in:** Previous, chronic, or acute *Histoplasma* infection, recent histoplasmin skin testing. Cross-reactions at low levels in patients with blastomycosis and coccidioidomycosis. | Histoplasmosis is usually seen in the Mississippi and Ohio River Valleys but may appear elsewhere.<br>Test is useful as a screening test or as an adjunct to complement fixation test (see below) in diagnosis of systemic histoplasmosis.<br>Ref: Rose NR et al (editors): *Manual of Clinical Laboratory Immunology*, 4th ed. American Society for Microbiology, 1992. |

| | *Histoplasma capsulatum* CF antibody | | |
|---|---|---|---|
| **Test/Range/Collection** | **Physiologic Basis** | **Interpretation** | **Comments** |
| ***Histoplasma capsulatum* complement fixation (CF) antibody,** serum<br><br>< 1:4 titer<br><br>Marbled<br><br>$$<br><br>Submit paired sera, one specimen collected within 1 week after onset of illness and another 2 weeks later. | Quantitates level of *Histoplasma* antibody.<br>Antibodies in primary pulmonary infections are generally found within 4 weeks after exposure and frequently are present at the time symptoms appear.<br>Two types of CF test are available based on mycelial antigen and yeast phase antigen. The yeast phase test is considerably more sensitive.<br>Latex agglutination (LA) and ELISA tests are also available but are less reliable. | **Increased in:** Previous, chronic, or acute *Histoplasma* infection (75–80%), recent histoplasmin skin testing (20%), other fungal disease, leishmaniasis.<br>Cross-reactions in patients with blastomycosis and coccidioidomycosis. | Elevated CF titers of > 1:16 are suggestive of infection. Titers of > 1:32 or rising titers are usually indicative of active infection.<br>Histoplasmin skin test is not recommended for diagnosis since it interferes with subsequent serologic tests. About 3.5–12% of clinically normal persons have positive titers, usually less than 1:16.<br>Ref: Hosp Pract (Off Ed) Feb 1991;26:41.<br>Ref: Rose NR et al (editors): *Manual of Clinical Laboratory Immunology*, 4th ed. American Society for Microbiology, 1992. |

| HIV antibody | | | |
|---|---|---|---|
| **HIV antibody,** serum<br><br>Negative<br><br>Marbled<br>$$ | This test detects antibody against the human immunodeficiency virus-1 (HIV-1), the etiologic agent of AIDS. HIV antibody test is considered positive only when a repeatedly reactive enzyme immunoassay (EIA) is confirmed by a Western blot analysis or immunofluorescent antibody test (IFA). | **Positive in:** HIV infection: EIA sensitivity > 99% after first 2–4 months of infection, specificity 99%. When combined with confirmatory test, specificity is 99.995%. | A positive p24 antigen test in an HIV antibody-negative individual must be confirmed by a viral neutralization assay.<br>While Western blot test is currently the most sensitive and specific assay for HIV serodiagnosis, it is highly dependent on the proficiency of the laboratory performing the test and on the standardization of the procedure.<br>Ref: Ann Intern Med 1987;106:671.<br>Ref: Arch Pathol Lab Med 1989;113: 975.<br>Ref: JAMA 1991;266:2861.<br>Ref: Infect Dis Clin North Am 1993;7: 203. |
| **HLA typing,** serum and blood (HLA)<br><br>Marbled (2 mL) and Yellow (40 mL)<br>$$$$<br>Specimens must be < 24 hours old. Refrigerate serum, but not blood in yellow tubes. | The human leukocyte antigen (HLA) system consists of four closely linked loci (HLA-A, -B, -C, and -DR) located on the short arm of chromosome 6.<br>The most widely used technique for HLA typing is the microlymphocyte toxicity test. This is a complement-mediated serologic assay in which HLA antibodies is added to peripheral blood lymphocytes. Cell death indicates that the lymphocytes carried the specific targeted antigen. | **Useful in:** Evaluation of transplant candidates and potential donors and for paternity and forensic testing. | While diseases associated with particular HLA antigens have been identified, HLA typing for the diagnosis of these diseases is not generally indicated.<br>Ref: Cell 1984;36:1. |

| | HLA-B27 typing | 5-Hydroxyindoleacetic acid |
|---|---|---|
| **Test/Range/Collection** | **HLA-B27 typing,** whole blood<br><br>Negative<br><br>Yellow<br>$$$<br>Specimens must be < 24 hours old. | **5-Hydroxyindoleacetic acid,** urine (5-HIAA)<br><br>2–8 mg/24 h<br>[10–40 μmol/d]<br><br>Urine bottle containing hydrochloric acid<br>$$ |
| **Physiologic Basis** | The HLA-B27 allele is found in approximately 8% of the US white population. It occurs less frequently in the African-American population. | Serotonin (5-hydroxytryptamine) is a neurotransmitter that is metabolized by monoamine oxidase (MAO) to 5-HIAA and then excreted into the urine.<br><br>Serotonin is secreted by most carcinoid tumors, which arise from neuroendocrine cells in locations derived from the embryonic gut. |
| **Interpretation** | There is an increased incidence of spondyloarthritis among patients who are HLA-B27-positive. HLA-B27 is present in 88% of patients with ankylosing spondylitis. It is also associated with the development of Reiter's syndrome (80%) following infection with *Shigella* or *Salmonella*. | **Increased in:** Metastatic carcinoid tumor (foregut, midgut, and bronchial). Nontropical sprue (slight increase). Diet of bananas, walnuts, avocado, eggplant, pineapple, plums. Drugs: reserpine.<br><br>**Negative in:** Rectal carcinoids (usually), renal insufficiency. Drugs: MAO inhibitors, phenothiazines. |
| **Comments** | The best diagnostic test for ankylosing spondylitis is a lumbar spine film and not HLA-B27 typing.<br>HLA-B27 testing is not usually clinically indicated.<br>Ref: Ann Intern Med 1980;92:208. | Since most carcinoid tumors drain into the portal vein and serotonin is rapidly cleared by the liver, the carcinoid syndrome (flushing, bronchial constriction, diarrhea, hypotension, and cardiac valvular lesions) is a late manifestation of carcinoid tumors, appearing only after hepatic metastasis has occurred.<br>Ref: N Engl J Med 1986;315:702.<br>Ref: Clin Chem 1992;38:1730.<br>Ref: Endocrinol Metab Clin North Am 1993;22:823.<br>Ref: Clin Chem 1994;40:86. |

|  | IgG index | Immunoelectrophoresis |
| --- | --- | --- |
| **Test / Specimen** | IgG index, serum and CSF<br><br>0.29–0.59 ratio<br><br>Marbled (for serum) and glass/plastic tube (for CSF)<br>$$$<br>Collect serum and CSF simultaneously. | Immunoelectrophoresis, serum (IEP)<br><br>Negative<br><br>Marbled<br>$$$ |
| **Physiologic Basis** | This test compares CSF IgG and albumin levels to serum levels. An increased ratio allegedly reflects synthesis of IgG within the central nervous system.<br><br>$$\text{IgG index} = \frac{\text{CSF IgG/CSF albumin}}{\text{Serum IgG/Serum albumin}}$$ | Immunoelectrophoresis is used to identify specific immunoglobulin (Ig) classes. Serum is separated electrophoretically and reacted with antisera of known specificity. Newer technique (immunofixation) is available and easier to interpret. |
| **Interpretation** | **Increased in:** Multiple sclerosis (80–90%), neurosyphilis, subacute sclerosing panencephalitis, other inflammatory and infectious CNS diseases. | **Positive in:** Presence of identifiable monoclonal paraprotein: multiple myeloma, Waldenström's macroglobulinemia, Franklin's disease (heavy chain disease), lymphoma, leukemia, monoclonal gammopathy of undetermined significance. The most common form of myeloma is the IgG type. |
| **Comments** | Test is reasonably sensitive but not specific for multiple sclerosis. (Compare with Oligoclonal bands, p 137.)<br>Ref: Ann Neurol 1980;8:426.<br>Ref: Mayo Clin Proc 1989;64:577. | Test is indicated to identify an Ig spike seen on serum protein electrophoresis, to differentiate a polyclonal from a monoclonal increase, and to identify the nature of a monoclonal increase. Test is not quantitative and is not sensitive enough to use for the evaluation of immunodeficiency. Order quantitative immunoglobulins for this purpose (see below).<br>Ref: Clin Lab Med 1986;6:403,601.<br>Ref: Am J Clin Pathol 1987;88(2):198. |

| | Immunoglobulins | |
|---|---|---|
| **Test/Range/Collection** | **Physiologic Basis** | **Interpretation** | **Comments** |

| Test/Range/Collection | Physiologic Basis | Interpretation | Comments |
|---|---|---|---|
| **Immunoglobulins, serum (Ig)**<br><br>IgA: 78–367 mg/dL<br>IgG: 583–1761 mg/dL<br>IgM: 52–335 mg/dL<br>[IgA: 0.78–3.67 g/L<br>IgG: 5.83–17.6 g/L<br>IgM: 0.52–3.35 g/L]<br><br>Marbled<br>$$$ | IgG makes up about 85% of total serum immunoglobulins and predominates late in immune responses. It is the only immunoglobulin to cross the placenta.<br>IgM antibody predominates early in immune responses.<br>Secretory IgA plays an important role in host defense mechanisms by blocking transport of microbes across mucosal surfaces. | ↑**IgG:** *Polyclonal:* Autoimmune diseases (eg, SLE, rheumatoid arthritis), sarcoidosis, chronic liver diseases, some parasitic diseases, chronic or recurrent infections.<br>*Monoclonal:* Multiple myeloma (IgG type), lymphomas, or other malignancies.<br>↑**IgM:** *Polyclonal:* Isolated infections such as viral hepatitis, infectious mononucleosis, early response to bacterial or parasitic infection.<br>*Monoclonal:* Waldenström's macroglobulinemia, lymphoma.<br>↑**IgA:** *Polyclonal:* Chronic liver disease, chronic infections (especially of the GI and respiratory tracts).<br>*Monoclonal:* Multiple myeloma (IgA).<br>↓**IgG:** Immunosuppressive therapy, genetic (SCID, Wiskott-Aldrich syndrome, common variable immunodeficiency).<br>↓**IgM:** Immunosuppressive therapy.<br>↓**IgA:** Inherited IgA deficiency (ataxia-telangiectasia, combined immunodeficiency disorders). | Quantitative immunoglobulin levels are indicated in the evaluation of immunodeficiency or the quantitation of a paraprotein.<br>IgG deficiency is associated with recurrent and occasionally severe pyogenic infections.<br>The most common form of multiple myeloma is the IgG type.<br>Ref: Science 1986;231:1241. |

| Test | Description | Interpretation | Notes |
|---|---|---|---|
| **Inhibitor screen,** plasma<br><br>Negative<br><br>Blue<br>$$<br>Fill tube completely. | Test is useful for evaluating a prolonged partial thromboplastin time (PTT), prothrombin time (PT), or thrombin time. (Presence of heparin should first be excluded.)<br>Patient's plasma is mixed with normal plasma and a PTT is performed. If the patient has a factor deficiency, the postmixing PTT will be normal. If an inhibitor is present, it will be prolonged. | **Positive in:** Presence of inhibitor: Antiphospholipid antibodies (lupus anticoagulant (LAC) or anticardiolipin antibodies), factor-specific antibodies.<br>**Negative in:** Factor deficiencies. | LAC prolongs a PTT immediately and is the most common inhibitor. Poor sensitivity for lupus anticoagulant owing to relatively high phospholipid levels in this assay system. 1–4 hour incubation period may be needed to detect factor-specific antibodies with low in vitro affinities. About 15% of hemophilia A patients develop inhibitor against factor VIII. Ref: Am J Clin Path 1993;99:653. |
| **Insulin antibody,** serum<br><br>Negative<br><br>Marbled<br>$$$ | Insulin antibodies develop in nearly all diabetics treated with insulin. Most antibodies are IgG and do not cause clinical problems. Occasionally, high-affinity antibodies can bind to exogenous insulin and cause insulin resistance. | **Increased in:** Insulin therapy, type I diabetics before treatment (secondary to autoimmune pancreatic B cell destruction). | Insulin antibodies interfere with most assays for insulin. Insulin antibody test is not sensitive or specific for the detection of surreptitious insulin use; use C-peptide level (see p 59). Anti-insulin and islet cell antibodies are poor predictors of IDDM and only roughly correlate with insulin requirements in patients with diabetes. Ref: Diabetes Care 1989;12:641. Ref: Diabetic Med 1991;8:97. Ref: Lancet 1994;343:1383. |

| Test/Range/Collection | Physiologic Basis | Interpretation | Comments |
|---|---|---|---|
| **Insulin, immunoreactive**, serum<br><br>6–35 µU/mL<br>[42–243 pmol/L]<br><br>Marbled<br>$$<br>Fasting sample required. Measure glucose concurrently. | Measures levels of insulin, either endogenous or exogenous. | **Increased in:** Insulin-resistant states (eg, obesity, type II diabetes mellitus, uremia, glucocorticoids, acromegaly), liver disease, surreptitious use of insulin or oral hypoglycemic agents, insulinoma (pancreatic islet cell tumor).<br>**Decreased in:** Type I diabetes mellitus, hypopituitarism. | **Insulin, immunoreactive**<br><br>Measurement of serum insulin level has little clinical value except in the diagnosis of fasting hypoglycemia. An insulin-to-glucose ratio of > 0.3 is presumptive evidence of insulinoma. C-peptide should be used as well as serum insulin to distinguish insulinoma from surreptitious insulin use, since C-peptide will be absent with exogenous insulin use (see C-peptide, p 59).<br>Ref: Mayo Clin Proc 1976;51:417. |

| Iron | | |
|---|---|---|
| **Iron,** serum ($Fe^{2+}$)<br><br>50–175 µg/dL<br>[9–31 µmol/L]<br><br>Marbled<br>$<br>Avoid hemolysis. | Plasma iron concentration is determined by absorption from the intestine; storage in the liver, spleen, bone marrow; rate of breakdown or loss of hemoglobin; and rate of synthesis of new hemoglobin. | **Increased in:** Hemosiderosis (eg, multiple iron transfusions, excess iron administration), hemolytic anemia, pernicious anemia, aplastic or hypoplastic anemia, viral hepatitis, lead poisoning, thalassemia, hemochromatosis. Drugs: estrogens, ethanol, oral contraceptives.<br>**Decreased in:** Iron deficiency, nephrotic syndrome, chronic renal failure, many infections, active hematopoiesis, remission of pernicious anemia, hypothyroidism, malignancy (carcinoma), postoperative state, kwashiorkor. | Absence of stainable iron on bone marrow aspirate differentiates iron deficiency from other causes of microcytic anemia (eg, thalassemia, sideroblastic anemia, some chronic disease anemias), but the procedure is invasive and expensive. Serum iron, iron-binding capacity, and transferrin saturation—or serum ferritin—may obviate the need for bone marrow examination.<br>Serum iron is useful (see p 87) in screening family members for hereditary hemochromatosis.<br>Recent transfusion will confound the test results.<br>Ref: Med Clin North Am 1992;76:549.<br>Ref: N Engl J Med 1993;328:1616.<br>Ref: Am J Med Sci 1994;307:353. |

| | Iron-binding capacity | | |
|---|---|---|---|
| **Test/Range/Collection** | **Physiologic Basis** | **Interpretation** | **Comments** |
| **Iron-binding capacity, total,** serum (TIBC)<br><br>250–460 µg/dL<br>[45–82 µmol/L]<br><br>Marbled<br>$$ | Iron is transported in plasma complexed to transferrin, which is synthesized in the liver.<br>Total iron-binding capacity is calculated from transferrin levels measured immunologically. Each molecule of transferrin has two iron-binding sites, so its iron-binding capacity is 1.47 mg/g.<br>Normally, transferrin carries an amount of iron representing about 16–60% of its capacity to bind iron (ie, % saturation of iron-binding capacity is 16–60%). | **Increased in:** Iron deficiency anemia, late pregnancy, infancy, hepatitis. Drugs: oral contraceptives.<br>**Decreased in:** Hypoproteinemic states (eg, nephrotic syndrome, starvation, malnutrition, cancer), hyperthyroidism, chronic inflammatory disorders, chronic liver disease, other chronic disease. | Increased % transferrin saturation with iron is seen in iron overload (iron poisoning, hemolytic anemia, sideroblastic anemia, thalassemia, hemochromatosis, pyridoxine deficiency, aplastic anemia).<br>Decreased % transferrin saturation with iron is seen in iron deficiency (usually saturation < 16%).<br>Transferrin levels can also be used to assess nutritional status.<br>Recent transfusion will confound the test results.<br>Ref: Am J Clin Pathol 1990;93:240.<br>Ref: Arch Pathol Lab Med 1993;117:622.<br>Ref: N Engl J Med 1993;328:1616. |

| Lactate dehydrogenase | | |
|---|---|---|
| **Lactate dehydrogenase,** serum (LDH)<br><br>88–230 U/L<br>[1.46–3.82 μkat/L] (laboratory-specific)<br><br>Marbled<br>$<br><br>Hemolyzed specimens are unacceptable. | LDH is an enzyme that catalyzes the interconversion of lactate and pyruvate in the presence of NAD/NADH. It is widely distributed in body cells and fluids.<br><br>Because LDH is highly concentrated in red blood cells (RBCs), spuriously elevated serum levels will occur if RBCs are hemolyzed during specimen collection. | **Increased in:** Tissue necrosis, especially in acute injury of cardiac muscle, RBCs, kidney, skeletal muscle, liver, lung, or skin. Commonly elevated in various carcinomas and in *Pneumocystis carinii* pneumonia (78–94%) and lymphoma in AIDS. Marked elevations occur in hemolytic anemias, vitamin B₁₂ deficiency anemia, folate deficiency anemia, polycythemia vera, thrombotic thrombocytopenic purpura (TTP), hepatitis, cirrhosis, obstructive jaundice, renal disease, musculoskeletal disease, CHF. Drugs causing hepatotoxicity (eg, acetaminophen) or hemolysis.<br>**Decreased in:** Drugs: clofibrate, fluoride (low dose). | LDH is elevated after myocardial infarction (for 2–7 days), in liver congestion (eg, in CHF), and in *P carinii* pneumonia.<br>LDH is not a useful liver function test, and it is not specific enough for the diagnosis of hemolytic or megaloblastic anemias.<br>Its main diagnostic use has been in myocardial infarction, when the creatine kinase-MB elevation has passed (see CK-MB, p 76, and Figure 8–17, p. 342). LDH isoenzymes are preferred over total serum LDH in late diagnosis of MI, but both tests are now being replaced by cardiac troponin I levels.<br>Ref: Am Rev Respir Dis 1988;137: 796.<br>Ref: Clin Biochem 1990;23:375. |

| Test/Range/Collection | Physiologic Basis | Interpretation | Comments |
|---|---|---|---|
| **Lactate dehydrogen-ase isoenzymes,** serum (LDH isoenzymes)<br><br>$LDH_1/LDH_2$: < 0.85<br><br>Marbled<br>$$<br>Hemolyzed specimens are unacceptable. | LDH consists of five isoenzymes separable by electrophoresis. The fraction with the greatest electrophoretic mobility is called $LDH_1$; the one with the least, $LDH_5$. $LDH_1$ is found in high concentrations in heart muscle, RBCs, and kidney cortex; $LDH_5$ in skeletal muscle and liver. | **Increased in:** $LDH_1/LDH_2 > 0.85$ in myocardial infarction, hemolysis (hemolytic or megaloblastic anemia) or acute renal infarction. $LDH_5$ is increased in liver disease, congestive heart failure, skeletal muscle injury, and essential thrombocythemia. | The only clinical indication for LDH isoenzyme measurement has been to rule out myocardial infarction in patients presenting more than 24 hours after onset of symptoms ($LDH_1$/$LDH_2 > 0.85$ is usually present within 12–48 hours). It may also be helpful if CK-MB results cannot be easily interpreted. The test is being replaced by measurement of cardiac troponin I (see CK-MB, p 76).<br>Ref: Clin Chem 1980;26:1241.<br>Ref: Ann Clin Lab Sci 1982;12:408.<br>Ref: Hum Pathol 1984;15:706. |
| **Lactate,** venous blood<br><br>0.5–2.0 meq/L [mmol/L]<br><br>Gray<br>$$<br>Collect on ice in gray tube containing fluoride to inhibit in vitro glycolysis and lactic acid production. | Severe tissue anoxia leads to anaerobic glucose metabolism with production of lactic acid. | **Increased in:** Lactic acidosis, ethanol ingestion, sepsis, shock, liver disease, diabetic ketoacidosis, muscular exercise, hypoxia; regional hypoperfusion (bowel ischemia); prolonged use of a tourniquet (spurious elevation); type I glycogen storage disease, fructose 1,6-diphosphatase deficiency (rare), pyruvate dehydrogenase deficiency. Drugs: phenformin, isoniazid toxicity. | Lactic acidosis should be suspected when there is a markedly increased anion gap (> 18 meq/L) in the absence of other causes (eg, renal failure, ketosis, ethanol, methanol, or salicylate). Lactic acidosis is characterized by lactate levels > 5 mmol/L in association with metabolic acidosis. Tissue hypoperfusion is the most common cause. Blood lactate levels may indicate whether perfusion is being restored by therapy.<br>Ref: Crit Care Med 1992;20:80. |

| | Lactate dehydrogenase isoenzymes | Lactate |

| Lead | | |
|---|---|---|
| **Lead,** whole blood (Pb)<br><br>Child (< 6 yrs): < 10 μg/dL<br>Child (> 6 yrs): < 25 μg/dL<br>Adult: < 40 μg/dL<br>[Child (< 6): < 0.48 μmol/L<br>Child (> 6): < 1.21 mol/L<br>Adult: < 1.93 μmol/L]<br><br>Navy<br>$$<br>Use trace metal-free navy blue top tube with heparin. | Lead salts are absorbed through ingestion, inhalation, or the skin. About 5–10% of ingested lead is found in blood and 95% of this is in erythrocytes. 80–90% is taken up by bone, where it is relatively inactive.<br>Lead poisons enzymes by binding to protein disulfide groups, leading to cell death.<br>Lead levels fluctuate. Several specimens may be needed to rule out lead poisoning. | **Increased in:** Lead poisoning, including abnormal ingestion (especially lead-containing paint, moonshine whiskey), occupational exposures (metal smelters, miners, welders, storage battery workers, auto manufacturers, ship builders, paint manufacturers, printing workers, pottery workers, gasoline refinery workers), retained bullets.<br><br>Subtle neurologic impairment may be detectable in children with lead levels of 15 μg/dL and in adults at 30 μg/dL; full-blown symptoms appear at > 60 μg/dL.<br>Most chronic lead poisoning leads to a moderate anemia with basophilic stippling of erythrocytes on peripheral blood smear.<br>Acute poisoning is rare and associated with abdominal pain and constipation. Blood lead levels are useful in the diagnosis.<br>Industrial workers' limit: < 50 μg/dL.<br>Ref: Medicine 1983;62:221.<br>Ref: Pediatrics 1994;93:201. |

| Test/Range/Collection | Physiologic Basis | Interpretation | Comments |
|---|---|---|---|
| **Lecithin/sphingomyelin ratio** | | | |
| **Lecithin/sphingomye-lin ratio,** amniotic fluid (L/S ratio)<br><br>> 2.0 (method-dependent)<br><br>$$$<br>Collect in a plastic tube. | This test is used to estimate lung maturity in fetuses at risk for hyaline membrane disease.<br>As fetal pulmonary surfactant matures, there is a rapid rise in amniotic fluid lecithin content. To circumvent the dependency of lecithin concentrations on amniotic fluid volume and analytic recovery of lecithin, the assay examines the lecithin/sphingomyelin ratio. | **Increased in:** Contamination of amniotic fluid by blood, meconium, or vaginal secretions that contain lecithin (false-positives).<br>**Decreased in:** Fetal lung immaturity; 95% of normal fetuses. | Test identifies fetal lung maturity effectively only 60% of the time: ie, 40% of fetuses with an L/S ratio of < 2.0 will not develop hyaline membrane disease.<br>Precision of L/S ratio test is poor: results on a single sample may vary by ± 25%.<br>Test is not reliable to assess fetal lung maturity in offspring of diabetic mothers.<br>Ref: Am J Clin Pathol 1983;79:52.<br>Ref: Med Decis Making 1990;10:201.<br>Ref: Clin Chem 1992;38:1523.<br>Ref: Clin Chem 1994;40:541. |

## *Legionella* antibody

| | | |
|---|---|---|
| **Legionella antibody,** serum<br><br>< 1:32 titer<br><br>Marbled<br>$$$<br>Submit paired sera, one collected within 2 weeks of illness and another 2–3 weeks later. | *Legionella pneumophila* is a weakly staining gram-negative bacillus that causes Pontiac fever (acute influenza-like illness) and Legionnaire's disease (a pneumonia that may progress to a severe multisystem illness). It does not grow on routine bacteriologic culture media.<br>Antibodies are detected by indirect immunofluorescent tests to serogroup 1 of *L pneumophila*.<br>There are at least six serogroups of *L pneumophila* and at least 22 species of *Legionella*. | **Increased in:** *Legionella* infection (80% of patients with pneumonia have a fourfold rise in titer); cross-reactions with other infectious agents (*Yersinia pestis* [plague], *Francisella tularensis* [tularemia], *Bacteroides fragilis*, *Mycoplasma pneumoniae*, or *Leptospira interrogans*). | A greater than fourfold rise in titer to > 1:128 in specimens gathered more than 3 weeks apart indicates recent infection. A single titer of > 1:256 is considered diagnostic.<br>About 50–60% of cases of legionellosis may have a positive direct fluorescent antibody test. Culture can have a sensitivity of 50%. All three methods may increase sensitivity to 90%.<br>This test is species-specific. Polyvalent antiserum is needed to test for all serogroups and species.<br>Ref: Am Rev Respir Dis 1980;121:317.<br>Ref: JAMA 1983;250:1981. |

| Test/Range/Collection | Physiologic Basis | Interpretation | Comments |
|---|---|---|---|
| | | **Leukocyte alkaline phosphatase** | |
| **Leukocyte alkaline phosphatase,** whole blood (LAP)<br><br>40–130<br>Based on 0–4+ rating of 100 PMNs<br><br>Green<br>$$<br><br>Blood smear from finger stick preferred. If collecting venous blood, make smear as soon as possible. | The test measures the amount of alkaline phosphatase in neutrophils in a semiquantitative fashion.<br>Neutrophilic leukocytes on a peripheral blood smear are stained for alkaline phosphatase activity and then 100 are scored on a scale from 0 to 4+ on the basis of the intensity of the dye in their cytoplasm. | **Increased in:** Leukemoid reaction (eg, severe infections), polycythemia vera, myelofibrosis with myeloid metaplasia.<br>**Decreased in:** Chronic myeloid leukemia, paroxysmal nocturnal hemoglobinuria. | Test may be helpful for distinguishing leukemoid reactions (high-normal or increased LAP) from chronic myeloid leukemia (decreased LAP), but it is poorly reproducible.<br>Ref: Am J Clin Pathol 1963;39:439. |
| | | **Leukocyte count, total** | |
| **Leukocyte (white blood cell) count, total,** whole blood (WBC count)<br><br>3.4–10 × 10³/µL<br>[× 10⁹/L]<br>*Panic:* < 1.5 × 10³/µL<br><br>Lavender<br>$ | Measure of the total number of leukocytes in whole blood.<br>Counted on automated instruments using light scattering or electrical impedance after lysis of red blood cells. WBCs are distinguished from platelets by size. | **Increased in:** Infection, inflammation, hematologic malignancy, leukemia, lymphoma. Drugs: corticosteroids.<br>**Decreased in:** Aplastic anemia (decreased production), B₁₂ or folate deficiency (maturation defect), sepsis (decreased survival). Drugs: phenothiazines, chloramphenicol, aminopyrine. | A spurious increase may be seen when there are a large number of nucleated red cells.<br>Ref: Lab Med 1983;14:509. |

| | Lipase | | Luteinizing hormone |
|---|---|---|---|
| **Lipase,** serum<br><br>0–160 U/L<br>[0–2.66 μkat/L] (laboratory-specific)<br><br>Marbled<br>$$ | Lipases are responsible for hydrolysis of glycerol esters of long-chain fatty acids to produce fatty acids and glycerol.<br><br>Lipases are produced in the liver, intestine, tongue, stomach, and many other cells.<br><br>Assays are highly dependent on the substrate used. | **Increased in:** Acute, recurrent, or chronic pancreatitis, pancreatic pseudocyst, pancreatic malignancy, peritonitis, biliary disease, hepatic disease, diabetes mellitus (especially diabetic ketoacidosis), intestinal disease, gastric malignancy or perforation. | The sensitivity of lipase in acute pancreatitis is similar to that of amylase; lipase remains elevated longer than amylase. The specificity of lipase and amylase in acute pancreatitis is similar, though both are poor.<br><br>Test sensitivity is not very good for chronic pancreatitis or pancreatic cancer.<br><br>Ref: Dig Dis Sci 1984;29:289.<br>Ref: Arch Pathol Lab Med 1991;115: 325.<br>Ref: Clin Chem 1991;37:447. |
| **Luteinizing hormone,** serum (LH)<br><br>Male: 1–10 mIU/mL<br>Female: (mIU/mL)<br>Follicular 1–18<br>Luteal 0.4–20<br>Midcycle peak 24–105<br>Postmenopausal 15–62<br>(laboratory-specific)<br><br>Marbled<br>$$ | LH is stimulated by the hypothalamic hormone gonadotropin-releasing hormone (GnRH). It is secreted from the anterior pituitary and acts on the gonads.<br><br>LH is the principal regulator of steroid biosynthesis in the ovary and testis. | **Increased in:** Primary hypogonadism, polycystic ovary syndrome, postmenopause.<br><br>**Decreased in:** Pituitary or hypothalamic failure, anorexia nervosa, severe stress, malnutrition, Kallman's syndrome (gonadotropin deficiency associated with anosmia). Drugs: digoxin, oral contraceptives, phenothiazines. | Intact human chorionic gonadotropin (hCG) cross-reacts with LH in most immunoassays so that LH levels appear to be falsely elevated in pregnancy or in individuals with hCG-secreting tumors.<br><br>Repeated measurement may be required to diagnose gonadotropin deficiencies.<br><br>Measurement of total testosterone is the test of choice to diagnose polycystic ovary syndrome.<br><br>Ref: Clin Obstet Gynecol 1990;33:576.<br>Ref: Br J Obstet Gynaecol 1992;99: 232.<br>Ref: J Clin Endocrinol Metab 1994;78: 1208. |

| | Lyme disease antibody | | |
|---|---|---|---|
| **Test/Range/Collection** | **Physiologic Basis** | **Interpretation** | **Comments** |
| **Lyme disease anti-body,** serum<br><br>ELISA: negative (< 1:8 titer)<br><br>Western blot: non-reactive<br><br>Marbled<br><br>$$ | Test detects the presence of antibody to *Borrelia burgdorferi*, the etiologic agent in Lyme disease, an inflammatory disorder transmitted by the ticks *Ixodes dammini*, *I pacificus*, and *I scapularis* in the northeastern and midwestern, western, and southeastern USA, respectively.<br><br>Detects IgM antibody, which develops within 3–6 weeks after the onset of rash; or IgG, which develops within 6–8 weeks after the onset of disease. IgG antibody may persist for months. | **Positive in:** Lyme disease, asymptomatic individuals living in endemic areas, syphilis (*Treponema pallidum*), tick-borne relapsing fever (*Borrelia hermsii*).<br><br>**Negative in:** During the first 5 weeks of infection or after antibiotic therapy. | Test is less sensitive in patients with only a rash.<br><br>Since culture or direct visualization of the organism is difficult, serologic diagnosis (by ELISA) is indicated, although sensitivity and specificity and standardization of procedure between laboratories need improvement.<br><br>Cross-reactions may occur with syphilis (should be excluded by RPR and treponemal antibody assays).<br><br>Ref: N Engl J Med 1989;321:586.<br>Ref: Ann Intern Med 1991;114:472. |

| | Magnesium | Mean corpuscular hemoglobin |
|---|---|---|
| | Hypomagnesemia is associated with tetany, weakness, disorientation, and somnolence.<br>A magnesium deficit may exist with little or no apparent change in serum level.<br>There is a progressive reduction in serum magnesium level during normal pregnancy (related to hemodilution).<br>Ref: Arch Intern Med 1988;148:2415.<br>Ref: Magnes Res 1990;3:267.<br>Ref: J Emerg Med 1992;10:735. | MCH is calculated from measured values of hemoglobin (Hb) and red cell count (RBC) by the formula:<br><br>$$MCH = \frac{Hb}{RBC}$$ |
| | **Increased in:** Dehydration, tissue trauma, renal failure, hypoadrenocorticism, hypothyroidisn. Drugs: aspirin (prolonged use), lithium, magnesium salts, progesterone, triamterene.<br>**Decreased in:** Chronic diarrhea, enteric fistula, starvation, chronic alcoholism, total parenteral nutrition with inadequate replacement, hypoparathyroidism (especially post parathyroid surgery), acute pancreatitis, chronic glomerulonephritis, hyperaldosteronism, diabetic ketoacidosis. Drugs: albuterol, amphotericin B, calcium salts, cisplatin, citrates (blood transfusion), cyclosporine, diuretics, ethacrynic acid. | **Increased in:** Macrocytosis.<br>**Decreased in:** Microcytosis (iron deficiency, thalassemia). Hypochromia (lead poisoning, sideroblastic anemia, anemia of chronic disease). |
| **Magnesium,** serum $(Mg^{2+})$<br><br>1.8–3.0 mg/dL<br>[0.75–1.25 mmol/L]<br>***Panic:*** < 0.5 or > 4.5 mg/dL<br><br>Marbled<br>$ | Magnesium is primarily an intracellular cation (second most abundant, 60% found in bone); it is a necessary cofactor in numerous enzyme systems, particularly ATPases.<br>In extracellular fluid, it influences neuromuscular response and irritability.<br>Magnesium concentration is determined by intestinal absorption, renal excretion, and exchange with bone and intracellular fluid. | |
| **Mean corpuscular hemoglobin,** blood (MCH)<br><br>26–34 pg<br><br>Lavender<br>$ | | MCH indicates the amount of hemoglobin per red blood cell in absolute units.<br>Low MCH can mean hypochromia or microcytosis or both.<br>High MCH is evidence of macrocytosis. |

| Test/Range/Collection | Physiologic Basis | Interpretation | Comments |
|---|---|---|---|
| **Mean corpuscular hemoglobin concentration,** blood (MCHC)<br><br>31–36 g/dL<br>[310–360 g/L]<br><br>Lavender<br>$ | MCHC describes how fully the erythrocyte volume is filled with hemoglobin and is calculated from measurement of hemoglobin (Hb), mean corpuscular volume (MCV), and red cell count (RBC) by the formula:<br><br>$$MCHC = \frac{Hb}{MCV \times RBC}$$ | **Increased in:** Marked spherocytosis. Spuriously increased in autoagglutination, hemolysis (with spuriously high Hb or low MCV or RBC), lipemia. Cellular dehydration syndromes, xerocytosis.<br>**Decreased in:** Hypochromic anemia (iron deficiency, thalassemia, lead poisoning), sideroblastic anemia, anemia of chronic disease. Spuriously decreased with high white blood cell count, low Hb, or high MCV or RBC. | Ref: N Engl J Med 1979;300:1277.<br>Ref: Lab Med 1983;14:509. |
| **Mean corpuscular volume,** blood (MCV)<br><br>80–100 fL<br><br>Lavender<br>$ | Average volume of the red cell is measured by automated instrument, by electrical impedance, or by light scatter. | **Increased in:** Liver disease, megaloblastic anemia (folate, $B_{12}$ deficiencies), reticulocytosis. Spurious increase in autoagglutination, high white blood cell count. Drugs: phenytoin.<br>**Decreased in:** Iron deficiency, thalassemia; decreased or normal in anemia of chronic disease. | MCV can be normal in combined iron and folate deficiency.<br>In patients with two red cell populations (macrocytic and microcytic), MCV may be normal.<br>MCV is an insensitive test in the evaluation of anemia. Patients with iron deficiency anemia or pernicious anemia commonly have a normal MCV.<br>Ref: J Gen Intern Med 1990;5:187. |

|  | **Metanephrines** | **Methanol** |
|---|---|---|
| **Metanephrines, urine**<br><br>0.3–0.9 mg/24 h<br>[1.6–4.9 µmol/24 h]<br><br>Urine bottle containing hydrochloric acid<br>$$$<br>Collect 24-hour urine. | Catecholamines, secreted in excess by pheochromocytomas, are metabolized by the enzyme catechol-O-methyltransferase to metanephrines, and these are excreted in the urine. | |
| | **Increased in:** Pheochromocytoma (96% sensitivity, 98% specificity), neuroblastoma, ganglioneuroma. Drugs: monoamine oxidase inhibitors. | First-line test for diagnosis of pheochromocytoma (see Pheochromocytoma algorithm, p 345).<br>Since < 0.1% of hypertensives have a pheochromocytoma, routine screening of all hypertensives would yield a positive predictive value of < 10%.<br>Avoid overutilization of tests. Do not order urine vanillylmandelic acid, urine catecholamines, and plasma catecholamines at the same time.<br>Plasma catecholamine levels are often spuriously increased when drawn in the hospital setting.<br>Ref: Mayo Clin Proc 1990;65:88.<br>Ref: Ann Intern Med 1995;123:101. |
| **Methanol, whole blood**<br><br>Negative<br><br>Green or lavender<br>$$ | Serum methanol levels > 20 mg/dL are toxic and levels > 40 mg/dL are life-threatening. | |
| | **Increased in:** Methanol intoxication. | Methanol intoxication is associated with metabolic acidosis and an osmolal gap (see p 343).<br>Methanol is commonly ingested in its pure form or in cleaning and copier solutions.<br>Acute ingestion causes an optic neuritis that may result in blindness.<br>Ref: Med Toxicol 1986;1:309. |

| | Methemoglobin | | |
|---|---|---|---|
| **Test/Range/Collection** | **Physiologic Basis** | **Interpretation** | **Comments** |
| **Methemoglobin, whole blood (MetHb)**<br><br>< 0.005 g/dL<br>[< 0.5 g/L]<br><br>Lavender<br>$$<br>Analyze promptly. | Methemoglobin has its heme iron in the oxidized ferric state and thus cannot combine with and transport oxygen.<br><br>Methemoglobin can be assayed spectrophotometrically by measuring the decrease in absorbance at 630–635 nm due to the conversion of methemoglobin to cyanmethemoglobin with cyanide. | **Increased in:** Hemoglobin variants (HbM) (rare), methemoglobin reductase deficiency. Oxidant drugs such as sulfonamides (dapsone, sulfasalazine), nitrites and nitrates, aniline dyes, phenacetin, anesthetics such as benzocaine. | Levels of 1.5 g/dL (10% of total Hb) result in visible cyanosis. Patients with levels of about 35% have headache, weakness, and breathlessness. Levels in excess of 70% are usually fatal.<br>Fetal methemoglobin is accurately measured using newer multiple-wavelength spectrophotometers.<br>Ref: Am J Med Sci 1985;289:200.<br>Ref: Am J Hematol 1993;42:7.<br>Ref: Ann Emerg Med 1994;24:626.<br>Ref: Clin Chem 1995;41:458. |

| Metyrapone test (overnight) | | |
|---|---|---|
| **Metyrapone test (overnight)**, plasma or serum<br><br>8 AM cortisol:<br>< 10 µg/dL<br>[< 280 nmol/L]<br>8 AM 11-deoxycortisol: > 7 µg/dL<br>[> 202 nmol/L]<br><br>Marbled, lavender, or green<br>$$$<br>Give 2.0–2.5 g of metyrapone PO at 12:00 midnight.<br>Draw serum cortisol and 11-deoxycortisol levels at 8:00 AM. | The metyrapone stimulation test assesses both pituitary and adrenal reserve and is mainly used to diagnose secondary adrenal insufficiency (see Adrenocortical Insufficiency algorithm, p 310).<br>Metyrapone is a drug that inhibits adrenal 11β-hydroxylase and blocks cortisol synthesis. The consequent fall in cortisol increases release of ACTH and hence production of steroids formed proximal to the block (eg, 11-deoxycortisol). | **Decreased in:** An 8 AM 11-deoxycortisol level ≤ 7 µg/dL indicates primary or secondary adrenal insufficiency.<br><br>The metyrapone test can be useful in steroid-treated patients to assess the extent of suppression of the pituitary-adrenal axis.<br>The use of an extended metyrapone test in the differential diagnosis of ACTH-dependent Cushing's syndrome (pituitary versus ectopic) has been questioned.<br>Ref: Arch Intern Med 1975;135:698.<br>Ref: JAMA 1979;241:1251.<br>Ref: Ann Intern Med 1994;121:318. |

| | β$_2$-Microglobulin | | |
|---|---|---|---|
| **Test/Range/Collection** | **Physiologic Basis** | **Interpretation** | **Comments** |
| **β$_2$-Microglobulin,** serum (β$_2$M)<br><br>< 0.2 mg/dL<br>[< 2.0 mg/L]<br><br>Marbled<br><br>$$$ | β$_2$-Microglobulin is a portion of the HLA molecule on cell surfaces synthesized by all nucleated cell types and is present in all body fluids.<br>It is increased in many conditions that are accompanied by high cell turnover. | **Increased in:** Any type of inflammation, autoimmune disorders, lymphoid malignancies, viral infections (HIV, CMV). Marked elevation in patients with amyloidosis and renal failure. | Of tests used to predict progression to AIDS in HIV-infected patients, CD4 cell number has the most predictive power, followed closely by β$_2$-microglobulin.<br>Asymptomatic HIV patients with elevated β$_2$-microglobulin levels have a two- to threefold increased chance of disease progression.<br>However, β$_2$-microglobulin does not provide information significantly more useful than the combination of serial CD4 count and serum IgA in predicting onset of AIDS.<br>Ref: AIDS 1994;8:911. |

| | Microhemagglutination-*Treponema pallidum* | Mitochondrial antibody |
|---|---|---|
| **Microhemagglutination-*Treponema pallidum*, serum (MHA-TP)** <br><br> Nonreactive <br><br> Marbled <br> $$ | The MHA-TP test measures specific antibody against *T pallidum* in a patient's serum by agglutination of *T pallidum* antigen-coated erythrocytes. Antibodies to nonpathogenic treponemes are first removed by binding to nonpathogenic treponemal antigens. | **Increased in:** Syphilis: primary (64–87%), secondary (96–100%), late latent (96–100%), tertiary (94–100%); infectious mononucleosis, collagen-vascular diseases, hyperglobulinemia and dysglobulinemia. | Test is used to confirm reactive serologic tests for syphilis (RPR or VDRL). <br> Compared to FTA-ABS, MHA-TP is slightly less sensitive in all stages of syphilis and becomes reactive somewhat later in the disease. <br> Because test usually remains positive for long periods of time regardless of therapy, it is not useful in assessing the effectiveness of therapy. <br> In one study, 36 months after treatment of syphilis, 13% of patients had nonreactive MHA-TP tests. <br> Ref: Ann Intern Med 1986;104:368. <br> Ref: J Infect Dis 1990;162:862. <br> Ref: Ann Intern Med 1991;114:1005. |
| **Mitochondrial antibody, serum** <br><br> Negative <br><br> Marbled <br> $$ | Qualitative measure of antibodies against hepatic mitochondria. <br> Rabbit hepatocytes are incubated first with serum and then (after washing) with a fluorescein-tagged antibody to human immunoglobulin. Hepatocytes are then viewed for presence of cytoplasmic staining. | **Increased in:** Primary biliary cirrhosis (87–98%), chronic active hepatitis (25–28%); lower titers in viral hepatitis, infectious mononucleosis, neoplasms, cryptogenic cirrhosis (25–30%). | Primarily used to distinguish primary biliary cirrhosis (antibody present) from extrahepatic biliary obstruction (antibody absent). <br> Ref: Hepatology 1986;6:381. <br> Ref: Acta Med Scand 1986;220:241. <br> Ref: Dig Dis 1992;10:85. |

| Test/Range/Collection | Physiologic Basis | Interpretation | Comments |
|---|---|---|---|
| **Neutrophil cytoplasmic antibodies** | | | |
| **Neutrophil cytoplasmic antibodies, serum (ANCA)**<br><br>Negative<br><br>Marbled<br><br>$$$ | Measurement of autoantibodies in serum against cytoplasmic constituents of neutrophils. (See also Autoantibodies table, p 316.) | **Positive in:** Wegener's granulomatosis, systemic vasculitis, crescentic glomerulonephritis, paraneoplastic vasculitis, ulcerative colitis. | Test sensitivity for Wegener's granulomatosis ranges from 56% to 96%, depending on the population studied. Test specificity for Wegener's granulomatosis is claimed to be high (99%) when requiring diffuse cytoplasmic staining for a positive result, but interpretation is highly technique-dependent.<br>In the patient with systemic vasculitis, elevated ANCA levels imply active disease and high likelihood of recurrence. However, ANCA levels can be persistently elevated and should be used in conjunction with other clinical indices in treatment decisions.<br>Ref: N Engl J Med 1988;318:1651.<br>Ref: Ann Intern Med 1989;111:28.<br>Ref: Am J Kidney Dis 1995;25:380.<br>Ref: Ann Intern Med 1995;123:925. |

| Test/Specimen | Method | Elevated/Positive in | Comments |
|---|---|---|---|
| **Nuclear antibody, serum (ANA)** < 1:20 Marbled $$ | Heterogeneous antibodies to nuclear antigens (DNA and RNA, histone and nonhistone proteins). Nuclear antibody is measured in serum by layering the patient's serum over human epithelial cells and detecting the antibody with fluorescein-conjugated polyvalent antihuman immunoglobulin. | **Elevated in:** Patients over age 65 (35–75%, usually in low titers), systemic lupus erythematosus (98%), drug-induced lupus (100%), Sjögren's syndrome (98%), rheumatoid arthritis (30–50%), scleroderma (60%), mixed connective tissue disease (100%), Felty's syndrome, mononucleosis, hepatic or biliary cirrhosis, hepatitis, leukemia, myasthenia gravis, dermatomyositis, polymyositis, chronic renal failure. | A negative ANA test does not completely rule out SLE, but alternative diagnoses should be considered. Pattern of ANA staining may give some clues to diagnoses, but since the pattern also changes with serum dilution, it is not routinely reported. Only the rim (peripheral) pattern is highly specific (for SLE). Not useful as a screening test. Should be used only when there is clinical evidence of a connective tissue disease. Ref: Ann Intern Med 1981;95:333. Ref: West J Med 1987;147:210. |
| **Oligoclonal bands, serum and CSF** Negative Marbled and glass or plastic tube for CSF $$ Collect serum and CSF simultaneously. | Electrophoretic examination of IgG found in CSF may show oligoclonal bands not found in serum. This suggests local production in CSF of limited species of IgG. | **Positive in:** Multiple sclerosis (88%), CNS syphilis, subacute sclerosing panencephalitis, other CNS inflammatory diseases. | Test is indicated only when multiple sclerosis is suspected clinically. Test interpretation is very subjective. IgG index is a more reliable test analytically, but neither test is specific for multiple sclerosis. Ref: Neurology 1985;35:212. Ref: Mayo Clin Proc 1989;64:577. |

| Test/Range/Collection | Physiologic Basis | Interpretation | Comments |
|---|---|---|---|
| **Osmolality, serum** (Osm) <br><br> 285–293 mosm/kg $H_2O$ [mmol/kg $H_2O$] <br> ***Panic:*** < 240 or > 320 mosm/kg $H_2O$ <br><br> Marbled <br> $$ | Test measures the osmotic pressure of serum by the freezing point depression method. <br><br> Plasma and urine osmolality are more useful indicators of degree of hydration than BUN, hematocrit, or serum proteins. <br><br> Serum osmolality can be estimated by the following formula: <br><br> $$Osm = 2(Na^+) + \frac{BUN}{2.8} + \frac{Glucose}{18}$$ <br><br> where $Na^+$ is in meq/L and BUN and glucose are in mg/dL. | **Increased in:** Diabetic ketoacidosis, nonketotic hyperosmolar hyperglycemic coma, hypernatremia secondary to dehydration (diarrhea, severe burns, vomiting, fever, hyperventilation, inadequate water intake, central or nephrogenic diabetes insipidus, or osmotic diuresis), hypernatremia with normal hydration (hypothalamic disorders, defective osmostat), hypernatremia with overhydration (iatrogenic or accidental excessive NaCl or $NaHCO_3$ intake), alcohol or other toxic ingestion (see Comments). hypercalcemia; tube feedings. Drugs: corticosteroids, mannitol, glycerin. <br> **Decreased in:** Pregnancy (third trimester), hyponatremia with hypovolemia (adrenal insufficiency, renal losses, diarrhea, vomiting, severe burns, peritonitis, pancreatitis), hyponatremia with normovolemia, hyponatremia with hypervolemia (congestive heart failure, cirrhosis, nephrotic syndrome, SIADH, postoperative state). Drugs: chlorthalidone, cyclophosphamide, thiazides. | If the difference between calculated and measured serum osmolality is greater than 10 mosm/kg $H_2O$, suspect the presence of a low-molecular-weight toxin (alcohol, methanol, isopropyl alcohol, ethylene glycol, acetone, ethyl ether, paraldehyde, or mannitol), ethanol being the most common. (See p 343 for further explanation.) <br> Every 100 mg/dL of ethanol increases serum osmolality by 22 mosm/kg $H_2O$. <br> While the osmolal gap may overestimate the blood alcohol level, a normal serum osmolality excludes ethanol intoxication. <br> Ref: Clin Chem 1990;36:2004. <br> Ref: J Emerg Med 1992;10:129. <br> Ref: Pharmacotherapy 1993;13:60. |

| | Osmolality, serum | Oxygen, partial pressure |
|---|---|---|
| **Osmolality, urine** (Urine Osm)<br><br>Random: 100–900 mosm/kg $H_2O$ [mmol/kg $H_2O$]<br><br>Urine container<br>$$ | Test measures renal tubular concentrating ability. | With average fluid intake, normal random urine osmolality is 100–900 mosm/kg $H_2O$.<br>After 12-hour fluid restriction, normal random urine osmolality is > 850 mosm/kg $H_2O$.<br>Ref: Am J Med 1982;72:308. |
| | **Increased in:** Hypovolemia. Drugs: anesthetic agents (during surgery), carbamazepine, chlorpropamide, cyclophosphamide, metolazone, vincristine. **Decreased in:** Diabetes insipidus, primary polydipsia, exercise, starvation. Drugs: acetohexamide, demeclocycline, glyburide, lithium, tolazamide. | |
| **Oxygen, partial pressure**, whole blood ($PO_2$)<br><br>83–108 mm Hg<br>[11.04–14.36 kPa]<br><br>Heparinized syringe<br>$$$<br>Collect arterial blood in a heparinized syringe. Send to laboratory immediately on ice. | Test measures the partial pressure of oxygen (oxygen tension) in arterial blood.<br>Partial pressure of oxygen is critical since it determines (along with hemoglobin and blood supply) tissue oxygen supply. | % saturation of hemoglobin ($SO_2$) represents the oxygen content divided by the oxygen carrying capacity of hemoglobin.<br>% saturation on blood gas reports is calculated not measured. It is calculated from $PO_2$ and pH using reference oxyhemoglobin dissociation curves for normal adult hemoglobin (lacking methemoglobin, carboxyhemoglobin, etc). At $PO_2$ < 60 mm Hg, the oxygen saturation (and content) cannot be reliably estimated from the $PO_2$. Therefore, oximetry should be used to determine % saturation directly.<br>Ref: JAMA 1990;264:244.<br>Ref: Chest 1990;98:1244.<br>Ref: Clin Chem 1992;38:1601. |
| | **Increased in:** Oxygen therapy. **Decreased in:** Ventilation/perfusion mismatching (asthma, COPD, atelectasis, pulmonary embolism, pneumonia, interstitial lung disease, airway obstruction by foreign body, shock); alveolar hypoventilation (kyphoscoliosis, neuromuscular disease, head injury, stroke); right-to-left shunt (congenital heart disease). Drugs: barbiturates, opioids. | |

| | Parathyroid hormone | | | |
|---|---|---|---|---|
| Test/Range/Collection | Physiologic Basis | Interpretation | Comments |

| Test/Range/Collection | Physiologic Basis | Interpretation | Comments |
|---|---|---|---|
| **Parathyroid hormone**, serum (PTH)<br><br>Intact PTH: 11–54 pg/mL<br>[1.2–5.7 pmol/L] (laboratory-specific)<br><br>Marbled<br>$$$$<br><br>Fasting sample preferred; simultaneous measurement of serum calcium and phosphorus is also required. | PTH is secreted from the parathyroid glands. It mobilizes calcium from bone, increases distal renal tubular reabsorption of calcium, decreases proximal renal tubular reabsorption of phosphorus, and stimulates 1,25-hydroxy vitamin D synthesis from 25-hydroxy vitamin D by renal 1α-hydroxylase.<br><br>The "intact" PTH molecule (84 amino acids) has a circulating half-life of about 5 minutes.<br><br>Carboxyl terminal and midmolecule fragments make up 90% of circulating PTH. They are biologically inactive, cleared by the kidney, and have half-lives of about 1–2 hours.<br><br>The amino terminal fragment is biologically active and has a half-life of 1–2 minutes.<br><br>Measurement of PTH by immunoassay depends on the specificity of the antibodies used. | **Increased in:** Primary hyperparathyroidism, secondary hyperparathyroidism due to renal disease. Drugs: lithium, furosemide, phosphates.<br><br>**Decreased in:** Hypoparathyroidism, sarcoidosis, hyperthyroidism, hypomagnesemia, malignancy with hypercalcemia, nonparathyroid hypercalcemia. | PTH results must always be evaluated in light of concurrent serum calcium levels (see PTH and Calcium Nomogram, p 344).<br><br>PTH tests differ in sensitivity and specificity from assay to assay and from laboratory to laboratory.<br><br>Carboxyl terminal antibody measures intact, carboxyl terminal and midmolecule fragments. It is 85% sensitive and 95% specific for primary hyperparathyroidism.<br><br>Amino terminal antibody measures intact and amino terminal fragments. It is about 75% sensitive for hyperparathyroidism.<br><br>Intact PTH assays are preferred because they detect PTH suppression in nonparathyroid hypercalcemia. Sensitivity of immunometric assays is 85–90% for primary hyperparathyroidism.<br><br>Ref: Arch Surg 1986;121:841.<br>Ref: Ann Intern Med 1987;106:559.<br>Ref: Endocrinol Metab Clin North Am 1989;18:647.<br>Ref: Mayo Clin Proc 1992;67:637. |

| Parathyroid hormone-related protein | | |
|---|---|---|
| **Parathyroid hormone-related protein** (PTHrP), plasma<br><br>Assay-specific (pmol/L or undetectable)<br><br>Tube containing anticoagulant and protease inhibitors; specimen drawn without a tourniquet.<br><br>$$ | Parathyroid hormone-related protein (PTHrP) is a 139- to 173-amino-acid protein with amino terminal homology to parathyroid hormone (PTH). The homology explains the ability of PTHrP to bind to the PTH receptor and have PTH-like effects on bone and kidney. PTHrP induces increased plasma calcium, decreased plasma phosphorus, and increased urinary cAMP.<br><br>PTHrP is found in keratinocytes, fibroblasts, placenta, brain, pituitary gland, adrenal gland, stomach, liver, testicular Leydig cells, and mammary glands. Its physiologic role in these diverse sites is unknown.<br><br>PTHrP is secreted by solid malignant tumors (lung, breast, kidney; other squamous tumors) and produces humoral hypercalcemia of malignancy.<br><br>PTHrP analysis is by immunoradiometric assay (IRMA). Assay of choice is amino terminal-specific IRMA. Two-site IRMA assays require sample collection in protease inhibitors because serum proteases destroy immunoreactivity. | **Increased in:** Humoral hypercalcemia of malignancy (80% of solid tumors). | Assays directed at the amino terminal portion of PTHrP are not influenced by renal failure.<br>Increases in PTHrP concentrations are readily detectable with most current assays in the majority of patients with humoral hypercalcemia of malignancy. About 20% of patients with malignancy and hypercalcemia will have low PTHrP levels because their hypercalcemia is caused by local osteolytic processes.<br>Ref: N Engl J Med 1990;322:1106.<br>Ref: West J Med 1990;153:635.<br>Ref: Clin Chem 1992;38:2171. |

| | Partial thromboplastin time | |
|---|---|---|
| **Test/Range/Collection** | **Physiologic Basis** | **Interpretation** | **Comments** |
| **Partial thromboplastin time,** activated, plasma (PTT)

25–35 seconds (range varies)
**Panic:** ≥ 60 seconds (off heparin)

Blue
$$
Fill tube adequately. Do not contaminate specimen with heparin. | Patient's plasma is activated to clot in vitro by mixing it with phospholipid and an activator substance.
Test screens the intrinsic coagulation pathway and adequacy of all coagulation factors except XIII and VII.
PTT is usually abnormal if any factor level drops below 30–40% of normal. | **Increased in:** Deficiency of any individual coagulation factor except XIII and VII; presence of nonspecific inhibitors (eg, lupus anticoagulant), specific factor inhibitors, von Willebrand's disease (PTT may also be normal), hemophilia A and B, disseminated intravascular coagulation (DIC). Drugs: heparin, warfarin.
**Decreased in:** Hypercoagulable states, DIC. | PTT is the best test to monitor adequacy of heparin therapy, but it does not reliably predict the risk of bleeding.
Test is not always abnormal in von Willebrand's disease.
Test may be normal in chronic DIC.
A very common cause of PTT prolongation is the spurious presence of heparin in the plasma sample.
Sensitivity and degree of prolongation of PTT depend on particular reagents used.
Therapeutic levels of heparin are best achieved using a weight-based dosing nomogram with dose adjustment based on the PTT at 6 hours.
Ref: JAMA 1989;262:2428.
Ref: Am J Med 1993;95:315.
Ref: Ann Intern Med 1993;119:874. |

| pH | | |
|---|---|---|
| **pH,** whole blood<br><br>Arterial: 7.35–7.45<br>Venous: 7.31–7.41<br><br>Heparinized syringe<br>$$$<br>Specimen must be collected in heparinized syringe and immediately transported on ice to lab without exposure to air. | pH assesses the acid-base status of blood, an extremely useful measure of integrated cardiorespiratory function.<br>The essential relationship between pH, $P_{CO_2}$ and bicarbonate ($HCO_3^-$) is expressed by the Henderson–Hasselbalch equation (at 37 °C):<br><br>$$pH = 6.1 + \log\left(\frac{HCO_3^-}{P_{CO_2} \times 0.03}\right)$$<br><br>Arteriovenous pH difference is 0.01–0.03 but is greater in patients with congestive heart failure and shock. | **Increased in:** *Respiratory alkalosis:* hyperventilation (eg, anxiety), sepsis, liver disease, fever, early salicylate poisoning, and excessive artificial ventilation.<br>*Metabolic alkalosis:* Loss of gastric HCl (eg, vomiting), potassium depletion, excessive alkali administration (eg, bicarbonate, antacids), diuretics, volume depletion.<br>**Decreased in:** *Respiratory acidosis:* decreased alveolar ventilation (eg, COPD, respiratory depressants), neuromuscular diseases (eg, myasthenia).<br>*Metabolic acidosis* (bicarbonate deficit): increased formation of acids (eg, ketosis [diabetes mellitus, alcohol, starvation], lactic acidosis); decreased $H^+$ excretion (eg, renal failure, renal tubular acidosis, Fanconi's syndrome); increased acid intake (eg, ion-exchange resins, salicylates, ammonium chloride, ethylene glycol, methanol); and increased loss of alkaline body fluids (eg, diarrhea, fistulas, aspiration of gastrointestinal contents, biliary drainage). | The pH of a standing sample decreases because of cellular metabolism.<br>The correction of pH (measured at 37 °C), based on the patient's temperature, is not clinically useful.<br>(See also Acid-Base Nomogram, p 309.)<br>Ref: Am J Med 1982;72:496. |

| | Phosphorus |
|---|---|
| | **Comments** |

| Test/Range/Collection | Physiologic Basis | Interpretation | Comments |
|---|---|---|---|
| **Phosphorus,** serum<br><br>2.5–4.5 mg/dL<br>[0.8–1.45 mmol/L]<br>***Panic:*** < 1.0 mg/dL<br><br>Marbled<br>$<br>Avoid hemolysis. | The plasma concentration of inorganic phosphate is determined by parathyroid gland function, action of vitamin D, intestinal absorption, renal function, bone metabolism, and nutrition. | **Increased in:** Renal failure, massive blood transfusion, hypoparathyroidism, sarcoidosis, neoplasms, adrenal insufficiency, acromegaly, hypervitaminosis D, osteolytic metastases to bone, leukemia, milk-alkali syndrome, healing bone fractures, pseudohypoparathyroidism, diabetes mellitus with ketosis, malignant hyperpyrexia, cirrhosis, lactic acidosis, respiratory acidosis. Drugs: phosphate infusions or enemas, anabolic steroids, ergocalciferol, furosemide, hydrochlorothiazide, clonidine, verapamil, potassium supplements, and others.<br><br>**Decreased in:** Hyperparathyroidism, hypovitaminosis D (rickets, osteomalacia), malabsorption (steatorrhea), malnutrition, starvation or cachexia, GH deficiency, chronic alcoholism, severe diarrhea, vomiting, nasogastric suction, severe hypercalcemia (any cause), acute gout, osteoblastic metastases to bone, severe burns (diuretic phase), respiratory alkalosis, hyperalimentation with inadequate phosphate repletion, carbohydrate administration (eg, intravenous $D_{50}W$ glucose bolus), renal tubular acidosis and other renal tubular defects, diabetic ketoacidosis (during recovery), acid-base disturbances, hypokalemia, pregnancy, hypothyroidism, hemodialysis. Drugs: acetazolamide, phosphate-binding antacids, anticonvulsants, beta-adrenergic agonists, catecholamines, estrogens, isoniazid, oral contraceptives, prolonged use of thiazides, glucose infusion, insulin therapy, salicylates (toxicity). | Thrombocytosis may cause spurious elevation of serum phosphate, but plasma phosphate levels are normal.<br>Ref: Clin Lab Med 1993;13:183.<br>Ref: Ann Pharmacother 1994;28:626.<br>Ref: Am J Med Sci 1994;307:255. |

| Platelet aggregation | | |
|---|---|---|
| **Platelet aggregation, whole blood**<br><br>Aggregation by adenosine diphosphate (ADP), collagen, epinephrine, thrombin, ristocetin, and arachidonic acid<br><br>Drawn by lab<br>$$$$<br>Whole blood in citrate is drawn into a plastic tube. Platelet-rich plasma (PRP) is obtained by centrifuging at 100 × g for 10–15 minutes. | Platelet aggregometry can provide information concerning possible qualitative platelet defects. Aggregation is measured as an increase in light transmission through stirred platelet-rich plasma (PRP) when a specific agonist is added. Test examines platelet aggregation response to various agonists (eg, ADP, collagen, epinephrine, thrombin, ristocetin, arachidonic acid). Newer lumiaggregation measures aggregation and simultaneous platelet ATP release—the so-called "platelet release reaction." | **Abnormal in:** Acquired defects in the platelet release reaction (eg, drugs, following cardiopulmonary bypass, uremia, paraproteinemias, myeloproliferative disorders), congenital release abnormalities, Glanzmann's thrombasthenia (absent aggregation to ADP, collagen, epinephrine), essential athrombia (similar to Glanzmann's disease except clot retraction is normal), storage pool disease (no secondary wave with ADP, epinephrine, and decreased aggregation with collagen), cyclooxygenase and thromboxane synthetase deficiencies (rare hereditary aspirin-like defects), von Willebrand's disease (normal aggregation with all factors except ristocetin). Drugs: aspirin (absent aggregation curves to ADP and epinephrine, collagen, arachidonate). | Acquired platelet dysfunction is more common than the hereditary form. Hereditary storage pool disease is common enough to be suspected in a child with easy or spontaneous bruising. Test should not be done if the patient has taken aspirin within the previous 10 days.<br>Direct PRP aggregation by ristocetin (1.5 mg/mL) may be normal or abnormal in von Willebrand's disease (vWD). Because this test has limited sensitivity for detection of vWD, it is no longer used for that purpose (see instead Bleeding time, p 56, and von Willebrand factor protein, p 188).<br>Ref: N Engl J Med 1991;324:27.<br>Ref: Semin Thromb Hemost 1992;18:167. |

| | Platelet count |
|---|---|

| Test/Range/Collection | Physiologic Basis | Interpretation | Comments |
|---|---|---|---|
| **Platelet count,** whole blood (Plt)<br><br>150–450 × $10^3$/μL [× $10^9$/L]<br>***Panic:*** < 25 × $10^3$/μL<br><br>Lavender<br>$ | Platelets are released from mega-karyocytes in bone marrow and are important for normal hemostasis. Platelet counting is done by a flow cytometry with size discrimination based on electrical impedance or electro-optical systems. | **Increased in:** Myeloproliferative disorders: polycythemia vera, chronic myeloid leukemia, essential thrombocythemia, myelofibrosis; after bleeding, postsplenectomy, reactive thrombocytosis secondary to inflammatory diseases, iron deficiency, malignancies, alkalosis.<br>**Decreased in:** Decreased production: bone marrow suppression or replacement, chemotherapeutic agents, drugs (eg, ethanol). Increased destruction or removal: splenomegaly, disseminated intravascular coagulation, platelet antibodies (idiopathic thrombocytopenic purpura, posttransfusion purpura, neonatal isoimmune thrombocytopenia, drugs [eg, quinidine, cephalosporins]). | Ref: Am J Clin Pathol 1965;44:678.<br>Ref: Med Lab Sci 1976;33:201.<br>Ref: N Engl J Med 1995;332:1132.<br>Ref: Am J Med 1995;98:436.<br>Ref: Am J Med 1995;98:551. |

## Platelet-associated IgG

| Platelet-associated IgG, whole blood<br><br>Negative<br><br>Yellow<br>$$$$<br>17 mL of blood is needed. | Antibody screening involves direct testing of a patient's platelets to demonstrate platelet-associated IgG (which may be directed against specific platelet antigens or may represent immune complexes nonspecifically absorbed to the platelet surface) in idiopathic (autoimmune) thrombocytopenic purpura (ITP). It also involves indirect testing of the patient's serum against a panel of reagent platelets to detect circulating antiplatelet antibodies. In alloimmune thrombocytopenia, the patient's direct test is negative and the patient's serum reacts with reagent platelets.<br><br>Antibody specificity can be identified, and platelets lacking the involved antigen can be transfused. | **Positive in:** Some autoimmune thrombocytopenias (eg, ITP) (90–95%). | In ITP, the direct antiplatelet antibody test may be useful to confirm the diagnosis and monitor subsequent response to therapy. It is also useful in diagnosing posttransfusion purpura and suspected neonatal isoimmune thrombocytopenia.<br><br>Platelet-associated IgG is also useful for patients with thrombocytopenia or as part of a platelet cross-match prior to transfusion of patients who have repeatedly failed to respond to random donor platelet transfusions.<br>Ref: N Engl J Med 1991;324:27.<br>Ref: Rose NR et al (editors): *Manual of Clinical Laboratory Immunology*, 4th ed. American Society for Microbiology, 1992. |

| Test/Range/Collection | Physiologic Basis | Interpretation | Comments |
|---|---|---|---|
| | | **Porphobilinogen** | |
| **Porphobilinogen, urine (PBG)**<br><br>Negative<br><br>$$<br><br>Protect from light. | Porphyrias are characterized clinically by neurologic and cutaneous manifestations and chemically by overproduction of porphyrin and other precursors of heme production.<br><br>PBG is a water-soluble precursor of heme whose urinary excretion is increased in symptomatic hepatic porphyrias.<br><br>PBG is detected qualitatively by a color reaction with Ehrlich's reagent and confirmed by extraction into chloroform (Watson-Schwartz test). | **Positive in:** Acute intermittent porphyria, variegate porphyria, coproporphyria, lead poisoning (rare).<br><br>**Negative in:** 20–30% of patients with hepatic porphyria between attacks. | Positive qualitative urinary PBG tests should be followed up by quantitative measurements. Many labs report frequent false positives with the Watson-Schwartz test.<br><br>A screening PBG test is insensitive, and a negative test does not rule out porphyria between attacks or the carrier state.<br><br>Specific porphyrias can be better defined by quantitative measurement of urine PBG and by measurement of erythrocyte uroporphyrinogen-1-synthetase.<br><br>Ref: Am J Clin Pathol 1989;92:644.<br>Ref: Mayo Clin Proc 1994;69:289. |

| Potassium | | |
|---|---|---|
| **Potassium,** serum ($K^+$)<br><br>3.5–5.0 meq/L [mmol/L]<br>**Panic:** < 3.0 or > 6.0 meq/L<br><br>Marbled<br>$<br>Avoid hemolysis. | Potassium is predominantly an intracellular cation whose plasma level is regulated by renal excretion.<br>Plasma potassium concentration determines neuromuscular irritability. Elevated or depressed potassium concentrations interfere with muscle contraction. | **Increased in:** Massive hemolysis, severe tissue damage, rhabdomyolysis, acidosis, dehydration, acute or chronic renal failure, Addison's disease, renal tubular acidosis type IV (hyporeninemic hypoaldosteronism), hyperkalemic familial periodic paralysis, exercise (transient). Drugs: potassium salts, potassium-sparing diuretics (eg, spironolactone, triamterene), non-steroidal anti-inflammatory drugs, beta-blockers, ACE inhibitors, high-dose trimethoprim-sulfamethoxazole.<br>**Decreased in:** Low potassium intake, prolonged vomiting or diarrhea, renal tubular acidosis types I and II, hyperaldosteronism, Cushing's syndrome, osmotic diuresis (eg, hyperglycemia), alkalosis, familial periodic paralysis, trauma (transient). Drugs: adrenergic agents (isoproterenol), diuretics. | Spurious hyperkalemia can occur with hemolysis of sample, delayed separation of serum from erythrocytes, prolonged fist clenching during blood drawing, and prolonged tourniquet placement. Very high white blood cell or platelet counts may cause spurious elevation of serum potassium, but plasma potassium levels are normal.<br>Ref: Crit Care Nurs Q 1990;13:34.<br>Ref: Ann Intern Med 1993;119:291.<br>Ref: Circulation 1994;89:1144. |

| | | Prolactin | Prostate-specific antigen |
|---|---|---|---|
| **Test/Range/Collection** | | | |
| **Prolactin,** serum (PRL)<br><br>< 20 ng/mL [µg/L]<br><br>Marbled<br>$$$ | **Physiologic Basis:** Prolactin is a polypeptide hormone secreted by the anterior pituitary. It functions in the initiation and maintenance of lactation in the postpartum period.<br>PRL secretion is inhibited by hypothalamic secretion of dopamine.<br>Prolactin levels increase with renal failure, hypothyroidism, and drugs that are dopamine antagonists. | **Interpretation:** **Increased in:** Sleep, nursing, nipple stimulation, exercise, hypoglycemia, stress, hypothyroidism, pituitary tumors (prolactinomas and others), hypothalamic/pituitary stalk lesions, renal failure. Drugs: phenothiazines, haloperidol, reserpine, methyldopa, estrogens, opiates, cimetidine.<br>**Decreased in:** Drugs: levodopa. | **Comments:** Serum PRL is used primarily in workup of suspected pituitary tumor (60% of pituitary adenomas secrete PRL). Clinical presentation is usually amenorrhea and galactorrhea in women and impotence in men. (See Amenorrhea algorithm, p 311.)<br>Only 4% of impotence is caused by hyperprolactinemia, and hyperprolactinemia is rare in the absence of low serum testosterone.<br>Ref: Lancet 1982;2:129.<br>Ref: N Engl J Med 1991;324:822. |
| **Prostate-specific antigen,** serum (PSA)<br><br>0–4 ng/mL [µg/L]<br><br>Marbled<br>$$$ | Prostate-specific antigen is a glycoprotein produced by cells of the prostatic ductal epithelium and is present in the serum of all men. It is absent from the serum of women. | **Increased in:** Prostate carcinoma, benign prostatic hypertrophy (BPH), following prostate examination.<br>**Negative in:** Metastatic prostate carcinoma treated with antiandrogen therapy, postprostatectomy. | PSA is used to monitor recurrence of treated prostate cancer.<br>Decrease in mortality rates resulting from use for cancer screening is unproven, and the risks of early therapy are significant. PSA is often increased in BPH, and the predictive value of a positive test in healthy older men is low.<br>PSA replaces the acid phosphatase test.<br>Ref: Clin Chem 1993;39:2540.<br>Ref: Urol Clin North Am 1993;20:637.<br>Ref: J Urol 1994;152:1689.<br>Ref: Semin Oncol 1994;21:542.<br>Ref: JAMA 1994;272:773. |

| Protein C | | |
|---|---|---|
| **Protein C, plasma**<br><br>71–176%<br><br>Blue<br><br>$$$ | Protein C is a vitamin K-dependent proenzyme synthesized in the liver. Following its activation by thrombin, it exerts an anticoagulant effect through inactivation of factors Va and VIIIa using protein S as cofactor. Tests to assay quantitative (antigenic) or functional activity are available. Deficiency is inherited in an autosomal dominant fashion with incomplete penetrance or is acquired. Deficient patients may present with a hypercoagulable state, with recurrent thrombophlebitis or pulmonary emboli. | **Decreased in:** Congenital deficiency, liver disease, cirrhosis (13–25%), warfarin use (28–60%), vitamin K deficiency, disseminated intravascular coagulation (DIC). | Homozygous deficiency of protein C (< 1% activity) is associated with fatal neonatal purpura fulminans and massive venous thrombosis. Heterozygous patients (one in 200–300 of the population, with levels 25–50% of normal) may be at risk for venous thrombosis.<br>Interpretation of an abnormally low protein C must be tempered by the clinical setting. Anticoagulant therapy, DIC, and liver disease must not be present. There is overlap between lower limits of normal values and values found in heterozygotes.<br>Kindred with dysfunctional protein C of normal quantity have been identified.<br>Ref: Semin Thromb Hemost 1984;10:162.<br>Ref: N Engl J Med 1986;314:1298.<br>Ref: Am J Clin Pathol 1993;99:677. |

## Protein electrophoresis

| Test/Range/Collection | Physiologic Basis | Interpretation | Comments |
|---|---|---|---|
| **Protein electrophoresis,** serum<br><br>Adults:<br>Albumin: 3.3–5.7 g/dL<br>$\alpha_1$: 0.1–0.4 g/dL<br>$\alpha_2$: 0.3–0.9 g/dL<br>$\beta_2$: 0.7–1.5 g/dL<br>$\gamma$: 0.5–1.4 g/dL<br><br>Marbled<br>$$ | Electrophoresis of serum proteins will separate serum proteins into albumin, $\alpha_1$, $\alpha_2$, $\beta_2$, and $\gamma$ fractions. Albumin is the principal serum protein (see Albumin, p 42). The term "globulin" generally refers to the non-albumin fraction of serum protein.<br><br>The $\alpha_1$ fraction contains $\alpha_1$-antiprotease (90%), $\alpha_1$-lipoprotein and $\alpha_1$-acid glycoprotein. The $\alpha_2$ fraction contains $\alpha_2$-macroglobulin, haptoglobin, and ceruloplasmin. The $\beta$ fraction contains transferrin, hemopexin, complement C3, and $\beta$-lipoproteins. The $\gamma$ fraction contains immunoglobulins G, A, D, E, and M. | ↑$\alpha_1$: inflammatory states ($\alpha_1$-antiprotease), pregnancy.<br>↑$\alpha_2$: nephrotic syndrome, inflammatory states, oral contraceptives, steroid therapy, hyperthyroidism.<br>↑$\beta$: hyperlipidemia, hemoglobinemia, iron deficiency anemia.<br>↑$\gamma$: polyclonal gammopathies (liver disease, cirrhosis [associated with $\beta$–$\gamma$ "bridging"], chronic infections, autoimmune disease); monoclonal gammopathies (multiple myeloma, Waldenström's macroglobulinemia, lymphoid malignancies, monoclonal gammopathy of undetermined significance).<br>↓$\alpha_1$: $\alpha_1$-antiprotease deficiency.<br>↓$\alpha_2$: in vivo hemolysis, liver disease.<br>↓$\beta$: hypo-$\beta$-lipoproteinemia.<br>↓$\gamma$: immune deficiency. | Presence of "spikes" in $\alpha_2$, $\beta_2$, or $\gamma$ regions necessitates the use of immunoelectrophoresis to verify the presence of a monoclonal gammopathy (see Immunoelectrophoresis, p 115). If Bence Jones proteins (light chains) are suspected, urine protein electrophoresis needs to be done.<br>Test is insensitive for detection of decreased levels of immunoglobulins and $\alpha_1$-antiprotease. Specific quantitation is required (see Immunoglobulins, p 116, and $\alpha_1$-Antiprotease, p 51).<br>If plasma is used, fibrinogen will be detected in the $\beta$–$\gamma$ region.<br>The "acute-phase protein pattern" seen with acute illness, surgery, infarction or trauma is characterized by an ↑$\alpha_2$ (haptoglobin) and ↑$\alpha_1$ ($\alpha_1$-antiprotease).<br>Ref: Mayo Clin Proc 1978;53:719. |

| Red cell volume | | | |
|---|---|---|---|
| **Red cell volume, whole blood (RCV)** Male: 24–32 Female: 22–28 mL/kg Yellow Lavender (for Hct) $$$ A sample of the patient's whole blood is labeled with radioactive $^{51}$Cr (which is taken up into red cells) and reinjected into the patient. Blood is sampled 10 and 60 minutes later to measure radioactivity. | Test measures absolute volume of red cells based on hemodilution of a known quantity of radioactivity in the circulation. Test can distinguish between absolute polycythemia (increased hematocrit [Hct], increased RCV) and relative polycythemia (hemoconcentration) (increased Hct, normal RCV). | **Increased in:** Polycythemia vera, secondary polycythemia due to tissue hypoxemia (pulmonary disease, congenital heart disease, carboxyhemoglobinemia [cigarette smoking], methemoglobinemia), or neoplasms (renal cell carcinoma, hepatoma, large uterine leiomyomas), high altitude, pregnancy. | Test is clinically indicated (but not always required) in the diagnosis of polycythemia vera. Ref: Semin Nucl Med 1975;5:63. Ref: J Nucl Med 1980;21:793. Ref: Mayo Clin Proc 1991;66:102. |

| Test/Range/Collection | Physiologic Basis | Interpretation | Comments |
|---|---|---|---|
| **Renin activity, plasma (PRA)**<br><br>*High-sodium diet* (75–150 meq Na⁺/d): supine, 0.2–2.3; standing, 1.3–4.0 ng/mL/h<br>*Low-sodium diet* (30–75 meq Na⁺/d): standing, 4.0–7.7 ng/mL/h<br><br>Lavender<br>$$ | The renal juxtaglomerular apparatus generates renin, an enzyme that converts angiotensinogen to angiotensin I.<br>The inactive angiotensin I is then converted to angiotensin II, which is a potent vasopressor.<br>Renin activity is measured by the ability of patient's plasma to generate angiotensin I from substrate (angiotensinogen).<br>Normal values depend on the patient's hydration, posture, and salt intake. | **Increased in:** Dehydration, some hypertensive states (eg, renal artery stenosis); edematous states (cirrhosis, nephrotic syndrome, congestive heart failure); hypokalemic states (gastrointestinal sodium and potassium loss, Bartter's syndrome); adrenal insufficiency. Drugs: ACE inhibitors, estrogen, hydralazine, nifedipine, minoxidil, oral contraceptives.<br>**Decreased in:** Hyporeninemic hypoaldosteronism, some hypertensive states (eg, primary aldosteronism). Drugs: beta-blockers, aspirin, clonidine, prazosin, reserpine, methyldopa, indomethacin. | PRA alone is not a satisfactory screening test for hyperaldosteronism because suppressed PRA has only 64% sensitivity and 83% specificity for primary hyperaldosteronism. However, when plasma aldosterone and PRA testing are combined, the sensitivity for primary hyperaldosteronism increases to 95% (see Aldosterone, plasma, p 43).<br>Test is also useful in evaluation of hypoaldosteronism (low-sodium diet, patient standing).<br>Measurement of peripheral vein renin activity is not useful in classification of hypertensive patients or in diagnosis of renal artery stenosis.<br>Bilateral renal vein sampling has been used to investigate renal artery stenosis. In general, a renal vein renin (RVR) ratio of 1.5 or more (affected/nonaffected side) is predictive of response to revascularization in >90% of cases, but 60% of cases with RVR ratios < 1.5 will also respond. Therefore, the test cannot reliably predict therapeutic response to a surgical procedure.<br>Ref: Am J Med 1983;74:641.<br>Ref: Mayo Clin Proc 1994;69:1172. |

**Renin activity**

| | Reptilase clotting time | Reticulocyte count |
|---|---|---|
| **Reptilase clotting time,** plasma<br><br>13–19 seconds<br><br>Blue<br>$$ | Reptilase is an enzyme derived from the venom of *Bothrops atrox* or *Bothrops jararaca*, South American pit vipers.<br>Reptilase cleaves a fibrinopeptide from fibrinogen directly, bypassing the heparin-antithrombin system, and produces a fibrin clot. The reptilase time will be normal in heparin toxicity, even when the thrombin time is infinite. | **Increased in:** Hypofibrinogenemia, dysfibrinogenemia, afibrinogenemia, and disseminated intravascular coagulation (DIC).<br>**Normal in:** Presence of heparin. | When the thrombin time is prolonged, the reptilase time is useful in distinguishing the presence of an antithrombin (normal reptilase time) from hypo- or dysfibrinogenemia (prolonged reptilase time).<br>The reptilase time is normal when heparin is the cause of a prolonged thrombin time.<br>The reptilase time is only slightly prolonged by fibrin degradation products.<br>Ref: Br J Haematol 1971;21:43. |
| **Reticulocyte count,** whole blood<br><br>33–137 × 10³/µL<br>[× 10⁹/L]<br><br>Lavender<br>$ | Reticulocytes are immature red blood cells that contain cytoplasmic mRNA. | **Increased in:** Hemolytic anemia, blood loss; recovery from iron, B₁₂, or folate deficiency or drug-induced anemia.<br>**Decreased in:** Iron deficiency anemia, aplastic anemia, anemia of chronic disease, megaloblastic anemia, sideroblastic anemia, bone marrow suppression. | This test is indicated in the evaluation of anemia to distinguish hypoproliferative from hemolytic anemia or blood loss.<br>The old method of measuring reticulocytes (manual staining and counting) has poor reproducibility. It has been replaced by automated methods (eg, flow cytometry), which are more precise. Method-specific reference ranges must be used.<br>Ref: Lab Med 1989;20:551.<br>Ref: Am J Hematol 1990;33:13.<br>Ref: Am J Clin Pathol 1994;102:623. |

| | Rh grouping | |
|---|---|---|
| **Test/Range/Collection** | **Physiologic Basis** | **Interpretation** | **Comments** |

| Test/Range/Collection | Physiologic Basis | Interpretation | Comments |
|---|---|---|---|
| **Rh grouping,** red cells (Rh)<br><br>Red<br><br>$<br><br>Proper identification of specimen is critical. | The Rhesus blood group system is second in importance only to the ABO system. Anti-Rh antibodies are the leading cause of hemolytic disease of the newborn and may also cause hemolytic transfusion reactions.<br><br>Although there are other Rhesus antigens, only tests for the D antigen are performed routinely in pretransfusion testing, since the D antigen is the most immunogenic.<br><br>The terms Rh-positive and -negative refer to the presence or absence of the red cell antigen, D, on the cell surface.<br><br>Persons whose red cells lack D do not regularly have anti-D in their serum. Formation of anti-D almost always results from exposure through transfusion or pregnancy to red cells possessing the D antigen. | Sixty percent of US whites are Rh(D)-positive, 40% negative; 72% of African-Americans are Rh(D)-positive, 28% negative; 95% of Asian-Americans are Rh(D)-positive, 5% negative. | Of D– persons receiving a single D+ unit, 50–75% will develop anti-D. The blood of all donors and recipients is therefore routinely tested for D, so that D– recipients can be given D– blood. Donor bloods must also be tested for a weak form of D antigen, called $D^u$, and must be labeled D+ if the $D^u$ test is positive. Recipient blood need not be tested for $D^u$.<br>Ref: *Technical Manual of the American Association of Blood Banks,* 11th ed. American Association of Blood Banks, 1993. |

|  | **Rheumatoid factor** | | **Ribonucleoprotein antibody** |
|---|---|---|---|
| **Rheumatoid factor,** serum (RF)<br><br>Negative (< 1:16)<br><br>Marbled<br><br>$ | Rheumatoid factor consists of heterogeneous autoantibodies usually of the IgM class that react against the Fc region of human IgG. | **Positive in:** Rheumatoid arthritis (75–90%), Sjögren's syndrome (80–90%), scleroderma, dermatomyositis, SLE (30%), sarcoidosis, Waldenström's macroglobulinemia. Drugs: methyldopa, others.<br><br>Low-titer RF can be found in healthy older patients (20%), in 1–4% of normal individuals, and in a variety of acute immune responses (eg, viral infections, including infectious mononucleosis and viral hepatitis), chronic bacterial infections (tuberculosis, leprosy, subacute infective endocarditis), and chronic active hepatitis. | Rheumatoid factor can be useful in differentiating rheumatoid arthritis from other chronic inflammatory arthritides. However, a positive RF test is only one of several criteria needed to make the diagnosis of rheumatoid arthritis.<br>(See also Autoantibodies table, p 316.)<br>RF must be ordered selectively because its predictive value is low (34%) if it is used as a screening test.<br>The test has poor positive predictive value because of its lack of specificity. The subset of patients with seronegative rheumatic disease limits its sensitivity and negative predictive value.<br>Ref: Geriatrics 1989;44:61.<br>Ref: Arch Intern Med 1992;152:2417. |
| **Ribonucleoprotein antibody,** serum (RNP)<br><br>Negative<br><br>Marbled<br><br>$$ | This is an antibody to a ribonucleoprotein-extractable nuclear antigen. | **Increased in:** Scleroderma (20–30% sensitivity, low specificity), mixed connective tissue disease (MCTD) (95–100% sensitivity, low specificity), SLE (30%), Sjögren's syndrome, rheumatoid arthritis (10%), discoid lupus (20–30%). | A negative test essentially excludes MCTD.<br>(See also Autoantibodies table, p 316.)<br>Ref: Rheum Dis Clin North Am 1992; 18:283.<br>Ref: Rheum Dis Clin North Am 1992; 18:311.<br>Ref: Rheum Dis Clin North Am 1994; 20:29. |

| Test/Range/Collection | Physiologic Basis | Interpretation | Comments |
|---|---|---|---|
| **Rubella antibody,** serum<br><br>< 1:8 titer<br><br>Marbled<br>$<br><br>For diagnosis of a recent infection, submit paired sera, one collected within 1 week of illness and another 2–4 weeks later. | Rubella (German measles) is a viral infection that causes fever, malaise, coryza, lymphadenopathy, fine maculopapular rash, and congenital birth defects when infection occurs in utero.<br>Antibodies to rubella can be detected by hemagglutination inhibition (HI), complement fixation (CF), indirect hemagglutination (IHA), ELISA, or latex agglutination (LA). Tests can detect IgG and IgM antibody.<br>Titers usually appear as rash fades (1 week) and peak at 10–14 days for HI and 2–3 weeks for other techniques. Baseline titers may remain elevated for life. | **Increased in:** Recent rubella infection, congenital rubella infection, previous rubella infection or vaccination (immunity). Spuriously increased IgM antibody occurs in the presence of rheumatoid factor. | Rubella titers of ≤ 1:8 indicate susceptibility and need for immunization to prevent infection during pregnancy. Titers of > 1:32 indicate immunity from prior infection or vaccination.<br>Definitive diagnosis is based on a fourfold rise in titer or the presence of IgM antibody.<br>To diagnose congenital infection, submit a single specimen for IgM. If positive, submit a second specimen 2–3 months later to rule out maternal antibody transmission across the placenta.<br>The recent resurgence of congenital rubella can largely be prevented with improved rubella testing and vaccination programs.<br>Ref: Rev Infect Dis 1985;7(Suppl 1): S108.<br>Ref: JAMA 1992;267:2616. |

| | Russell's viper venom clotting time | | Salicylate |
|---|---|---|---|
| **Russell's viper venom clotting time** (dilute), plasma (RVVT)<br><br>24–37 seconds<br><br>Blue<br><br>$$ | Russell viper venom is extracted from a pit viper (*Vipera russelli*), which is common in Southeast Asia (especially Burma) and which causes a rapidly fatal syndrome of consumptive coagulopathy with hemorrhage, shock, rhabdomyolysis, and renal failure.<br><br>Approximately 70% of the protein content of the venom is phospholipase $A_2$ which activates factor X in the presence of phospholipid, bypassing factor VII.<br><br>RVVT is a phospholipid-dependent coagulation test used in detection of antiphospholipid antibodies (so-called lupus anticoagulants). It should be noted that the anticoagulant detected in vitro may be associated with thrombosis (and not bleeding) in vivo. | **Increased in:** Circulating lupus anticoagulants (LAC), severe fibrinogen deficiency (< 50 mg/dL), deficiencies in prothrombin, factor V, factor X, and heparin therapy.<br><br>**Normal in:** Factor VII deficiency and all intrinsic pathway factor deficiencies. | The lupus anticoagulant may be associated with a prolonged PTT and a positive inhibitor screen (mixing study). If heparin is not present, a dilute Russell viper venom test may be indicated to confirm that the inhibitor is an LAC. Since specific factor inhibitors against factors VIII and IX are associated with clinically significant bleeding and require specific treatment, they must not be missed.<br><br>The LAC is associated with an increased risk of thrombosis (venous > arterial), recurrent spontaneous abortion, and the primary antiphospholipid syndrome of arterial thrombosis.<br><br>Ref: Haemostasis 1990;20:208.<br>Ref: Blood Coagul Fibrinolysis 1990; 1:627.<br>Ref: Int J Biochem 1994;26:79. |
| **Salicylate,** serum (aspirin)<br><br>20–30 mg/dL<br>[200–300 mg/L]<br>***Panic:*** > 35 mg/dL<br><br>Marbled<br><br>$$ | At high concentrations, salicylate stimulates hyperventilation, uncouples oxidative phosphorylation, and impairs glucose and fatty acid metabolism. Salicylate toxicity is thus marked by respiratory alkalosis and metabolic acidosis. | **Increased in:** Acute or chronic salicylate intoxication. | The potential toxicity of salicylate levels after acute ingestion can be determined by using the Salicylate nomogram, p 356. Nomograms have become less valid with the increasing popularity of enteric-coated slow-release aspirin preparations.<br>Ref: Pediatrics 1960;26:800. |

| | Scleroderma-associated antibody |
|---|---|

| Test/Range/Collection | Physiologic Basis | Interpretation | Comments |
|---|---|---|---|
| **Scleroderma-associated antibody (Scl-70 antibody)**, serum<br><br>Negative<br><br>Marbled<br>$$ | This antibody reacts with a cellular antigen (DNA topoisomerase 1) that is responsible for the relaxation of supercoiled DNA. | **Increased in:** Scleroderma (15–20% sensitivity, high specificity). | Predictive value of a positive test is > 95% for scleroderma. Test has prognostic significance for severe digital ischemia in patients with Raynaud's disease and scleroderma. (See also Autoantibodies table, p 316.)<br>Ref: Rheum Dis Clin North Am 1990; 16:169.<br>Ref: J Rheumatol 1991;18:1826.<br>Ref: Rheum Dis Clin North Am 1992; 18:483.<br>Ref: Ann Rheum Dis 1994;53:540. |

| | Semen analysis | Smith (anti-Sm) antibody |
|---|---|---|
| **Semen analysis,** ejaculate<br><br>Sperm count: > 20 × $10^6$/mL [$10^9$/L]<br>Motility score: > 60% motile<br>Volume: 2–5 mL<br>Normal morphology: > 60%<br><br>$$<br><br>Semen is collected in a urine container after masturbation following 3 days of abstinence from ejaculation. Specimen must be examined promptly. | Sperm are viewed under the microscope for motility and morphology. Infertility can be associated with low counts or with sperm of abnormal morphology or decreased motility.<br><br>**Decreased in:** Primary or secondary testicular failure, cryptorchidism, following vasectomy, drugs. | A low sperm count should be confirmed by sending two other appropriately collected semen specimens for evaluation.<br>Functional and computer-assisted sperm analyses increase diagnostic accuracy but are not yet widely available.<br>Ref: Fertil Steril 1975;26:492.<br>Ref: Endocrinol Metab Clin North Am 1994;23:725. |
| **Smith (anti-Sm) antibody,** serum<br><br>Negative<br><br>Marbled<br>$$ | This antibody to Smith antigen (an extractable nuclear antigen) is a marker antibody for SLE.<br><br>**Positive in:** SLE (30–40% sensitivity, high specificity). | A positive test substantially increases posttest probability of SLE. Test rarely needed for the diagnosis of SLE.<br>(See also Autoantibodies table, p 316.)<br>Ref: Clin Rheumatol 1990;9:346.<br>Ref: Rheum Dis Clin North Am 1992; 18:311.<br>Ref: Clin Rheumatol 1993;12:350. |

| | Smooth muscle antibodies | | |
|---|---|---|---|
| Test/Range/Collection | Physiologic Basis | Interpretation | Comments |
| **Smooth muscle anti-bodies,** serum<br><br>Negative<br><br>Marbled<br>$$ | Antibodies against smooth muscle proteins are found in patients with chronic active hepatitis and primary biliary cirrhosis. | **Positive in:** Autoimmune chronic active hepatitis (40–70%, predominantly IgG antibodies), lower titers in primary biliary cirrhosis (50%, predominantly IgM antibodies), viral hepatitis, infectious mononucleosis, cryptogenic cirrhosis (28%), HIV infection, vitiligo (25%), endometriosis, Behçet's disease (< 2% of normal individuals). | The presence of high titers of smooth muscle antibodies (> 1:80) is useful in distinguishing autoimmune chronic active hepatitis from other forms of hepatitis.<br>Ref: Gut 1980;21:878.<br>Ref: J Clin Pathol 1991;44:64.<br>Ref: Br J Obstet Gynaecol 1991;98: 680.<br>Ref: J Dermatol 1993;20:679.<br>Ref: Br J Rheumatol 1993;32:908. |

| Sodium | | |
|---|---|---|
| **Sodium,** serum (Na⁺) 135–145 meq/L [mmol/L] *Panic:* < 125 or > 155 meq/L Marbled $ | Sodium is the predominant extracellular cation. The serum sodium level is primarily determined by the volume status of the individual. Hyponatremia can be divided into hypovolemia, euvolemia, and hypervolemia categories (see Hyponatremia algorithm, p 339). | **Increased in:** Dehydration (excessive sweating, severe vomiting or diarrhea), polyuria (diabetes mellitus, diabetes insipidus), hyperaldosteronism, inadequate water intake (coma, hypothalamic disease). Drugs: steroids, licorice, oral contraceptives. **Decreased in:** Congestive heart failure, cirrhosis, vomiting, diarrhea, excessive sweating (with replacement of water but not salt), salt-losing nephropathy, adrenal insufficiency, nephrotic syndrome, water intoxication, SIADH. Drugs: thiazides, diuretics, ACE inhibitors, chlorpropamide, carbamazepine. | Spurious hyponatremia may be produced by severe lipemia or hyperproteinemia if sodium analysis involves a dilution step. The serum sodium falls about 1.6 meq/L for each 100 mg/dL increase in blood glucose. Hyponatremia in a normovolemic patient with urine osmolality higher than plasma osmolality suggests the possibility of SIADH, myxedema, hypopituitarism, or reset osmostat. Treatment of disorders of sodium balance relies on clinical assessment of the patient's extracellular fluid volume rather than the serum sodium. Sodium is commonly measured by ion-selective electrode. Ref: Am J Med 1982;72:496. Ref: Am Intern Med 1985;102:164. Ref: Postgrad Med 1993;93:227. Ref: Clin Chem 1994;40:1528. |

| | Somatomedin C | | |
|---|---|---|---|
| Test/Range/Collection | Physiologic Basis | Interpretation | Comments |
| **Somatomedin C,** plasma<br><br>123–463 ng/mL (age- and sex-dependent)<br><br>Lavender<br>$$$$ | Somatomedin C is a growth hormone-dependent plasma peptide produced by the liver. It is believed to mediate the growth-promoting effect of growth hormone (GH). It has an anabolic, insulin-like action on fat and muscle and stimulates collagen and protein synthesis. Its level is relatively constant throughout the day. | **Increased in:** Acromegaly (level correlates with disease activity better than GH level).<br>**Decreased in:** Pituitary dwarfism, hypopituitarism, Laron dwarfism (end-organ resistance to GH), fasting for 5–6 days, poor nutrition, hypothyroidism, cirrhosis. Values may be normal in growth hormone-deficient patients with hyperprolactinemia or craniopharyngioma. | A normal somatomedin C level in children is strong evidence that GH deficiency is not present and precludes the need for extensive pituitary function testing.<br>A low level does not prove that GH deficiency is present, since levels may be reduced in malnutrition, malabsorption, chronic systemic illness, and hypothyroidism.<br>Reference range here is for an immunoassay done following displacement of somatomedin C from its binding protein (acid-ethanol extraction).<br>Ref: N Engl J Med 1979;301:1138.<br>Ref: J Pediatr 1981;99:720.<br>Ref: J Clin Endocrinol 1988;66:538.<br>Ref: Endocrinol Metab Clin North Am 1992;21:649. |

| | | SS-A/Ro antibody | SS-B/La antibody |
|---|---|---|---|
| **SS-A/Ro antibody,** serum<br><br>Negative<br><br>Marbled<br><br>$$ | Antibodies to Ro (SSA) cellular ribonucleoprotein complexes are found in connective tissue diseases such as Sjögren's syndrome (SS), SLE, rheumatoid arthritis (RA), and vasculitis. | **Increased in:** Sjögren's (60–70% sensitivity, low specificity), SLE (30–40%), RA (10%), subacute cutaneous lupus, vasculitis. | Useful in counseling women of child-bearing age with known connective tissue disease, since a positive test is associated with a small but real risk of neonatal SLE and congenital heart block. The few (< 10%) patients with SLE who do not have a positive ANA commonly have antibodies to SS-A. (See also Autoantibodies table, p 316.) Ref: Rheum Dis Clin North Am 1992; 18:337. |
| **SS-B/La antibody,** serum<br><br>Negative<br><br>Marbled<br><br>$$ | Antibodies to La (SSB) cellular ribonucleoprotein complexes are found in Sjögren's syndrome (SS) and appear to be relatively more specific for SS than are antibodies to SSA. They are quantitated by immunoassay. | **Increased in:** Sjögren's (50% sensitivity, higher specificity than anti-SS-A), SLE (10%). | Direct pathogenicity and usefulness of autoantibody test in predicting disease exacerbation not proved. (See also Autoantibodies table, p 316.) Ref: Clin Rheumatol 1990;9:123. Ref: Rheum Dis Clin North Am 1992; 18:359. |

| | T cell receptor gene rearrangement |
|---|---|

| Test/Range/Collection | Physiologic Basis | Interpretation | Comments |
|---|---|---|---|
| **T cell receptor gene rearrangement**<br>Whole blood, bone marrow, or frozen tissue<br><br>Lavender<br>$$$$ | In general, the percentage of T lymphocytes with identical T cell receptors is very low; in malignancies, however, the clonal expansion of one population leads to a large number of cells with identical T cell receptor gene rearrangement. Southern blot is used to identify a monoclonal population. | Positive test results may be seen in T cell neoplasms such as T cell lymphocytic leukemia and cutaneous or nodal T cell lymphomas. | Samples with > 10% of cells showing a given T cell rearrangement are considered positive. However, a large monoclonal population is not absolutely diagnostic of malignancy.<br>Ref: Arch Path Lab Med 1988;112: 117. |

|  | Testosterone | Thrombin time |
| --- | --- | --- |
| **Testosterone, serum**<br><br>Males: 3.0–10.0 ng/mL<br>Females: 0.3–0.7 ng/mL<br>[Males: 10–35 nmol/L]<br>Females: 1.0–2.4 nmol/L]<br><br>Marbled<br><br>$$$ | Testosterone is the principal male sex hormone, produced by the Leydig cells of the testes. Dehydroepiandrosterone (DHEA) is produced in the adrenal cortex, testes and ovaries and is the main precursor for serum testosterone in women. In normal males after puberty, the testosterone level is twice as high as all androgens in females.<br>In serum, it is largely bound to albumin (38%) and to a specific steroid hormone-binding globulin (SHBG) (60%) but it is the free hormone (2%) that is physiologically active. The total testosterone level measures both bound and free testosterone in the serum (by immunoassay). | **Increased in:** Idiopathic sexual precocity (in boys, levels may be in adult range), adrenal hyperplasia (boys), adrenocortical tumors, trophoblastic disease during pregnancy, idiopathic hirsutism, virilizing ovarian tumors, arrhenoblastoma, virilizing luteoma, testicular feminization (normal or moderately elevated), cirrhosis (through increased SHBG), hyperthyroidism (through increased SHBG). Drugs: anticonvulsants, barbiturates, estrogens, oral contraceptives (through increased SHBG).<br><br>**Decreased in:** Hypogonadism (primary and secondary, orchidectomy, Klinefelter's, uremia, hepatic insufficiency, ethanol [men]). Drugs: digoxin, spironolactone. | Serum testosterone levels decrease in men after age 50.<br>A free testosterone level is indicated when a normal total testosterone level is thought not to reflect free testosterone levels because of increases in SHBG.<br>In men, there is a small diurnal variation in serum testosterone with a 20% elevation in levels in the evenings.<br>Ref: N Engl J Med 1980;303:682.<br>Ref: Endocrinol Metab Clin North Am 1992;21:921.<br>Ref: Endocrinol Metab Clin North Am 1994;23:709. |
| **Thrombin time, plasma**<br><br>24–35 seconds (laboratory-specific)<br><br>Blue<br><br>$ | Prolongation of the thrombin time indicates a defect in conversion of fibrinogen to fibrin. | **Increased in:** Low fibrinogen (< 50 mg/dL), abnormal fibrinogen (dysfibrinogenemia), increased fibrin degradation products (eg, disseminated intravascular coagulation), heparin, fibrinolytic agents (streptokinase, urokinase, tissue plasminogen activator), primary systemic amyloidosis (40%). | Thrombin time can be used to monitor fibrinolytic therapy and to screen for dysfibrinogenemia or circulating anticoagulants.<br>Ref: Blood 1991;77:2637. |

| Test/Range/Collection | Physiologic Basis | Interpretation | Comments |
|---|---|---|---|
| **Thyroglobulin,** serum<br><br>3–42 ng/mL [µg/L]<br><br>Marbled<br>$$$ | Thyroglobulin is a large protein specific to the thyroid gland from which thyroxine is synthesized and cleaved. | **Increased in:** Hyperthyroidism, subacute thyroiditis, untreated thyroid carcinomas (except medullary carcinoma). **Decreased in:** Factitious hyperthyroidism, presence of thyroglobulin autoantibodies, after total thyroidectomy. | Thyroglobulin is useful to follow patients after treatment of nonmedullary thyroid carcinomas. Levels fall after successful therapy and rise when metastases develop.<br><br>Sensitivity of the test is increased if patients are off thyroid replacement for 6 weeks prior to testing or if given $T_3$ (Cytomel) for the first 4 weeks, then no medication for the last 2 weeks.<br><br>Athyrotic patients on $T_4$ (levothyroxine) should have values < 5 ng/mL and those off $T_4$ should have values < 10 ng/mL.<br>Ref: Cancer 1983;52:1856.<br>Ref: JAMA 1983;250:2352. |
| **Thyroglobulin antibody,** serum<br><br>< 1:10 (highly method-dependent)<br><br>Marbled<br>$$ | Antibodies against thyroglobulin are produced in autoimmune diseases of the thyroid and other organs. Ten percent of the normal population have slightly elevated titers (especially women and the elderly). | **Increased in:** Hashimoto's thyroiditis (> 90%), thyroid carcinoma (45%), thyrotoxicosis, pernicious anemia (50%), SLE (20%), subacute thyroiditis, Graves' disease. **Not increased in:** Multinodular goiter, thyroid adenomas, and some carcinomas. | The antithyroid peroxidase antibody test is more sensitive than the thyroglobulin antibody test in autoimmune thyroid disease.<br><br>There is little indication for this test. (See Thyroid Peroxidase Antibody, below.)<br>Ref: Am J Med 1983;74:941.<br>Ref: Med Clin North Am 1991;75:1. |

|  | | | |
|---|---|---|---|
| **Thyroid peroxidase antibody**, serum<br><br>Negative<br><br>Marbled<br>$$ | Thyroid peroxidase is a membrane-bound glycoprotein. This enzyme mediates the oxidation of iodide ions and incorporation of iodine into tyrosine residues of thyroglobulin. Its synthesis is stimulated by thyroid-stimulating hormone (TSH). Antithyroid peroxidase antibody assays are performed by ELISA or radioimmunoassay. | **Increased in:** Hashimoto's thyroiditis (> 99%), idiopathic myxedema (> 99%), Graves' disease (75–85%), Addison's disease (50%) and Riedel's thyroiditis. Low titers are present in approximately 10% of normal individuals and patients with nonimmune thyroid disease. | Thyroid peroxidase antibody is an antibody to the main autoantigenic component of microsomes and is a more sensitive and specific test than hemagglutination assays for microsomal antibodies in the diagnosis of autoimmune thyroid disease. Thyroid peroxidase antibody testing alone is almost always sufficient to detect autoimmune thyroid disease.<br>Ref: J Clin Endocrinol Metab 1990;71:661.<br>Ref: Arch Intern Med 1993;153:862. |
| **Thyroid-stimulating hormone**, serum (TSH; thyrotropin)<br><br>0.4–6 µU/mL [mU/L]<br><br>Marbled<br>$$ | TSH is an anterior pituitary hormone that stimulates the thyroid gland to produce thyroid hormones. Secretion is stimulated by thyrotropin-releasing hormone from the hypothalamus. There is negative feedback on TSH secretion by circulating thyroid hormone. | **Increased in:** Hypothyroidism. Mild increases in recovery phase of acute illness.<br>**Decreased in:** Hyperthyroidism, acute medical or surgical illness, pituitary hypothyroidism. Drugs: dopamine, high-dose corticosteroids. | Newer sensitive assays can detect low enough levels of TSH to be useful in the diagnosis of hyperthyroidism as well as hypothyroidism and in distinguishing hyperthyroidism from subnormal TSH values occasionally found in euthyroid sick patients. (See also Thyroid function table, p 361.) Test is useful for following patients taking thyroid medication. Neonatal and cord blood levels are 2–4 times higher than adult levels.<br>Ref: J Nucl Med 1985;26:1248.<br>Ref: Endocrinol Metab Clin North Am 1992;21:903.<br>Ref: Postgrad Med 1993;94:81. |

| Test/Range/Collection | Physiologic Basis | Interpretation | Comments |
|---|---|---|---|
| **Thyroid-stimulating hormone receptor antibody**, serum (TSH-R [stim] Ab) < 130% basal activity of adenylyl cyclase Marbled $$$$ | Test detects heterogeneous IgG antibodies directed against the TSH receptor on thyroid cells. Frequently, they cause excess release of hormone from the thyroid. Test measures antibodies indirectly by their stimulation of adenylyl cyclase to produce cAMP. | **Increased in:** Graves' disease. | Although TSH-R [stim] Ab is a marker of Graves' disease, the test is not necessary for the diagnosis in most cases. Test is very rarely indicated but may be helpful in (1) pregnant women with a history of Graves' disease, because TSH-R [stim] Ab may have some predictive value for neonatal thyrotoxicosis; (2) patients presenting with exophthalmos who are euthyroid, to confirm Graves' disease. Use of the test to predict relapse of hyperthyroidism at the end of a course of antithyroid drugs is controversial. Ref: J Clin Endocrinol Metab 1989;69:1093. |
| **Thyroxine, total**, serum ($T_4$) 5.0–11.0 µg/dL [64–142 nmol/L] Marbled $ | Total $T_4$ is a measure of thyroid gland secretion of $T_4$, bound and free, and thus is influenced by serum thyroid hormone binding activity. | **Increased in:** Hyperthyroidism, increased thyroid-binding globulin (TBG) (eg, pregnancy, drug). Drugs: amiodarone, high-dose beta-blockers (especially propranolol). **Decreased in:** Hypothyroidism, low TBG due to illness or drugs, congenital absence of TBG. Drugs: phenytoin, carbamazepine, androgens. | Total $T_4$ should be interpreted with the TBG level or as part of a free thyroxine index. Ref: Med Clin North Am 1991;75:1. Ref: Med Clin North Am 1991;75:27. |

| | Thyroxine, free | Thyroxine index, free |
|---|---|---|
| **Thyroxine, free, serum (FT₄)** $$ Varies with method $$ Marbled $$ | FT$_4$ (if done by equilibrium dialysis or ultrafiltration method) is a more direct measure of the free T$_4$ hormone concentration (biologically available hormone) than the free T$_4$ index. FT$_4$ done by a two-step immunoassay is similar to the free thyroxine index. | **Increased in:** Hyperthyroidism, nonthyroidal illness, especially psychiatric. Drugs: amiodarone, beta-blockers (high dose). **Decreased in:** Hypothyroidism, nonthyroidal illness. Drugs: phenytoin. |
| | | FT$_4$ is functionally equivalent to the FT$_4$I (see below). Free T$_4$ is a good single test for initial evaluation of thyroid disease. Confirmation of hyper- or hypothyroidism with a sensitive TSH assay is indicated. Ref: JAMA 1990;263:1529. |
| **Thyroxine index, free, serum (FT₄I)** $$ 6.5–12.5 $$ Marbled $$ | Free thyroxine index is expressed as total T$_4$ × T$_3$ (or T$_4$) resin uptake and provides an estimate of the level of free T$_4$, since the T$_3$ (or T$_4$) resin uptake (ie, thyroid hormone binding ratio) is an indirect estimate of the thyroid binding globulin (TBG) concentration. (TBG binds 70% of circulating thyroid hormone.) The unbound form of circulating T$_4$, normally 0.03% of total serum T$_4$, determines the amount of T$_4$ available to cells. | **Increased in:** Hyperthyroidism, nonthyroidal illness, especially psychiatric. Drugs: amiodarone, beta-blockers (high dose). **Decreased in:** Hypothyroidism, nonthyroidal illness. Drugs: phenytoin. |
| | | Test is useful in patients with clinically suspected hyper- or hypothyroidism, in elderly patients admitted to geriatric units, or in women over 40 with one or more somatic complaints. (See Thyroid function table, p 361.) Screening for thyroid disease is not indicated in younger women, men, or patients admitted with acute medical or psychiatric illnesses because transient abnormalities are indistinguishable from true thyroid disease. FT$_4$I is functionally equivalent to the FT$_4$ (see above). Ref: Ann Intern Med 1990;112:840. |

| | *Toxoplasma* antibody | | |
|---|---|---|---|
| Test/Range/Collection | Physiologic Basis | Interpretation | Comments |
| *Toxoplasma* anti-body, serum or CSF (Toxo)<br><br>IgG: < 1:16<br>IgM:<br>Infant < 1:2<br>Adult < 1:8 titer<br><br>Marbled or CSF<br>$$$<br><br>Submit paired sera, one collected within 1 week of illness and another 2–3 weeks later. | *Toxoplasma gondii* is an obligate intracellular protozoan that causes human infection via ingestion, trans-placental transfer, blood products, or organ transplantation. Cats are the definitive hosts of *T gondii* and pass oocysts in their feces. Human infection occurs through ingestion of sporulated oocysts or via the trans-placental route.<br><br>In the immunodeficient host, acute infection may progress to lethal men-ingoencephalitis, pneumonitis, or myocarditis.<br><br>In acute primary infection, IgM anti-bodies develop 1–2 weeks after onset of illness, peak in 6–8 weeks, and then decline. IgG antibodies develop on a similar time-course but persist for years.<br><br>In adult infection, the disease usually represents a reactivation, not a pri-mary infection. Therefore, the IgM test is less useful.<br><br>Approximately 30% of all US adults have antibodies to *T gondii*. | **Increased in:** Acute or congenital toxo-plasmosis (IgM), previous *Toxoplasma* exposure (IgG), and false-positive reac-tions (SLE, rheumatoid arthritis). | Single IgG titers of > 1:256 are consid-ered diagnostic of active infection; titers of > 1:128 are suspicious. Titers of 1:16–1:64 may merely represent past exposure. If titers subsequently rise, they probably represent early dis-ease.<br><br>IgM titer > 1:16 is very important in the diagnosis of congenital toxoplas-mosis.<br><br>High titer IgG antibody results should prompt an IgM test. IgM, however, is generally not found in adult AIDS patients since the disease usually rep-resents a reactivation.<br><br>Some recommend ordering baseline *Toxoplasma* IgG titers in all asymp-tomatic HIV-positive patients because a rising *Toxoplasma* titer can help diagnose CNS toxoplasmosis in the future.<br><br>Culture of the *T gondii* organism is dif-ficult, and most laboratories are not equipped for the procedure.<br><br>(See also Brain abscess, p 201.)<br>Ref: Ann Intern Med 1984;100:36.<br>Ref: N Engl J Med 1988;318:271.<br>Ref: Clin Infect Dis 1994:18:14. |

| | Triglycerides | |
|---|---|---|
| **Triglycerides, serum** (TG)<br><br>< 165 mg/dL<br>[< 1.65 g/L]<br><br>Marbled<br><br>$<br><br>Fasting specimen required. | Dietary fat is hydrolyzed in the small intestine, absorbed and resynthesized by mucosal cells, and secreted into lacteals as chylomicrons. Triglycerides in the chylomicrons are cleared from the blood by tissue lipoprotein lipase.<br>Endogenous triglyceride production occurs in the liver. These triglycerides are transported in association with β-lipoproteins in very low density lipoproteins (VLDL). | **Increased in:** Hypothyroidism, diabetes mellitus, nephrotic syndrome, chronic alcoholism (fatty liver), biliary tract obstruction, stress, familial dysbetalipoproteinemia, familial combined hyperlipidemia, obesity, viral hepatitis, cirrhosis, pancreatitis, chronic renal failure, gout, pregnancy, glycogen storage diseases types I, III, and VI, anorexia nervosa, dietary excess. Drugs: beta-blockers, cholestyramine, corticosteroids, diazepam, diuretics, estrogens, oral contraceptives.<br>**Decreased in:** Tangier disease (α-lipoprotein deficiency), hypo- and abetalipoproteinemia, malnutrition, malabsorption, parenchymal liver disease, hyperthyroidism, intestinal lymphangiectasia. Drugs: ascorbic acid, clofibrate, nicotinic acid, gemfibrozil. | If serum is clear, the serum triglyceride level is generally < 350 mg/dL.<br>Hypertriglyceridemia in an asymptomatic person who does not have a strong family history of coronary heart disease or a personal history of hypercholesterolemia is not a definite risk factor for coronary heart disease.<br>A high serum triglyceride level is a predictor of mortality following coronary artery bypass surgery.<br>Triglycerides > 1000 mg/dL can be seen when a primary lipid disorder is exacerbated by alcohol or fat intake or by corticosteroid or estrogen therapy.<br>Ref: JAMA 1993;269:505.<br>Ref: Lancet 1993;342:781.<br>Ref: N Engl J Med 1993;328:1220.<br>Ref: Med Clin North Am 1994;78:117. |

| Test/Range/Collection | Physiologic Basis | Interpretation | Comments |
|---|---|---|---|
| **Triiodothyronine, total, serum ($T_3$)**<br><br>95–190 ng/dL<br>[1.5–2.9 nmol/L]<br><br>Marbled<br>$$ | $T_3$ reflects the metabolically active form of thyroid hormone and is influenced by thyroid hormone-binding activity. | **Increased in:** Hyperthyroidism (some), increased thyroid-binding globulin.<br>**Decreased in:** Hypothyroidism, nonthyroidal illness, decreased thyroid-binding globulin. Drugs: amiodarone. | $T_3$ may be increased in approximately 5% of hyperthyroid patients in whom $T_4$ is normal ($T_3$ toxicosis). Therefore, test is indicated when hyperthyroidism is suspected and $T_4$ value is normal. Test is of no value in the diagnosis of hypothyroidism.<br>Ref: Ann Intern Med 1990;112:840.<br>Ref: JAMA 1990;263:1529.<br>Ref: Am J Med 1994;96:229. |
| **Troponin-I, cardiac, serum (cTnI)**<br><br>< 1.5 ng/mL<br><br>Marbled<br>$$ | Troponin is the contractile regulatory protein of striated muscle. It contains three subunits: T, C, and I. Subunit I consists of three forms, which are found in slow-twitch skeletal muscle, fast-twitch skeletal muscle, and cardiac muscle, respectively. Troponin I is predominantly a structural protein and is released into the circulation after cellular necrosis. Cardiac troponin I is expressed only in cardiac muscle, throughout development and despite pathology, and thus its presence in serum can distinguish between myocardial injury and skeletal muscle injury.<br>cTnI is measured by immunoassay using monoclonal antibodies. | **Increased in:** Myocardial infarction (sensitivity 50% at 4 hours, 97% at 6 hours; specificity 95%), cardiac trauma or cardiac surgery. Slight elevations rarely noted in patients with recent aggravated unstable angina.<br>**Not increased in:** Skeletal muscle disease (myopathy, myositis, dystrophy), noncardiac trauma or surgery, rhabdomyolysis, severe muscular exertion, chronic renal failure. | Cardiac troponin I is a more specific marker for myocardial infarction than CKMB with roughly equivalent sensitivity early in the course of infarction (4–36 hours). cTnI appears in serum approximately 4 hours after onset of chest pain, peaks at 8–12 hours, and persists for 5–7 days. This prolonged persistence gives it much greater sensitivity than CKMB for diagnosis of myocardial infarction beyond the first 36–48 hours, and it replaces the use of LDH isoenzymes for the detection of infarction at these times. (See Figure 8–17, p 342.)<br>Ref: Clin Chem 1994;40:1291.<br>Ref: N Engl J Med 1994;330:670.<br>Ref: Clin Chem 1995;41:1266. |

| Tularemia agglutinins | | |
|---|---|---|
| **Tularemia agglutinins,** serum<br><br>< 1:80 titer<br><br>Marbled<br><br>$$ | *Francisella tularensis* is an organism of wild rodents (rabbits and hares) that infects humans (eg, trappers and skinners) via contact with animal tissues, by the bite of certain ticks and flies, and by consumption of undercooked meat or contaminated water. Agglutinating antibodies appear in 10–14 days and peak in 5–10 weeks. A four-fold rise in titers is typically needed to prove acute infection. Titers decrease over years. | **Increased in:** Tularemia; cross-reaction with *Brucella* antigens and *Proteus* OX-19 antigen (but at lower titers). | Single titers of > 1:160 are indicative of infection. Maximum titers are > 1:1280.<br>A history of exposure to rabbits, ticks, dogs, cats, or skunks is suggestive of—but is not a requirement for—the diagnosis. Most common presentation is a single area of painful lymphadenopathy with low-grade fever. Initial treatment should be empiric. Culture of the organism is difficult, requiring special media, and hazardous to laboratory personnel. Serologic tests are the mainstay of diagnosis.<br>Ref: Medicine 1985;64:251.<br>Ref: N Engl J Med 1993;329:936. |

| Test/Range/Collection | Physiologic Basis | Interpretation | Comments |
|---|---|---|---|
| **Type and cross-match**, serum and red cells (Type and cross)<br><br>Red<br>$$<br><br>Specimen label must be signed by the person drawing the blood.<br><br>A second "check" specimen is needed at some hospitals. | A type and cross-match involves ABO and Rh grouping (see pp. 37 and 160, respectively), antibody screen (see p. 48), and cross-match. (Compare with Type and Screen, below.)<br><br>A major cross-match involves testing recipient serum against donor cells. It uses antihuman globulin to detect recipient's antibodies on donor red cells.<br><br>If the recipient's serum contains a clinically significant alloantibody by antibody screen, a cross-match is required. | | A type and screen is adequate preparation for operative procedures unlikely to require transfusion.<br><br>Unnecessary type and cross-match orders reduce blood availability and add to costs.<br><br>In addition, a preordering system should be in place, indicating the number of units of blood likely to be needed for each operative procedure.<br><br>Ref: *Technical Manual of the American Association of Blood Banks*, 11th ed. American Association of Blood Banks, 1993. |
| **Type and screen,** serum and red cells<br><br>Red or lavender<br>$$<br><br>Specimen label must be signed by the person drawing the blood.<br><br>A second "check" specimen is needed at some hospitals. | Type and screen includes ABO and Rh grouping (see pp. 37 and 160, respectively) and antibody screen (see p. 48). (Compare with Type and Cross-Match, above.) | | Type and screen is indicated for patients undergoing operative procedures unlikely to require transfusion.<br><br>A negative antibody screen implies that a recipient can receive un-cross-matched type-specific blood with minimal risk.<br><br>If the recipient's serum contains a clinically significant alloantibody by antibody screen, a cross-match is required.<br><br>Ref: *Technical Manual of the American Association of Blood Banks*, 11th ed. American Association of Blood Banks, 1993. |

| | Uric acid | | | Vanillylmandelic acid |
|---|---|---|---|---|
| **Uric acid, serum**<br><br>Males: 2.4–7.4<br>Females 1.4–5.8 mg/dL<br>[Males: 140–440.<br>Females: 80–350 µmol/L]<br><br>Marbled<br>$ | Uric acid is an end product of nucleoprotein metabolism and is excreted by the kidney.<br>An increase in serum uric acid concentration occurs with increased nucleoprotein synthesis or catabolism (blood dyscrasias, therapy of leukemia) or decreased renal uric acid excretion (eg, thiazide diuretic therapy or renal failure). | **Increased in:** Renal failure, gout, myeloproliferative disorders (leukemia, lymphoma, myeloma, polycythemia vera), psoriasis, glycogen storage disease (type I), Lesch-Nyhan syndrome (X-linked hypoxanthine–guanine phosphoribosyltransferase deficiency), lead nephropathy. Drugs: antimetabolite and chemotherapeutic agents, diuretics, ethanol, nicotinic acid, salicylates (low dose), theophylline.<br>**Decreased in:** SIADH, xanthine oxidase deficiency, low-purine diet, Fanconi's syndrome, neoplastic disease (various, causing increased renal excretion), liver disease. Drugs: salicylates (high dose), allopurinol (xanthine oxidase inhibitor). | | Sex, age, and renal function affect uric acid levels.<br>The incidence of hyperuricemia is greater in some ethnic groups (eg, Filipinos) than others (whites).<br>Hyperuricemia may be a marker for excess cardiovascular risk.<br>Ref: Clin Chem 1992;38:1350.<br>Ref: Postgrad Med J 1994;70:486. |
| **Vanillylmandelic acid, urine (VMA)**<br><br>2–7 mg/24 h<br>[10–35 µmol/d]<br><br>Urine bottle containing hydrochloric acid<br>$$<br>Collect 24-hour urine. | Catecholamines secreted in excess by pheochromocytomas are metabolized by the enzymes monoamine oxidase and catechol-O-methyltransferase to VMA, which is excreted in urine. | **Increased in:** Pheochromocytoma (96% sensitivity, 100% specificity), neuroblastoma, ganglioneuroma.<br>**Decreased in:** Drugs: monoamine oxidase inhibitors. | | A 24-hour urine metanephrine test (p 131) is the recommended test for the diagnosis of pheochromocytoma. (See also Pheochromocytoma algorithm, p 345.)<br>A special diet is not needed when VMA test is done by the usual method.<br>< 0.1% of hypertensive patients have a pheochromocytoma.<br>Ref: Am J Cardiol 1970;26:270.<br>Ref: Ann Surg 1974;179:740. |

## VDRL test, serum

| Test/Range/Collection | Physiologic Basis | Interpretation | Comments |
|---|---|---|---|
| **Venereal Disease Research Laboratory test**, serum (VDRL)<br><br>Nonreactive<br><br>Marbled<br><br>$ | This syphilis test measures nontreponemal antibodies that are produced when *Treponema pallidum* interacts with host tissues. The VDRL usually becomes reactive at a titer of > 1:32 within 1–3 weeks after the genital chancre appears. | **Increased in:** Syphilis: primary (59–87%), secondary (100%), late latent (79–91%), tertiary (37–94%); collagen-vascular diseases (rheumatoid arthritis, SLE), infections (mononucleosis, leprosy, malaria), pregnancy, drug abuse. | VDRL is used as a syphilis screening test and in suspected cases of primary and secondary syphilis. Positive tests should be confirmed with an FTA-ABS or MHA-TP test (see pp 90 and 135, respectively).<br>The VDRL has similar sensitivity and specificity to the RPR (see Syphilis test table, p 359).<br>Ref: Ann Intern Med 1986;104:368.<br>Ref: Ann Intern Med 1991;114:1005. |

| VDRL test, CSF | | |
|---|---|---|
| **Venereal Disease Research Laboratory test,** CSF (VDRL)<br><br>Nonreactive<br><br>$$<br><br>Deliver in a clean plastic or glass tube. | The CSF VDRL test measures nontreponemal antibodies that develop in the CSF when *Treponema pallidum* interacts with the central nervous system. | **Increased in:** Tertiary neurosyphilis (10%).<br><br>The quantitative VDRL is the test of choice for CNS syphilis. Treponemal tests (FTA-ABS, MHA-TP) are not helpful in CSF.<br><br>Since the sensitivity of CSF VDRL is very low, a negative test does not rule out neurosyphilis. Clinical features, CSF white cell count, and CSF protein should be used together to make the diagnosis (see CSF profiles, p 318).<br><br>Because the specificity of the CSF VDRL test is high, a positive test confirms the presence of neurosyphilis. Patients being screened for neurosyphilis with CSF VDRL testing should have a positive serum RPR, VDRL, FTA-ABS, MHA-TP test or other evidence of infection.<br><br>Repeat testing may be indicated in HIV-infected patients in whom neurosyphilis is suspected.<br>Ref: Neurology 1985;35:1368.<br>Ref: West J Med 1988;149:47.<br>Ref: Neurology 1990;40:541.<br>Ref: Am J Clin Pathol 1991;95:397. |

| Test/Range/Collection | Physiologic Basis | Interpretation | Comments |
|---|---|---|---|
| **Vitamin B$_{12}$, serum**<br><br>140–820 pg/mL<br>[100–600 pmol/L]<br><br>Marbled<br>$$ | Vitamin B$_{12}$ is a necessary cofactor for three important biochemical processes: conversion of methylmalonyl-CoA to succinyl-CoA and methylation of homocysteine to methionine and demethylation of methyltetrahydrofolate to tetrahydrofolate (THF). Consequent deficiency of folate coenzymes derived from THF is probably the crucial lesion caused by B$_{12}$ deficiency.<br><br>All vitamin B$_{12}$ comes from ingestion of foods of animal origin.<br><br>Vitamin B$_{12}$ in serum is protein-bound, 70% to transcobalamin I (TC I) and 30% to transcobalamin II (TC II). The B$_{12}$ bound to TC II is physiologically active; that bound to TC I is not. | **Increased in:** Leukemia (acute myelocytic, chronic myelocytic, chronic lymphocytic, monocytic), marked leukocytosis, polycythemia vera. (Increased B$_{12}$ levels are not diagnostically useful.)<br><br>**Decreased in:** Pernicious anemia, gastrectomy, gastric carcinoma, malabsorption (sprue, celiac disease, steatorrhea, regional enteritis, fistulas, bowel resection, *Diphyllobothrium latum* [fish tapeworm] infestation, small bowel bacterial overgrowth), pregnancy, dietary deficiency, HIV infection (with or without malabsorption), drugs (eg, omeprazole, metformin). | Confirmation of suspected vitamin B$_{12}$ deficiency requires a vitamin B$_{12}$ absorption (Schilling's) test (see below).<br><br>The commonly available competitive protein binding assay measures total B$_{12}$. It is insensitive to significant decreases in physiologically significant B$_{12}$ bound to TC II.<br><br>Specificity of the serum vitamin B$_{12}$ test (approximately 73%) has not been systematically studied.<br><br>Neuropsychiatric disorders caused by low serum B$_{12}$ level can occur in the absence of anemia or macrocytosis.<br>Ref: Br J Haematol 1993;83:643.<br>Ref: Essays Biochem 1994;28:63.<br>Ref: JAMA 1994;272:1233.<br>Ref: Ann Intern Med 1994;120:211. |

| Vitamin B$_{12}$ absorption test | | |
|---|---|---|
| **Vitamin B$_{12}$ absorption test, 24-hour urine** (Schilling's test)<br><br>Excretion of > 8% of administered dose<br><br>$$$$<br><br>Stage I: 0.5–1.0 μCi of $^{52}$Co-B$_{12}$ is given orally, followed by 1.0 mg of unlabeled B$_{12}$ IM 2 hours later. A 24-hour urine is collected.<br>Stage II: After 5 days, test is repeated with 60 mg active hog intrinsic factor added to the oral labeled B$_{12}$. | Absorption of vitamin B$_{12}$ is dependent on two factors: adequate intrinsic factor produced by the stomach antrum and normal ileal absorption. Lack of either can lead to B$_{12}$ deficiency. | **Decreased in:** Ileal disease or resection, bacterial overgrowth, B$_{12}$ deficiency (because megaloblastosis of the intestinal wall leads to decreased B$_{12}$ absorption), pernicious anemia (< 2.5% excretion of administered dose), postgastrectomy, chronic pancreatitis, cystic fibrosis, giardiasis, Crohn's disease. | If the patient's creatinine clearance is < 60 mL/min, a 48-hour urine should be collected.<br>Pernicious anemia is suggested by an abnormal stage I test, followed by a normal stage II test (ie, addition of intrinsic factor leads to normal intestinal absorption and urinary excretion). Ileal malabsorption gives abnormal results in stages I and II.<br>Low intrinsic factor contributing to B$_{12}$ deficiency is common in AIDS.<br>Egg yolk-bound B$_{12}$ should be used rather than crystalline B$_{12}$ to avoid false negative tests.<br>Ref: CRC Crit Rev Clin Lab Sci 1988; 26:263.<br>Ref: Am J Gastroenterol 1992;87:1781.<br>Ref: Mayo Clin Proc 1994;69:144. |

| | Vitamin D₃, 25-hydroxy | | |
|---|---|---|---|
| **Test/Range/Collection** | **Physiologic Basis** | **Interpretation** | **Comments** |
| **Vitamin D₃, 25-hydroxy**, serum or plasma (25[OH]D₃)<br><br>10–50 ng/mL [25–125 nmol/L]<br><br>Marbled or green<br>$$$ | The vitamin D system functions to maintain serum calcium levels. Vitamin D is a fat-soluble steroid hormone. Two molecular forms exist: D₃ (cholecalciferol), synthesized in the epidermis, and D₂ (ergocalciferol), derived from plant sources. To become active, both need to be further metabolized. Two sequential hydroxylations occur: in the liver to 25(OH)D₃ and then, in the kidney, to 1,25[OH]₂D₃.<br><br>Plasma levels increase with sun exposure. | **Increased in:** Heavy milk drinkers (up to 64 ng/mL), vitamin D intoxication, sun exposure.<br>**Decreased in:** Dietary deficiency, malabsorption (rickets, osteomalacia), biliary and portal cirrhosis, nephrotic syndrome, lack of sun exposure. Drugs: phenytoin, phenobarbital. | Measurement of 25(OH)D₃ is the best indicator of both vitamin D deficiency and toxicity. It is indicated in hypocalcemic disorders associated with increased PTH levels, in children with rickets and in adults with osteomalacia. In hypercalcemic disorders, 25(OH)D₃ is useful in disorders associated with decreased PTH levels, or possible vitamin D overdose (hypervitaminosis D).<br><br>Vitamin D toxicity is manifested by hypercalcemia, hyperphosphatemia, soft tissue calcification and renal failure.<br><br>Ref: Adv Intern Med 1982;27:45.<br>Ref: Mayo Clin Proc 1985;60:851.<br>Ref: Endocrinol Metab Clin North Am 1989;18:765. |

| Vitamin D$_3$, 1,25-dihydroxy | | |
|---|---|---|
| **Vitamin D$_3$, 1,25-dihydroxy,** serum or plasma (1,25[OH]$_2$D$_3$)<br><br>20–76 pg/mL<br><br>Marbled or green<br>$$$$ | 1,25-Dihydroxy vitamin D$_3$ is the most potent form of vitamin D.<br>The main actions of vitamin D are the acceleration of calcium and phosphate absorption in the intestine and stimulation of bone resorption. | **Increased in:** Primary hyperparathyroidism, idiopathic hypercalciuria, sarcoidosis, some lymphomas, 1,25(OH)$_2$D$_3$-resistant rickets, normal growth (children), pregnancy, and lactation.<br>**Decreased in:** Chronic renal failure, anephric patients, hypoparathyroidism, pseudohypoparathyroidism, 1α-hydroxylase deficiency, postmenopausal osteoporosis. | Test is rarely needed.<br>Measurement of 1,25(OH)$_2$D$_3$ is only useful in distinguishing 1α-hydroxylase deficiency from 1,25(OH)$_2$D$_3$-resistant rickets or in monitoring vitamin D status of patients with chronic renal failure.<br>Test is not useful for assessment of vitamin D intoxication, because of efficient feedback regulation of 1,25(OH)$_2$D$_3$ synthesis.<br>Ref: Adv Intern Med 1982;27:45.<br>Ref: N Engl J Med 1989;320:980. |

| | von Willebrand's factor protein | | |
|---|---|---|---|
| **Test/Range/Collection** | **Physiologic Basis** | **Interpretation** | **Comments** |
| **von Willebrand's factor protein (immunologic)**, plasma (vWF)<br><br>44–158% units<br><br>Blue<br>$$$ | von Willebrand's factor (vWF) is produced by endothelial cells, circulates in the plasma complexed to factor VIII coagulant protein, and mediates platelet adhesion.<br><br>Both quantitative and qualitative changes can cause disease.<br><br>vWF can be measured as protein antigen (immunologic measure) or by ristocetin cofactor activity (functional assay). | **Increased in:** Inflammatory states (acute phase reactant).<br><br>**Decreased in:** von Willebrand's disease. | In von Willebrand's disease, the platelet count and morphology are generally normal and the bleeding time is usually prolonged (markedly prolonged by aspirin). Variant forms associated with mild thrombocytopenia and angiodysplasia are described. The PTT may not be prolonged if factor VIII coagulant level is > 30%. Diagnosis is suggested by bleeding symptoms and family history. Laboratory diagnosis of von Willebrand's disease has become more difficult because of the identification of numerous variant forms. In the classic type I disease, vWF antigen is decreased.<br><br>Ref: Blood 1987;70:895.<br>Ref: Mayo Clin Proc 1991;66:832. |

| D-Xylose absorption test |
|---|

| **D-Xylose absorption test,** urine | Xylose is normally easily absorbed from the small intestine. Measuring xylose in serum or its excretion in urine after ingestion evaluates the carbohydrate absorption ability of the proximal small intestine. | **Decreased in:** Intestinal malabsorption, small intestinal bacterial overgrowth, renal insufficiency, AIDS wasting syndrome, cryptosporidiosis. | Test can be helpful in distinguishing intestinal malabsorption (decreased D-xylose absorption) from pancreatic insufficiency (normal D-xylose absorption). |
|---|---|---|---|
| > 5 g per 5-hour urine (> 20% excreted in 5 hours) | | | Urinary xylose excretion may be spuriously decreased in renal failure, thus limiting the specificity and usefulness of the test. In this case, a serum xylose level (gray top tube) obtained 1 hour after administration of a 25-g dose of D-xylose can be used to evaluate xylose absorption. The normal level should be > 29 mg/dL (1.9 mmol/L). |
| $$$ | | | Ref: Dig Dis Sci 1991;36:188. |
| Fasting patient is given D-xylose, 25 g in two glasses of water, followed by four glasses of water over the next 2 hours. Urine is collected for 5 hours and refrigerated. | | | Ref: J Acquir Immune Defic Syndr 1992;5:1047. |
| | | | Ref: Gastroenterology 1995;108:1075. |

# 4

# Therapeutic Drug Monitoring: Principles and Test Interpretation

*Diana Nicoll, MD, PhD*

## UNDERLYING ASSUMPTIONS

The basic assumptions underlying therapeutic drug monitoring are that drug metabolism varies from patient to patient and that the plasma level of a drug is more closely related to the drug's therapeutic effect or toxicity than is the dosage.

## INDICATIONS FOR DRUG MONITORING

Drugs with a **narrow therapeutic index** (where therapeutic drug levels do not differ greatly from levels associated with serious toxicity) should be monitored. *Example:* Lithium.

Patients who have **impaired clearance** of a drug with a narrow therapeutic index are candidates for drug monitoring. The clearance mechanism of the drug involved must be known. *Example:* Patients with renal failure have decreased clearance of gentamicin and therefore are at a higher risk for gentamicin toxicity.

Drugs whose **toxicity is difficult to distinguish from a patient's underlying disease** may require monitoring. *Example:* Theophylline in patients with chronic obstructive pulmonary disease.

Drugs whose **efficacy is difficult to establish clinically** may require monitoring of plasma levels. *Example:* Phenytoin.

## SITUATIONS IN WHICH DRUG MONITORING MAY NOT BE USEFUL

Drugs that can be given in extremely high doses before toxicity is apparent are not candidates for monitoring. *Example:* Penicillin.

If there are better means of assessing drug effects, drug level monitoring may not be appropriate. *Example:* Warfarin is monitored by prothrombin time and INR (International Normalized Ratio) determinations, not by serum levels.

Drug level monitoring to assess compliance is limited by the inability to distinguish compliance from rapid metabolism without direct inpatient scrutiny of drug administration.

Drug toxicity cannot be diagnosed with drug levels alone; it is a clinical diagnosis. Drug levels within the usual therapeutic range do not rule out drug toxicity in a given patient. *Example:* Digoxin, where other physiologic variables (eg, hypokalemia) affect drug toxicity.

In summary, therapeutic drug monitoring may be useful to guide dosage adjustment of certain drugs in certain patients. Patient compliance is essential if drug monitoring data are to be correctly interpreted.

## OTHER INFORMATION REQUIRED FOR EFFECTIVE DRUG MONITORING

### Reliability of the Analytic Method

The **analytic sensitivity** of the drug monitoring method must be adequate. For some drugs, plasma levels are in the nanogram per milliliter range. *Example:* Tricyclic antidepressants, digoxin.

The **specificity** of the method must be known, since the drug's metabolites or other drugs may interfere. Interference by metabolites—which may or may not be pharmacologically active—is of particular concern in immunologic assay methods using antibodies to the parent drug.

The **precision** of the method must be known in order to assess whether changes in levels are caused by method imprecision or by clinical changes.

### Reliability of the Therapeutic Range

Establishing the therapeutic range for a drug requires a reliable clinical assessment of its therapeutic and toxic effects, together with plasma drug level measurements by a particular analytic method. In practice, as newer, more specific analytic methods are introduced, the therapeutic ranges for those methods are estimated by comparing the old and new methodologies—without clinical correlation.

### Pharmacokinetic Parameters

Five pharmacokinetic parameters that are important in therapeutic drug monitoring include:

1. *Bioavailability.* The bioavailability of a drug depends in part on its formulation. A drug that is significantly metabolized as it first passes through the liver exhibits a marked "first-pass effect," reducing the effective oral absorption of the drug. A reduction in this first-pass effect (eg, because of decreased hepatic blood flow in heart failure) could cause a clinically significant increase in effective oral drug absorption.

2. *Volume of distribution and distribution phases.* The volume of distribution of a drug determines the plasma concentration reached after a loading dose. The distribution phase is the time taken for a drug to distribute from the plasma to the periphery. Drug levels drawn before completion of a long distribution phase may not reflect levels of pharmacologically active drug at sites of action. *Examples:* Digoxin, lithium.

3. *Clearance.* Clearance is either renal or nonrenal (usually hepatic). Whereas changes in renal clearance can be predicted on the basis of serum creatinine or creatinine clearance, there is no routine liver function test for assessment of hepatic drug metabolism. For most therapeutic drugs measured, clearance is independent of plasma drug concentration, so that a change in dose is reflected in a similar change in plasma level. If, however, clearance is dose-dependent, dosage adjustments produce disproportionately large changes in plasma levels and must be made cautiously. *Example:* Phenytoin.

4. *Half-life.* The half-life of a drug depends on its volume of distribution and its clearance and determines the time taken to reach a steady state level. In three or four half-lives, the drug level will be 87.5% to 93.75% of the way to steady state. Patients with decreased drug clearance and therefore increased drug half-lives will take longer to reach a higher steady state level. In general, since non-steady state drug levels are potentially misleading and can be difficult to interpret, it is recommended that most clinical monitoring be done at steady state.

5. *Protein binding of drugs.* All routine drug level analysis involves assessment of both protein-bound and free drug. However, pharmacologic activity depends on only the free drug level. Changes in protein binding (eg, in uremia or hypoalbuminemia) may significantly affect interpretation of reported levels for drugs that are highly protein-bound. *Example:* Phenytoin. In such cases, where the ratio of free to total measured drug level is increased, the usual therapeutic range based on total drug level will not apply.

## Drug Interactions

For patients receiving several medications, the possibility of drug interactions affecting drug elimination must be considered. *Example:* Quinidine decreases digoxin clearance.

## Time to Draw Levels

In general, the specimen should be drawn after steady state is reached (at least 3 or 4 half-lives after a dosage adjustment) and just before the next dose (trough level).

Peak and trough levels may be indicated to evaluate the dosage of drugs whose half-lives are much shorter than the dosing interval. *Example:* Gentamicin.

## Reference

Winter M: *Basic Clinical Pharmacokinetics,* 3rd ed. Applied Therapeutics, 1994.

**TABLE 4–1. THERAPEUTIC DRUG MONITORING.**

| Drug | Effective Concentrations | Half-Life (hours) | Dosage Adjustment | Comments |
|---|---|---|---|---|
| Amikacin | Peak: 10–25 µg/mL Trough: < 10 µg/mL | 2–3 ↑ in uremia | ↓ in renal dysfunction | Concomitant kanamycin or tobramycin therapy may give falsely elevated amikacin results by immunoassay. |
| Amitriptyline | 160–240 ng/mL | 9–46 | | Drug is highly protein-bound. Patient-specific decrease in protein binding may invalidate quoted range of effective concentration. |
| Carbamazepine | 4–8 µg/mL | 10–30 | | Induces its own metabolism. Metabolite 10,11-epoxide exhibits 13% cross-reactivity by immunoassay. Toxicity: diplopia, drowsiness, nausea, vomiting, and ataxia. |
| Cyclosporine | 150–400 mg/mL (ng/L) whole blood | 6–12 | Need to know specimen and methodology used | Cyclosporine is lipid-soluble (20% bound to leukocytes; 40% to erythrocytes; 40% in plasma, highly bound to lipoproteins). Binding is temperature-dependent, so whole blood is preferred to plasma or serum as specimen. High-performance liquid chromatography or monoclonal fluorescence polarization immunoassay measures cyclosporine reliably. Polyclonal fluorescence polarization immunoassays cross-react with metabolites, so the therapeutic range used with those assays is higher. Anticonvulsants and rifampin increase metabolism. Erythromycin, ketoconazole, and calcium channel blockers decrease metabolism. |
| Desipramine | 100–250 ng/mL | 13–23 | | Drug is highly protein-bound. Patient-specific decrease in protein binding may invalidate quoted range of effective concentration. |

↔ = unchanged; ↑ = increased; ↓ = decreased; CHF = congestive heart failure

*(continued)*

**TABLE 4–1 (CONT'D). THERAPEUTIC DRUG MONITORING.**

| Drug | Effective Concentrations | Half-Life (hours) | Dosage Adjustment | Comments |
|---|---|---|---|---|
| Digoxin | 0.8–2.0 ng/mL | 42 ↑ in uremia, CHF, hypothyroidism; ↓ in hyperthyroidism | ↓ in renal dysfunction, CHF | Bioavailability of digoxin tablets is 50–90%. Specimen must not be drawn within 6 hours of dose. Dialysis does not remove a significant amount. Hypokalemia potentiates toxicity. Digitalis toxicity is a clinical and *not* a laboratory diagnosis. Digibind (digoxin-specific antibody) therapy of digoxin overdose can interfere with measurement of digoxin levels depending on the digoxin assay. Elimination reduced by quinidine, verapamil, and amiodarone. |
| Ethosuximide | 40–100 mg/L | Child: 30 Adult: 50 | | Levels used primarily to assess compliance. Toxicity is rare and does not correlate well with plasma concentrations. |
| Gentamicin | Peak: 4–8 μg/mL Trough: < 2 μg/mL | 2–5 ↑ in uremia (7.3 on dialysis) | ↓ in renal dysfunction | Draw peak specimen 30 minutes after end of infusion. Draw trough just before next dose. In uremic patients, carbenicillin may reduce gentamicin half-life from 46 to 22 hours. |
| Imipramine | 180–350 ng/mL | 10–16 | | Drug is highly protein-bound. Patient-specific decrease in protein binding may invalidate quoted range of effective concentration. |
| Lidocaine | 1–5 μg/mL | 1.8 ↔ in uremia, CHF ↑ in cirrhosis | ↓ in CHF, liver disease | Levels increased with cimetidine therapy. CNS toxicity common in the elderly. |
| Lithium | 0.7–1.5 meq/L | 22 ↑ in uremia | ↓ in renal dysfunction | Thiazides and loop diuretics may increase serum lithium levels. |
| Methotrexate | | 8.4 ↑ in uremia | ↓ in renal dysfunction | 7-Hydroxymethotrexate cross-reacts 1.5% in immunoassay. To minimize toxicity, leucovorin should be continued if methotrexate level is > 0.1 μmol/L at 48 hours after start of therapy. Methotrexate > 1 μmol/L at > 48 hours requires an increase in leucovorin rescue therapy. |

↔ = unchanged; ↑ = increased; ↓ = decreased; CHF = congestive heart failure

**TABLE 4–1 (CONT'D). THERAPEUTIC DRUG MONITORING.**

| Drug | Effective Concentrations | Half-Life (hours) | Dosage Adjustment | Comments |
|---|---|---|---|---|
| Nortriptyline | 50–40 ng/mL | 18–44 | | Drug is highly protein-bound. Patient-specific decrease in protein binding may invalidate quoted range of effective concentration. |
| Phenobarbital | 10–30 µg/mL | 86 ↑ in cirrhosis | ↓ in liver disease | Metabolized principally by the hepatic microsomal enzyme system. Many drug-drug interactions. |
| Phenytoin | 10–20 µg/mL ↓ in uremia, hypoalbuminemia | Dose-dependent | | Metabolite cross-reacts 10% in immunoassay. Metabolism is capacity-limited. Increase dose *cautiously* when level approaches therapeutic range, since new steady state level may be disproportionately higher. Drug is very highly protein-bound, and when protein-binding is decreased in uremia and hypoalbuminemia, the usual therapeutic range does not apply. In this situation, use a reference range of 5–10 µg/mL. |
| Primidone | 5–10 µg/mL | 8 | | Phenobarbital cross-reacts 0.5%. Metabolized to phenobarbital. Primidone/phenobarbital ratio > 1:2 suggests poor compliance. |
| Procainamide | 4–8 µg/mL | 3 ↑ in uremia | ↓ in renal dysfunction | Thirty percent of patients with plasma levels of 12–16 µg/mL have ECG changes; 40% of patients with plasma levels of 16 µg/mL have severe toxicity. Metabolite *N*-acetylprocainamide is active. |
| Quinidine | 1–5 µ/mL | 7 ↔ in CHF ↑ in liver disease | ↓ in liver disease, CHF | Effective concentration is lower in chronic liver disease and nephrosis where binding is decreased. |
| Salicylate | 150–300 µg/mL (15–30 mg/dL) | Dose-dependent | | See Figure 8–23, p 356, for nomogram of salicylate toxicity. |
| Theophylline | 5–20 µg/mL | 9 | ↓ in CHF, cirrhosis, and with cimetidine | Caffeine cross-reacts 10%. Elimination is increased 1.5–2 times in smokers. 1,3-Dimethyl uric acid metabolite increased in uremia and because of cross-reactivity may cause an apparent slight increase in serum theophylline. |

↔ = unchanged; ↑ = increased; ↓ = decreased; CHF = congestive heart failure

*(continued)*

**TABLE 4–1 (CONT'D). THERAPEUTIC DRUG MONITORING.**

| Drug | Effective Concen- trations | Half-Life (hours) | Dosage Adjust- ment | Comments |
|------|----------------------------|-------------------|---------------------|----------|
| Tobra- mycin | Peak: 5–10 µg/mL Trough: < 2 µg/mL | 2–3 ↑ in uremia | ↓ in renal dysfunc- tion | Tobramycin, kanamycin, and amika- cin may cross-react in immunoassay. |
| Valproic acid | 55–100 µg/mL | 13–19 | | Ninety-five percent protein-bound. Reduced binding in uremia and cir- rhosis. |
| Vanco- mycin | Trough: 5– 15 µg/mL | 6 ↑ in uremia | ↓ in renal dysfunc- tion | Toxicity in uremic patients leads to irreversible deafness. Keep peak level < 30–40 µg/mL to avoid toxicity. |

↔ = unchanged; ↑ = increased; ↓ = decreased; CHF = congestive heart failure

# 5

# Microbiology: Test Selection

*Tony M. Chou, MD, William M. Detmer, MD,*
*Stephen J. McPhee, MD, and Lynn Pulliam, PhD*

## HOW TO USE THIS SECTION

This section displays information about clinically important infectious diseases in tabular form. Included in these tables are the *Organisms* involved in the disease/syndrome listed; *Specimens/Diagnostic Tests* that are useful in the evaluation; and *Comments* regarding the tests and diagnoses discussed. Topics are listed by body area/organ system: Central Nervous System, Eye, Ear, Sinus, Upper Airway, Lung, Heart and Vessels, Abdomen, Genitourinary, Bone, Joint, Muscle, Skin, and Blood.

## Organisms

This column lists organisms that are known to cause the stated illness. Scientific names are abbreviated according to common usage (eg, *Streptococcus pneumoniae* as *S pneumoniae* or pneumococcus). Specific age or risk groups are listed in order of increasing age or frequency (eg, Infant, Child, Adult, AIDS).

When bacteria are listed, Gram's stain characteristics follow the organism name in parentheses—eg, "*S pneumoniae* (GPDC)." The following abbreviations are used:

| | | | |
|---|---|---|---|
| **GPC** | Gram-positive cocci | **GNC** | Gram-negative cocci |
| **GPDC** | Gram-positive diplococci | **GNDC** | Gram-negative diplococci |
| **GPCB** | Gram-positive coccobacilli | **GNCB** | Gram-negative coccobacilli |
| **GPR** | Gram-positive rods | **GNR** | Gram-negative rods |
| **GVCB** | Gram-variable coccobacilli | **AFB** | Acid-fast bacilli |

When known, the frequency of the specific organism's involve-
ment in the disease process is also provided in parentheses—eg, "*S
pneumoniae* (GPDC) (50%)."

## Specimen Collection/Diagnostic Tests

This column describes the collection of specimens, laboratory pro-
cessing, useful radiographic procedures, and other diagnostic tests.
Culture or test sensitivities with respect to the diagnosis in question
are placed in parentheses immediately following the test when
known—eg, "Gram's stain (60%)." Pertinent serologic tests are also
listed. Keep in mind that few infections can be identified by definitive
diagnostic tests and that clinical judgement is critical to making difficult diagnoses when test results are equivocal.

## Comments

This column includes general information about the utility of the tests
and may include useful information about patient management.
Appropriate general references are also listed.

## Syndrome Name/Body Area

In the last 2 columns the syndrome name and body area are placed
perpendicular to the rest of the table to allow for quick referencing.

| | **CENTRAL NERVOUS SYSTEM** | |
|---|---|---|
| | **Brain Abscess** | |
| **Organism** | **Specimens/Diagnostic Tests** | **Comments** |
| **Brain Abscess** | Blood for bacterial cultures. | Common in patients with cyanotic congenital heart disease and right-to-left shunting (eg, tetralogy of Fallot) or arteriovenous vascular abnormalities of the lung (eg, Osler-Weber-Rendu). |
| Usually polymicrobial: Viridans group and anaerobic streptococci (GPC in chains) (60–70%), *Bacteroides* (20–40%), Entero-bacteriaceae (GNR) (23–33%), *S aureus* (GPC) (10–15%), fungus (10–15%), cysticercosis. | Brain abscess aspirate for Gram's stain (82%), bacterial (88%), AFB, fungal cultures, and cytology. CSF profile is nonspecific, resembling that of aseptic meningitis (10% have normal CSF). Lumbar puncture is potentially dangerous. | Majority of toxoplasmosis abscesses are multiple and are best seen on MRI in the basal ganglia, parietal and frontal lobes. |
| HIV infection: *Toxoplasma gondii.* | Sources of infection in the ears, sinuses, lungs or bloodstream should be sought for culture when abscess is found. | $^{99m}$Technetium brain scan is a very sensitive test for abscess and the test of choice where CT or MRI are unavailable. |
| Post-traumatic: *S aureus* (GPC), Enterobacteriaceae (GNR). | CT scan and MRI are the most valuable imaging procedures and can guide biopsy if a specimen is needed. (See CT scan, MRI of head, p 243.) | Ref: J Med Microbiol 1993;38:187. |
| | Serum *Toxoplasma* antibody in HIV-infected patients may not be positive at outset of presumptive therapy. If negative or if no response to empiric therapy, biopsy may be needed to rule out lymphoma or tuberculosis. Biopsy material should be sent for *Toxoplasma* antigen (DFA). | Ref: J Clin Microbiol 1993;31:1866. |
| | Detection of *Toxoplasma* DNA in blood or CSF samples by PCR techniques is now available from specialized or reference laboratories. A positive PCR result must be interpreted in the context of the clinical presentation. Active or recent infection is indicated by a positive IgM antibody test. (See also *Toxoplasma* antibody, p 176.) | Ref: Clin Infect Dis 1993;16:661. |

## CENTRAL NERVOUS SYSTEM

### Encephalitis

| Organism | Specimens/Diagnostic Tests | Comments |
|---|---|---|
| **Encephalitis**<br><br>Arboviruses (California, St. Louis, western equine), enteroviruses (coxsackie, echo, polio), herpes simplex HSV (predominantly type 1), lymphocytic choriomeningitis, mumps, postinfectious (following influenza, measles, mumps, rubella, varicella-zoster), rabies.<br><br>Post-vaccination: Rabies, pertussis.<br><br>AIDS: Cytomegalovirus (CMV), toxoplasmosis. | CSF for pressure (elevated), cell count (WBCs elevated but variable [10–2000/μL], mostly lymphocytes), protein (elevated, especially IgG fraction), glucose (normal), RBCs (especially in herpesvirus). Repeat exam of CSF after 24 hours often useful. (See CSF profiles, p 318.)<br>CSF cultures for virus (low yield for herpes) and bacteria (low yield).<br>Identification of CMV genome in CSF by PCR techniques in 33% of cases.<br>Identification of HSV DNA in CSF by PCR techniques is now the definitive diagnostic test.<br>Throat swab for enterovirus, mumps.<br>Stool culture for enterovirus, which is frequently shed for weeks (especially in children).<br>Urine culture for mumps.<br>Culture of both skin biopsy from hairline and saliva for rabies.<br>Paired sera for arboviruses, mumps, or rabies should be drawn acutely and after 1–3 weeks of illness. Serologic tests are often of academic interest only. Not indicated for herpes simplex. | Controversy exists over whether brain biopsy is necessary for diagnosis and treatment of herpes simplex. CT scan with contrast or MRI with gadolinium reveals temporal lobe lesions consistent with herpes simplex.<br>In AIDS-related CMV encephalitis, CT scans show periventricular enhancement; MRI shows periventricular lesions with meningeal enhancement.<br>Ref: Drugs 1991;42:406.<br>Ref: Clin Infect Dis 1992;15:211.<br>Ref: Neurology 1994;44(3 Part 1):507.<br>Ref: J Infect Dis 1995;17:857. |

## CENTRAL NERVOUS SYSTEM
### Aseptic Meningitis

| **Aseptic Meningitis**

Enteroviruses (coxsackie, echo, polio) (90%), mumps, herpes simplex (HSV, predominantly type 2), varicella-zoster (VZV), leptospirosis (rare), lymphocytic choriomeningitis virus (rare). | CSF for pressure (elevated), cell count (WBCs 10–100/μL, PMNs early, lymphocytes later), protein (normal or slightly elevated), and glucose (normal). (See CSF profiles, p 318).

CSF viral culture can be negative despite active viral infection. Enteroviruses can be isolated from the CSF in the first few days after onset but only rarely after the first week.

Detection of enteroviral RNA in CSF and in rectal swabs by PCR techniques is now available from specialized or reference laboratories.

Urine viral culture for mumps.

Vesicle culture for HSV or VZV.

Paired sera for viral titers: poliovirus, mumps, and VZV. Not practical for other organisms unless actual isolate known and then only useful epidemiologically.

Blood or urine for serologic test for leptospirosis (very expensive; should be ordered only with very high index of suspicion).

Vesicle fluid for direct fluorescent antibody testing for HSV or VZV.

Detection of VZV or HSV DNA sequences in CSF by PCR techniques is now possible. | Aseptic meningitis is acute meningeal irritation in the absence of pyogenic bacteria or fungi. Diagnosis is usually made by the examination of the CSF and by ruling out other infectious causes (eg, syphilis, tuberculosis).

Enteroviral aseptic meningitis is rare after age 40. Patients with deficiency of the complement regulatory protein factor I may have recurrent aseptic meningitis.

Ref: Curr Clin Top Infect Dis 1992;12:1.
Ref: J Med Microbiol 1992;38:54.
Ref: Scand J Infect Dis 1993;25:547.
Ref: J Med Virol 1994;43:331. |

| | CENTRAL NERVOUS SYSTEM |
|---|---|
| | **Bacterial Meningitis** |

| Organism | Specimens/Diagnostic Tests | Comments |
|---|---|---|
| **Bacterial Meningitis**<br><br>Neonate: *E coli* (GNR), group B or D streptococci (GPC).<br>Infant: Group B or D streptococci, *H influenzae* (GNCB), *S pneumoniae* (GPC), *N meningitidis* (GNDC), *Listeria moncytogenes* (GPR).<br>Child: *H influenzae*, *S pneumoniae*, *N meningitidis*.<br>Adult: *S pneumoniae*, *N meningitidis*, *L monocytogenes*.<br>Post-neurosurgical: *S aureus* (GPC), *S pneumoniae*, *Pseudomonas* (GNR), *E coli* (GNR), other Enterobacteriaceae.<br>Alcoholic patients and the elderly: Enterobacteriaceae, *Pseudomonas*, *H influenzae*. | CSF for pressure (> 180 mm $H_2O$), cell count (WBCs 1000–100,000/µL, > 50% PMNs), protein (150–500 mg/dL), glucose (< 40% of serum). (See CSF profiles, p 318.)<br>CSF sediment for Gram's stain (positive in 70–80%).<br>CSF culture for bacteria.<br>Blood culture positive in 40–60% of patients with pneumococcal, meningococcal, and *H influenzae* meningitis.<br>CSF CIE or latex agglutination antigen test may be useful for detection of pneumococcus, *H influenzae* type B capsular polysaccharide, group B Streptococcus, or meningococcus in patients who have already received antibiotic therapy. False-negative results are common. Antigen tests on concentrated urine may be more sensitive in systemic infection but are not necessarily indicative of CSF infection. | The first priority in the care of the patient with suspected acute meningitis is therapy, then diagnosis. Antibiotics should be started within 30 minutes of presentation. The death rate for meningitis is about 30%.<br>With recurrent *N meningitidis* meningitis, suspect a terminal complement component deficiency. With other recurrent bacterial meningitides, suspect a CSF leak.<br>Ref: N Engl J Med 1993;328:21.<br>Ref: Clin Infect Dis 1993;17:603.<br>Ref: Pediatr Rev 1993;14:11. |

| CENTRAL NERVOUS SYSTEM |
|---|
| **Fungal Meningitis** |

**Fungal Meningitis**

*Cryptococcus neoformans* (spherical, budding yeast), *Coccidioides immitis* (spherules), *Histoplasma capsulatum*.

CSF for pressure (normal or elevated), cell count (WBCs 50–1000/μL, mostly lymphocytes), protein (elevated), and glucose (decreased).

CSF for fungal culture (collect at least 5 mL). Initial cultures are positive in 75% of cases of cryptococcal meningitis, 40% of *Coccidioides* cases and 27–65% of *Histoplasma* cases. Repeat cultures are frequently needed.

Culture of blood and sputum for fungus should also be performed to rule out extraneural infection.

CSF India ink prep for *Cryptococcus* is not recommended because it is positive in only 50% of cases. CSF cryptococcal antigen (CrAg) is a latex agglutination test. It is positive in 98% of AIDS patients and 85% of non-AIDS patients with cryptococcal meningitis.

Serum coccidioidal serology is a concentrated serum immunodiffusion test for the organism (75–95%). CSF serologic testing is rarely necessary. (See *Coccidioides* serology, p 72.)

Complement fixation test for *Histoplasma* is available from public health department laboratories (see p 112).

*Histoplasma* antigen can be detected in urine, blood, or CSF in 61% of cases of *Histoplasma* meningitis.

The clinical presentation of fungal meningitis is that of an indolent chronic meningitis.

Prior to AIDS, cryptococcal meningitis was seen both in patients with cellular immunologic deficiencies and in patients who lacked obvious defects (about 50% of cases).

*Cryptococcus* is the most common cause of meningitis in AIDS patients. HIV-related cryptococcal meningitis may present with totally normal CSF findings.

Titer of CSF CrAg can be used to monitor therapeutic success (falling titer) or failure (unchanged or rising titer) or to predict relapse during suppressive therapy (rising titer).

Ref: Medicine 1990;69:244.
Ref: West J Med 1993;159:153.
Ref: Infect Dis Clin North Am 1994;8:383.
Ref: Clin Infect Dis 1994;18:789.

| CENTRAL NERVOUS SYSTEM |
| --- |
| **Spirochetal Meningitis** |

| Organism | Specimens/Diagnostic Tests | Comments |
| --- | --- | --- |
| **Spirochetal Meningitis/ Neurosyphilis**<br><br>*Treponema pallidum* | **Acute syphilitic meningitis:**<br>CSF for pressure (elevated), cell count (WBCs 25–2000/μL, mostly lymphocytes), protein (elevated), and glucose (normal or low). (See CSF profiles, p 318.)<br>Serum VDRL. (See VDRL, serum, p 182.)<br>CSF VDRL is the preferred test (see p 183), but is only 66% sensitive for acute syphilitic meningitis.<br>**Neurosyphilis:**<br>CSF for pressure (normal), cell count (WBCs normal or slightly increased, mostly lymphocytes), protein (normal or elevated). glucose (normal), and CSF VDRL.<br>Serum VDRL, FTA-ABS, or MHA-TP should be done. | Neurosyphilis is a late stage of infection and can present with meningovascular (hemiparesis, seizures, aphasia), parenchymal (general paresis, tabes dorsalis), or asymptomatic (latent) disease. Because there is no single highly sensitive or specific test for neurosyphilis, the diagnosis must depend on a combination of clinical and laboratory data. Therapy of suspected neurosyphilis should not be withheld on the basis of a negative CSF VDRL if clinical suspicion is high.<br>Ref: Infect Dis Clin North Am 1994;8:769.<br>Ref: Clin Infect Dis 1994;18:288. |

| CENTRAL NERVOUS SYSTEM | |
|---|---|
| **Tuberculous Meningitis** | **Subdural Empyema** |
| **Tuberculous Meningitis**<br><br>*Mycobacterium tuberculosis* (MTb) (acid-fast bacilli [AFB] seen on Kinyoun stain) | CSF for pressure (elevated), cell count (WBCs 100–500/μL, PMNs early, lymphocytes later), protein (elevated), glucose (decreased). (See CSF profiles, p 318.)<br>CSF for AFB stain (see Kinyoun stain, p 22). Stain is positive in only 30%.<br>CSF for AFB culture (positive in < 70%). Repeated sampling of the CSF during the first week of therapy is recommended: ideally, 3–4 specimens of 5–10 mL each should be obtained (87% yield with 4 specimens). Standard cultures for MTb take 6–8 weeks to turn positive. New culture systems can detect mycobacterial growth in several days. DNA probes are available for rapid confirmation from mycobacterial growth. | Tuberculous meningitis is usually secondary to rupture of a subependymal tubercle rather than bloodborne invasion.<br>Since CSF stain and culture are not sensitive for tuberculosis, diagnosis and treatment should be based on a combination of clinical and microbiologic data.<br>Evidence of inactive or active extrameningeal tuberculosis, especially pulmonary, is seen in 75% of patients.<br>Ref: Tuber Lung Dis 1994;75:149.<br>Ref: J Neurol Sci 1994;123:173.<br>Ref: Neurology 1994;44:1161. |
| **Subdural Empyema**<br><br>Infant and Child: Group B or D streptococci (GPC), *H influenzae* (GNCB), *S pneumoniae* (GPC), *N meningitidis* (GNDC).<br>Adult: Usually polymicrobial: Viridans group streptococci (GPC in chains) (35%), *S aureus* (GPC) (17%), anaerobic streptococci (GPC in chains) (12%), *Bacteroides* (GPR), Enterobacteriaceae (GNR). | CSF changes are nonspecific. Lumbar puncture is contraindicated because of the danger of transtentorial herniation. | Subdural empyema usually occurs as an extension of paranasal sinus infection, osteomyelitis of the skull with epidural abscess, middle ear or mastoid infection, trauma, or neurosurgery. Occurs in males four times more frequently than in females.<br>Sinusitis or otitis is present on x-rays or CT scans in over two-thirds of patients. MRI with gadolinium is superior to CT in detection of subdural empyema.<br>Ref: Curr Opin Neurol 1994;7:223.<br>Ref: Clin Infect Dis 1995;20:372. |

| EYE |
|---|
| **Conjunctivitis** |

| Organism | Specimens/Diagnostic Tests | Comments |
|---|---|---|
| **Conjunctivitis**<br><br>Neonate (ophthalmia neonatorum): *N gonorrhoeae* (GNDC), *Chlamydia trachomatis*, herpes simplex type 2.<br>Adult: Adenovirus, *H influenzae* (GNCB), *S pneumoniae* (GPC), group A streptococcus (GPC), *N gonorrhoeae* (GNDC), *Moraxella lacunata* (GNCB).<br>Adult inclusion conjunctivitis/Trachoma: *Chlamydia trachomatis*.<br>Acute hemorrhagic conjunctivitis (acute epidemic keratoconjunctivitis): Enterovirus, coxsackievirus. | Conjunctival Gram's stain is especially useful if gonococcal infection suspected.<br>Bacterial culture for severe cases (routine bacterial culture) or suspected gonococcal infection (chocolate agar).<br>Conjunctival scrapings or smears show epithelial intracytoplasmic inclusions by Giemsa stain (10–60% sensitivity) or positive direct immunofluorescent monoclonal antibody staining for *Chlamydia trachomatis*.<br>Cell culture for *Chlamydia*.<br>Detection of chlamydial DNA on ocular swabs by PCR techniques is now available. | The causes of conjunctivitis change with the season. Adenovirus occurs mainly in the fall. *H influenzae* in the winter.<br>Gonococcal conjunctivitis is an ophthalmologic emergency.<br>Cultures are usually unnecessary unless *Chlamydia* or gonorrhea is suspected, or the case is severe.<br>Ref: Am J Ophthalmol 1990;109:138.<br>Ref: Am J Ophthalmol 1992;114:685.<br>Ref: Infect Dis Clin North Am 1992;6:807. |

| EYE | |
| --- | --- |
| **Keratitis** | **Endophthalmitis** |
| **Keratitis**<br><br>Bacteria: *Pseudomonas aeruginosa* (GNR), *S pneumoniae* (GPDC), *Moraxella* sp, *Staphylococcus* sp (GPC).<br>Virus: Herpes simplex (HSV) (dendritic pattern on fluorescein slitlamp exam)<br>Contact lens: *Acanthamoeba*.<br>Fungus: *Candida*. | **Endophthalmitis**<br><br>Spontaneous or postoperative: *S aureus* (GPC), *S epidermidis* (GPC), Enterobacteriaceae (GPC), *Pseudomonas* sp (GNR), anaerobes, fungus (especially in neutropenic or critically ill patients).<br>Post-filtering bleb: Viridans group streptococcus (57%), *S pneumoniae* (GPDC), *H influenzae* (GNCB).<br>IV drug abuse: Add *B cereus* to above. |
| Corneal scrapings for Gram's stain and culture. Routine bacterial culture is used for most bacterial causes, viral culture for herpes, and special media for *Acanthamoeba* (can be detected with trichrome or Giemsa stain of smears). Treatment depends on Gram's stain appearance and culture. | Culture material from anterior chamber, vitreous cavity, and wound abscess for bacteria, mycobacteria, and fungi. Traumatic and postoperative cases should have aqueous and vitreous aspiration for culture and smear (56%). Conjunctival cultures are inadequate and misleading. |
| Prompt ophthalmologic consultation is mandatory. *Acanthamoeba* infection occurs in soft contact (extended-wear) lens wearers and may resemble HIV infection on fluorescein examination (dendritic ["branching"] ulcer).<br>Ref: Am J Ophthalmol 1991;112(4 Suppl):2S.<br>Ref: Br J Biomed Sci 1994;51:65. | Endophthalmitis is an inflammatory process of the ocular cavity and adjacent structures. Rapid diagnosis is critical, since vision may be compromised. Bacterial endophthalmitis usually occurs as a consequence of ocular surgery. Prophylactic antibiotic use is of unproven benefit, though topical antibiotics are widely used.<br>Ref: Ophthalmology 1995;102:705.<br>Ref: Infect Dis Clin North Am 1995;9:195. |

| | EAR | |
|---|---|---|
| | **Otitis Media** | |
| **Organism** | **Specimens/Diagnostic Tests** | **Comments** |
| **Otitis Media**<br><br>Infant, Child, and Adult: *S pneumoniae* (GPC), *H influenzae* (GNCB), *M catarrhalis* (GNDC), *S aureus* (GPC), group A *Streptococcus* (GPC), "sterile."<br><br>Neonate: Same as above plus Enterobacteriaceae (GNR), group B *Streptococcus* (GPC).<br><br>Endotracheal intubation: *Pseudomonas* sp (GNR), *Klebsiella* (GNR), Enterobacteriaceae (GNR). | Tympanocentesis aspirate for Gram's stain and bacterial culture in the patient who has a toxic appearance. Otherwise, microbiologic studies of effusions are so consistent that empiric treatment is acceptable.<br><br>Blood culture in the toxic patient. | Peak incidence of otitis media occurs in the first 3 years of life, especially between 6 and 24 months of age.<br><br>In neonates, predisposing factors include cleft palate, hypotonia, mental retardation (Down's syndrome).<br><br>Tympanocentesis is indicated if the patient fails to improve after 48 hours or develops fever. It may hasten resolution and decrease sterile effusion. Persistent middle ear effusion may require placement of ventilating or tympanostomy tubes.<br>Ref: Otolaryngol Clin North Am 1991;24:905.<br>Ref: Arch Intern Med 1992;152:2301.<br>Ref: Clin Infect Dis 1994;19:823. |

| EYE | | |
|---|---|---|
| **Otitis Externa** | | |

| **Otitis Externa** | Ear drainage for Gram's stain and bacterial culture, especially in malignant otitis externa. CT or MRI can aid in diagnosis by demonstrating cortical bone erosion or meningeal enhancement. | Infection of the external auditory canal is similar to infection of skin and soft tissue elsewhere. If malignant otitis externa is present, exclusion of associated osteomyelitis and surgical drainage may be required. Ref: Ear Nose Throat J 1994;73:772. Ref: Infect Dis Clin North Am 1995;9:195. Ref: Radiology 1995;196:499. |
|---|---|---|
| Acute localized: *S aureus* (GPC), group A *Streptococcus* (GPC in chains). "Swimmer's ear": *Pseudomonas* sp (GNR), Enterobacteriaceae (GNR), fungi (rare). Chronic: Usually secondary to seborrhea. Diabetes mellitus, AIDS ("malignant otitis externa"): *Pseudomonas aeruginosa* (GNR), *Aspergillus* spp. Furuncle of external canal: *S aureus*. | | |

| | SINUS | |
|---|---|---|
| | **Sinusitis** | |
| **Organism** | **Specimens/Diagnostic Tests** | **Comments** |
| **Sinusitis** | Nasal aspirate for bacterial culture is not usually helpful. Maxillary sinus aspirate for bacterial culture may be helpful in severe or atypical cases. | Diagnosis and treatment of sinusitis is usually based on clinical and radiologic features. Microbiologic studies can be helpful in severe or atypical cases. Sinus CT scan (or MRI) is better than plain x-ray for diagnosing sinusitis, particularly if sphenoid sinusitis is suspected. However, sinus CT scans should be interpreted cautiously, since abnormalities are also seen in patients with the common cold. Acute and chronic sinusitis occur frequently in HIV-infected patients, may be recurrent or refractory, and may involve multiple sinuses (especially when the CD4 cell count is < 200/μL). Ref: Am J Med 1992;93:157, 163. Ref: Ear Nose Throat J 1994;73:532. Ref: Medicine 1994;73:69. Ref: N Engl J Med 1994;330:25. |
| Acute: *S pneumoniae* (GPC) (31%), *H influenzae* (GNCB) (21%), *M catarrhalis* (GNDC), group A *Streptococcus* (GPC), anaerobes, viruses (rhinovirus, influenza, parainfluenza), *S aureus* (GPC) (rare). Chronic (child): *S pneumoniae, H influenzae, M catarrhalis.* Chronic (adult): *Bacteroides* sp, Prevotella sp (GNR), *Peptostreptococcus* (GPC), *Fusobacterium* sp (GNR). Hospitalized with nasogastric tube or nasotracheal intubation: Enterobacteriaceae (GNR), *Pseudomonas* sp (GNR). Fungal: Zygomycetes (*Mucor*), *Aspergillus, Pseudallescheria boydii.* | | |

| UPPER AIRWAY | |
| --- | --- |
| **Pharyngitis** | **Laryngitis** |
| **Pharyngitis**<br><br>Exudative: Group A *Streptococcus* (GPC) (15–30%), viruses (rhinovirus, coronavirus, adenovirus) (25%), group C *Streptococcus* (GPC), Epstein-Barr virus (mononucleosis), *N gonorrhoeae* (GNDC), *Arcanobacterium (Corynebacterium) hemolyticum* (GPR).<br><br>Membranous: *C diphtheriae* (GPR), Epstein-Barr virus. | **Laryngitis**<br><br>Virus (90%), group A *Streptococcus* (GPC) (10%), *Moraxella catarrhalis* (GNDC) (55% of adults), *Mycobacterium tuberculosis*, fungus (cryptococcosis, histoplasmosis). |
| Throat swab for culture. Place in sterile tube or transport medium. If *N gonorrhoeae* suspected, use chocolate agar or Thayer-Martin media. If *C diphtheriae* suspected, use Tinsdale or blood agar.<br><br>Throat swabs are routinely cultured for group A *Streptococcus* only. If other organisms are suspected, this must be stated.<br><br>Throat culture is about 70% sensitive for group A *Streptococcus*.<br><br>"Rapid" tests for group A *Streptococcus* can speed diagnosis and aid in the treatment of family members. However, they are insensitive and false negative results may lead to underdiagnosis and failure to treat. New immunoassay kits for antigen detection are more sensitive. | Diagnosis is made by clinical picture of upper respiratory infection with hoarseness. |
| Controversy exists over how to evaluate patients with sore throat. Some authors suggest culturing all patients and then treating only those with positive cultures.<br><br>In patients with compatible histories, be sure to consider pharyngeal abscess or epiglottitis, both of which may be life-threatening.<br><br>Ref: JAMA 1992;267:695.<br>Ref: J Emerg Med 1992;10:607.<br>Ref: Med J Aust 1992;156:572.<br>Ref: J Emerg Med 1994;12:665.<br>Ref: J Pediatr 1995;126:933. | Laryngitis usually occurs in association with common cold or influenzal syndromes.<br><br>Fungal laryngeal infections occur most commonly in immunocompromised patients (AIDS, cancer, organ transplants, corticosteroid therapy, diabetes mellitus).<br><br>Ref: Otolaryngal Clin North Am 1993;26:1091. |

| | UPPER AIRWAY | | |
|---|---|---|---|
| | Tracheobronchitis | | Epiglottitis |

| Organism | Specimens/Diagnostic Tests | Comments |
|---|---|---|
| **Tracheobronchitis**<br><br>Infant/child (bronchiolitis): Respiratory syncytial virus (50–75%), parainfluenza virus, adenovirus.<br>Adolescent/adult: Usually viruses, *Mycoplasma pneumoniae*, *Chlamydia pneumoniae*, *Bordetella pertussis*.<br>Chronic adult (smokers): Viral (25–50%), *S pneumoniae* (GPC), *H influenzae* (GNCB), *S aureus* (GPC), Enterobacteriaceae (GNR), anaerobes (< 10%). | Throat swab or nasopharyngeal aspirate for viral, *Mycoplasma* or *Bordetella* culture can be considered in severe cases but is rarely indicated. Cellular exam of early morning sputum will show many PMNs in chronic bronchitis.<br>Sputum Gram's stain and culture for ill adults. In chronic bronchitis, mixed flora are usually seen with oral flora or colonized *H influenzae* or *S pneumoniae* on culture.<br>Paired sera for viral titers can help make a diagnosis retrospectively in infants and children but are not clinically useful except for seriously ill patients. | Chronic bronchitis by definition is diagnosed when sputum is coughed up on most days for at least 3 consecutive months for more than 2 successive years.<br>Bacterial infections are usually secondary infections of initial viral or *Mycoplasma*-induced inflammation.<br>Airway endoscopy can aid in the diagnosis of bacterial tracheitis in children.<br>Ref: Int J Pediatr Otolaryngol 1993;27:147. |
| **Epiglottitis**<br><br>Child: *H influenzae* type B (GNCB).<br>Adult: Group A *Streptococcus* (GPC), *H influenzae*. | Blood for bacterial culture: positive in 50–100% of children with *H influenzae*.<br>Throat/epiglottis swab for Gram's stain and bacterial culture can be helpful in adults but is not indicated in children because it can precipitate laryngospasm and acute airway obstruction.<br>Lateral neck x-ray may show an enlarged epiglottis but has a low sensitivity (31%). | Acute epiglottitis is a rapidly moving cellulitis of the epiglottis and represents an airway emergency. Epiglottitis can be confused with croup, a viral infection of gradual onset that affects infants and causes inspiratory and expiratory stridor. Airway management is the primary concern, and an endotracheal tube should be placed or tracheostomy performed as soon as the diagnosis is made in children. A tracheostomy set should be at the bedside for adults.<br>Ref: JAMA 1994;272:1358.<br>Ref: Pediatr Clin North Am 1994;41:265. |

| LUNG | | |
|---|---|---|
| **Community-Acquired Pneumonia** | | |
| **Community-Acquired Pneumonia**<br><br>Neonate: E coli (GNR), group A or B Streptococcus (GPC), S aureus (GPC), Pseudomonas sp (GNR), Chlamydia trachomatis.<br><br>Infant/child (< 5 years): Virus S pneumoniae (GPC), H influenzae (GNCB), S aureus.<br><br>Age 5–40 years: Virus, Mycoplasma pneumoniae, Chlamydia pneumoniae (formerly known as TWAR strain), C psittaci, S pneumoniae, Legionella sp.<br><br>Age > 40 without other disease: S pneumoniae, group A Streptococcus, H influenzae, Legionella sp. Chlamydia pneumoniae (TWAR strain), C psittaci, viruses (eg, influenza).<br><br>Chronic bronchitis: S pneumoniae, group A streptococcus, H influenzae, Klebsiella (GNR), other Enterobacteriaceae (GNR), virus (eg, influenza). Underlying disease (alcoholism, diabetes, CHF): As in chronic bronchitis with addition of M pneumoniae, Legionella sp, C pneumoniae, S aureus.<br><br>Cystic fibrosis: Pseudomonas aeruginosa, P cepacia.<br><br>Exposure to deer mice (contaminated aerosols): Hantavirus. | Sputum for Gram's stain and culture. An adequate specimen should have < 10 epithelial cells and > 25 PMNs per low-power field. Special sputum cultures for C trachomatis, C pneumoniae, and Legionella are available. DFA for Legionella spp has a sensitivity of 25–70% and a specificity of 95%. (Positive predictive value is low in areas of low disease prevalence.)<br><br>Blood for bacterial cultures, especially in ill patients.<br><br>Pleural fluid for bacterial culture if significant effusion is present.<br><br>Bronchoalveolar lavage or brushings for bacterial, fungal, and AFB culture in immunocompromised patients and atypical cases.<br><br>Paired sera for M pneumoniae complement fixation testing can diagnose infection retrospectively.<br><br>Serologic tests for C pneumoniae and C psittaci strains are available. Serologic tests for hantavirus (IgM and IgG) are available.<br><br>Other special techniques (bronchoscopy with telescoping plugged catheter on protected brush, transtracheal aspiration, transthoracic fine-needle aspiration, or, rarely, open lung biopsy) can be used to obtain specimens for culture (or detection of bacterial antigens) in severe cases, in immunocompromised patients, or in cases with negative conventional cultures and progression despite empiric antibiotic therapy. | About 60% of cases of community-acquired pneumonia have an identifiable microbial etiology. Pneumatoceles suggest S aureus but are also reported with pneumococcus, group A Streptococcus, H influenzae, and Enterobacteriaceae (in neonates).<br><br>An "atypical pneumonia" presentation (diffuse pattern on chest x-ray with lack of organisms on Gram's stain of sputum) should raise suspicion of Mycoplasma, Legionella, or chlamydial infection. Consider hantavirus pulmonary syndrome if pulmonary symptoms follow afebrile illness.<br>Ref: Am Rev Resp Dis 1993;148:1418.<br>Ref: Med Clin North Am 1994;78:1035.<br>Ref: Chest 1994;105:1487.<br>Ref: N Engl J Med 1994;330:949. |

| | | LUNG | |
|---|---|---|---|
| | **Organism** | **Specimens/Diagnostic Tests** | **Comments** |

### LUNG — Anaerobic Pneumonia

| Organism | Specimens/Diagnostic Tests | Comments |
|---|---|---|
| **Anaerobic Pneumonia/ Lung Abscess**<br><br>Usually polymicrobial: *Bacteroides* spp (15% *B fragilis*), *Peptostreptococcus*, microaerophilic streptococcus, *Veillonella*, *Staphylococcus aureus*, *Pseudomonas aeruginosa*, type 3 *S pneumoniae* (rare), *Klebsiella* (rare). | Sputum Gram's stain and culture for anaerobes are of little value because of contaminating oral flora. Bronchoalveolar sampling (brush or aspirate) for bacterial culture will usually make an accurate diagnosis. As contamination is likely with a bronchoscope alone, a Bartlett tube should be used. Percutaneous transthoracic needle aspiration may be useful for culture and for cytology to demonstrate coexistence of an underlying carcinoma. Blood cultures are usually negative. | Aspiration is the most important background feature of lung abscess. Without clear-cut risk factors such as alcoholism, coma, or seizures, bronchoscopy is often performed to rule out neoplasm.<br>Ref: Chest 1987;91:901.<br>Ref: Chest 1990;97:69.<br>Ref: Intern Med 1993;32:278. |

### LUNG — Aspiration Pneumonia

| Organism | Specimens/Diagnostic Tests | Comments |
|---|---|---|
| **Aspiration Pneumonia**<br><br>Community-acquired: *S pneumoniae* (GPC), *Klebsiella pneumoniae* (GNR), Enterobacteriaceae (GNR), *Bacteroides* sp and other oral anaerobes.<br>Hospital-associated: *Pseudomonas* sp (GNR), *Klebsiella*.<br>Neutropenic: *Pseudomonas* sp (GNR), *Klebsiella*, *Enterobacter* (GNR), *Bacteroides* sp and other oral anaerobes, *Legionella*, *Candida*, *Aspergillus*, *Mucor*.<br>Mendelson's syndrome (see comments): No organisms initially, then *Pseudomonas*, Enterobacteriaceae, *S aureus*, *S pneumoniae*. | Sputum Gram's stain and culture for bacteria (aerobic and anaerobic) and fungus (if suspected). Blood cultures for bacteria are often negative. Endotracheal aspirate or bronchoalveolar sample for bacterial and fungal culture in selected patients. | Community-acquired aspirations are most commonly associated with stroke, alcoholism, drug abuse, sedation, and periodontal disease. Hospital-associated aspiration pneumonia is associated with intubation and the use of broad-spectrum antibiotics.<br>A strong association between aspiration pneumonia and swallowing dysfunction is demonstrable by videofluoroscopy.<br>Mendelson's syndrome is due to acute aspiration of gastric contents (eg, during anesthesia or drowning).<br>Ref: Rev Infect Dis 1991;13(Suppl 9):S737.<br>Ref: Dysphagia 1994;9:1. |

## LUNG

### Pneumonia in AIDS

| | | |
|---|---|---|
| **Pneumonia in the HIV-Infected Host**<br><br>Child: *Lymphoid interstitial pneumonia* (LIP).<br>Adult: *Pneumocystis carinii* (PCP), *S pneumoniae* (GPC), *H influenzae* (GNCB), *Staphylococcus aureus*, gram-negative bacilli, *Pseudomonas aeruginosa*, *M tuberculosis* (AFB), *Histoplasma*, *Coccidioides*, *Cryptococcus*, cytomegalovirus, *Rhodococcus equi* (GPR) (rare). | Expectorated sputum for Gram's stain and bacterial culture, if purulent.<br>Sputum induction or bronchiolar lavage for Giemsa or methenamine silver staining or direct fluorescent antibody (DFA) for *Pneumocystis carinii* trophozoites or cysts; and for mycobacterial and fungal staining and culture.<br>Blood or bone marrow fungal culture for histoplasmosis (positive in 50%), coccidioidomycosis (positive in 30%).<br>Blood culture for bacteria. Blood cultures are more frequently positive in HIV-infected patients with bacterial pneumonia and often are the only source where a specific organism is identified; bacteremic patients have higher mortality rates.<br>*Histoplasma* polysaccharide antigen positive in 90% of AIDS patients with disseminated histoplasmosis; antigen increases ≥ 2 RIA units with relapse.<br>Immunodiffusion or CIE is useful for screening for, and CF for confirmation of, suspected histoplasmosis or coccidioidomycosis.<br>Cryptococcal antigen when pulmonary cryptococcosis is suspected.<br>Serum lactate dehydrogenase (LDH) levels are elevated in 63% and hypoxemia (PaO$_2$ < 75 mm Hg) occurs in 57% of PCP cases. | In PCP the sensitivities of the various diagnostic tests are: sputum induction 80% (in experienced labs), bronchoscopy with lavage 90–97%, transbronchial biopsy 94–97%.<br>In PCP, chest x-ray may show interstitial (36%) or alveolar (25%) infiltrates or may be normal (39%), particularly if leukopenia is present.<br>Recurrent episodes of bacterial pneumonia are common.<br>Kaposi's sarcoma of the lung is a common neoplastic process that can imitate infection in homosexual and African HIV-infected patients.<br>Ref: Eur Resp J 1994;7:235.<br>Ref: Thorax 1994;49:367.<br>Ref: J Acquir Immune Defic Syndr 1994;7:39.<br>Ref: Arch Intern Med 1994;154:2589.<br>Ref: Chest 1994;105:816.<br>Ref: Arch Pathol Lab Med 1994;118:1205.<br>Ref: J Med Microbiol 1995;42:231. |

## LUNG

### Mycobacterial Pneumonia

| Organism | Specimens/Diagnostic Tests | Comments |
|---|---|---|
| **Mycobacterial Pneumonia**<br><br>*Mycobacterium tuberculosis* (MTb), *M kansasii*, *M avium-intracellulare* complex (AFB, acid-fast beaded rods). | Sputum for AFB stain and culture. First morning samples are best, and at least 3 samples are required. Standard cultures for MTb take 6–8 weeks to turn positive. New culture systems detect mycobacterial growth in as little as several days. Bronchoalveolar lavage for AFB stain and culture or gastric washings for AFB culture can be used if sputum tests are negative.<br>CT- or ultrasound-guided transthoracic fine-needle aspiration cytology can be used if clinical or radiographic features are nonspecific or if malignancy is suspected. | AFB found on sputum stain do not necessarily make the diagnosis of tuberculosis, because *M kansasii* and *M avium-intracellulare* look identical.<br>Tuberculosis is very common in HIV-infected patients, in whom the chest x-ray appearance may be atypical and occasionally (4%) may mimic PCP (especially in patients with CD4 cell counts < 200/µL). In one study, only 2% of patients sent for sputum induction for PCP had tuberculosis.<br>Delayed diagnosis of pulmonary tuberculosis is common (up to 20% of cases), especially among patients who are older or who lack respiratory symptoms.<br>In any patient with suspected tuberculosis, respiratory isolation is required.<br>Ref: Chest 1992;102:428.<br>Ref: AIDS 1993;7:1351.<br>Ref: Arch Intern Med 1994;154:306.<br>Ref: Tubercle Lung Dis 1995;76:84. |

| | LUNG — Empyema | HEART AND VESSELS — Pericarditis |
|---|---|---|

**Empyema**

| Organisms | Diagnostic Tests | Comments |
|---|---|---|
| Neonate: *E coli* (GNR), group A or B *Streptococcus* (GPC), *S aureus* (GPC), *Pseudomonas* sp (GNR). Infant/child (< 5 years): *S aureus* (GPC), *S pneumoniae* (GPC), *H influenzae* (GNCB), anaerobes. Child (> 5 years)/adult, Acute: *S pneumoniae* (GPC), group A *Streptococcus* (GPC), *S aureus* (GPC), *H influenzae* (GNCB), *Legionella*. Child (> 5 years)/adult, chronic: Anaerobic streptococci, *Bacteroides* sp, *Prevotella* sp, *Porphyromonas* sp, *Fusobacterium* sp, Enterobacteriaceae, *E coli*, *Klebsiella pneumoniae*. | Pleural fluid for cell count (WBCs 25,000–100,000/ µL, mostly PMNs), protein (> 50% of serum), glucose (< serum, often very low), pH (< 7.20), LDH (> 60% of serum). (See Pleural fluid profiles, p 346.) Pleural fluid for Gram's stain and bacterial culture (aerobic and anaerobic). Blood cultures for bacteria. Sputum for Gram's stain and bacterial culture. Special culture can also be performed for *Legionella* when suspected. Fluid can be tested for *Legionella* by direct fluorescent antibody and culture. | The clinical presentation of empyema is nonspecific. Chest CT with contrast is helpful in demonstrating pleural fluid accumulations due to mediastinal or subdiaphragmatic processes and can identify loculated effusions, bronchopleural fistulae, and lung abscesses. About 25% of cases result from trauma or surgery. Chest tube drainage is paramount. Bronchoscopy is indicated when the infection is unexplained. Occasionally, multiple thoracenteses may be needed to diagnose empyema. Ref: Pediatrics 1990;85:722. Ref: Chest 1993;103:1502. Ref: South Med J 1994;87:1103. Ref: Semin Resp Med 1992;13:167. |

**Pericarditis**

| Organisms | Diagnostic Tests | Comments |
|---|---|---|
| Viruses: Enteroviruses (coxsackie, echo), influenza, Epstein-Barr, herpes zoster, mumps, HIV, CMV. Bacteria: *S aureus* (GPC), *S pneumoniae* (GPC), group A *Streptococcus* (GPC), Enterobacteriaceae (GNR), *N meningitidis* (GNDC). | In acute pericarditis, specific bacterial diagnosis is made in only 19%. Pericardial fluid aspirate for viral culture (rarely positive) or Gram's stain and bacterial culture (aerobic and anaerobic). In acute pericarditis, only 54% have pericardial effusions. Stool or throat swab for viral culture (if enteroviruses suspected). Surgical pericardial drainage with biopsy of pericardium for culture (22%) and histologic examination. Paired sera for enteroviruses can be helpful. | Viral pericarditis is usually diagnosed clinically (precordial pain, muffled heart sounds, pericardial friction rub, cardiomegaly). The diagnosis is rarely aided by microbiologic tests. Bacterial pericarditis is usually secondary to surgery, immunosuppression (including HIV), esophageal rupture, endocarditis with ruptured ring abscess, extension from lung abscess, aspiration pneumonia or empyema, or sepsis with pericarditis. Ref: J Am Coll Cardiol 1993;22:1661. Ref: Am J Cardiol 1994;74:807. Ref: Chest 1994;105:615. |

| HEART AND VESSELS |
|---|
| **Tuberculous Pericarditis** |

| Organism | Specimens/Diagnostic Tests | Comments |
|---|---|---|
| **Tuberculous Pericarditis**<br><br>*Mycobacterium tuberculosis* (MTb, AFB, acid-fast beaded rods) | PPD skin testing should be performed (negative in a sizeable minority).<br>Pericardial fluid obtained by needle aspiration can show AFB by smear (rare) or culture (low yield). The yield is improved by obtaining three or four repeated specimens for smear and culture.<br>Pericardial biopsy may be needed to make diagnosis and initiate early drug therapy.<br>Other sources of culture for MTb besides pericardium are available in 50% of patients.<br>Pericardial fluid may show markedly elevated levels of adenosine deaminase, an enzyme associated with purine metabolism. | Spread from nearby caseous mediastinal lymph nodes or pleurisy is the most common route of infection. Acutely, serofibrinous pericardial effusion develops with substernal pain, fever, and friction rub. Tamponade may occur.<br>Tuberculosis accounts for 4% of cases of acute pericarditis, 7% of cases of cardiac tamponade, and 6% of cases of constrictive pericarditis.<br>One-third to one-half of patients develop constrictive pericarditis despite drug therapy. Constrictive pericarditis occurs 2–4 years after acute infection.<br>Ref: JAMA 1991;266:91.<br>Ref: Intern Med 1993;32:675.<br>Ref: Am Heart J 1993;126:249. |

| HEART AND VESSELS | |
| --- | --- |
| **Infectious Myocarditis** | **Infective Endocarditis** |
| Acute infectious myocarditis should be suspected in a patient with dynamically evolving changes in ECG, echocardiography, and serum CK levels and symptoms of an infection. The value of endomyocardial biopsy in such cases has not been established.<br>In contrast, an endomyocardial biopsy is needed to diagnose lymphocytic or giant cell myocarditis.<br>The incidence of myocarditis in AIDS may be as high as 46%.<br>Many patients with acute myocarditis progress to dilated cardiomyopathy.<br>Ref: West J Med 1989;150:431.<br>Ref: N Engl J Med 1991;325:763.<br>Ref: Am Heart J 1991;122:537.<br>Ref: Scand J Infect Dis 1993;88(Suppl):33.<br>Ref: Chest 1993;104:1427. | Patients with congenital or valvular heart disease should receive prophylaxis before dental procedures or surgery of the upper respiratory, genitourinary, or gastrointestinal tract.<br>In left-sided endocarditis, patients should be watched carefully for development of valvular regurgitation or ring abscess.<br>The size and mobility of valvular vegetations on TEE can help to predict the risk of arterial embolization.<br>Ref: Medicine 1993;72:90.<br>Ref: Infect Dis Clin North Am 1993;7:877.<br>Ref: Curr Opin Cardiol 1994;9:389. |
| Endomyocardial biopsy for pathologic examination and culture in selected cases. Indium-111 antimyosin antibody imaging is more sensitive than endomyocardial biopsy.<br>Stool or throat swab for coxsackievirus.<br>Paired sera for enteroviruses, scrub typhus, *Rickettsia rickettsii*, *Coxiella burnetii*, *Trichinella*, *Toxoplasma*.<br>Single serum for HIV, *Borrelia burgdorferi*, *Trypanosoma cruzi*.<br>Gallium scanning is sensitive but not specific for myocardial inflammation. | Blood cultures for bacteria. Three blood cultures are sufficient in 97% of cases. Blood cultures are frequently positive with Gram-positive organisms but can be negative with Gram-negative or anaerobic organisms.<br>If the patient is not acutely ill, therapy can begin after cultures identify an organism.<br>Transesophageal echocardiography (TEE) can help in diagnosis by demonstrating the presence of valvular vegetations (sensitivity > 90%), prosthetic valve dysfunction, valvular regurgitation, secondary "jet" or "kissing" lesions, and paravalvular abscess. |
| **Infectious Myocarditis**<br>Enteroviruses (coxsackie A, echo, polio), HIV, *Borrelia burgdorferi* (Lyme disease), scrub typhus, *Rickettsia rickettsii* (Rocky Mountain spotted fever), *Coxiella burnetii* (Q fever), *C diphtheriae*, *Trichinella spiralis* (trichinosis), *Trypanosoma cruzi* (Chagas' disease), *Toxoplasma*. | **Infective Endocarditis**<br>Viridans group *Streptococci* (GPC), *Enterococcus* (GPC), nutritionally deficient *Streptococcus* (GPC), *S aureus* (GPC), *S pneumoniae* (GPC).<br>Slow-growing fastidious GNRs: *H parainfluenzae*, *H aphrophilus*, *Actinobacillus*, *Cardiobacterium*, *Eikenella*, *Kingella*. |

| HEART AND VESSELS |
|---|
| **Prosthetic Valve Infective Endocarditis** |

| Organism | Specimens/Diagnostic Tests | Comments |
|---|---|---|
| **Prosthetic Valve Infective Endocarditis (PVE)**<br><br>Early (< 2 months): *S epidermidis* (GPC) (27%), *S aureus* (GPC) (20%), Enterobacteriaceae (GNR), diphtheroids (GPR), *Candida*, *Aspergillus*.<br><br>Late (> 2 months): Viridans group *Streptococci* (GPC) (42%), *S epidermidis* (21%), *S aureus* (11%), Enterococcus (GPC), Enterobacteriaceae. | Blood cultures for bacteria. Three sets of blood cultures are sufficient in 97% of cases. Draw before temperature spike.<br><br>Blood for fungal culture in suspected cases (eg, large vegetations on echocardiogram). | In a large series using perioperative prophylaxis the incidences of early-onset and late-onset prosthetic valve endocarditis were 0.78% and 1.1%, respectively.<br><br>The portals of entry of early-onset PVE are intraoperative contamination and postoperative wound infections. The portals of entry of late-onset PVE appear to be the same as those of native valve endocarditis, and the microbiologic profiles are also similar.<br><br>Clinically, patients with late-onset PVE resemble those with native valve disease. However, those with early-onset infection are often critically ill, more often have other complicating problems, are more likely to go into shock and are more likely to have conduction abnormalities due to ring abscess.<br>Ref: Medicine 1993;72:90. |

| HEART AND VESSELS | ABDOMEN |
|---|---|
| **Infectious Thrombophlebitis** | **Infectious Esophagitis** |
| Thrombophlebitis is an inflammation of the vein wall. Infectious thrombophlebitis is associated with microbial invasion of the vessel and is associated with bacteremia and thrombosis. Risk of infection from an indwelling peripheral venous catheter goes up significantly after 4 days. Ref: Clin Infect Dis 1993;16:778. Ref: Br J Hosp Med 1994;52:50. | Thrush and odynophagia in an immunocompromised patient warrants empiric therapy for *Candida*. Factors predisposing to infectious esophagitis include HIV infection, exposure to radiation, cytotoxic chemotherapy, recent antibiotic therapy, corticosteroid therapy, and neutropenia. Ref: Gastrointest Endosc Clin North Am 1994;4:713. Ref: Semin Radiol 1994;29:341. Ref: Radiol Clin North Am 1994;32:1135. Ref: Gastroenterology 1994;106:509. |
| Blood cultures for bacteria (positive in 80–90%). Catheter tip for bacterial culture. More than 15 colonies (CFUs) suggests colonization or infection. | Barium esophagram reveals abnormalities in the majority of cases of candidal esophagitis. Endoscopy with biopsy and brushings for culture and cytology has the highest diagnostic yield (57%) and should be performed if clinically indicated or if empiric antifungal therapy is unsuccessful. |
| **Infectious Thrombophlebitis**<br>Associated with venous catheters: *S aureus* (GPC) (65–78%), *S epidermidis* (GPC), *Candida* sp, *Pseudomonas* sp (GNR), Enterobacteriaceae (GNR).<br>Hyperalimentation with catheter: *Candida* sp.<br>Indwelling venous catheter (eg, Broviac, Hickman, Gershom): *S aureus, S epidermidis, Pseudomonas* sp, Enterobacteriaceae, *Candida* sp.<br>Postpartum or post-abortion pelvic thrombophlebitis: *Bacteroides* (GNR), Enterobacteriaceae, *Clostridium* (GPR), *Streptococcus* (GPC). | **Infectious Esophagitis**<br>*Candida* sp, herpes simplex (HSV), cytomegalovirus (CMV), varicella-zoster (VZV), *Cryptosporidium*.<br>(Rare causes: *Mycobacterium tuberculosis, Aspergillus, Histoplasma, Blastomyces*, HIV). |

| | ABDOMEN | |
|---|---|---|
| | **Infectious Colitis/Dysentery** | |
| **Organism** | **Specimens/Diagnostic Tests** | **Comments** |
| **Infectious Colitis/Dysentery**<br><br>Premature Infant (necrotizing enterocolitis); *E coli* (GNR), *S epidermidis* (GPC in clusters), *Pseudomonas aeruginosa* (GNR), *Clostridium perfringens* (GPR).<br><br>Infant: *E coli* (enteropathogenic).<br><br>Child/Adult without travel, afebrile, no gross blood or WBCs in stool: Rotavirus, Norwalk agent, *E coli* (GNR).<br><br>Child/Adult with fever, bloody stool or WBCs in stool or history of travel to subtropics/tropics (varies with epidemiology): *Campylobacter jejuni* (GNR), *E coli* (GNR), (enterotoxigenic, enteroinvasive, enterohemorrhagic O157:H7), *Shigella* (GNR), *Salmonella* (GNR), *Yersinia enterocolitica* (GNR), *Clostridium difficile* (GPR), *Aeromonas* (GNR), *Vibrio cholerae* (GNR), *Cryptosporidium*, *Entamoeba histolytica, Giardia lamblia*. | Stool collected for Wright or methylene blue stain (WBCs suggests invasion of the mucosa), culture, ova and parasites examination. Multiple samples are often needed. Special culture technique is needed for *Yersinia*. Cultures for *Salmonella* or *Shigella* are not helpful in patients hospitalized more than 72 hours.<br><br>Proctosigmoidoscopy is indicated in patients with chronic or recurrent diarrhea or in diarrhea of unknown cause for smears of aspirates (may show organisms) and biopsy. Cultures of biopsy specimens have higher sensitivities than stool cultures. Rectal and jejunal biopsies may be necessary in HIV-infected patients. Need modified acid-fast stain for *Cryptosporidium*.<br><br>Immunodiagnosis of *G lamblia, Cryptosporidium,* or *E histolytica* cysts in stool is highly sensitive and specific. | Acute dysentery is diarrhea with bloody, mucoid stools, tenesmus, and pain on defecation and implies an inflammatory invasion of the colonic mucosa.<br><br>Necrotizing enterocolitis is a fulminant disease of premature newborns. Air in the intestinal wall (pneumatosis intestinalis), in the portal venous system, or in the peritoneal cavity seen on plain x-ray can confirm diagnosis. 30–50% of these infants will have bacteremia or peritonitis.<br><br>Risk factors for infectious colitis include poor hygiene and immune compromise (infancy, advanced age, corticosteroid or immunosuppressive therapy, HIV infection).<br><br>Ref: Gastrointest Endosc 1994;40(2 Part 1):184.<br>Ref: Surg Clin North Am 1993;73:1055. |

| ABDOMEN | |
|---|---|
| **Antibiotic-associated Colitis** | |
| **Antibiotic-associated/ Pseudomembranous Colitis** *Clostridium difficile* (GPR) toxin. | Send stool for fecal leukocytes and *C difficile* toxin titers. Fecal WBCs are present in 30–50% of cases. The toxin is very labile and can be present in patients with no disease. Stool culture is not recommended because nontoxigenic strains occur. Colonoscopy and visualization of characteristic 1–5 mm raised yellow plaques provides the most rapid diagnosis. | Pseudomembranous colitis typically occurs after antibiotic use, although many patients have received no antibiotics, suggesting other predispositions. Antibiotics cause changes in normal intestinal flora, allowing overgrowth of *C difficile* and elaboration of toxin. Other risk factors for *C difficile*-induced colitis are GI manipulations, advanced age, female sex, inflammatory bowel disease, chemotherapy, and renal disease. Ref: JAMA 1993;269:71. Ref: J Clin Microbiol 1994;32:51. Ref: Postgrad Med 1994;95:111. |

| | ABDOMEN |
| --- | --- |
| | Diarrhea in HIV |

| Organism | Specimens/Diagnostic Tests | Comments |
| --- | --- | --- |
| **Diarrhea in the HIV-infected Host**<br><br>Same as Child-Adult Infectious Colitis with addition of cytomegalovirus, *Cryptosporidium, Isospora belli*, microsporidia (*Enterocytozoon bieneusi*), *Cyclospora* sp, *Giardia intestinalis, Mycobacterium avium-intracellulare* complex, herpes simplex (HSV). *Entamoeba histolytica*, ?HIV. | Stool for stain for fecal leukocytes (Wright's or methylene blue-stained smear showing WBCs suggests invasion of the mucosa), culture (especially for *Salmonella, Shigella, Yersinia,* and *Campylobacter*), ovum and parasite examination, and AFB smear. Multiple samples are often needed.<br><br>Proctosigmoidoscopy with fluid aspiration and biopsy is indicated in patients with chronic or recurrent diarrhea or in diarrhea of unknown cause for smears of aspirates (may show organisms) and histologic examination and culture of tissue.<br><br>Rectal and jejunal biopsies may be necessary, especially in patients with tenesmus or bloody stools. Need modified acid-fast stain for *Cryptosporidium*. Intranuclear inclusion bodies on histologic exam suggest CMV.<br><br>Immunodiagnosis of *Giardia, Cryptosporidium,* and *E histolytica* cysts in stool is highly sensitive and specific. | Most patients with HIV infection will develop diarrhea at some point in their illness.<br><br>*Cryptosporidium* causes a chronic debilitating diarrheal infection that rarely remits spontaneously and is still without effective treatment. Diarrhea seems to be the result of malabsorption and produces a cholera-like syndrome.<br><br>Between 15% and 50% of HIV-infected patients with diarrhea have no identifiable pathogen.<br><br>Ref: Ann Intern Med 1993;119:895.<br>Ref: Ann Intern Med 1994;121:654.<br>Ref: J Clin Microbiol 1995;33:745. |

| ABDOMEN | | |
|---|---|---|
| **Peritonitis** | | |

**Peritonitis**

Spontaneous or primary (associated with nephrosis or cirrhosis) peritonitis (SBP): Enterobacteriaceae (GNR) (69%), *S pneumoniae* (GPC), group A *Streptococcus* (GPC), *S aureus* (GPC), anacrobes (5%).
Secondary (bowel perforation, hospital-acquired, or antecedent antibiotic therapy): Enterobacteriaceae, *Enterococcus* (GPC), *Bacteroides* sp, *Pseudomonas aeruginosa* (3–15%).
Chronic ambulatory peritoneal dialysis: *S epidermidis* (43%), *S aureus* (14%), *Streptococcus* sp (12%), Enterobacteriaceae (14%), *Candida* (2%) *Aspergillus* (rare), *Cryptococcus* (rare).

Peritoneal fluid sent for PMN count (86% > 500/μL, 98% specific for SBP), WBC (> 1000/μL, mostly PMNs), pH (< 7.35 in 57%, 96% specific for SBP, Gram stain (22–77% for SBP) and bacterial culture (65–85% for SBP). (See Ascitic fluid profiles, p 314.)
Blood cultures for bacteria positive in 75% of SBP cases.
Catheter-related infection is associated with a WBC > 500/μL.

In nephrotic patients, Enterobacteriaceae and *S aureus* are most frequent. In cirrhotics, 69% of cases are due to Enterobacteriaceae.
"Bacterascites," a positive ascitic fluid culture without an elevated PMN count, is seen in 8% of cases of SBP and probably represents early infection.
Ref: Am J Med 1994;97:169.
Ref: Mayo Clin Proc 1995;70:365.

| | ABDOMEN |
|---|---|
| | **Tuberculous Peritonitis/Enterocolitis** |

| Organism | Specimens/Diagnostic Tests | Comments |
|---|---|---|
| **Tuberculous Peritonitis/ Enterocolitis**<br><br>*Mycobacterium tuberculosis* (MTb, AFB, acid-fast beaded rods). | Ascitic fluid for appearance (clear, hemorrhagic or chylous), RBCs (can be high), WBCs (> 1000/μL, > 70% lymphs), protein (> 2.5 g/dL), serum/ascites albumin ratio (< 1.1), AFB stain (rarely positive), culture (< 50% positive). (See Ascitic fluid profiles, p 314.)<br>Culture or AFB smear from other sources (especially from respiratory tract) can help confirm diagnosis.<br>Abdominal ultrasound may demonstrate free or loculated intra-abdominal fluid, intra-abdominal abscess, ileocecal mass, and retroperitoneal lymphadenopathy.<br>Marked elevations of serum CA 125 have been noted; levels decline to normal with antituberculous therapy.<br>Diagnosis of enterocolitis rests on biopsy of colonic lesions via endoscopy if pulmonary or other extrapulmonary infection cannot be documented.<br>Diagnosis of peritonitis relies upon biopsy of peritoneal lesions via laparoscopy or laparotomy (88%).<br>Operative procedure may be needed to relieve obstruction or for diagnosis. | Infection of the intestines can occur anywhere along the GI tract but occurs most commonly in the ileocecal area or mesenteric lymph nodes. It often complicates pulmonary infection. Peritoneal infection usually is an extension of intestinal disease. Symptoms may be minimal even with extensive disease. In the US, 29% of patients with abdominal tuberculosis have a normal chest x-ray. Presence of AFB in the feces does not correlate with intestinal involvement.<br>Ref: Gut 1990;31:1130.<br>Ref: Abdom Imaging 1993;18:23. |

| ABDOMEN | |
| --- | --- |
| **Diverticulitis** | **Liver Abscess** |
| Pain usually is localized to the left lower quadrant because the sigmoid and descending colon are the most common sites for diverticula. It is important to rule out other abdominal disease (eg, colon carcinoma, Crohn's disease, ischemic colitis). Ref: Am J Gastroenterol 1994;89:455. Ref: Am J Roentgenol 1994;163:81. | 60% of patients have a single lesion; 40% have multiple lesions. Biliary tract disease is the most common underlying disease, followed by malignancy (biliary tract or pancreatic), colonic disease (diverticulitis), diabetes mellitus, liver disease, and alcoholism. Ref: Trop Gastroenterol 1993;14:3. Ref: Int Surg 1993;78:40. Ref: Postgrad Med J 1994;70:436. |
| Identification of organism is not usually sought. Ultrasonography or flat and upright x-rays of abdomen are crucial to rule out perforation (free air under diaphragm) and to localize abscess (air-fluid collections). Barium enema can show presence of diverticuli. Avoid enemas in acute disease because increased intraluminal pressure may cause perforation. CT scan findings of fluid at the root of the mesentery and vascular engorgement have positive predictive values of 89% and 100% (respectively) for sigmoid diverticulitis. Urinalysis will reveal urinary tract involvement, if present. | CT scan with contrast and ultrasonography are the most accurate tests for the diagnosis of liver abscess. Antibodies against *E histolytica* should be obtained on all patients. (See Amebic serology, p 45.) Abscess material obtained via surgery or percutaneous aspiration is recommended for culture and direct examination for *E histolytica*. Chest x-ray is often useful with raised hemidiaphragm, right pleural effusion, or right basilar atelectasis in 41% of patients. Elevation of serum alkaline phosphatase level in 78%. |
| **Diverticulitis** Enterobacteriaceae (GNR), *Bacteroides* sp (GNR), *Enterococcus* (GPC in chains). | **Liver Abscess** Usually polymicrobial: Enterobacteriaceae, especially *Klebsiella* (GNR), *Enterococcus* (GPC in chains), *Bacteroides* sp (GNR), *S aureus* (GPC in clusters), *Candida* sp, *Entamoeba histolytica*. |

| | ABDOMEN | GENITOURINARY |
|---|---|---|
| | **Cholangitis/Cholecystitis** | **Urinary Tract Infection** |

| Organism | Specimens/Diagnostic Tests | Comments |
|---|---|---|
| **Cholangitis/Cholecystitis**<br><br>Enterobacteriaceae (GNR) (68%), *Enterococcus* (GPC in chains) (14%), *Bacteroides* (GNR) (10%), *Clostridium* sp (GPR) (7%), microsporidia (*Enterocytozoon bieneusi*). | Ultrasonography is the best test to quickly demonstrate gallstones or phlegmon around the gallbladder or dilation of biliary tree. (See Abdominal ultrasound, p 262.)<br><br>CT scanning is useful in cholangitis in detecting the site and cause of obstruction but may fail to detect stones in the common bile duct.<br><br>Radionuclide scans can demonstrate cystic duct obstruction. (See p 262.)<br><br>Blood cultures for bacteria. | 90% of cases of acute cholecystitis are calculous, 10% are acalculous. Risk factors for acalculous disease include prolonged illness, fasting, hyperalimentation, HIV, and carcinoma of the gallbladder or bile ducts.<br><br>Biliary obstruction and cholangitis can develop before biliary dilation is detected.<br><br>Common bile duct obstruction secondary to tumor or pancreatitis seldom results in infection (0–15%).<br>Ref: Surg Clin North Am 1990;70:1297.<br>Ref: N Engl J Med 1993;328:95.<br>Ref: Dig Dis 1993;11:55. |
| **Urinary Tract Infection (UTI)/ Cystitis/Pyuria-Dysuria Syndrome**<br><br>Enterobacteriaceae (GNR, especially *E coli*), *Chlamydia trachomatis*, *Staphylococcus saprophyticus* (GPC) (in young women), *Enterococcus* (GPC), *N gonorrhoeae* (GNCB), HSV. | Urinalysis and culture reveal the 2 most important signs: bacteriuria (> $10^5$ CFU/mL urine) and pyuria (> 10 WBCs/μL). 30% of patients have hematuria. It is generally accepted that > $10^5$ CFU/mL urine represents infection, although women with dysuria and > $10^2$ CFU/mL are also considered to have infection.<br><br>Intravenous pyelogram and cystoscopy should be performed in women with recurrent or childhood infections, all young boys with UTI, men with recurrent or complicated infection, and patients with symptoms suggestive of obstruction or renal stones. (See Intravenous pyelogram, p 269.) | Most men with urinary tract infections have a functional or anatomic genitourinary abnormality.<br><br>In catheter-related UTI, cure is unlikely unless the catheter is removed. In asymptomatic catheter-related UTI, antibiotics should be given only if patients are at risk for sepsis (old age, underlying disease, diabetes mellitus, pregnancy).<br><br>Up to one-third of cases of acute cystitis have "silent" upper tract involvement.<br>Ref: Am Intern Med 1989;111:906.<br>Ref: Ann Intern Med 1989;110:138.<br>Ref: Med Clin North Am 1991;75:313.<br>Ref: Am J Clin Pathol 1994;101:100. |

| GENITOURINARY | |
| --- | --- |
| **Prostatitis** | **Pyelonephritis** |
| **Prostatitis**<br><br>Acute and Chronic: Enterobacteriaceae (GNR), *Pseudomonas* sp (GNR), *Enterococcus* (GPC in chains), cytomegalovirus (CMV). | Acute prostatitis is a severe illness characterized by fever, dysuria, and a boggy or tender prostate. Chronic prostatitis often has no symptoms of dysuria or perineal discomfort and a normal prostate exam.<br>Nonbacterial prostatitis (prostatodynia) represents 90% of prostatitis cases. Its etiology is unknown and it is refractory to therapy.<br>Ref: Med Clin North Am 1991;75:405.<br>Ref: J Antimicrob Chemother 1993;32(Suppl A):1.<br>Ref: Urology 1993;41:301. |
| Urinalysis shows pyuria.<br>Urine culture usually identifies causative organism. Prostatic massage is useful in chronic prostatitis to retrieve organisms but is contraindicated in acute prostatitis (it may cause bacteremia). Bacteriuria is first cleared by antibiotic treatment. Then urine cultures are obtained from first-void, bladder, and post-prostatic massage urine specimens. A higher organism count in the post-prostatic massage specimen localizes infection to the prostate. | |
| **Pyelonephritis**<br><br>Acute, uncomplicated (usually young women): Enterobacteriaceae (especially *E coli*) (GNR).<br>Complicated (older women, men; post-catheterization, obstruction, post-renal transplant): Enterobacteriaceae (especially *E coli*), *Pseudomonas aeruginosa* (GNR), *Enterococcus* (GPC), *Staphylococcus saprophyticus* (GPC). | Patients usually present with fever, chills, nausea, vomiting, and costovertebral angle tenderness.<br>20–30% of pregnant women with untreated bacteriuria develop pyelonephritis.<br>Ref: Ann Emerg Med 1991;20:253.<br>Ref: Pediatr Infect Dis J 1994;13:777. |
| Urine culture is indicated when pyelonephritis is suspected.<br>Urinalysis will usually show pyuria (≥ 5 WBC/hpf) and may show WBC casts.<br>Blood cultures for bacteria if sepsis is suspected. Intravenous pyelogram in patients with recurrent infection will show irregularly outlined renal pelvis with caliectasis and cortical scars. (See Intravenous pyelogram, p 269.) | |

| GENITOURINARY | | |
| --- | --- | --- |
| **Organism** | **Specimens/Diagnostic Tests** | **Comments** |
| **Perinephric Abscess**<br><br>Associated with staphylococcal bacteremia: *Staphylococcus aureus* (GPC).<br>Associated with pyelonephritis: Enterobacteriaceae (GNR). | CT scan with contrast is more sensitive than ultrasound in imaging abscess and confirming diagnosis. (See Abdominal CT, p 255.)<br>Urinalysis may be normal or may show pyuria.<br>Urine culture (positive in 60%).<br>Blood cultures for bacteria (positive in 20–40%).<br>Bacterial culture of abscess fluid via drainage (percutaneous or surgical). | Most perinephric abscesses are the result of extension of an ascending urinary tract infection. Often they are very difficult to diagnose.<br>They should be considered in patients who fail to respond to antibiotic therapy, in patients with anatomic abnormalities of the urinary tract, and in patients with diabetes mellitus.<br>Ref: Infect Dis Clin North Am 1987;1:907.<br>Ref: Med Clin North Am 1988;72:993. |
| **Urethritis (Gonococcal and Non-gonococcal)**<br><br>Gonococcal (GC): *Neisseria gonorrhoeae* (GNDC).<br>Non-gonococcal (NGU): *Chlamydia trachomatis* (50%), *Ureaplasma urealyticum*.<br>*Trichomonas vaginalis*, herpes simplex (HSV), *Mycoplasma genitalium*, unknown (35%). | Urethral discharge collected with urethral swab usually shows ≥ 4 WBCs per oil immersion field.<br>Gram stain (identify gonococcal organisms as Gram-negative intracellular diplococci). PMNs (in GC, > 95% of WBCs are PMNs, in NGU usually < 80% are PMNs).<br>Urethral discharge for culture of GC and *Chlamydia* (cell culture).<br>Urethral discharge can be tested for chlamydial antigens by ELISA or for *Chlamydia* by direct immunofluorescence; detection of *C trachomatis* DNA by PCR technique is also possible.<br>VDRL should be checked in all patients because of high incidence of associated syphilis. | About 50% of patients with GC will have concomitant NGU infection.<br>Always treat sexual partners. Recurrence may be secondary to failure to treat partners.<br>Persistent or recurrent episodes with adequate treatment of patient and partners may warrant further evaluation for other causes (eg, prostatitis).<br>Ref: Med Clin North Am 1990;74:1543.<br>Ref: J Clin Pathol 1991;44:564.<br>Ref: Lancet 1993;342:582. |

| GENITOURINARY | |
| --- | --- |
| **Epididymitis/Orchitis** | **Vaginitis/Vaginosis** |
| Testicular torsion is a surgical emergency that is often confused with orchitis or epididymitis. Sexual partners should be examined for signs of sexually transmitted diseases. In non-sexually transmitted disease, evaluation for underlying urinary tract infection or structural defect is recommended. Ref: Med Clin North Am 1990;74:1543. Ref: Semin Urol 1991;9:28. Ref: J Urol 1993;150:81. | Bacterial vaginosis results from massive overgrowth of anaerobic vaginal bacterial flora (especially *Gardnerella*). Serious infectious sequelae associated with bacterial vaginosis include abscesses, endometritis and pelvic inflammatory disease. There is also a danger of premature rupture of the membranes and premature labor. Ref: Am J Obstet Gynecol 1991;165(4 Part 2):1161. Ref: Clin Obstet Gynecol 1993;36:177. Ref: Curr Opin Obstet Gynecol 1994;6:389. |
| Urinalysis may reveal pyuria. Patients aged > 35 years will often have mid-stream pyuria and scrotal edema. Culture urine and expressible urethral discharge when present. Prostatic secretions for Gram stain and bacterial culture are helpful in older patients. When testicular torsion is considered, Doppler ultrasound or radionuclide scan can be useful in diagnosis. Ultrasonography in tuberculous epididymitis shows enlargement of the epididymis (predominantly in the tail) and marked heterogeneity in texture. | Vaginal discharge for appearance (in candidiasis, area is pruritic with thick "cheesy" discharge; in trichomoniasis, copious foamy discharge), pH (about 4.5 for *Candida*; 5.0–7.0 in *Trichomonas*; 5.0–6.0 for bacterial), KOH preparation (hyphae in *Candida*; "fishy" odor on reaction with *Gardnerella* infection), saline ("wet") preparation (motile organisms seen in *Trichomonas*; cells covered with organisms—"clue" cells—in *Gardnerella*). (See Vaginitis table, p 365.) Atrophic vaginitis is seen in postmenopausal patients, often with bleeding, scant discharge, and pH 6.0–7.0. Cultures for *Gardnerella* are not useful and are not recommended. |
| **Epididymitis/Orchitis**<br>Age < 35 years, homosexual men: *Chlamydia trachomatis*, *N gonorrhoeae* (GNDC).<br>Age > 35 years, or children: Enterobacteriaceae (especially *E coli*) (GNR), *Pseudomonas sp* (GNR), *Salmonella* (GNR), *Haemophilus influenzae* (GNCB), varicella (VZV), mumps.<br>Immunosuppression: *H influenzae*, *Mycobacterium tuberculosis*, *Candida sp*, cytomegalovirus (CMV). | **Vaginitis/Vaginosis**<br>*Candida sp*, *Trichomonas vaginalis*, *Gardnerella vaginalis* (GPR), *Bacteroides* (non-fragilis) (GNR), *Mobiluncus* (GPR), *Peptostreptococcus* (GPC), herpes simplex (HSV). |

| | GENITOURINARY | | |
|---|---|---|---|
| | **Cervicitis** | **Salpingitis** | |
| **Organism** | **Specimens/Diagnostic Tests** | **Comments** | |

**Cervicitis, Mucopurulent**

*Chlamydia trachomatis* (50%), *N gonorrhoeae* (GNDC) (8%).

Cervical swab specimen for appearance (yellow or green purulent material), Gram stain (for identification of gonococcus [GC]), cell count (> 10 WBCs per high-power oil immersion field seen in 91% of *C trachomatis*), and culture (for GC and *Chlamydia*).

Mucopurulent discharge may persist for 3 months or more even after appropriate therapy.
Ref: APMIS 1993;101:37.
Ref: Adv Contracept 1994;10:309.
Ref: JAMA 1994;272:867.

**Salpingitis/Pelvic Inflammatory Disease (PID)**

Usually polymicrobial: *N gonorrhoeae* (GNDC), *Chlamydia trachomatis*, *Bacteroides*, *Peptostreptococcus*, *G. vaginalis*, and other anaerobes, Enterobacteriaceae (GNR), Streptococci (GPC in chains), *Mycoplasma hominis* (debatable).

Gram's stain and culture of urethral or endocervical exudate.
*Chlamydia* can also be detected by endocervical smears stained with Giemsa stain; chlamydial antigens, by enzyme immunoassay; and *C trachomatis* DNA detection, by techniques such as PCR. Endometrial biopsy and transvaginal ultrasonography improve diagnostic accuracy. Ultrasonographic findings include thickened fluid-filled tubes, polycystic-like ovaries, and free pelvic fluid. Laparoscopy is the most specific test to confirm the diagnosis of PID.
VDRL should be checked in all patients because of high incidence of associated syphilis.

PID typically progresses from cervicitis to endometritis to salpingitis. PID is a sexually transmitted disease in some cases, not in others.
All sexual partners should be examined.
All IUDs should be removed.
Some recommend that all patients with PID be hospitalized.
Ref: Obstet Gynecol 1992;80:912.
Ref: Am J Obstet Gynecol 1993;168:1438.
Ref: Infect Dis Clin North Am 1994;8:821.
Ref: N Engl J Med 1994;330:115.
Ref: Am J Obstet Gynecol 1994;170:1008.

| BONE | | |
| --- | --- | --- |
| **Osteomyelitis** | | |

| Osteomyelitis | | |
| --- | --- | --- |
| *Staphylococcus aureus* (GPC) (about 60% of all cases).<br>Infant: *S aureus*, Enterobacteriaceae (GNR), groups A and B streptococci (GPC).<br>Child (< 3 years): *H influenzae* (GNCB), *S aureus*, Streptococci.<br>Child (> 3 years) to Adult: *S aureus*, *Pseudomonas aeruginosa*.<br>Postoperative: *S aureus*, Enterobacteriaceae, *Pseudomonas* sp (GNR).<br>Joint prosthesis: *S epidermidis*. | Blood cultures for bacteria are positive in about 60%.<br>Cultures of percutaneous needle biopsy or open bone biopsy are needed if blood cultures are negative and osteomyelitis is suspected.<br>Imaging with bone scan or gallium/indium scan (sensitivity 95%, specificity 60–70%) can localize areas of suspicion. Technetium ($^{99m}$Tc)-Methylene diphosphonate (MDP) bone scan can suggest osteomyelitis days or weeks before plain bone films. Plain bone films are abnormal in acute cases after about 2 weeks of illness (33%). Indium-labeled WBC scan is useful in detecting abscesses.<br>CT scan aids in detecting sequestra.<br>MRI is useful in defining extent and in distinguishing osteomyelitis from cellulitis.<br>Myelography, CT, or MRI is indicated to rule out epidural abscess in vertebral osteomyelitis. | Hematogenous or contiguous infection (eg, infected prosthetic joint, chronic cutaneous ulcer) may lead to osteomyelitis in children (metaphyses of long bones) or adults (vertebrae, metaphyses of long bones).<br>Hematogenous osteomyelitis in drug addicts occurs in unusual locations (vertebrae, clavicle, ribs).<br>In infants, osteomyelitis is often associated with contiguous joint involvement.<br>Ref: Am J Dis Child 1991;145:65.<br>Ref: Am J Roentgenol 1991;157:365.<br>Ref: Clin Infect Dis 1995;20:320. |

| | JOINT | |
| --- | --- | --- |
| | **Bacterial/Septic Arthritis** | |
| **Organism** | **Specimens/Diagnostic Tests** | **Comments** |
| **Bacterial/Septic Arthritis**<br><br>Infant (< 3 months): *S aureus* (GPC), Enterobacteriaceae (GNR), *Kingella kingae* (GNCB), *Haemophilus influenzae* (GNCB).<br><br>Child (3 months to 6 years): *S aureus* (35%), *H influenzae* (GNCB) (15%), *Streptococcus* (10%), Enterobacteriaceae (6%). Adult, venereal disease not likely: *S aureus* (40%), group A *Streptococcus* (27%), Enterobacteriaceae (23%).<br><br>Adult, venereal disease likely: *N gonorrhoeae* (GNCB) (disseminated gonococcal infection, DGI). Prosthetic joint, postoperative or following intraarticular injection: *S epidermidis* (40%), *S aureus* (20%), Enterobacteriaceae, *Pseudomonas* sp. | Joint aspiration (synovial) fluid for WBCs (in non-gonococcal infection, mean WBC is 100,000/µL). Gram stain (best on centrifuged concentrated specimen; positive in one-third of cases), culture (nongonococcal infection in adults [85–95%], DGI [25%]). (See Synovial fluid profiles, p 357.)<br><br>Blood cultures for bacteria may be useful, especially in infants; nongonococcal infection in adults (50%); DGI (1–3%).<br><br>Genitourinary, throat, or rectal culture: DGI may be diagnosed by positive culture from a nonarticular source and by a compatible clinical picture. Gram stain of skin lesions is rarely positive. | Septic arthritis is usually hematogenously acquired. Prosthetic joint and diminished host defenses secondary to cancer, HIV, liver disease, or hypogammaglobulinemia are common predisposing factors. Nongonococcal bacterial arthritis is usually monarticular (and typically affects one knee joint).<br><br>DGI is the most common cause of septic arthritis in urban centers and is usually polyarticular with associated tenosynovitis.<br><br>Ref: Rheumat Dis Clin North Am 1993;19:311.<br>Ref: Curr Opin Rheumatol 1994;6:394.<br>Ref: Arch Pediatr Adolesc Med 1995;149:537. |

| | MUSCLE — Gas Gangrene | SKIN — Impetigo |
|---|---|---|
| **Organisms** | **Gas Gangrene**<br>*Clostridium perfringens* (GPR), (80–95%), other *Clostridium* sp. | **Impetigo**<br>Infant (impetigo neonatorum): *Staphylococcus* (GPC). Nonbullous or "vesicular": Group A *Streptococcus* (GPC), *S aureus* (GPC). Bullous: *S aureus*. |
| **Diagnostic Tests** | Diagnosis should be suspected in areas of devitalized tissue when gas is discovered by palpation (subcutaneous crepitation) or x-ray. Gram stain of foul-smelling, brown/blood-tinged watery exudate can be diagnostic with Gram-positive rods and a remarkable absence of neutrophils. Anaerobic culture of discharge is confirmatory. | Gram stain and Tzanck smear of scrapings from lesions may be useful in differentiating impetigo from other vesicular or pustular lesions (HSV, VZV, contact dermatitis). Tzanck preparation can be performed by scraping the contents, base, and roof of vesicle and applying to glass slide. After fixing, the slide is stained with Wright or Giemsa stain and inspected for giant cells. (See Tzanck smear, p 25.) Many laboratories offer direct fluorescent antibody (DFA) for identification of HSV or VZV on slides from scrapings. |
| **Comments** | Gas gangrene occurs in the setting of a contaminated wound. *Clostridium perfringens* produces potent exotoxins, including alpha toxin and theta toxin, which depresses myocardial contractility, induces shock, and causes direct vascular injury at the site of infection. Infections with *Enterobacter* or *E coli* and anaerobic infections can also cause gas formation. These agents cause cellulitis rather than myonecrosis. Ref: Clin Infect Dis 1993;16(Suppl 4):S195. Ref: Orthop Rev 1990;19:333. | Impetigo neonatorum requires prompt treatment and protection of other infants (isolation). Patients with recurrent impetigo should have cultures of the anterior nares to exclude carriage of *S aureus*. Ref: Pediatr Ann 1993;22:235. Ref: Pediatr Dermatol 1994;11:293. |

| | SKIN | |
|---|---|---|
| | **Cellulitis** | |
| **Organism** | **Specimens/Diagnostic Tests** | **Comments** |

| Organism | Specimens/Diagnostic Tests | Comments |
|---|---|---|
| **Cellulitis**<br><br>Spontaneous, traumatic wound: Polymicrobial: *S aureus* (GPC), groups A, C, D, and G streptococci (GPC), Enterobacteriaceae (GNR), *Clostridium perfringens* (GPR), *Clostridium tetani*, *Pseudomonas* sp (GNR) (if water exposure).<br><br>Postoperative wound (not GI or GU): *S aureus*, group A *Streptococcus*, Enterobacteriaceae, *Pseudomonas* sp.<br><br>Postoperative wound (GI or GU): must add *Bacteroides* sp, anaerobes, *Enterococcus* (GPC), groups B or C streptococci.<br><br>Diabetes mellitus: Polymicrobial: Group A *Streptococcus*, *Enterococcus*, *S aureus*, Enterobacteriaceae, anaerobes.<br><br>Bullous lesions, sea water contaminated abrasion, after raw seafood consumption: *Vibrio vulnificus*.<br><br>Vein graft donor site: *Streptococcus*.<br><br>Decubitus ulcers: Polymicrobial: *S aureus*, anaerobic streptococci, Enterobacteriaceae, *Pseudomonas* sp, *Bacteroides* sp.<br><br>Necrotizing fasciitis, type 1: *Streptococcus*, anaerobes, Enterobacteriaceae; type 2: group A *Streptococcus* (hemolytic streptococcal gangrene). | Skin culture: In spontaneous cellulitis, isolation of the causative organism is difficult. In traumatic and postoperative wounds, Gram stain may allow rapid diagnosis of staphylococcal or clostridial infection. Culture of wound or abscess material will almost always yield the diagnosis.<br><br>MRI can aid in diagnosis of secondary abscess formation, necrotizing fasciitis, or pyomyositis. Frozen section of biopsy specimen may be useful. | Cellulitis has long been considered to be the result of an antecedent bacterial invasion with subsequent bacterial proliferation. However, the difficulty in isolating putative pathogens from cellulitic skin has cast doubt on this theory.<br><br>Consider updating antitetanus prophylaxis for all wounds.<br><br>In the diabetic, and in post-operative and traumatic wounds, consider prompt surgical debridement for necrotizing fasciitis. With abscess formation, surgical drainage is the mainstay of therapy and may be sufficient. Hemolytic streptococcal gangrene may follow minor trauma and involves specific strains of *Streptococcus*.<br><br>Ref: Clin Infect Dis 1992;14:2.<br>Ref: Clin Infect Dis 1993;16:792.<br>Ref: Hosp Pract (Off Ed) 1993 Jul;28(Suppl 2):10.<br>Ref: Radiology 1994;192:493.<br>Ref: Arch Dermatol 1994;130:1150. |

| BLOOD |
| --- |
| **Bacteremia of Unknown Source** |

| Bacteremia of Unknown Source | | |
| --- | --- | --- |
| Neonate (< 4 days): Group B Streptococcus (GPC), E coli (GNR), Klebsiella (GNR), Enterobacter (GNR), S aureus (GPC). Neonate (> 5 days): add H influenzae (GNCB). Child (nonimmunocompromised): H influenzae, S pneumoniae (GPDC), N meningitidis (GNDC), S aureus. Adult (IV drug use): S aureus or viridans group streptococci (GPC). Adult (catheter-related, "line" sepsis): S aureus, S epidermidis, Pseudomonas sp, Candida sp. Adult (splenectomized): S pneumoniae, H influenzae, N meningitidis. Neutropenia (< 500 PMN): Enterobacteriaceae, Pseudomonas sp, S aureus, S epidermidis, viridans group Streptococcus. | Blood cultures are mandatory for all patients with fever and no obvious source of infection. Often they are negative, especially in neonates. Cultures should be drawn at onset of febrile episode. Culture should never be drawn from an IV or from a femoral site. | Predisposing factors include IV drug use, neutropenia, cancer, diabetes mellitus, venous catheterization, hemodialysis, and plasmapheresis. Catheter-related infection in patients with long-term venous access (Broviac, Hickman, etc) may be treated successfully without removal of the line, but recurrence of bacteremia is frequent. Switching needles during blood cultures does not decrease contamination rates and increases the risk of needle-stick injuries. Ref: Rev Infect Dis 1991;13:613. Ref: Clin Infect Dis 1992;14:436. Ref: Infect Control Hosp Epidemiol 1992;13:215. |

# 6

# Diagnostic Imaging: Test Selection and Interpretation

*Susan D. Wall, MD*

## HOW TO USE THIS SECTION

Information in this chapter is arranged anatomically from superior to inferior. It would not be feasible to include all available diagnostic tests in one chapter in a book this size, but we have attempted to summarize the essential features of those examinations that are most frequently ordered in modern clinical practice or those that may be associated with difficulty or risk. Indications, advantages and disadvantages, contraindications, and patient preparation are presented. Costs of the studies are approximate and represent averages reported from several large medical centers.

$$\$ = < \$250$$
$$\$\$ = \$250–\$750$$
$$\$\$\$ = \$750–\$1000$$
$$\$\$\$\$ = > \$1000$$

## Risks of Intravenous Contrast Studies

While intravenous contrast is an important tool in radiology, it is not without substantial risks. Minor reactions (nausea, vomiting, hives) occur in about 5% of patients. Major reactions (laryngeal edema, bronchospasm, cardiac arrest) occur in about 1:3000 patients. Patients with an allergic history (asthma, hay fever, allergy to foods or drugs) are at increased risk. A history of reaction to contrast material is associated with an increased risk of a subsequent severe reaction. Prophylactic measures that may be required in such cases include $H_1$ and $H_2$ blockers and corticosteroids.

In addition, there is a risk of contrast-induced renal failure, which is usually mild and reversible. Persons at increased risk for potentially *irreversible* renal damage include patients with preexisting renal disease (particularly diabetics with high serum creatinine concentrations), multiple myeloma, and severe hyperuricemia.

In summary, intravenous contrast should be viewed in the same manner as other medications—ie, risks and benefits must be balanced before an examination using this pharmaceutical is ordered.

| | HEAD | |
|---|---|---|
| | **CT** | **MRI** |
| **Test** | **Computed tomography (CT)** $$$ <br> HEAD | **Magnetic resonance imaging (MRI)** $$$$ <br> HEAD |
| **Indications** | Evaluation of acute craniofacial trauma, acute neurologic dysfunction (< 72 hours) from suspected intracranial or subarachnoid hemorrhage. <br> Further characterization of intracranial masses identified by MRI (presence or absence of calcium or involvement of the bony calvarium). <br> Evaluation of sinus disease and temporal bone disease. | Evaluation of essentially all intracranial disease except those listed above for CT. |
| **Advantages** | Rapid acquisition makes it the modality of choice for trauma. <br> Superb spatial resolution. <br> Superior to MRI in detection of hemorrhage within the first 24–48 hours. | Provides exquisite spatial resolution, multiplanar capability. <br> Can detect flowing blood and cryptic vascular malformations. <br> Can detect demyelinating and dysmyelinating disease. <br> No beam-hardening artifacts such as can be seen with CT. <br> No ionizing radiation. |
| **Disadvantages/Contraindications** | Artifacts from bone may interfere with detection of disease at the skull base and in the posterior fossa. <br> Limited to transaxial views. <br> **Contraindications and risks:** Contraindicated in pregnancy because of the potential harm of ionizing radiation to the fetus. Use of intravenous contrast agents is associated with infrequent but substantial risks (see p 241.) | Subject to motion artifacts. <br> Inferior to CT in the setting of acute trauma because it is insensitive to acute hemorrhage, incompatible with life support and traction devices, inferior in detection of bony injury and foreign bodies, and requires longer imaging acquisition time. <br> **Contraindications and risks:** Contraindicated in patients with cardiac pacemakers, intracranial metallic foreign bodies, intracranial aneurysm clips, cochlear implants, some artificial heart valves, and life support devices. |
| **Preparation** | Normal hydration. <br> Sedation of agitated patients. <br> Recent serum creatinine determination if intravenous contrast is to be used. | Sedation of agitated patients. <br> Screening CT of the orbits if history suggests possible metallic foreign body in the eye. |

| | BRAIN | |
| --- | --- | --- |
| | **Radionuclide scan** | **Cisternography** |

| Test | Indications | Advantages | Disadvantages/Contraindications | Preparation |
| --- | --- | --- | --- | --- |
| BRAIN<br><br>**Brain scan** (radionuclide)<br><br>$$ | Establishment of brain death. Evaluation of suspected herpes simplex encephalitis, dementia, seizures. Single photon emission computed tomography (SPECT) imaging can be used to distinguish ischemia from infarct. | Provides functional information. Can be portable. | Limited resolution. Delayed imaging (1–4 hours) often required. **Contraindications and risks:** Caution in pregnancy because of the potential harm of ionizing radiation to the fetus. | Sedation of agitated patients. Premedicate with potassium perchlorate when using TcO$_4$ in order to block choroid plexus uptake. |
| BRAIN<br><br>**Cisternography** (radionuclide)<br><br>$$ | Evaluation of hydrocephalus (particularly normal pressure), CSF rhinorrhea or otorrhea, and ventricular shunt patency. | Provides functional information. Can help distinguish normal pressure hydrocephalus from senile atrophy. Can detect CSF leaks. | Requires multiple delayed imaging sessions up to 48–72 hours after injection. **Contraindications and risks:** Caution in pregnancy because of the potential harm of ionizing radiation to the fetus. | Sedation of agitated patients. For suspected CSF leak, pack the patient's nose or ears with cotton pledgets prior to administration of dose. Must follow strict sterile precautions for intrathecal injection. |

| NECK | | | | |
|---|---|---|---|---|
| **MRI** | | | | |
| NECK<br><br>**Magnetic resonance imaging (MRI)**<br><br>$$$$ | Evaluation of the upper aerodigestive tract.<br>Staging of neck masses.<br>Differentiation of lymphadenopathy from blood vessels.<br>Evaluation of head and neck malignancy, thyroid nodules, parathyroid adenoma, lymphadenopathy, retropharyngeal abscess, brachial plexopathy. | Superb spatial resolution and better tissue contrast compared with CT.<br>Tissue differentiation of malignancy or abscess from benign tumor often possible.<br>Sagittal and coronal planar imaging possible. Multiplanar capability especially advantageous regarding brachial plexus.<br>No iodinated contrast needed to distinguish lymphadenopathy from blood vessels.<br>Magnetic resonance angiography of carotid arteries can be sufficient preoperative evaluation regarding critical stenosis when local expertise exists. | Subject to motion artifacts, particularly those of carotid pulsation.<br>**Contraindications and risks:** Contraindicated in patients with cardiac pacemakers, intraocular metallic foreign bodies, intracranial aneurysm clips, cochlear implants, some artificial heart valves, and life support devices. | Sedation of agitated patients.<br>Screening CT of orbits if history suggests possible metallic foreign body in the eye. |

|  | NECK | | THYROID |
| --- | --- | --- | --- |
|  | CT | Ultrasound | Ultrasound |

| Test | Indications | Advantages | Disadvantages/Contraindications | Preparation |
| --- | --- | --- | --- | --- |
| **NECK** Computed tomography (CT) $$$$ | Evaluation of the upper acrodigestive tract. Staging of neck masses. Evaluation of suspected abscess. | Rapid. Superb spatial resolution. Can guide percutaneous fine-needle aspiration of possible tumor or abscess. | Adequate intravenous contrast enhancement of vascular structures is mandatory for accurate interpretation. **Contraindications and risks:** Contraindicated in pregnancy because of the potential harm of ionizing radiation to the fetus. Use of intravenous contrast agents is associated with infrequent but substantial risks (see p 241). | Normal hydration. Sedation of agitated patients. Recent serum creatinine determination. |
| **NECK** Ultrasound (US) $$ | Patency and morphology of arteries and veins. Evaluation of thyroid and parathyroid. Guidance for percutaneous fine-needle aspiration biopsy of neck lesions. | Can detect and monitor atherosclerotic stenosis of carotid arteries noninvasively and without iodinated contrast. | Technically demanding, operator-dependent. Patient must lie supine and still for 1 hour. | None. |
| **THYROID** Ultrasound (US) $$ | Determination as to whether a palpable nodule is a thyroid nodule and whether single or multiple nodules are present. Assessment of response to suppressive therapy. Screening patients with a history of prior radiation to the head and neck. Guidance for biopsy. | Noninvasive. No ionizing radiation. Can be portable. Can image in all planes. | Cannot distinguish between benign and malignant lesions unless local invasion is demonstrated. Technique very operator-dependent. **Contraindications and risks:** None. | None. |

| THYROID | | | | |
|---|---|---|---|---|
| **Thyroid uptake and scan** | | | | |
| THYROID<br><br>**Thyroid uptake and scan** (radionuclide)<br><br>$$ | Uptake indicated for evaluation of clinical hypothyroidism, hyperthyroidism, thyroiditis, effects of thyroid-stimulating and suppressing medications, and for calculation of therapeutic radiation dosage. Scanning indicated for above as well as evaluation of palpable nodules, mediastinal mass, and screening of patients with history of head and neck irradiation. Total body scanning used for postoperative evaluation of thyroid metastases. | Demonstrates both morphology and functional information. Can identify ectopic thyroid tissue and "cold" nodules that have a greater risk of malignancy. Imaging of total body with one dose ($^{131}$I). | Substances interfering with test include iodides in vitamins and medicines, antithyroid drugs, steroids, and intravascular contrast agents. Delayed imaging is required with iodides ($^{123}$I, 6 hours; $^{131}$I total body, 72 hours). Test may not visualize thyroid gland in acute thyroiditis. **Contraindications and risks:** Not advised in pregnancy because of the risk of ionizing radiation to the fetus (iodides cross placenta and concentrate in fetal thyroid). Significant radiation exposure occurs in total body scanning with $^{131}$I; patients should be instructed about precautionary measures by nuclear medicine personnel. | Administration of dose after a 4- to 6-hour fast aids absorption. Discontinue all interfering substances prior to test, especially thyroid-suppressing medications: $T_3$ (1 week), $T_4$ (4–6 weeks), propylthiouracil (2 weeks). |

| Test | Indications | Advantages | Disadvantages/Contraindications | Preparation |
|---|---|---|---|---|
| **THYROID** | | Radionuclide therapy | | |
| THYROID<br><br>**Thyroid therapy** (radio-nuclide)<br><br>$-$$ | Hyperthyroidism and some thyroid carcinomas (papillary and follicular types are amenable to treatment, whereas medullary and anaplastic types are not). | Noninvasive alternative to surgery. | Rarely, radiation thyroiditis may occur 1–3 days after therapy. Hypothyroidism occurs commonly as a long-term complication. Higher doses that are required to treat thyroid carcinoma may result in pulmonary fibrosis. **Contraindications and risks:** Contraindicated in pregnancy and lactation. Contraindicated in patients with metastatic disease to the brain, because treatment may result in brain edema and subsequent herniation, and in those < 20 years of age because of possible increased risk of thyroid cancer later in life. Patients receiving high doses for treatment of thyroid carcinoma must be hospitalized until radioactive level is < 30 mCi. | After treatment, patients must isolate all bodily secretions from household members. |
| **PARATHYROID** | | | | Radionuclide scan |
| PARATHY-ROID<br><br>**Parathyroid scan** (radio-nuclide)<br><br>$$ | Evaluation of suspected parathyroid adenoma. | Identifies hyperfunctioning tissue, which is useful when planning surgery. | Small adenomas (< 500 mg) may not be detected. **Contraindications and risks:** Caution in pregnancy is advised because of the risk of ionizing radiation to the fetus. | Requires strict patient immobility during scanning. |

| CHEST | | |
|---|---|---|
| | **Chest radiograph** | **CT** |

| CHEST **Chest radiograph** $ | Evaluation of pleural and parenchymal pulmonary disease, mediastinal disease, cardiogenic and noncardiogenic pulmonary edema, congenital and acquired cardiac disease. Screening for traumatic aortic rupture (though angiogram is the gold standard). Evaluation of possible pneumothorax (expiratory upright film) or free flowing fluid (decubitus views). | Inexpensive. Widely available. | Difficult to distinguish between causes of hilar enlargement (ie, vasculature vs adenopathy). **Contraindications and risks:** Caution in pregnancy because of the potential harm of ionizing radiation to the fetus. | None. |
| CHEST **Computed tomography (CT)** $$$ | Differentiation of mediastinal and hilar lymphadenopathy from vascular structures. Evaluation and staging of primary and metastatic lung neoplasm. Characterization of pulmonary nodules. Differentiation of parenchymal vs pleural process (ie, lung abscess vs empyema). Evaluation of interstitial lung disease (1.5 mm thin sections), aortic dissection, and aneurysm. Evaluation of pulmonary embolism with spiral CT. | Rapid. Superb spatial resolution. Can guide percutaneous fine-needle aspiration of possible tumor or abscess. | Patient cooperation required for appropriate breath-holding. Generally limited to transaxial views. **Contraindications and risks:** Contraindicated in pregnancy because of the potential harm of ionizing radiation to the fetus. Use of intravenous contrast agents is associated with infrequent but substantial risks (see p 241). | Preferably NPO for 2 hours prior to study. Normal hydration. Sedation of agitated patients. Recent serum creatinine determination. |

| Test | Indications | Advantages | Disadvantages/Contraindications | Preparation |
|---|---|---|---|---|
| **CHEST** | | | | |
| | | | **MRI** | |
| CHEST Magnetic resonance imaging (MRI) $$$$ | Evaluation of mediastinal masses. Discrimination between hilar vessels and enlarged lymph nodes. Tumor staging (especially when invasion of vessels or pericardium is suspected). Evaluation of aortic dissection, aortic aneurysm, congenital and acquired cardiac disease. | Provides exquisite spatial resolution, multiplanar capability. No beam-hardening artifacts such as can be seen with CT. No ionizing radiation. | Subject to motion artifacts. **Contraindications and risks:** Contraindicated in patients with cardiac pacemakers, intraocular metallic foreign bodies, intracranial aneurysm clips, cochlear implants, some artificial heart valves, and life support devices. | Sedation of agitated patients. Screening CT of the orbits if history suggests possible metallic foreign body in the eye. |
| **LUNG** | | | | |
| | | | **Ventilation-perfusion scan** | |
| LUNG Ventilation-perfusion scan (radionuclide) $\dot{V} = \$\$$ $\dot{Q} = \$\$$ $\dot{V} + \dot{Q} = \$\$\$$— $$$$ | Evaluation of pulmonary embolism or burn inhalation injury. Preoperative evaluation of patients with chronic obstructive pulmonary disease and of those who are candidates for pneumonectomy. | Noninvasive. Provides functional information in preoperative assessment. | Patients must be able to cooperate for ventilation portion of the examination. There is a high proportion of indeterminate studies in patients with underlying lung disease. A patient who has a low probability scan still has a 10% chance of having a pulmonary embolus. **Contraindications and risks:** Patients with severe pulmonary artery hypertension or significant right-to-left shunts should have fewer particles injected. Caution advised in pregnancy because of risk of ionizing radiation to the fetus. | Current chest radiograph is mandatory for interpretation. |

| | LUNG | | | | BREAST |
|---|---|---|---|---|---|
| | **Pulmonary angiography** | | | | **Mammogram** |
| LUNG<br>**Pulmonary angiography**<br>$$$$ | Suspected pulmonary embolism with equivocal results on ventilation/perfusion scan or when diagnosis especially important because of contraindication to anticoagulation.<br>Arteriovenous malformation, pulmonary sequestration, vasculitides, vascular occlusion by tumor or inflammatory disease. | Remains the standard for diagnosis of acute and chronic pulmonary embolism. | Invasive. Requires catheterization of the right heart and pulmonary artery. **Contraindication:** Pulmonary artery hypertension. | Ventilation/perfusion scan for localization of right versus left lung. Electrocardiogram, especially for possible left bundle branch block (when temporary cardiac pacemaker should be placed before the catheter is introduced into the pulmonary artery). | |
| BREAST<br>**Mammogram**<br>$ | Screening for breast cancer in asymptomatic women: (1) baseline between ages 35 and 40 (at age 30 for women with a first-degree relative with premenopausal breast cancer); (2) every 1–2 years between ages 40 and 49; (3) every year after age 50. If prior history of breast cancer, mammogram should be performed yearly. Indicated at any age for symptoms (palpable mass, bloody discharge) or before planned breast surgery. | Newer film screen techniques generate lower radiation doses (0.1–0.2 rad per film, mean glandular dose). | Detection of breast masses is more difficult in patients with dense breasts. Breast compression may cause patient discomfort. **Contraindications and risks:** Radiation from repeated mammograms can theoretically cause breast cancer; however, the benefits of screening mammograms greatly outweigh the risks. | None. | |

| | HEART | | | |
|---|---|---|---|---|
| | **Thallium scan** | | | |
| Test | Indications | Advantages | Disadvantages/Contraindications | Preparation |
| HEART<br><br>**Myocardial perfusion scan** (thallium scan)<br><br>$–$$–$$$ (broad range) | Evaluation of atypical chest pain. Detection of presence, location, and extent of myocardial ischemia. | Highly sensitive for detecting physiologically significant coronary stenosis.<br><br>Noninvasive. | The patient must be carefully monitored during treadmill or pharmacologic stress—optimally, under the supervision of a cardiologist.<br><br>False-positive results may be caused by exercise-induced spasm, aortic stenosis, or left bundle branch block; false-negative results may be caused by inadequate exercise, mild or distal disease, or diffuse ischemia.<br><br>**Contraindications and risks:** Aminophylline (inhibitor of dipyridamole) is a contraindication to the use of dipyridamole. Treadmill or pharmacologic stress carries a risk of arrhythmia, ischemia, infarct, and, rarely, death. Caution in pregnancy because of the risk of ionizing radiation to the fetus. | Patient should be able to exercise on a treadmill.<br><br>In case of severe peripheral vascular disease, severe pulmonary disease, or musculoskeletal disorder, pharmacologic stress with dipyridamole or other agents may be used.<br><br>Tests should be performed in the fasting state.<br><br>Patient should not exercise between stress and redistribution. |

| | HEART | |
|---|---|---|
| | **Pyrophosphate scan** | **Ventriculography** |
| **HEART**<br><br>**Myocardial infarct scan** (pyrophosphate scan)<br><br>$$ | Determination of location and extent of acute myocardial infarction. | Pyrophosphate imaging identifies acute myocardial infarction, including perioperative infarcts following cardiac surgery, where CK and ECG findings may be misleading. | Pyrophosphate scan is most sensitive at 48–72 hours after myocardial injury. Sensitivity is lower for nontransmural infarcts.<br>Sensitivity is also affected by location of infarct (highest for anterior wall, lowest for inferior wall).<br>Pyrophosphate scan may be positive in patients with unstable angina, myocardial contusion, pericarditis, myocarditis, or recent cardioversion. Scan may be persistently positive in up to 20% of patients with remote history of infarct. **Contraindications and risks:** Caution in pregnancy because of the risk of ionizing radiation to the fetus. | Sedation of agitated patients. |
| **HEART**<br><br>**Radionuclide ventriculography** (multigated acquisition [MUGA])<br><br>$$–$$$–$$$$ | Evaluation of patients with ischemic heart disease and other cardiomyopathies.<br>Evaluation of response to pharmacologic therapy and effects of cardiotoxic drugs. | Noninvasive.<br>Resting ejection fraction is a reproducible index that can be used to follow course of disease and response to therapy. | Gated data acquisition may be difficult in patients with severe arrhythmias.<br>Limited to resting study in patients who are unable to exercise on a supine bicycle.<br>**Contraindications and risks:** Recent infarct is a contraindication to exercise ventriculography (arrhythmia, ischemia, infarct, and rarely death may occur with exercise). Caution is advised in pregnancy because of the risk of ionizing radiation to the fetus. | May require harvesting, labeling, and reinjecting the patient's red blood cells.<br>Sterile technique required in handling of red cells. |

| | ABDOMEN | |
| --- | --- | --- |
| | **KUB** | **Ultrasound** |
| **Test** | ABDOMEN **Abdominal plain radiograph** (KUB [Kidneys, ureters, bladder] x-ray) $ | ABDOMEN **Ultrasound** (US) $$ |
| **Indications** | Assessment of bowel gas patterns (eg, to distinguish ileus from obstruction). To rule out pneumoperitoneum, order an upright abdomen and chest radiograph (acute abdominal series). Good screening test for renal calculi (90% are radiopaque), but not for gallstones (only 15% are radiopaque). | Differentiation of cystic vs solid lesions of the liver and kidneys, intra- and extrahepatic biliary ductal dilation, cholelithiasis, gallbladder wall thickness, pericholecystic fluid, peripancreatic fluid and pseudocyst, primary and metastatic liver carcinoma, hydronephrosis, abdominal aortic aneurysm, ascites. |
| **Advantages** | Inexpensive. Widely available. | Noninvasive. No ionizing radiation. Can be portable. Imaging in all planes. Can guide percutaneous fine-needle aspiration of tumor or abscess. |
| **Disadvantages/Contraindications** | Supine film alone is inadequate to rule out pneumoperitoneum (see indications). Obstipation may obscure lesions. **Contraindications and risks:** Contraindicated in pregnancy because of the risk of ionizing radiation to the fetus. | Technique very operator-dependent. Organs (particularly pancreas and distal aorta) may be obscured by bowel gas. Presence of barium obscures sound waves. **Contraindications and risks:** None. |
| **Preparation** | None. | NPO for 6 hours. |

| ABDOMEN | | | | |
|---|---|---|---|---|
| **CT** | | | | |
| ABDOMEN<br><br>**Computed tomography** (CT)<br><br>$$$–$$$$ | Morphologic evaluation of all abdominal and pelvic organs. Differentiation of intraperitoneal vs retroperitoneal disorders. Evaluation of abscess, trauma, mesenteric and retroperitoneal lymphadenopathy, bowel wall thickening, obstructive biliary disease, pancreatitis, site of gastrointestinal obstruction, pancreatic carcinoma, appendicitis, peritonitis and carcinomatosis, abdominal aortic aneurysm, splenic infarction, retroperitoneal hemorrhage, aortoenteric fistula.<br>Staging of renal cell carcinoma, carcinomas of the GI tract, and metastatic liver disease.<br>Spiral CT can help in evaluation of the aorta and its branches. | Rapid.<br>Superb spatial resolution.<br>Not limited by overlying bowel gas as with ultrasound.<br>Can guide fine-needle aspiration and percutaneous drainage procedures. | Barium or Hypaque, surgical clips, and metallic prostheses can cause artifacts and degrade image quality.<br>**Contraindications and risks:** Contraindicated in pregnancy because of the potential harm of ionizing radiation to the fetus. Use of intravenous contrast agents is associated with infrequent but substantial risks (see p 241). | Preferably NPO for 4–6 hours. Normal hydration.<br>Opacification of GI tract with water-soluble oral contrast (Gastrografin).<br>Sedation of agitated patients.<br>Recent serum creatinine determination. |

| | ABDOMEN |
|---|---|
| | **MRI** |

| Test | Indications | Advantages | Disadvantages/Contraindications | Preparation |
|---|---|---|---|---|
| **ABDOMEN**<br><br>**Magnetic resonance imaging** (MRI)<br><br>$$$$ | Clarification of CT findings when surgical clip artifacts are present. Differentiation of retroperitoneal lymphadenopathy from blood vessels or the diaphragmatic crus. Preoperative staging of renal cell carcinoma. Differentiation of benign nonhyperfunctioning adrenal adenoma from malignant adrenal mass. Complementary to CT in evaluation of liver lesions (especially metastatic disease and possible tumor invasion of hepatic or portal veins). Differentiation of benign cavernous hemangioma (> 2 cm in diameter) from malignancy. Evaluation of stenosis or obstruction of the aorta and its branches, including (sometimes) peripheral leg vessels. | Provides exquisite spatial resolution, multiplanar capability. No beam-hardening artifacts such as can be seen with CT. No ionizing radiation. | Subject to motion artifacts. Gastrointestinal opacification not yet readily available. **Contraindications and risks:** Contraindicated in patients with cardiac pacemakers, intraocular metallic foreign bodies, intracranial aneurysm clips, cochlear implants, some artificial heart valves or life support devices. | NPO for 4–6 hours. Intramuscular glucagon to inhibit peristalsis. Sedation of agitated patients. Screening CT of the orbits if history suggests possible metallic foreign body in the eye. |

| ABDOMEN | | | |
| --- | --- | --- | --- |
| **Mesenteric angiography** | | | |
| ABDOMEN<br>**Mesenteric angiography**<br>$$$$ | Gastrointestinal hemorrhage that does not resolve with conservative therapy and cannot be treated endoscopically.<br>Localization of gastrointestinal bleeding site.<br>Acute mesenteric ischemia, intestinal angina, splenic or other splanchnic artery aneurysm.<br>Evaluation of possible vasculitis, such as polyarteritis nodosa.<br>Detection of islet cell tumors not identified by other studies.<br>Abdominal trauma. | Therapeutic embolization of gastrointestinal hemorrhage is often possible. | Invasive. Patient must remain supine with leg extended for 6 hours following the procedure in order to protect the common femoral artery at the catheter entry site. **Contraindications and risks:** Allergy to iodinated contrast material may require corticosteroid and $H_1$ blocker or $H_2$ blocker premedication. Contraindicated in pregnancy because of the potential harm of ionizing radiation to the fetus. Contrast nephrotoxicity, especially with preexisting impaired renal function due to diabetes mellitus or multiple myeloma; however, any creatinine elevation following the procedure is usually reversible. | NPO for 4–6 hours.<br>Good hydration to limit possible renal insult due to iodinated contrast material.<br>Recent serum creatinine determination, assessment of clotting parameters, reversal of anticoagulation.<br>Performed with conscious sedation.<br>Requires cardiac, respiratory, blood pressure, and pulse oximetry monitoring. |

| | | Test | Indications | Advantages | Disadvantages/Contraindications | Preparation |
|---|---|---|---|---|---|---|
| **GASTROINTESTINAL** | | | | | | |
| **UGI** | | | | | | |
| GI | **Upper GI study (UGI)** $$ | | Double-contrast barium technique demonstrates esophageal, gastric, and duodenal mucosa for evaluation of inflammatory disease and other subtle mucosal abnormalities. Single-contrast technique is suitable for evaluation of possible outlet obstruction, peristalsis, gastroesophageal reflux and hiatal hernia, esophageal cancer and varices. Water-soluble contrast (Gastrografin) is suitable for evaluation of anastomotic leak or gastrointestinal perforation. | Good evaluation of mucosa with double-contrast examination. No sedation required. Less expensive than endoscopy. | Aspiration of water-soluble contrast material may occur, inciting severe pulmonary edema. Leakage of barium from a perforation may cause granulomatous inflammatory reaction. Identification of a lesion does not prove it to be the site of blood loss in patients with GI bleeding. Barium precludes endoscopy and body CT examination. Retained gastric secretions prevent mucosal coating with barium. **Contraindications and risks:** Contraindicated in pregnancy because of the potential harm of ionizing radiation to the fetus. | NPO for 8 hours. |
| GI | **Enteroclysis** $$ | | Barium fluoroscopic study for location of site of intermittent partial small bowel obstruction. Evaluation of extent of Crohn's disease or small bowel disease in patient with persistent gastrointestinal bleeding and normal upper gastrointestinal and colonic evaluations. Evaluation of metastatic disease to the small bowel. | Clarifies lesions noted on more traditional barium examination of the small bowel. Best means of establishing small bowel as normal. Controlled high rate of flow of barium can dilate a partial obstruction. | Requires nasogastric or orogastric tube placement and manipulation to beyond the ligament of Treitz. **Contraindications and risks:** Radiation exposure is substantial, since lengthy fluoroscopic examination is required. Therefore, the test is contraindicated in pregnant women and should be used sparingly in children and women of childbearing age. | Clear liquid diet for 24 hours. Colonic cleansing. |

| GASTROINTESTINAL | | | | |
|---|---|---|---|---|
| | **Imaging technique** | | | **Preparation** |
| **GI**<br>**Peroral pneumocolon**<br>$ | Fluoroscopic evaluation of the terminal ileum by insufflating air per rectum after orally ingested barium has reached the cecum. | Best evaluation of the terminal ileum. Can be performed concurrently with upper GI series. | Undigested food in the small bowel interferes with the evaluation. **Contraindications and risks:** Contraindicated in pregnancy because of the potential harm of ionizing radiation to the fetus. | Clear liquid diet for 24 hours. |
| **GI**<br>**Barium enema** (BE)<br>$$ | Double-contrast technique for evaluation of colonic mucosa in patients with suspected inflammatory bowel disease or neoplasm. Single-contrast technique for investigation of possible fistulous tracts, bowel obstruction, large palpable masses in the abdomen, and for examination of diverticulitis and for examination of debilitated patients. | Good mucosal evaluation. No sedation required. | Retained fecal material limits study. Requires patient cooperation. Marked diverticulosis precludes evaluation of possible neoplasm in that area. Evaluation of right colon occasionally incomplete or limited by reflux of barium across ileocecal valve and overlapping opacified small bowel. Use of barium delays subsequent colonoscopy and body CT. **Contraindications and risks:** Contraindicated in patients with toxic megacolon and immediately after full-thickness colonoscopic biopsy. | Colon cleansing with enemas, cathartic, and clear liquid diet (1 day in young patients, 2 days in older patients). Intravenous glucagon (which inhibits peristalsis) is given to distinguish colonic spasm from a mass lesion. |

| | | GASTROINTESTINAL | | | | |
|---|---|---|---|---|---|---|
| | | **Hypaque enema** | | **Esophageal reflux study** | | |

| Test | Indications | Advantages | Disadvantages/Contraindications | Preparation |
|---|---|---|---|---|
| GI<br><br>**Hypaque enema**<br><br>$$ | Water-soluble contrast for fluoroscopic evaluation of sigmoid or cecal volvulus, anastomotic leak or other perforation.<br>Differentiation of colonic versus small bowel obstruction.<br>Therapy for obstipation. | Water-soluble contrast medium is evacuated much faster than barium because it does not adhere to the mucosa. Therefore, Hypaque enema can be followed immediately by oral ingestion of barium for evaluation of possible distal small bowel obstruction. | Demonstrates only colonic morphologic features and not mucosal changes. **Contraindicated in patients with toxic megacolon. Hypertonic solution may lead to fluid imbalance in debilitated patients and children.** | Colonic cleansing is desirable but not always necessary. |
| GI<br><br>**Esophageal reflux study** (radionuclide)<br><br>$$ | Evaluation of heartburn, regurgitation, recurrent aspiration pneumonia. | Noninvasive and well tolerated.<br>More sensitive for reflux than fluoroscopy, endoscopy, and manometry; similar sensitivity to acid reflux test.<br>Permits quantitation of reflux.<br>Can also identify aspiration into the lung fields. | Incomplete emptying of esophagus may mimic reflux.<br>Abdominal binder—used to increase pressure in the lower esophagus—may not be tolerated in patients who have undergone recent abdominal surgery. **Contraindications and risks:** Contraindicated in pregnancy because of the potential harm of ionizing radiation to the fetus. | NPO for 4–6 hours. During test, patient must be able to consume 300 mL of liquid. |

| GASTROINTESTINAL | | | | |
|---|---|---|---|---|
| **Gastric emptying study** | | | | **GI bleeding scan** |
| GI<br><br>**Gastric emptying study** (radionuclide)<br><br>$$ | Evaluation of dumping syndrome, vagotomy, gastric outlet obstruction due to inflammatory or neoplastic disease, effects of drugs, and other causes of gastroparesis (eg, diabetes mellitus). | Gives functional information not available by other means. | Reporting of meaningful data requires adherence to standard protocol and establishment of normal values. **Contraindications and risks:** Contraindicated in pregnancy because of the potential harm of ionizing radiation to the fetus. | NPO for 4–6 hours. During test, patient must be able to eat a 300-g meal consisting of both liquids and solids. |
| GI<br><br>**GI bleeding scan** (labeled red cell or sulfur colloid scan, radionuclide)<br><br>$$–$$$ | Evaluation of upper or lower GI blood loss. | Noninvasive compared to angiography. Longer period of imaging possible, which aids in detection of intermittent bleeding. Both labeled red cells and sulfur colloid can detect bleeding rates as low as 0.05–0.10 mL/min (angiography requires rate of about 0.5 mL/min). Labeled red cell scan is more sensitive but less specific than sulfur colloid for detecting GI bleeding. | Bleeding must be active during time of imaging. **Sulfur colloid:** Imaging time limited to approximately 1 hour, whereas red cells can be imaged for up to 24 hours. Upper GI bleeding can be obscured by liver and spleen activity. **Labeled red cells:** Longer imaging time required because of higher background activity. Presence of free $TcO_4$ (poor labeling efficiency) can lead to gastric, kidney, and bladder activity that can be misinterpreted as sites of bleeding. **Contraindications and risks:** Contraindicated in pregnancy because of the potential harm of ionizing radiation to the fetus. | Sterile technique required during in vitro labeling of red cells. |

| | | GALLBLADDER | |
| | | Ultrasound | HIDA scan |
|---|---|---|---|
| **Test** | | GALL-BLADDER **Ultrasound (US)** $ | GALL-BLADDER **⁹⁹ᵐTc N-substituted iminodiacetic acid scan (dimethyliminodiacetic acid [IDA] scan)** $$ |
| **Indications** | | Demonstrates cholelithiasis (95% sensitive), gallbladder wall thickening, pericholecystic fluid, intra- and extrahepatic biliary dilatation. | Evaluation of suspected acute cholecystitis or common bile duct obstruction. Evaluation of bile leaks, biliary atresia, and biliary enteric bypass patency. |
| **Advantages** | | Noninvasive. No ionizing radiation. Can be portable. Imaging in all planes. Can guide fine-needle aspiration, percutaneous transhepatic cholangiography, and biliary drainage procedures. | Hepatobiliary function assessed. Rapid. Not dependent on intestinal absorption. Can be performed in patients with elevated serum bilirubin. No intravenous contrast used. |
| **Disadvantages/Contraindications** | | Technique very operator-dependent. Presence of barium obscures sound waves. Difficult in obese patients. **Contraindications and risks:** None. | Does not demonstrate the cause of obstruction (eg, tumor or gallstone). Not able to evaluate biliary excretion if hepatocellular function is severely impaired. May require up to 24 hours to distinguish acute from chronic cholecystitis. Sensitivity may be lower in acalculous cholecystitis. False-positive results can occur with hyperalimentation, prolonged fasting, and acute pancreatitis. **Contraindications and risks:** Contraindicated in pregnancy because of the potential harm of ionizing radiation to the fetus. |
| **Preparation** | | Preferably NPO for 6 hours to enhance visualization of gallbladder. | NPO for 4–6 hours. Some radiologists premedicate patients with cholecystokinin. |

| | GALLBLADDER | PANCREAS/BILIARY TREE |
|---|---|---|
| | **Oral cholecystogram** | **ERCP** |

| Study | Indications | Advantages | Disadvantages/Risks | Comments / Preparation |
|---|---|---|---|---|
| GALL-BLADDER **Oral cholecystogram** (OCG) $ | Fluoroscopic evaluation of suspected cholelithiasis when clinical symptoms are highly suggestive but the ultrasound is normal or equivocal. Can assess gallbladder function and possible chronic cholecystitis. | Wide availability. Complements ultrasound. | Test sensitivity depends on intestinal absorption and liver function. Nonvisualization of the gallbladder can be caused by other factors besides obstruction of the cystic duct (eg, Telepaque tablets not absorbed by the gut). Requires up to 24–48 hours to perform. Nausea, vomiting, diarrhea, or headache occurs in up to 50% of patients. Exposure to ionizing radiation. **Contraindications and risks:** Contraindicated in pregnancy because of the potential harm of ionizing radiation to the fetus. Cannot be performed in patients with elevated bilirubin (> 3 mg/dL). | Iopanoic acid (Telepaque) or tyropanoate sodium (Bilopaque) is taken orally the night before the exam. Test may be repeated in 24 hours for "double-dose" examination if gallbladder is not visualized initially. |
| PANCREAS/BILIARY TREE **Endoscopic retrograde cholangiopancreatography** (ERCP) $$ | Primary sclerosing cholangitis, AIDS-associated cholangitis, and cholangiocarcinomas. Demonstrates cause, location, and extent of extrahepatic biliary obstruction (eg, choledocholithiasis). Can diagnose chronic pancreatitis. | Avoids surgery. If stone is suspected, ERCP offers therapeutic potential (sphincterotomy and extraction of common bile duct stone). Finds gallstones in up to 14% of patients with symptoms but negative ultrasound and oral cholecystogram. | Requires endoscopy. May cause pancreatitis (1%), cholangitis (< 1%), peritonitis, hemorrhage (if sphincterotomy performed), and death (rare). **Contraindications and risks:** Relatively contraindicated in patients with concurrent or recent (< 6 weeks) acute pancreatitis or suspected pancreatic pseudocyst. Contraindicated in pregnancy because of the potential harm of ionizing radiation to the fetus. | NPO for 6 hours. Sedation required. Vital signs should be monitored by the nursing staff. |

| Test | Indications | Advantages | Disadvantages/Contraindications | Preparation |
|------|-------------|------------|----------------------------------|-------------|
| | | **LIVER** | | |
| | **Ultrasound** | | | **CT** |
| LIVER **Ultrasound (US)** $ | Differentiation of cystic vs solid intrahepatic lesions. Evaluation of intra- and extrahepatic biliary dilatation, primary and metastatic liver tumors, and ascites. Evaluation of patency of portal vein, hepatic arteries, and hepatic veins. | Noninvasive. No radiation. Can be portable. Imaging in all planes. Can guide fine-needle aspiration, percutaneous transhepatic cholangiography, and biliary drainage procedures. | Technique very operator-dependent. Presence of barium obscures sound waves. More difficult in obese patients. **Contraindications and risks:** None. | Preferably NPO for 6 hours. |
| LIVER **Computed tomography (CT)** $$$–$$$$ | Suspected metastatic or primary tumor, gallbladder carcinoma, biliary obstruction, abscess. | Excellent spatial resolution. Can direct percutaneous fine-needle aspiration biopsy. | Requires iodinated contrast material administered intravenously. | NPO for 4–6 hours. Recent creatinine determination. Administration of oral contrast material for opacification of stomach and small bowel. |

| | | | LIVER | |
|---|---|---|---|---|
| | | | **CTAP** | **MRI** |
| LIVER<br>**Computed tomographic arterial portography (CTAP)**<br>$$$$ | Assessment of number, location, and resectability of metastatic liver tumors. | Greatest sensitivity to number of liver lesions.<br>Best cross-sectional imaging for segmental localization of liver tumors. | Invasive, requiring percutaneous catheter placement in the superior mesenteric artery.<br>Patient must remain supine with leg extended for 6 hours following the procedure to protect the common femoral artery at the catheter entry site. | NPO for 4–6 hours.<br>Recent creatinine determination.<br>Requires some conscious sedation. |
| LIVER<br>**Magnetic resonance imaging (MRI)**<br>$$$$ | Suspected metastatic or primary tumor.<br>Differentiation of benign cavernous hemangioma from malignant tumor, hemochromatosis. | Requires no iodinated contrast material. | Subject to motion artifacts, particularly those of respiration.<br>Contraindicated in patients with cardiac pacemakers, intraocular metallic foreign bodies, intracranial aneurysm clips, cochlear implants, some artificial heart valves, and life support devices. | Screening CT of orbits if history suggests possible metallic foreign body in the eye.<br>Intramuscular glucagon is used to inhibit intestinal peristalsis. |

| | | | LIVER | | |
|---|---|---|---|---|---|
| | | | PTC | | |
| Test | Indications | Advantages | Disadvantages/Contraindications | Preparation |
| LIVER/ BILIARY TREE<br><br>Percutaneous transhepatic cholangiogram (PTC)<br><br>$$$ | Biliary obstruction. | Best exam to assess site and morphology of obstruction close to the hilum (as opposed to endoscopic retrograde cholangiopancreatography [ERCP], which is better for distal obstruction). Can characterize the nature of diffuse intrahepatic biliary disease such as primary sclerosing cholangitis. Provides guidance and access for percutaneous transhepatic biliary drainage (PTBD) and possible stent placement to treat obstruction. | Invasive; requires special training. Performed with conscious sedation. Ascites may present a contraindication. | NPO for 4–6 hours. Sterile technique, assessment of clotting parameters, correction of coagulopathy. Performed with conscious sedation. |

| | LIVER | | | LIVER/SPLEEN |
|---|---|---|---|---|
| | **Hepatic angiography** | | | **Liver, spleen scan** |
| **LIVER**<br>**Hepatic angiography**<br>$$$$ | Preoperative evaluation for liver transplantation, vascular malformations, trauma, Budd-Chiari syndrome, portal vein patency (when ultrasound equivocal) prior to transjugular intrahepatic portosystemic shunt (TIPS) procedure. In some cases, evaluation of hepatic neoplasm or transcatheter embolotherapy of hepatic malignancy. | Best assessment of hepatic arterial anatomy, which is highly variable. More accurate than ultrasound with respect to portal vein patency when the latter suggests occlusion. | Invasive. Patient must remain supine with leg extended for 6 hours following the procedure in order to protect the common femoral artery at the catheter entry site. **Contraindications and risks:** Allergy to iodinated contrast material may require corticosteroid and $H_1$ blocker or $H_2$ blocker premedication. Contraindicated in pregnancy because of the potential harm of ionizing radiation to the fetus. Contrast nephrotoxicity, especially with preexisting impaired renal function due to diabetes mellitus or multiple myeloma; however, any creatinine elevation following the procedure is usually reversible. | NPO for 4–6 hours. Good hydration to limit possible renal insult due to iodinated contrast material. Recent serum creatinine determination, assessment of clotting parameters, reversal of anticoagulation. Performed with conscious sedation. Requires cardiac, respiratory, blood pressure, and pulse oximetry monitoring. |
| **LIVER,**<br>**SPLEEN**<br>**Liver,**<br>**spleen scan**<br>(radionuclide)<br>$$ | Evaluation of metastatic or primary tumor, inflammatory process, palpable mass, organomegaly, elevated hepatic enzymes, alcoholic liver disease, and thrombocytopenia.<br>Assist in location of an accessory spleen or suspected subphrenic abscess. | Better sampling and more sensitive than ultrasound. May detect isodense lesions missed by CT. Reproducible means of following response to chemotherapy. | Diminished sensitivity for small lesions (less than 1.5–2 cm) and deep lesions. Single photon emission computed tomography (SPECT) increases sensitivity (can detect lesions of 1–1.5 cm). Nonspecific; unable to distinguish solid vs cystic or inflammatory vs neoplastic tissue. Lower sensitivity for diffuse hepatic tumors. **Contraindications and risks:** Caution in pregnancy advised because of the risk of ionizing radiation to the fetus. | None. |

| Test | Indications | Advantages | Disadvantages/Contraindications | Preparation | |
|---|---|---|---|---|---|
| PANCREAS<br><br>**Computed tomography** (CT)<br><br>$$$–$$$$ | Evaluation of biliary obstruction and possible adenocarcinoma.<br>Staging of pancreatic carcinoma.<br>Diagnosis and staging of acute pancreatitis. | Best means of imaging the pancreas.<br>Can guide fine-needle biopsy or placement of a drainage catheter.<br>Can identify early necrosis in pancreatitis. | Optimal imaging requires intravenous contrast and thin section imaging (5 mm contiguous cuts).<br>**Contraindications and risks:** Contraindicated in pregnancy because of the potential harm of ionizing radiation to the fetus. Use of intravenous contrast agents is associated with infrequent but substantial risks. | Preferably NPO for 4–6 hours.<br>Normal hydration.<br>Opacification of GI tract with Gastrografin.<br>Sedation of agitated patients.<br>Recent serum creatinine determination. | PANCREAS — CT |
| PANCREAS<br><br>**Ultrasound** (US)<br><br>$ | Identification of peripancreatic fluid collections, pseudocysts, and pancreatic ductal dilatation. | Noninvasive.<br>No radiation.<br>Can be portable.<br>Imaging in all planes.<br>Can guide fine-needle aspiration or placement of drainage catheter. | Pancreas may be obscured by overlying bowel gas.<br>Technique very operator-dependent.<br>Presence of barium obscures sound waves.<br>Less sensitive than CT.<br>**Contraindications and risks:** None. | Preferably NPO for 6 hours. | PANCREAS — Ultrasound |

| | | ADRENAL | GENITOURINARY |
| --- | --- | --- | --- |
| | | **MIBG scan** | **IVP** |

| Test | Indications | Comments | Contraindications and risks | Patient preparation |
| --- | --- | --- | --- | --- |
| **ADRENAL**<br>**MIBG (metaiodo-benzyl-guanidine)** (radio-nuclide)<br>$$$$ | Suspected pheochromocytoma when CT is negative or equivocal. | Test is useful for localization of pheochromocytomas (particularly extra-adrenal). | High radiation dose to adrenal gland. High cost and limited availability of MIBG. Delayed imaging (1–3 days) necessitates return of patient. **Contraindications and risks:** Contraindicated in pregnancy because of the risk of ionizing radiation to the fetus. Because of the relatively high dose of $^{131}I$, patients should be instructed about precautionary measures by nuclear medicine personnel. | Administration of Lugol's iodine solution (to block thyroid uptake) prior to and following administration of dose. |
| **GENITO-URINARY**<br>**Intravenous pyelogram (IVP)**<br>$$$ | Fluoroscopic evaluation of uroepithelial neoplasm, calculus, papillary necrosis, and medullary sponge kidney.<br>Screening for urinary system injury after trauma. | Best method for evaluating collecting system.<br>Can assess both renal morphology and function. | Suboptimal evaluation of the renal parenchyma.<br>Does not adequately evaluate cause of ureteral deviation.<br>**Contraindications and risks:** Caution in pregnancy is advised because of the risk of ionizing radiation to the fetus. Use of intravenous contrast agents is associated with infrequent but substantial risks (see p 241). | Adequate hydration.<br>Colonic cleansing is preferred but not essential.<br>Recent serum creatinine determination. |

| | GENITOURINARY | |
|---|---|---|
| | **Ultrasound** | **MRI** |

| Test | Indications | Advantages | Disadvantages/Contraindications | Preparation |
|---|---|---|---|---|
| GENITO-URINARY **Ultrasound (US)** $$ | Evaluation of renal morphology, hydronephrosis, size of prostate, and residual urine volume. Differentiation of cystic vs solid renal lesions. | Noninvasive. No radiation. Can be portable. Imaging in all planes. Can guide fine-needle aspiration or placement of drainage catheter. | Technique very operator-dependent. More difficult in obese patients. **Contraindications and risks:** None. | Preferably NPO for 6 hours. Full urinary bladder required for pelvic studies. |
| GENITO-URINARY **Magnetic resonance imaging (MRI)** $$$$ | Staging of cancers of the uterus, cervix, and prostate. Can provide additional information in difficult CT cases of cancer of the kidney and urinary bladder. | Provides exquisite spatial resolution, multiplanar capability. No beam-hardening artifacts such as can be seen with CT. No ionizing radiation. | Subject to motion artifacts. Gastrointestinal opacification not yet readily available. **Contraindications and risks:** Contraindicated in patients with cardiac pacemakers, intraocular metallic foreign bodies, intracranial aneurysm clips, cochlear implants, some artificial heart valves, and life support devices. | Sedation of agitated patients. Screening CT of the orbits if history suggests possible metallic foreign body in the eye. |

| | GENITOURINARY | | PELVIS |
|---|---|---|---|
| | Radionuclide scan | | Ultrasound |
| GENITO-URINARY **Renal scan** (radionuclide) $$ | Evaluation of renal blood flow and function in acute or chronic renal failure. Evaluation of both medical and surgical complications of renal transplant. Estimation of glomerular filtration rate (GFR) and effective renal plasma flow (ERPF). Determination of relative renal function prior to nephrectomy. Parenchymal agents useful in assessment of obstruction. Captopril used in suspected renovascular hypertension. | Provides functional information without risk of iodinated contrast used in IVP. Provides quantitative information not available by other means. | Finding of poor renal blood flow does not pinpoint an etiologic diagnosis. Limited utility when renal function is extremely poor. Estimation of glomerular filtration rate and renal plasma flow often is inaccurate. One- to 4-hour delayed images are necessary with parenchymal agents. Parenchymal agents are nonspecific and do not give information about solid vs cystic nature of lesions. **Contraindications and risks:** Caution in pregnancy because of the risk of ionizing radiation to the fetus. Relatively high radiation dose with $^{131}$I Hippuran, so that good hydration and frequent bladder emptying are advised. |
| PELVIS **Ultrasound** (US) $$ | Evaluation of palpable ovarian mass, enlarged uterus, vaginal bleeding, pelvic pain, possible ectopic pregnancy, and infertility. Monitoring of follicular development. Localization of intrauterine device. Evaluation of appendicitis, ascites. | Use of a vaginal probe enables very early detection of intrauterine pregnancy and ectopic pregnancy and does not require a full bladder. | Transabdominal scan has limited sensitivity for uterine or ovarian pathology. Vaginal probe has limited field of view and therefore may miss large masses outside the pelvis. **Contraindications and risks:** None. Distended bladder required (only in transabdominal examination). |

| | PELVIS | | | |
| | MRI | | | |
| Test | Indications | Advantages | Disadvantages/Contraindications | Preparation |
|---|---|---|---|---|
| **PELVIS**<br><br>**Magnetic resonance imaging** (MRI)<br><br>$$$$ | Evaluation of gynecologic malignancies, particularly endometrial, cervical, and vaginal carcinoma. Evaluation of prostate, bladder, and rectal carcinoma. Evaluation of congenital anomalies of the genitourinary tract. Useful in distinguishing lymphadenopathy from vasculature. | Provides exquisite spatial resolution, multiplanar capability. No beam-hardening artifacts such as can be seen with CT. No ionizing radiation. | Subject to motion artifacts. **Contraindications and risks:** Contraindicated in patients with cardiac pacemakers, intraocular metallic foreign bodies, intracranial aneurysm clips, cochlear implants, some artificial heart valves, and life support devices. | Intramuscular glucagon is used to inhibit intestinal peristalsis. Air is used in some cases to distend the rectum. Sedation of agitated patients. Screening CT of orbits if history suggests possible metallic foreign body in the eye. |

| BONE | | | | |
| --- | --- | --- | --- | --- |
| **Bone scan** | | | | |
| BONE<br><br>**Bone scan, whole body** (radionuclide)<br><br>$$–$$$ | Evaluation of primary or metastatic neoplasm, osteomyelitis, arthritis, metabolic disorders, trauma, avascular necrosis, joint prosthesis, and reflex sympathetic dystrophy. | Can examine entire osseous skeleton or specific area of interest.<br>Highly sensitive compared with plain film radiography for detection of bone neoplasm.<br>In osteomyelitis, bone scan may be positive much earlier (24 hours) than plain film (10–14 days). | Nonspecific. Correlation with plain film radiographs often necessary.<br>Limited utility in patients with poor renal function.<br>Poor resolution in distal extremities, head, and spine; in these instances, single photon emission computed tomography (SPECT) is often useful.<br>Sometimes difficult to distinguish osteomyelitis from cellulitis or septic joint; dual imaging with gallium or with indium-labeled leukocytes can be helpful.<br>False-negative results for osteomyelitis can occur following antibiotic therapy and within the first 24 hours after trauma.<br>In avascular necrosis, bone scan may be hot, cold, or normal, depending on the stage.<br>**Contraindications and risks:** Caution in pregnancy because of the risk of ionizing radiation to the fetus. | None. |

| Test | Indications | Advantages | Disadvantages/Contraindications | Preparation |
|------|-------------|-----------|--------------------------------|-------------|
| **SPINE** | | | | |
| **SPINE** **Computed tomography (CT)** $$$ | Evaluation of structures that are not well visualized on MRI, including ossification of the posterior longitudinal ligament, tumoral calcification, osteophytic spurring, retropulsed bone fragments after trauma. Also used for patients in whom MRI is contraindicated. | Rapid. Superb spatial resolution. Can guide percutaneous fine-needle aspiration of possible tumor or abscess. | Generally limited to transaxial views. MRI unequivocally superior in evaluation of the spine and cord except for conditions mentioned in Indications. Artifacts from metal prostheses degrade images. **Contraindications and risks:** Contraindicated in pregnancy because of the potential harm of ionizing radiation to the fetus. Use of contrast agents for CT myelography is associated with infrequent but substantial risks (see p 241). | Normal hydration. Sedation of agitated patients. |
| **SPINE** **Magnetic resonance imaging (MRI)** $$$$ | Diseases involving the spine and cord except where CT is superior (ossification of the posterior longitudinal ligament, tumoral calcification, osteophytic spurring, retropulsed bone fragments after trauma). | Provides exquisite spatial resolution, multiplanar capability. No beam-hardening artifacts such as can be seen with CT. No ionizing radiation. | Less useful in detection of calcification, small spinal vascular malformations, acute spinal trauma (because of longer acquisition time, incompatibility with life support devices, and inferior detection of bony injury). Subject to motion artifacts. **Contraindications and risks:** Contraindicated in patients with cardiac pacemakers, intraocular metallic foreign bodies, intracranial aneurysm clips, cochlear implants, some artificial heart valves, and life support devices. | Sedation of agitated patients. Screening CT of orbits if history suggests possible metallic foreign body in the eye. |

| MUSCULOSKELETAL | | | | VASCULATURE |
| --- | --- | --- | --- | --- |
| MRI | | | | Ultrasound |
| MUSCULO-SKELETAL SYSTEM  **Magnetic resonance imaging (MRI)**  $$$$ | Evaluation of joints except where a prosthesis is in place. Extent of primary or malignant tumor (bone and soft tissue). Evaluation of aseptic necrosis, bone and soft tissue infections, marrow space disease, and traumatic derangements. | Provides exquisite spatial resolution. multiplanar capability. No beam-hardening artifacts such as can be seen with CT. No ionizing radiation. | Subject to motion artifacts. Less able than CT to detect calcification, ossification, and periosteal reaction. **Contraindications and risks:** Contraindicated in patients with cardiac pacemakers, intraocular metallic foreign bodies, intracranial aneurysm clips, cochlear implants, some artificial heart valves, and life support devices. | Sedation of agitated patients. Screening CT of the orbits if history suggests possible metallic foreign body in the eye. |
| VASCULA-TURE  **Ultrasound (US)**  $$ | Evaluation of deep venous thrombosis, extremity grafts, patency of inferior vena cava, portal vein, and hepatic veins. Carotid doppler indicated for symptomatic carotid bruit, atypical transient ischemic attack, monitoring after endarterectomy, and baseline prior to major vascular surgery. Surveillance of transjugular intrahepatic portosystemic shunt (TIPS) patency and flow. | Noninvasive. No radiation. Can be portable. Imaging in all planes. | Technique operator-dependent. Ultrasound not sensitive to detection of ulcerated plaque. May be difficult to diagnose tight stenosis vs occlusion. May be difficult to distinguish acute from chronic deep venous thrombosis. **Contraindications and risks:** None. | None. |

| | | AORTA |
|---|---|---|
| | | Angiography |

| Test | Indications | Advantages | Disadvantages/Contraindications | Preparation |
|---|---|---|---|---|
| AORTA AND ITS BRANCHES **Angiography** $$$ | Peripheral vascular disease, abdominal aortic aneurysm, renal artery stenosis (atherosclerotic and fibromuscular disease), polyarteritis nodosa, visceral ischemia, thoracic aortic dissection, gastrointestinal hemorrhage, thromboangiitis obliterans (Buerger's disease), popliteal entrapment syndrome, cystic adventitial disease, abdominal tumors, arteriovenous malformations, abdominal trauma. Preoperative evaluation for aortofemoral bypass reconstructive surgery. Postoperative assessment of possible graft stenosis, especially femoral to popliteal or femoral to distal (foot or ankle). | Can localize atherosclerotic stenosis and assess the severity by morphology, flow, and pressure gradient. Provides assessment of and access for percutaneous transluminal balloon dilation of stenotic lesions as well as possible stent treatment of iliac stenoses. Provides access for thrombolytic therapy of acute or subacute occlusion of native artery or bypass graft. | Invasive. Patient must remain supine with leg extended for 6 hours following the procedure in order to protect the common femoral artery at the catheter entry site. **Contraindications and risks:** Allergy to iodinated contrast material may require corticosteroid and H₁ blocker or H₂ blocker premedication. Contraindicated in pregnancy because of the potential harm of ionizing radiation to the fetus. Contrast nephrotoxicity, especially with preexisting impaired renal function due to diabetes mellitus or multiple myeloma; however, any creatinine elevation that occurs after the procedure is usually reversible. | NPO for 4–6 hours. Good hydration to limit possible renal insult due to iodinated contrast material. Recent serum creatinine determination, assessment of clotting parameters, reversal of anticoagulation. Performed with conscious sedation. Requires cardiac, respiratory, blood pressure, and pulse oximetry monitoring as well as noninvasive studies of peripheral vascular disease to verify indication for angiography and to guide the examination. |

| BLOOD | | | |
|---|---|---|---|
| | | **Indium scan** | |
| BLOOD<br><br>**Leukocyte scan** (indium scan, radionuclide)<br><br>$$$–$$$$ | Evaluation of fever of unknown origin, suspected abscess, pyelonephritis, and osteomyelitis. | Highly specific (98%) for infection (in contrast to gallium). Highly sensitive in detecting abdominal source of infection. In patients with fever of unknown origin, total body imaging is advantageous compared with CT scan or ultrasound. Preliminary imaging as early as 4 hours is possible but less sensitive (30–50% of abscesses are detected at 24 hours). | 24-hour delayed imaging may limit its utility in critically ill patients. False-negative scans occur with antibiotic administration or in chronic infection. Perihepatic or splenic infection can be missed because of normal leukocyte accumulation in these organs; liver and spleen scan is necessary adjunct in this situation. False-positive scans occur with swallowed leukocytes, bleeding, indwelling tubes and catheters, surgical skin wound uptake, and bowel activity due to inflammatory processes. Pulmonary uptake is nonspecific and has low predictive value for infection. Patients must be able to hold still during relatively long acquisition times (5–10 minutes). **Contraindications and risks:** Contraindicated in pregnancy because of the hazard of ionizing radiation to the fetus. High radiation dose to spleen. | Leukocytes from the patient are harvested, labeled in vitro, and then reinjected; process requires 1–2 hours. Scanning takes place 24 hours later. Homologous donor leukocytes should be used in neutropenic patients. |

# 7

# Basic Electrocardiography*

*Stuart J. Hutchison, MD, FRCP(C),*
*Tony M. Chou, MD, and G. Thomas Evans Jr., MD*

## HOW TO USE THIS SECTION

This chapter presents information about the interpretation of the basic 12-lead electrocardiogram (ECG). It is intended to be used as a reference and assumes a basic understanding of the PQRST complex. The authors' goal is to provide a condensed database from which useful interpretation of the ECG can be drawn or extrapolated. Included are sections discussing the following:

Rate and Rhythm

Conduction

Axis

P wave, PR interval

QRS complex

S–T–U complex and QT interval

Myocardial ischemia and infarction

Ventricular hypertrophy

Miscellaneous disease patterns

Arrhythmia differentials and algorithms

## RATES AND BASIC RHYTHMS

Rhythm = "three or more of anything in a row."

### Sinus Rhythms (usually upright P waves in leads I, II, aVF)

Normal sinus rhythm (60–100/min)

Sinus bradycardia (< 60/min)

*Adapted from Evans GT Jr: *ECG Interpretation Crib Sheets.* Ring Mountain Press, 232 Granada Drive, Corte Madera, CA 94925.

Sinus tachycardia (> 100/min)

Sinus arrhythmia (> 10% variation in P–P interval)

## Atrial Rhythms

Ectopic atrial rhythm (single, nonsinus P wave shape; atrial rate < 101/min)

Multiform atrial rhythm (≥ two P wave shapes; atrial rate < 101/min)

Atrial tachycardia (nonsinus P waves; atrial rate > 100/min)

Multifocal atrial tachycardia (MAT) (three or more different P waves; ventricular rate > 100/min)

Atrial fibrillation (variable atrial morphology; atrial rate ≥ 350/min)

Atrial flutter (identical repetitive atrial waveforms; atrial rate 300 ± 50/min)

## Premature Complexes

Premature atrial complexes (PACs) (either conducted or nonconducted)

Premature junctional complexes (PJCs)

Premature ventricular complexes (PVCs)

## Atrioventricular (AV) Dissociation

May be complete or incomplete (presence of capture or fusion complexes). There are four major causes:

1. Slowing of the primary pacemaker, eg, sinus bradycardia with junctional escape rhythm (JER)
2. Speeding of a subsidiary pacemaker, eg, ventricular or junctional tachycardia (JT)
3. Third-degree AV block
4. Combinations of the first two (ie, some sinus slowing with accelerated JER or JT)

## Paroxysmal Supraventricular Tachycardia (PSVT)

1. **Atrioventricular reentry tachycardia (AVRT):** Inverted P separate from QRS in the ST segment, or short R–P tachycardia, also known as orthodromic reciprocating tachycardia (ORT)

## Incomplete RBBB

**Criteria:** QRS: 0.10–0.12 s, with otherwise typical features of RBBB

## Incomplete LBBB

**Criteria:** QRS: 0.10–0.12 s, with otherwise typical features of LBBB

## Monofascicular Blocks

1. **Left Anterior Fascicular (or Hemi-) Block (LAFB or LAHB):**
   a. **Criteria**:
      Exclude other causes of left axis deviation (LAD) (see below)
      QRS axis: −45° to +90°; width: < 0.12 s
      aVL and I: 0.02 s Q waves
      II, III, aVF: 0.02 s R waves, deep S waves, S > R in II
   b. **Causes:** Nearly always indicates organic disease of the left ventricle.
2. **Left Posterior Fascicular (or Hemi-) Block (LPFB or LPHB):** Much less frequent than LAFB. Often associated with RBBB, inferior myocardial infarction (MI).
   a. **Criteria:**
      Exclude other causes of right axis deviation (RAD); see below
      QRS axis: 90° to 120°; width: < 0.12 s
      aVL and I: 0.02 s R waves, prominent S waves
      II, III, aVF: 0.02 s Q waves, tall R waves
   b. **Causes:** Usually indicates organic disease of the left ventricle.

## Wolff-Parkinson-White Syndrome

Classically, this form of preexcitation is described as an absent PR segment with initial slurring of the QRS segment ("delta wave") in any lead. Deformation of the QRS provides a delta wave "axis" that may help localize the anatomic site of the accessory pathway.

2. **Atrioventricular nodal reentry tachycardia (AVNRT):** P hidden in QRS or distorting the end of the QRST complex.

## Atrioventricular Block (AV Block)

**Differential diagnosis:** Ischemia, infarction, degeneration, medications

1. **First-degree (1°):** PR prolongation (PR ≥ 0.21 s) with all P waves followed by QRST
2. **Second-degree (2°):** Nonconducted QRST with on-time P waves
   a. **Mobitz type I (Wenckebach):**
      hjkhjk
      A pause follows progressively shorter R–R intervals.
      The first R–R interval following the pause is longer than the one before it.
      The length of the pause is shorter than any two consecutive short R–R intervals.
   b. **Mobitz type II:** Intermittent blocked P wave with constant PR intervals.
      2:1 AV block:
         May be seen with type 1 or type 2 block, or by itself.
         Constant PR intervals, with every second P wave dropped.
   c. **High-grade (advanced):**
      Two or more successive P waves are blocked.
      The atrial rate exceeds the ventricular rate.
3. **Third-degree (3°):** Complete AV dissociation.
   a. Complete dissociation of the P waves and QRST complexes.
   b. The atrial rate exceeds the ventricular rate.

## Other Categories Not Listed Above

| Classification | Junctional | Ventricular |
|---|---|---|
| Escape | 40–60 bpm* | 25–40 bpm |
| Accelerated | 61–100 bpm | 41–100 bpm |
| Tachycardia | > 100 bpm | > 100 bpm |

*bpm = beats per minute

# CONDUCTION

## Sinoatrial Block

Commonly secondary to digitalis, hyperkalemia, class 1a antiarrhythmics.

1. **First-degree:** Not ordinarily discernible.
2. **Second-degree Mobitz type 1 (Wenckebach):**
   P–P intervals before a pause shorten.
   P–P interval following a pause is shorter than the P–P following it.
   The duration of the pause is less than the sum of any two consecutive short cycles.
3. **Second-degree Mobitz type 2:**
   The pause equals two or more cycles.
   During pauses, there are either escape beats or no P or QRST complexes.
4. **Third-degree:** Atrial standstill.

## Intraventricular Block and Bundle Branch Blocks

Defined as prolonged QRS duration of most common QRS complex (adult normal range 70–113 ms).

### Right Bundle Branch Block (RBBB)

1. **Criteria:**
   QRS $\geq 0.12$ s in the limb leads
   Right precordial leads:
   QRS: wide RSR′ (90%), notched R (10%)
   ST segment: depressed
   T wave: inverted
   Left precordial leads and lead I:
   QRS: wide, with wide slurred S wave
   ST segment: normal
   T wave: upright
2. **Causes:** Usually associated with organic heart disease. Sometimes seen in healthy individuals.

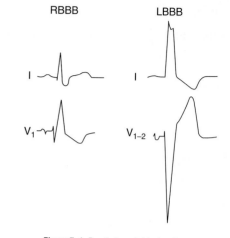

**Figure 7–1.** Bundle branch block patterns.

### Left Bundle Branch Block (LBBB)

1. **Criteria:**
   QRS $\geq 0.12$ s in the limb leads
   Right and midprecordial leads:
   QRS: rS (wide S) (67%), or wide QS (33%)
   ST segment: elevated
   T wave: upright
   Left precordial leads and lead I:
   QRS: wide, notched or slurred R or RsR′; Q waves unusual
   ST segment: depressed
   T wave: inverted
2. **Causes:** Almost always associated with organic heart disease. Rarely seen in healthy individuals.

### Nonspecific Intraventricular Conduction Delay (IVCD)

**Criteria:** QRS $\geq 0.12$ s in the limb leads without the typical tures of BBBs

Absent PR segment
and initial slurring of
the QRS in any lead

Posteroseptal
accessory
pathway

Left ventricular
free wall accessory
pathway

**Figure 7–2.** Wolff-Parkinson-White (WPW) patterns. Example complex on the left displays absent PR segment and initial slurring or "delta wave" in early QRS complex. Preexcitation patterns typically seen with posteroseptal and left ventricular free wall pathways are shown at right.

## AXIS

### Normal Axis in Adults –30° to +90°

The term "axis" refers to the spatial orientation of an electrical vector. Since the major electrical forces of the heart are ventricular, the major electrical vector is the QRS; therefore, when "axis" is unspecified, the vector referred to is the (frontal plane) QRS. The P wave and the T wave also have normal and abnormal axes, but these are rarely discussed. In adults, the range of normal of the QRS axis (which is calculated with the first 0.06 s of the QRS only) is –30° to +90°. Deviations outside this range indicate structural or conduction disease of the heart.

Axis is derived from vertical plane standard limb leads and augmented limb leads—the hexaxial reference system; see Figures 7–3 and 7–4. The direction of the axis is depicted by the direction of the largest positive vectors.

### Four Main Causes of Left Axis Deviation

1. Left anterior fascicular block
2. Inferior MI (q wave ≥ 0.03 s in aVF)
3. Ventricular preexcitation (posteroseptal accessory pathway)
4. COPD (uncommon; 10%)

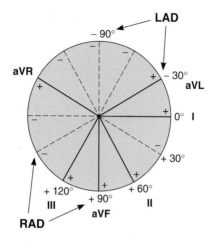

**Figure 7–3.** Axis determination. Frontal plane hexaxial reference system.

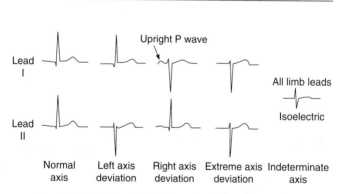

**Figure 7–4.** Axis deviation. Examples of axis deviation based on leads I and II.

## Four Main Causes of Right Axis Deviation

1. Right ventricular hypertrophy is the most common cause; however, one must first exclude inferior or posterior MI and acute inferior injury with LPFB in addition to the next two entities.
2. Anterolateral MI, extensive (QS or Qr in I or aVL or both)
3. Ventricular preexcitation (freewall accessory pathway)
4. Left posterior fascicular block

## P WAVE AND PR INTERVAL

### P Wave

The P wave represents atrial depolarization.

1. **Normal:**
   Positive in leads I, II, aVF
   Amplitude: 0.5–2.5 mm (largest in lead I or II)
2. **Causes of negative P waves in lead I:**
   Right-left reversal of arm leads
   Dextrocardia
   Left atrial rhythm; other causes

## Atrial "Abnormality" or "Enlargement"

Increased voltage or duration of a P wave usually indicates atrial abnormality. The term "abnormality" is less specific, therefore less apt to give rise to error, and is preferable to "hypertrophy" or "enlargement," both of which denote very specific states.

1. **Left Atrial Abnormality (LAA):**
   a. **Criteria:** Increased P terminal forces (lead V1), wide notching (lead II)
   b. **Causes:**
      Mitral disease, LVH, coronary artery disease (CAD)
      May be seen with right atrial enlargement, chronic obstructive pulmonary disease (COPD)

2. **Right Atrial Abnormality (RAA):**
   a. **Criteria:** Increased P initial forces (lead V1) tall and peaked (lead II)
   b. **Causes:**
      Right atrial enlargement (RAE), COPD
      Increased sympathetic tone

## PR Interval

The PR interval is the time required for the electrical wavefront to pass from the SA node to the ventricles. The normal range is 0.12–0.21 s. A PR > 0.21 s is seen with a 1:1 AV ratio in first degree AV block.

## QRS COMPLEX

The QRS interval represents the period of ventricular depolarization.

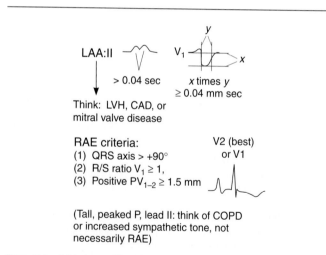

**Figure 7–5.** Atrial abnormalities. Examples of P wave morphologies seen in atrial abnormalities.

## Q Waves

Whether a Q wave is normal or abnormal depends largely on its size and to some extent on which lead it occurs in. Q waves > 0.04 s are often abnormal.

1. **Probably abnormal:**
   > 2 mm in leads I and II
   > 6 mm in lead III
   > 2 mm in lead aVF
   > 2 mm and > 25% of the R wave in lead aVF
   Any Q waves in leads $V_{1-3}$
   > 2 mm and > 15% of R wave height in leads $V_{4-6}$

2. **Causes:**
   Infarction
   Severe ischemia
   Dextrocardia or dextroversion
   Cor pulmonale, acute or chronic
   LVH, RVH
   Altered activation:
       LBBB
       Ventricular pacing
       Ventricular preexcitation
   Diffuse severe myocardial disease

## Low QRS Voltage

1. **Criteria:** < 5 mm in all three limb leads
2. **Causes:** Diffuse myocardial damage or disease

## R Wave Progression in the Precordial Leads

1. **Normal:** R wave height increases progressively from $V_1$ to $V_4$ or $V_5$.
2. **Causes of abnormal or "late" R wave progression:**
   LVH (most commonly)
   LAFB
   COPD

Anterior MI, especially loss of R wave height between $V_{1-2}$ and $V_{2-3}$

RVH, posterior MI, or WPW, especially if tall R in $V_1$ (as Rs or R wave)

## ST–T–U COMPLEX AND THE QT INTERVAL

These features of the ECG represent the period of ventricular repolarization.

## ST Segment Elevation or ST in the Same Direction as the QRS

**Causes:**

Normal variant (early repolarization)
Infarction with subepicardial injury
Pericarditis (stage 1), especially if widespread
Altered depolarization: LBBB
Altered depolarization: ventricular pacemaker
Left ventricular hypertrophy
Left ventricular aneurysm
Acute injury, infarction, or Prinzmetal's vasospasm
Hyperkalemia

## ST Segment Depression or ST Opposite to the QRS

**Causes:**

Ischemia
Infarction with subendocardial injury
Hypertrophy:
    LVH gives ST segments widely opposite to the QRS
    RVH gives ST segments opposite to the QRS in leads $V_{1-3}$
Altered conduction:
    LBBB gives ST segments widely opposite to the QRS
    RBBB
Metabolic abnormalities (electrolytes, catecholamines)
Drug effect, especially digitalis and antiarrhythmics
Subarachnoid hemorrhage (wide T wave with long QT)

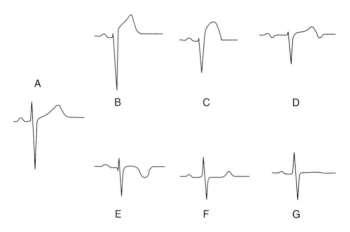

A. Normal ST segment (asymmetric sloping of ST)
B. Abnormal ST segment elevation or lack of normal upward concavity in the first part of the ST–T segment (as seen in LVH with acute ischemia)
C. ST–T segment typical of acute or recent myocardial infarction, ie, the ST–T segment is an upside-down, bowl-shaped, or "tombstone" waveform
D. Negative amplitudes in the latter part of the ST–T segment (may be seen in ischemia or old infarction)
E. Negative T wave (may be a nonspecific sign but may be seen in ischemia or old MI)
F. Downward sloping in the first part of the ST–T segment (may be seen with ischemia or drug or electrolyte effects)
G. Flat ST–T segment (a nonspecific sign)

**Figure 7–6.** ST morphologies. Examples of various contours of ST–T abnormalities in lead $V_2$. Figures adapted from Edenbrandt L, Devine B and MacFarlane PW: Classification of electrocardiographic ST-T segments. Eur Heart J 1993;14:464.

## QT Interval

The length of the QT interval is inversely related to the heart rate; hence, measure the QT interval (use $V_2$ or $V_3$) referenced to the preceding RR interval.

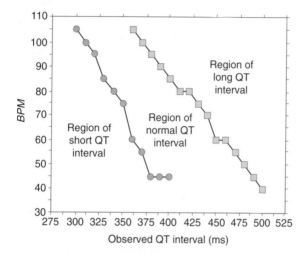

**Figure 7–7.** QT interval. Normal range of the QT interval as it varies with the heart rate. (Derived from data in MacFarlane and Veitch-Lawrie, using Hodges' correction.) Heart rate expressed in BPM = beats per minute.

## Prolonged QT

**Causes:**

Hypocalcemia or hypokalemia
Left ventricular enlargement
Myocardial infarction
Myocarditis
Diffuse myocardial disease
Intracranial hemorrhage
Drugs (class Ia and III antiarrhythmics)
Hypothermia
Familial
Conduction defect
Complete heart block

## Shortened QT Interval

Causes include hypercalcemia and digitalis toxicity.

## U Wave

When prominent, usually suggests digitalis toxicity or hypokalemia.

## ST–T Wave Abnormalities

See Figure 7–8.

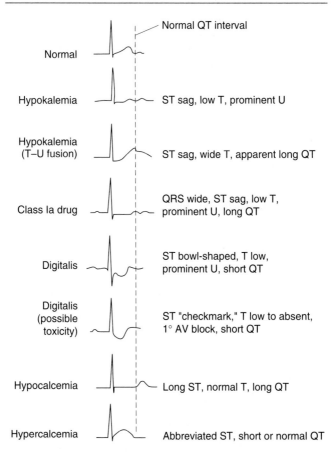

**Figure 7–8.** ST–T wave changes. Various classes of ST–T abnormalities as seen in lead $V_4$.

# MYOCARDIAL ISCHEMIA AND INFARCTION MANIFESTATIONS

## Myocardial Ischemia

May produce transient and variable abnormalities

1. **T wave changes** (accentuation, inversion, prolongation) are common
2. **ST changes** (depression ≥ 1 mm) are characteristic. The greater the ST depression, the more suggestive of ischemia.
   Up-sloping: the least specific
   Horizontal: more specific
   Down-sloping: the most specific, though least sensitive
3. **Q waves** are rarely produced by ischemia

## Acute Subendocardial Myocardial Infarction (MI) (Tables 7–1 and 7–2)

T waves changes: elevation, inversion
ST segment depression common, ≥ 1 mm in any two contiguous leads

## "Prior" or "Nonacute" or "Indeterminate-Age" Transmural MI (Table 7–3)

Q waves of pathologic size
ST isoelectric or elevated (if aneurysm)
T waves variable

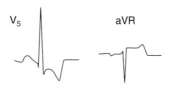

**Figure 7–9.** Ischemia. ST depression typical of ischemia or subendocardial infarction.

**TABLE 7–1. ACUTE TRANSMURAL MI. The characteristic ECG changes and their evolution.**

| Phase | Time | ST Segment | T Waves | R or Q Waves |
|---|---|---|---|---|
| Initial | First several hours | Elevated | Accentuated | Not yet |
| Early | First day | Elevated | Inverting | Q waves form |
| Mid | First days | Elevated or normalizing | Inverted | Q waves formed |
| Late | After first days | Elevated or normal | Variable | Q waves persist Loss of R waves persists |

**TABLE 7–2. ACUTE TRANSMURAL MI. The characteristic ECG changes and their location.**

| Territory | Artery Usually Responsible | ST Elevation in Contiguous Leads | Amount of ST Elevation |
|---|---|---|---|
| Anterior | LAD, diagonal, proximal marginal | Two leads of $V_{1-4}$ | 2 mm |
| Apical Inferior | PDA Origin: RCA 90%, LCx 10% | Two of: II, III, aVF | 2 mm 1 mm |
| Lateral High lateral | LCx LCx, distal RCA | $V_{5-6}$ I, aVL | 2 mm 2 mm |
| Posterior | RCA or LCx | ST depression in $V_1$, $V_2$ | 2 mm |
| Right ventricular | Acute marginal branch of RCA | $V_4R$ | 1 mm |

**KEY:** LAD = left anterior descending coronary artery; PDA = posterior descending coronary artery; RCA = right coronary artery; LCx = left circumflex coronary artery.

**TABLE 7–3. ACUTE TRANSMURAL MI LOCALIZATION.**

| Territory | ECG Lead | ECG Criteria[1] |
|---|---|---|
| Anterior | $V_2$ | Any Q, or $R \leq 1$ mm and $> 10$ ms, or R in $V_2 \geq$ R in $V_1$ |
| | $V_3$ | Any Q, or $R \leq 2$ mm and $> 20$ ms |
| Apical | $V_5$ | $Q \geq 30$ ms or $Q \geq \frac{1}{2}$ R height |
| | $V_6$ | $Q \geq 30$ ms or $Q \geq \frac{1}{3}$ R height |
| High lateral | I, aVL | Either I or aVL: $Q \geq$ ms |
| Inferior | II, III, aVF | II or aVF: $Q \geq 30$ ms III: Q depth $> \frac{1}{3}$ R height |
| Posterior | $V_1$ $V_2$ | $R \geq 40$ ms or $\geq 6$ mm $R \geq 50$ ms or $\geq 15$ mm |

[1] In the absence of LVH, LAFB, LBBB, RBBB, RVH, COPD, W-P-W, the criteria listed are $\geq 93\%$ specific.

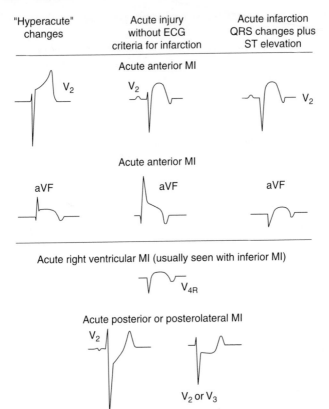

| "Hyperacute" changes | Acute injury without ECG criteria for infarction | Acute infarction QRS changes plus ST elevation |
|---|---|---|

Acute anterior MI

Acute anterior MI

Acute right ventricular MI (usually seen with inferior MI)

Acute posterior or posterolateral MI

**Figure 7–10.** Patterns with acute myocardial infarction.

## Factors That May Affect the Ability of the ECG to Diagnose MI

1. Is normal interventricular conduction present without ECG changes of emphysema, COPD, RVH or LVH? Use criteria as stated above.

2. **LVH:** The presence of LVH leads to false-positive diagnoses of infarction:

For anterior MI in presence of LVH: qrS in $V_{1-3}$, or R $\leq$ 1 mm in $V_3$

3. **LAFB (with QRS duration of $\geq$ 100 ms):** Small anterior infarcts may be overestimated (LPFB does not affect the accuracy).

4. **RVH:** Standard criteria for diagnosing posterior MI (leads $V_1$ and $V_2$), and for anterior or apical MI (using R/S ratio criteria leads $V_{4-6}$) may give false-positive results.

5. **RBBB (complete):** Gives false-positive diagnosis of posterior MI (leads $V_1$ and $V_2$).

6. **LBBB (complete):** With QRS duration $\geq$ 140 ms standard criteria for diagnosis of MI are invalid.

## VENTRICULAR HYPERTROPHY

### Left Ventricular Hypertrophy

**Criteria** (for adults)

(Suggested order of use. All criteria have $\geq$ 93% specificity.)

R in aVL > 11 mm

R in aVL plus S in $V_3$ > 20 mm (female), > 28 mm (male)

R in aVL plus S in $V_3$ (+8 for female) times QRS duration > 2436

R in I plus S in III > 25 mm

$V_1$ plus R in $V_{5-6}$ > 35 mm (age > 35)

Romhilt-Estes score > 5 points (LAA and ST segments of "strain," patient not taking digoxin)

R in $V_6$ > R in $V_5$ (occurs in the setting of a dilated LV)

I, aVL, $V_{5-6}$

**Figure 7–11.** Electrocardiographic changes seen with LVH.

## Right Ventricular Hypertrophy

> **Criteria** (for adults) With or without associated ST–T
> abnormalities
>> (First, exclude inferior MI, acute inferior injury with LPFB,
>> anterolateral MI, or WPW pattern. Then, any of the follow-
>> ing criteria has 97% specificity.)
>>
>> Right axis deviation (> 90°)
>>
>> An R/S ratio ≥ 1 in lead $V_1$ (absent posterior MI or RBBB)
>>
>> An R wave > 7 mm tall in $V_1$ (not R′ of RBBB)
>>
>> An rsR′ complex in $V_1$, with a QRS duration of < 0.12 s
>> (incomplete RBBB)
>>
>> An S wave > 7 mm deep in leads $V_5$ or $V_6$ (in the absence of
>> left axis deviation)
>>
>> RBBB with either RAD (first 0.06 s of the QRS) or an R/S ratio
>> < 2 in lead I

## Low QRS Voltage

Usually suggests lung disease.

> **Criteria:**
>> < 5 mm peak-to-peak in all limb leads, or
>>
>> < 10 mm in precordial leads

# MISCELLANEOUS DISEASE PATTERNS

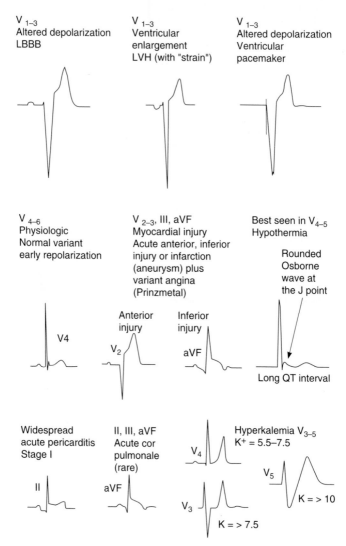

V 1–3
Altered depolarization
LBBB

V 1–3
Ventricular
enlargement
LVH (with "strain")

V 1–3
Altered depolarization
Ventricular
pacemaker

V 4–6
Physiologic
Normal variant
early repolarization

V 2–3, III, aVF
Myocardial injury
Acute anterior, inferior
injury or infarction
(aneurysm) plus
variant angina
(Prinzmetal)

Best seen in V 4–5
Hypothermia

Rounded
Osborne
wave at
the J point

V4

Anterior
injury

V₂

Inferior
injury

aVF

Long QT interval

Widespread
acute pericarditis
Stage I

II

II, III, aVF
Acute cor
pulmonale
(rare)

aVF

V₄

V₃

K = > 7.5

Hyperkalemia V 3–5
K⁺ = 5.5–7.5

V₅

K = > 10

**Figure 7–12.** Major causes of ST segment elevation.

$V_{1-3}$
Altered depolarization
RBBB

$V_{1-3}$
Ventricular
enlargement
RVH

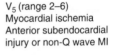

$V_{4-6}$
Altered depolarization
LBBB

$V_{4-6}$
Ventricular
enlargement
LVH (with "strain")

$V_{2-5}$
Subarachnoid
hemorrhage

II, III, aVF
Myocardial
ischemia
Inferior
subendocardial
injury

$V_{1-3}$
Myocardial
ischemia
Posterior
subepicardial
injury

$V_5$ (range 2–6)
Myocardial ischemia
Anterior subendocardial
injury or non-Q wave MI

All leads,
including $V_{1-3}$
Hypokalemia

$K = \leq 2.8$

I, L, $V_{4-6}$
Digitalis

I, L, II, F, $V_{4-6}$
Class Ia
Antiarrhythmics

Widespread
J point depression
2° to catecholamines

Baseline is
T–P segment

**Figure 7–13.** Major causes of ST segment depression.

## ARRHYTHMIA DIFFERENTIALS AND ALGORITHMS

## Tachycardias: Narrow, Irregular

### Causes:

Sinus tachycardia with extra beats: PACs, PJCs, PVCs

Sinus tachycardia with dropped beats

Atrial fibrillation (the most common sustained abnormal cardiac rhythm)

Atrial flutter with irregular or variable conduction

Multifocal atrial tachycardia

## Tachycardias: Narrow, Regular

### Causes:

Sinus tachycardia

Atrial flutter with regular conduction (1:1, 2:1)

Atrial tachycardia

Junctional tachycardia

Orthodromic reciprocating tachycardia

## Tachycardias: Wide, Irregular

### Causes:

Atrial fibrillation with underlying BBB, IVCD

Atrial fibrillation with rate-related BBB or IVCD

Atrial fibrillation with ventricular preexcitation

## Tachycardias: Wide, Regular

### Causes:

Sinus tachycardia with underlying BBB, IVCD

Sinus tachycardia with rate-related BBB or IVCD

Sinus tachycardia with ventricular preexcitation

Antidromic reciprocating tachycardia

Ventricular tachycardia

Ventricular pacing at rate > 100/min

## Notes

The most common cause of a premature QRS initiating a pause is:

Narrow premature QRS: a PAC or PJC

Wide premature QRS: PVC or aberrantly conducted PAC (BBB, access pathway)

Grouped beating suggests

PVCs in a repetitive pattern: bigeminy, trigeminy, quadrigeminy

PACs or PJCs in a repetitive pattern: bigeminy, trigeminy, quadrigeminy

Nonconduction of P waves: 2° AV block Mobitz type 1 or type 2

## Arrhythmias With Accelerating-Decelerating Pattern

Sinus arrhythmia, usually

Sinoatrial exit block with Wenckebach pattern

Brugada criteria in the differential between ventricular tachycardia or supraventricular tachycardia when wide complex with regular rhythm is present. Sinus or atrial tachycardia with RBBB or LBBB should first be excluded by examining for P waves, usually best seen in $V_1$. In patients taking antiarrhythmic medications, QRS widening may be present, giving a false-positive diagnosis of ventricular tachycardia (criterion No. 2 below).

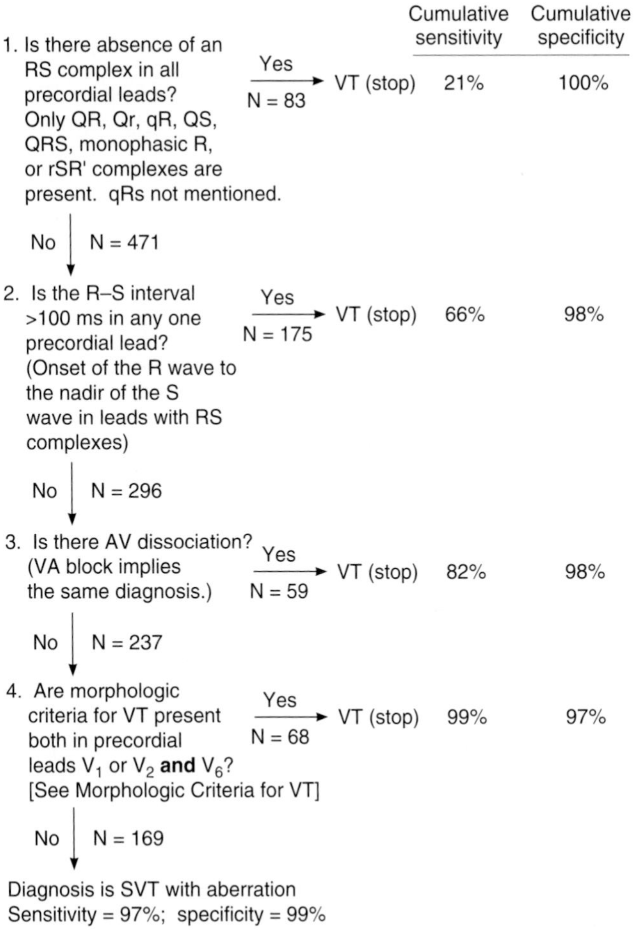

|  | Cumulative sensitivity | Cumulative specificity |
|---|---|---|

1. Is there absence of an RS complex in all precordial leads? Only QR, Qr, qR, QS, QRS, monophasic R, or rSR' complexes are present.  qRs not mentioned.

→ Yes  N = 83 → VT (stop)    21%    100%

No | N = 471

2. Is the R–S interval >100 ms in any one precordial lead? (Onset of the R wave to the nadir of the S wave in leads with RS complexes)

→ Yes  N = 175 → VT (stop)    66%    98%

No | N = 296

3. Is there AV dissociation? (VA block implies the same diagnosis.)

→ Yes  N = 59 → VT (stop)    82%    98%

No | N = 237

4. Are morphologic criteria for VT present both in precordial leads $V_1$ or $V_2$ **and** $V_6$? [See Morphologic Criteria for VT]

→ Yes  N = 68 → VT (stop)    99%    97%

No | N = 169

Diagnosis is SVT with aberration
Sensitivity = 97%;  specificity = 99%

**Figure 7–14.** Differentiation of wide complex tachycardia. Diagnosis of wide QRS complex tachycardia with regular rhythm (from Brugada P et al: A new approach to the differential diagnosis of a regular tachycardia with a wide QRS complex. Circulation 1991; 83:1649–1659). VT = ventricular tachycardia; SVT = supraventricular tachycardia.

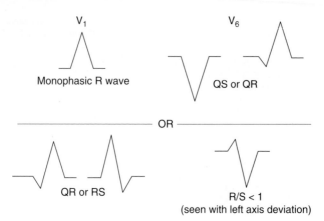

**Figure 7–15.** Morphologic criteria in differentiation of wide complex tachycardia with RBBB-type QRS (dominant positive in $V_1$). In leads $V_1$ and $V_6$, both criteria must be met to favor VT.

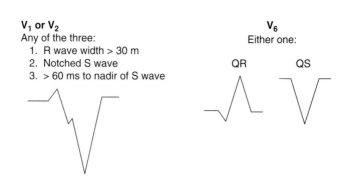

**Figure 7–16.** Morphologic criteria in differentiation of wide complex tachycardia with LBBB-type QRS (dominant negative in $V_1$). In leads $V_1$ and $V_6$, both criteria must both be met to favor VT.

# 8

# Diagnostic Testing: Algorithms, Nomograms, and Tables

*Stephen J. McPhee, MD, and Diana Nicoll, MD, PhD*

## HOW TO USE THIS SECTION

This section includes algorithms, nomograms, and tables, arranged alphabetically by subject, designed to be used in the selection and interpretation of appropriate laboratory tests.

A conventional algorithm layout is displayed below. Diagnostic tests are enclosed in ovals; diagnoses in italics; and treatment recommendations in rectangles.

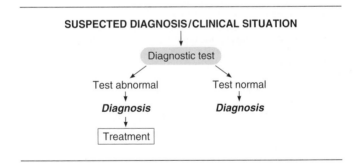

**SUSPECTED DIAGNOSIS/CLINICAL SITUATION**

Diagnostic test

Test abnormal
*Diagnosis*
Treatment

Test normal
*Diagnosis*

Abbreviations used throughout this section include the following:

**N** = normal
**Abn** = abnormal
**Pos** = positive
**Neg** = negative
**Occ** = occasional
↑ = increased or high
↓ = decreased or low

## *Contents*                                                        *Page*

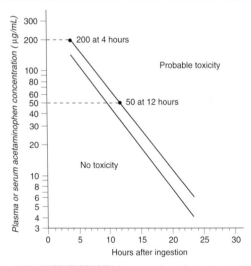

**Figure 8–1. ACETAMINOPHEN TOXICITY:** Nomogram for prediction of acetaminophen hepatotoxicity following acute overdosage. The upper line defines serum acetaminophen concentrations known to be associated with hepatotoxicity; the lower line defines serum levels 25% below those expected to cause hepatotoxicity. To give a margin for error, the lower line should be used as a guide to treatment. (Modified and reproduced, with permission, from Rumack BH, Matthew H: Acetaminophen poisoning and toxicity. Pediatrics 1975;55:871. Reproduced by permission of Pediatrics Vol 55 page 873, Copyright © 1975. Permission obtained also from Saunders CE, Ho MT [editors]: *Current Emergency Diagnosis & Treatment,* 4th ed. Appleton & Lange, 1992.)

**TABLE 8–1. ACID-BASE DISTURBANCES: LABORATORY CHARACTERISTICS OF PRIMARY SINGLE DISTURBANCES OF ACID-BASE BALANCE.[1]**

| Disturbance | Acute Primary Change | Arterial pH | [K⁺] (meq/L) | Anion Gap[2] (meq) | Clinical Features |
|---|---|---|---|---|---|
| Normal | None | 7.35–7.45 | 3.5–5.0 | 8–12 | None. |
| Respiratory acidosis | $P_{CO_2}$ retention | ↓ | ↑ | N | Dyspnea, polypnea, respiratory outflow obstruction, ↑ anterior-posterior chest diameter, musical rales, wheezes. In severe cases, stupor, disorientation, coma. |
| Respiratory alkalosis | $P_{CO_2}$ depletion | ↑ | → | N or ↓ | Anxiety, breathlessness, frequent sighing, lungs usually clear to examination, positive Chvostek and Trousseau signs. |
| Metabolic acidosis | $HCO_3^-$ depletion | ↓ | ↑ or ↓ | N or ↑ | Weakness, air hunger, Kussmaul respiration, dry skin and mucous membranes. In severe cases, poor skin turgor, coma, hypotension, death. |
| Metabolic alkalosis | $HCO_3^-$ retention | ↑ | → | N | Weakness, positive Chvostek and Trousseau signs, hyporeflexia. |

[1]Reproduced, with permission, from Harvey AM et al (editors): The Principles and Practice of Medicine, 22nd ed. Appleton & Lange, 1988.
[2]Anion gap = $[Na^+]-([HCO_3^-] + [Cl^-])$ = 8–12 meq normally.

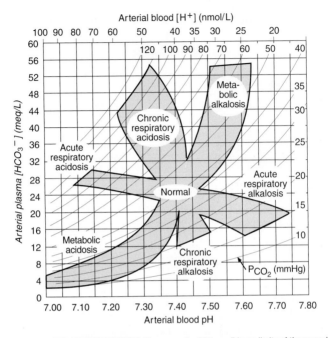

**Figure 8–2. ACID-BASE NOMOGRAM:** Shown are the 95% confidence limits of the normal respiratory and metabolic compensations for primary acid-base disturbances. (Reproduced, with permission, from Cogan MG (editor): *Fluid and Electrolytes: Physiology and Pathophysiology.* Appleton & Lange, 1991.)

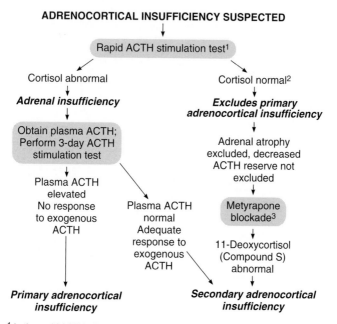

**ADRENOCORTICAL INSUFFICIENCY SUSPECTED**

<sub>1</sub> In the rapid ACTH stimulation test, a baseline cortisol sample is obtained; cosyntropin 0.25 mg is given IM or IV; and plasma cortisol samples are obtained 30 or 60 minutes later.

[2] The normal response is a cortisol increment > 7 μg/dL. If a cortisol level of > 18 μg/dL is obtained, the response is normal regardless of the increment.

[3] Metyrapone blockade is performed by giving 2.0–2.5 g metyrapone PO at 12 midnight. Draw cortisol and 11-deoxycortisol levels at 8 AM. 11-Deoxycortisol level < 7 μg/dL indicates secondary adrenal insufficiency (as long as there is adequate blockade of cortisol synthesis [cortisol level < 10 μg/dL]).

**Figure 8–3. ADRENOCORTICAL INSUFFICIENCY:** Laboratory evaluation of suspected adrenocortical insufficiency. **ACTH** = adrenocorticotropic hormone. (Modified, with permission, from Baxter JD, Tyrrell JB: The adrenal cortex. In: *Endocrinology and Metabolism,* 3rd ed. Felig P, Baxter JD, Frohman LA [editors]. McGraw-Hill, 1995; and from Harvey AM et al: *The Principles and Practice of Medicine,* 22nd ed. Appleton & Lange, 1988.)

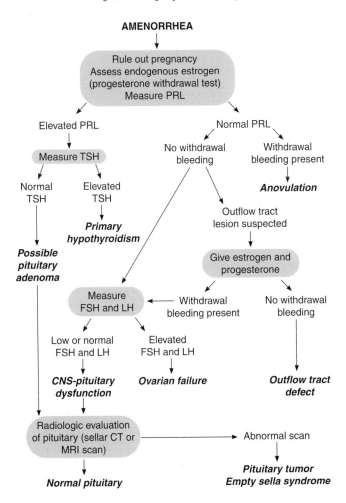

**Figure 8–4. AMENORRHEA:** Diagnostic evaluation of amenorrhea. **PRL** = prolactin; **FT₄I** = free thyroxine index; **TSH** = thyroid-stimulating hormone; **FSH** = follicle-stimulating hormone; **LH** = luteinizing hormone; **CT** = computed tomography; **MRI** = magnetic resonance imaging. (Modified, with permission, from Greenspan FS, Baxter JD [editors]: *Basic and Clinical Endocrinology*, 4th ed. Appleton & Lange, 1994.)

**TABLE 8-2. ANEMIA: DIAGNOSIS OF COMMON ANEMIAS BASED ON RED BLOOD CELL (RBC) INDICES.[1]**

| Type of Anemia | MCV (fL) | MCHC (g/dL) | Common Causes | Common Laboratory Abnormalities | Other Clinical Findings |
|---|---|---|---|---|---|
| Microcytic, hypochromic | < 80 | < 32 | Iron deficiency | Low reticulocyte count, low serum and bone marrow iron, high TIBC. | Mucositis, blood loss. |
| | | | Thalassemias | Reticulocytosis, abnormal red cell morphology, normal serum iron levels. | Asian, African, or Mediterranean descent. |
| | | | Chronic lead poisoning | Basophilic stippling of RBCs, elevated lead and free erythrocyte protoporphyrin levels. | Peripheral neuropathy, history of exposure to lead. |
| | | | Sideroblastic anemia | High serum iron, ringed sideroblasts in bone marrow. | Population of hypochromic RBCs on smear. |
| Normocytic, normochromic | 81–100 | 32–36 | Acute blood loss | Blood in stool. | Recent blood loss. |
| | | | Hemolysis | Haptoglobin low or absent, reticulocytosis, hyperbilirubinemia. | Hemoglobinuria, splenomegaly. |
| | | | Chronic disease | Low serum iron, TIBC low or low normal. | Depends on cause. |
| Macrocytic, normochromic | > 101[2] | > 36 | Vitamin $B_{12}$ deficiency | Hypersegmented PMNs; low serum vitamin $B_{12}$ levels; achlorhydria. | Peripheral neuropathy; glossitis. |
| | | | Folate deficiency | Hypersegmented PMNs; low folate levels. | Alcoholism; malnutrition. |
| | | | Liver disease | Mean corpuscular volume usually < 120 fL, normal serum vitamin $B_{12}$ and folate levels. | Signs of liver disease. |
| | | | Reticulocytosis | Marked (> 15%) reticulocytosis. | Variable. |

[1]Modified, with permission, from Saunders CE, Ho MT (editors): Current Emergency Diagnosis & Treatment, 4th ed. Appleton & Lange, 1992.
[2]If MCV > 120–130, vitamin $B_{12}$ or folate deficiency is likely.
**MCV** = mean corpuscular volume; **MCHC** = mean corpuscular hemoglobin concentration; **TIBC** = total iron-binding capacity, serum; **PMN** = polymorphonuclear cell.

**TABLE 8-3. ANEMIA, MICROCYTIC: LABORATORY EVALUATION OF MICROCYTIC, HYPOCHROMIC ANEMIAS.[1]**

| Diagnosis | MCV (fL) | Serum Iron (μg/dL) | Iron-binding Capacity (μg/dL) | Transferrin Saturation (%) | Serum Ferritin (μg/L) | Free Erythrocyte Protoporphyrin (μg/dL) | Basophilic Stippling | Bone Marrow Iron Stores |
|---|---|---|---|---|---|---|---|---|
| Normal | 80–100 | 50–175 | 250–460 | 16–60 | 16–300 | <35 | Absent | Present |
| Iron deficiency anemia | ↓ | <30 | ↑ | <16 | <12 | ↑ | Absent | Absent |
| Anemia of chronic disease | N or ↓ | <30 | N or ↓ | N or ↓ | N or ↑ | ↑ | Absent | Present |
| Thalassemia minor | ↓ | N | N | N | N | N | Usually present | Present |

[1] Modified, with permission, from Harvey AM et al (editors): The Principles and Practice of Medicine, 22nd ed. Appleton & Lange, 1988.

**TABLE 8-4. ASCITES: ASCITIC FLUID PROFILES IN VARIOUS DISEASE STATES.[1]**

| Diagnosis | Appearance | Fluid Protein (g/dL) | Fluid Glucose (mg/dL) | WBC and Differential (per µL) | RBC (per µL) | Bacteriologic Gram's Stain & Culture | Cytology | Comments |
|---|---|---|---|---|---|---|---|---|
| Normal | Clear | < 3.0 | Equal to plasma glucose | < 250 | Few or none | Neg | Neg | |
| **TRANSUDATES[2]** | | | | | | | | |
| Cirrhosis | Clear | < 3.0 | N | < 250, MN | Few | Neg | Neg | Occ turbid, rarely bloody. Fluid LDH/Serum LDH ratio < 0.6. |
| Congestive heart failure | Clear | < 2.5 | N | < 250, MN | Few | Neg | Neg | |
| Nephrotic syndrome | Clear | < 2.5 | N | < 250, MN | Few | Neg | Neg | |
| Pseudo-myxoma peritonei | Gelatinous | < 2.5 | N | < 250 | Few | Neg | Occ Pos | |
| **EXUDATES[3]** | | | | | | | | |
| Bacterial peritonitis | Cloudy | > 3.0 | < 50 with perforation | > 500, PMN | Few | Pos | Neg | Blood cultures frequently positive. |
| Tuberculous peritonitis | Clear | > 3.0 | < 60 | > 500, MN | Few, occ many | Stain Pos in 25%; culture Pos in 65% | Neg | Occ chylous. Peritoneal biopsy positive in 65%. |
| Malignancy | Clear or bloody | > 3.0 | < 60 | > 500, MN, PMN | Many | Neg | Pos in 60–90% | Occ chylous. Fluid LDH/Serum LDH ratio > 0.6. Peritoneal biopsy diagnostic. |

| | | | | | | | | |
|---|---|---|---|---|---|---|---|---|
| Pancreatitis | Clear or bloody | > 2.5 | N | > 500, PMN, MN | Many | Neg | Neg | Occ chylous. Fluid amylase > 1000 IU/L, sometimes > 10,000 IU/L. Fluid amylase > serum amylase. |
| Chylous ascites | Turbid | Varies, often > 2.5 | N | Few | Few | Neg | Neg | Fluid TG > 400 mg/dL (turbid). Fluid TG > serum TG. |

[1]Modified, with permission, from Harvey AM et al (editors): The Principles and Practice of Medicine, 22nd ed. Appleton & Lange, 1988; and Schiff L, Schiff ER (editors): Diseases of the Liver. 7th ed. Lippincott, 1993.

[2]Transudates have protein concentration below 2.5–3.0 g/dL; fluid LDH/serum LDH ratio < 0.6 (may be useful in difficult cases).

[3]Exudates have fluid protein concentration above 2.5–3.0 g/dL; fluid LDH serum LDH ratio > 0.6 (may be useful in difficult cases). **MN** = mononuclear cells (lymphocytes or monocytes); **PMN** = polymorphonuclear cells; **TG** = triglycerides.

TABLE 8–5. AUTOANTIBODIES: ASSOCIATIONS WITH CONNECTIVE TISSUE DISEASES.[1]

| Suspected Disease State | Test | Primary Disease Association (Sensitivity, Specificity) | Other Disease Associations | Comments |
|---|---|---|---|---|
| CREST syndrome | Anti-centromere antibody | CREST (70–90%, high) | Scleroderma (10–15%), Raynaud's disease (10–30%). | Predictive value of a positive test is > 95% for scleroderma or related disease (CREST, Raynaud's). Diagnosis of CREST is made clinically. |
| Systemic lupus erythematosus (SLE) | Anti-nuclear antibody (ANA) | SLE (> 95%, low) | RA (30–50%), discoid lupus, scleroderma (60%), drug-induced lupus (100%), Sjögren's syndrome (80%), miscellaneous inflammatory disorders. | Often used as a screening test; a negative test virtually excludes SLE; a positive test, while nonspecific, increases posttest probability. Titer does not correlate with disease activity. |
| | Anti-double-stranded-DNA (anti-ds-DNA) | SLE (60–70%, high) | Lupus nephritis, rarely RA, CTD, usually in low titer. | Predictive value of a positive test is > 90% for SLE if present in high titer; a decreasing titer may correlate with worsening renal disease. Titer generally correlates with disease activity. |
| | Anti-Smith antibody (anti-SM) | SLE (30–40%, high) | | SLE-specific. A positive test substantially increases posttest probability of SLE. Test rarely indicated. |
| Mixed connective tissue disease (MCTD) | Anti-ribonucleoprotein antibody (RNP) | Scleroderma (20–30%, low) MCTD (95–100%, low) | SLE (30%), Sjögren's syndrome, RA (10%), discoid lupus (20–30%). | A negative test essentially excludes MCTD; a positive test in high titer, while nonspecific, increases posttest probability of MCTD. |
| Rheumatoid arthritis (RA) | Rheumatoid factor (RF) | Rheumatoid arthritis (50–90%) | Other rheumatic diseases, chronic infections, some malignancies, some healthy individuals, elderly patients. | Titer does not correlate with disease activity. |
| Scleroderma | Anti-Scl-70 antibody | Scleroderma (15–20%, high) | | Predictive value of a positive test is > 95% for scleroderma. |

| | | | |
|---|---|---|---|
| Sjögren's syndrome | Anti-SS-A/Ro antibody | Sjögren's (60–70%, low) | Useful in counseling women of child-bearing age with known CTD, since a positive test is associated with a small but real risk of neonatal SLE and congenital heart block. |
| | | SLE (30–40%), RA (10%), subacute cutaneous lupus, vasculitis. | |
| Wegener's granulomatosis | Anti-neutrophil cytoplasmic antibody (ANCA) | Wegener's granulomatosis (systemic necrotizing vasculitis) (56–96%, high) | Ability of this assay to reflect disease activity remains unclear. |
| | | Crescentic glomerulonephritis or other systemic vasculitis (eg, polyarteritis nodosa). | |

[1]Modified, with permission, from Harvey AM et al (editors): *The Principles and Practice of Medicine,* 22nd ed. Appleton & Lange, 1988; from White RH, Robbins DL: *Clinical significance and interpretation of antinuclear antibodies.* West J Med 1987;147:210; and from Tan EM: *Autoantibodies to nuclear antigens (ANA): Their immunobiology and medicine.* Adv Immunol 1982;33:173.

**RA** = rheumatoid arthritis; **SLE** = systemic lupus erythematosus; **CTD** = connective tissue disease; **MCTD** = mixed connective tissue disease; **SSA** = Sjögren's syndrome A antibody; **CREST** = calcinosis, Raynaud's phenomenon, esophageal dysmotility, sclerodactyly and telangiectasia.

**TABLE 8–6. CEREBROSPINAL FLUID (CSF): CSF PROFILES IN CENTRAL NERVOUS SYSTEM DISEASE.[1]**

| Diagnosis | Appearance | Opening Pressure (mm $H_2O$) | RBC (per µL) | WBC & Diff (per µL) | CSF Glucose (mg/dL) | CSF Protein (mg/dL) | Smears | Culture | Comments |
|---|---|---|---|---|---|---|---|---|---|
| Normal | Clear, colorless | 70–200 | 0 | ≤ 5 MN, 0 PMN | 45–85 | 15–45 | Neg | Neg | |
| Bacterial meningitis | Cloudy | ↑↑↑ | 0 | 200–20,000, mostly PMN | < 45 | > 50 | Gram's stain Pos | Pos | |
| Tuberculous meningitis | N or cloudy | ↑↑↑ | 0 | 100–1000, mostly MN | < 45 | > 50 | AFB stain Pos | ± | PMN predominance may be seen early in course. |
| Fungal meningitis | N or cloudy | N or ↑ | 0 | 100–1000, mostly MN | < 45 | > 50 | Neg | ± | Counterimmunoelectrophoresis or latex agglutination may be diagnostic. CSF and serum cryptococcal antigen positive in cryptococcal meningitis. |
| Viral (aseptic) meningitis | N | N or ↑ | 0 | 100–1000, mostly MN | 45–85 | N or ↑ | Neg | Neg | RBC count may be elevated in herpes simplex encephalitis. Glucose may be decreased in herpes simplex or mumps infections. Viral cultures may be helpful. |

| | Appearance | | RBC | WBC | Glucose | | Smear / Cytology | ± / Neg | Comments |
|---|---|---|---|---|---|---|---|---|---|
| Parasitic meningitis | N or cloudy | N or ↑ | 0 | 100–1000, mostly MN, E | <45 | N or ↑ | Amebae may be seen on wet smear | ± | |
| Carcinomatous meningitis | N or cloudy | N or ↑ | 0 | N or 100–1000, mostly MN | <45 | N or ↑ | Cytology Pos | Neg | |
| Cerebral lupus erythematosus | N | N or ↑ | 0 | N or ↑, mostly MN | N | N or ↑ | Neg | Neg | |
| Subarachnoid hemorrhage | Pink-red, supernatant yellow | ↑ | ↑ crenated or fresh | N or 100–1000, mostly PMN | | N or ↑ | Neg | Neg | Blood in all tubes equally. Pleocytosis and low glucose sometimes seen several days after subarachnoid hemorrhage, reflecting chemical meningitis caused by subarachnoid blood. |
| "Traumatic" tap | Bloody, supernatant clear | N | ↑↑↑, fresh | ↑ | N | ↑ | Neg | Neg | Most blood in tube #1, least blood in tube #4. |
| Spirochetal, early, acute syphilitic meningitis | Clear to turbid | ↑ | 0 | 25–2000, mostly MN | 15–75 | >50 | Neg | Neg | PMN may predominate early. Positive serum RPR or VDRL. CSF VDRL insensitive. If clinical suspicion is high, institute treatment despite negative CSF VDRL. |
| Late CNS syphilis | Clear | Usually N | 0 | N or ↑ | N | N or ↑ | Neg | Neg | CSF VDRL insensitive (see p 183). |

**TABLE 8-6 (CONTINUED).**

| Diagnosis | Appearance | Opening Pressure (mm H$_2$O) | RBC (per µL) | WBC & Diff (per µL) | CSF Glucose (mg/dL) | CSF Protein (mg/dL) | Smears | Culture | Comments |
|---|---|---|---|---|---|---|---|---|---|
| "Neighborhood" meningeal reaction | Clear or turbid, often xantho-chromic | Variable, usually N | Variable | ↑ | N | N or ↑ | | Usually Neg | May occur in mastoiditis, brain abscess, sinusitis, septic throm-bophlebitis, brain tumor, intra-thecal drug therapy. |
| Hepatic encephalopathy | N | N | 0 | ≤ 5 | N | N | Neg | Neg | CSF glutamine > 15 mg/dL. |
| Uremia | N | Usually ↑ | 0 | N or ↑ | N or ↑ | N or ↑ | Neg | Neg | |
| Diabetic coma | N | Low | 0 | N or ↑ | ↑ | N | Neg | Neg | |

[1]Modified, with permission, from Aminoff MJ, Greenberg DA, Simon RP: Clinical Neurology, 3rd ed. Appleton & Lange, 1996; Tierney LM Jr, McPhee SJ, Papadakis MA (editors): Current Medical Diagnosis & Treatment 1996. Appleton & Lange, 1996; and from Krupp MA et al: Physician's Handbook, 21st ed. Appleton & Lange, 1985.
**MN** = mononuclear cells (lymphocytes or monocytes); **PMN** = polymorphonuclear cells; **E** = eosinophils; **CNS** = central nervous system.

**TABLE 8–7. CHILD'S CRITERIA: RELATIONSHIP OF HEPATIC FUNCTION AND NUTRITION TO OPERATIVE DEATH RATE AFTER PORTACAVAL SHUNT.[1]**

|  | Group | | |
|---|---|---|---|
|  | A | B | C |
| Operative death rate | 2% | 10% | 50% |
| Serum bilirubin (mg/dL) | < 2 | 2–3.0 | > 3 |
| Serum albumin (g/dL) | > 3.5 | 3–3.5 | < 3 |
| Ascites | None | Easily controlled | Poorly controlled |
| Encephalopathy | None | Minimal | Advanced |
| Nutrition | Excellent | Good | Poor |

[1]Reproduced, with permission, from Way LW (editor): Current Surgical Diagnosis & Treatment, 10th ed. Appleton & Lange, 1994.

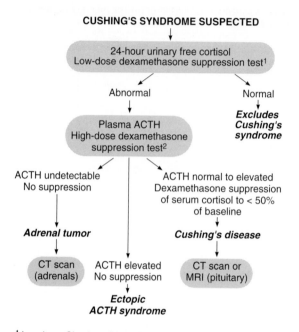

**CUSHING'S SYNDROME SUSPECTED**

24-hour urinary free cortisol
Low-dose dexamethasone suppression test[1]

Abnormal → Normal → *Excludes Cushing's syndrome*

Plasma ACTH
High-dose dexamethasone suppression test[2]

ACTH undetectable
No suppression → *Adrenal tumor* → CT scan (adrenals)

ACTH elevated
No suppression → *Ectopic ACTH syndrome*

ACTH normal to elevated
Dexamethasone suppression of serum cortisol to < 50% of baseline → *Cushing's disease* → CT scan or MRI (pituitary)

[1] Low dose: Give 1 mg dexamethasone at 11 PM; draw serum cortisol at 8 AM. Normally, AM cortisol is < 5 μg/dL.
[2] High dose: Give 8 mg dexamethasone at 11 PM; draw serum cortisol at 8 AM or collect 24-hour urinary free cortisol. Normally, AM cortisol is < 5 μg/dL.

**Figure 8–5. CUSHING'S SYNDROME:** Diagnostic evaluation of Cushing's syndrome. **ACTH** = adrenocorticotropic hormone; **CT** = computed tomography; **MRI** = magnetic resonance imaging. (Modified, with permission, from Baxter JD, Tyrrell JB: The adrenal cortex. In: *Endocrinology and Metabolism,* 3rd ed. Felig P, Baxter JD, Frohman LA [editors]. McGraw-Hill, 1995; from Harvey AM et al [editors]: *The Principles and Practice of Medicine,* 22nd ed. Appleton & Lange, 1988; and from Greenspan FS, Baxter JD [editors]: *Basic and Clinical Endocrinology,* 4th ed. Appleton & Lange, 1994.)

**Nerve root**

**Peripheral nerve**

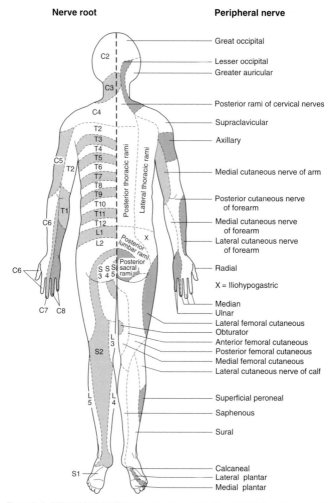

**Figure 8–6. DERMATOME CHART:** Cutaneous innervation. The segmental or radicular (root) distribution is shown on the left side of the body and the peripheral nerve distribution on the right side. ***Above:*** posterior view; ***next page:*** anterior view. (Reproduced, with permission, from Aminoff MJ, Greenberg DA, Simon RP: *Clinical Neurology,* 3rd ed. Appleton & Lange, 1996.)

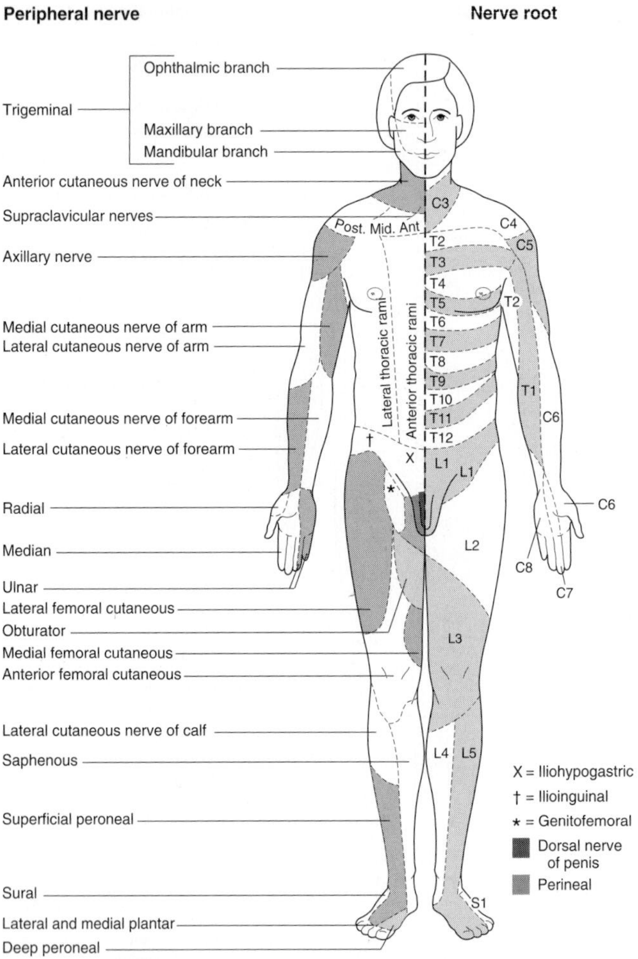

**Peripheral nerve**

**Nerve root**

Trigeminal
- Ophthalmic branch
- Maxillary branch
- Mandibular branch

Anterior cutaneous nerve of neck

Supraclavicular nerves

Axillary nerve

Medial cutaneous nerve of arm
Lateral cutaneous nerve of arm

Medial cutaneous nerve of forearm
Lateral cutaneous nerve of forearm

Radial

Median

Ulnar
Lateral femoral cutaneous
Obturator
Medial femoral cutaneous
Anterior femoral cutaneous

Lateral cutaneous nerve of calf

Saphenous

Superficial peroneal

Sural
Lateral and medial plantar
Deep peroneal

Post. Mid. Ant.

Lateral thoracic rami

Anterior thoracic rami

C3
C4
C5
T2
T3
T4
T5
T6
T7
T8
T9
T10
T11
T12
L1
L2
L3
L4 L5
S1
T2
T1
C6
C6
C8
C7

X = Iliohypogastric
† = Ilioinguinal
★ = Genitofemoral
■ Dorsal nerve of penis
■ Perineal

**Figure 8–6. Continued**

**TABLE 8–8. GENETIC DISEASES DIAGNOSED BY MOLECULAR DIAGNOSTIC TECHNIQUES.[1]**

| Test/Range/Collection | Physiologic Basis | Interpretation | Comments |
|---|---|---|---|
| **Cystic fibrosis mutation**<br><br>PCR+ reverse dot blot<br><br>Blood<br><br>Lavender<br>$$$$ | Cystic fibrosis is caused by a mutation in the cystic fibrosis transmembrane regulator gene (CFTR). Over 300 mutations have been found, with the most common being ΔF508, present in 68% of cases. | Test specificity approaches 100%, so a positive result should be considered diagnostic of a cystic fibrosis mutation. Because of the wide range of mutations, an assay for the ΔF508 mutation alone is 68% sensitive; a combined panel encompassing the 31 most common mutations is about 90% sensitive. The test can distinguish between heterozygous carriers and homozygous patients. | Cystic fibrosis is the most common inherited disease in North American Caucasians, affecting one in 2500 births. Caucasians have a carrier frequency of one in 25. The disease is autosomal recessive.<br>Ref: Proc Natl Acad Sci U S A 1989;86:6230.<br>Ref: Hum Mutations 1995;5:333.<br>Ref: J Lab Clin Med 1995;125:421. |
| **Fragile X syndrome**<br><br>Blood<br><br>Lavender<br>$$$$ | Fragile X syndrome results from a mutation in the familial mental retardation–1 gene (FMR-1), located at Xq27.3. Fully symptomatic patients have abnormal methylation of the gene (which blocks transcription) during oogenesis. The gene contains a variable number of repeating CGG sequences and, as the number of sequences increases, the probability of abnormal methylation increases. The number of copies increases with subsequent generations so that females who are unaffected carriers may have offspring who are affected. | Normal patients have 6–52 CGG repeat sequences. Patients with 52–230 repeat sequences are asymptomatic carriers. Patients with more than 230 repeat sequences are very likely to have abnormal methylation and to be symptomatic. | Fragile X syndrome is the most common cause of inherited mental retardation, occurring in one in 1000–1500 males and one in 2000–2500 females. Full mutations can show variable penetrance in females, but most of such females will be at least mildly retarded.<br>Ref: N Engl J Med 1991;325:1673.<br>Ref: Am J Hum Genet 1995;56:1147. |

**TABLE 8–8 (CONTINUED).**

| Test/Range/Collection | Physiologic Basis | Interpretation | Comments |
|---|---|---|---|
| **Hemophilia A**<br><br>Southern blot<br><br>Blood<br><br>Lavender<br>$$$$ | Approximately half of severe hemophilia A cases are caused by an inversion mutation within the factor VIII gene. The resulting rearrangement of *BCL1* sites can be detected by Southern blot hybridization assays. | Test specificity approaches 100%, so a positive result should be considered diagnostic of a hemophilia A inversion mutation. Because of a variety of mutations, however, test sensitivity is only about 50%. | Hemophilia A is one of the most common X-linked diseases in humans, affecting one in 5000 males.<br>Ref: Nature Genet 1993;5:236. |
| **Huntington's disease**<br><br>PCR+ Southern blot<br><br>Blood, amniocytes, or buccal cells<br><br>Lavender<br>$$$$ | Huntington's disease is an inherited neurodegenerative disorder associated with an autosomal dominant mutation on chromosome 4. The disease is highly penetrant, but symptoms (disordered movements, cognitive decline, and emotional disturbance) are often not expressed until middle age. The mutation results in the expansion of a CAG trinucleotide repeat sequence within the gene. | Normal patients will have fewer than 34 CAG repeats, while patients with disease usually have more than 37 repeats and may have 80 or more. Occasional affected patients can be seen with "high normal" (32–34) numbers of repeats. Tests showing 34–37 repeats are indeterminate. | Huntington's disease testing involves ethical dilemmas. Counseling is recommended prior to testing.<br>Ref: Hum Molec Genet 1993;2:633. |
| **α-Thalassemia**<br><br>PCR+ Southern blot<br><br>Blood, amniocytes, chorionic villi<br><br>Lavender<br>$$$$ | A deletion mutation in the α-globin gene region of chromosome 16 due to unequal crossing-over events can lead to defective synthesis of the α-globin chain of hemoglobin. Normally, there are 2 copies of the α-globin gene on each chromosome 16, and the severity of disease increases with the number of defective genes. | This assay is highly specific (approaches 100%). Sensitivity, however, can vary since detection of different mutations may require the use of different probes. α-Thalassemia due to point mutations may not be detected. | Patients with one deleted gene are usually normal or very slightly anemic; patients with two deletions usually have a hypochromic microcytic anemia; patients with three deletions have elevated hemoglobin H and a moderately severe hemolytic anemia; patients with four deletions generally die in utero with hydrops fetalis.<br>Ref: Eur J Clin Invest 1990;20:340. |

| β-Thalassemia | β-Thalassemia results from a mutation in the gene encoding the β-globin subunit of hemoglobin A (which is composed of a pair of α-chains and a pair of β-chains). A relative excess of α-globin chains precipitates within red blood cells, causing hemolysis and anemia. Over 100 different mutations have been described; testing usually covers a panel of the more common mutations. The test can distinguish between heterozygous and homozygous individuals. | Test specificity approaches 100%, so a positive result should be considered diagnostic of a thalassemia mutation. Because of the large number of mutations, sensitivity can be poor. A panel with the 41 most common mutations has a sensitivity that approaches 95%. | β-Thalassemia is very common; about 3% of the world's population are carriers. The incidence is increased in persons of Mediterranean, African, and Asian descent. The mutations may vary from population to population, and different testing panels may be needed for patients of different ethnicities. Ref: Semin Hematol 1990;27:209. |
|---|---|---|---|
| PCR+ reverse dot blot | | | |
| Blood, chorionic villi, amniocytes | | | |
| Lavender | | | |
| $$$$ | | | |

[1]Adapted, with permission, by Lindeman N from Wall J, Chehab F, Kan YW: Clinical Laboratory Manual. UCSF, 1996.

**PCR (polymerase chain reaction)** is a method for amplifying the amount of a particular DNA sequence in a specimen, facilitating detection by hybridization-based assay (ie, Southern blot, reverse dot blot).

**Southern blot** is a molecular hybridization technique whereby DNA is extracted from the sample and digested by different restriction enzymes. The resulting fragments are separated by electrophoresis and identified by labeled probes.

**Reverse dot blot** is a molecular hybridization technique in which a specific oligonucleotide probe is bound to a solid membrane prior to reaction with PCR-amplified DNA.

**$$$$ = > $100.00.**

**TABLE 8–9. HEMOSTATIC FUNCTION: LABORATORY EVALUATION.[1]**

| Suspected Diagnosis | Platelet Count | PT | PTT | TT | Further Diagnostic Tests |
|---|---|---|---|---|---|
| Idiopathic thrombocytopenic purpura, drug sensitivity, bone marrow depression | ↓ | N | N | N | Platelet antibody, marrow aspirate. |
| Disseminated intravascular coagulation | ↓ | ↑ | ↑ | ↑ | Fibrinogen assays, fibrin D-dimers. |
| Platelet function defect, salicylates, or uremia | N | N | N | N | Bleeding time, platelet aggregation, blood urea nitrogen (BUN), creatinine. |
| von Willebrand's disease | N | N | ↑ or N | N | Bleeding time, factor VIII assay, factor VIII antigen. |
| Factor VII deficiency or inhibitor | N | ↑ | N | N | Factor VII assay (normal plasma should correct PT if no inhibitor is present). |
| Factor V, X, II, I deficiencies as in liver disease or with anticoagulants | N | ↑ | ↑ | N or ↑ | Liver function tests. |
| Factor VIII (hemophilia), IX, XI, or XII deficiencies or inhibitor | N | N | ↑ | N | Inhibitor screen, individual factor assays. |
| Factor XIII deficiency | N | N | N | N | Urea stabilizing test, factor XIII assay. |

[1]Modified, with permission, from Tierney LM, Jr, McPhee SJ, Papadakis MA (editors): Current Medical Diagnosis & Treatment 1996. Appleton & Lange, 1996; and from Harvey AM et al: The Principles and Practice of Medicine, 22nd ed. Appleton & Lange, 1988.

**Note:** In approaching patients with bleeding disorders, try to distinguish clinically between platelet disorders (eg, patient has petechiae, mucosal bleeding) and factor deficiency states (eg, patient has hemarthrosis).

**PT** = prothrombin time; **PTT** = activated partial thromboplastin time; **TT** = thrombin time.

**TABLE 8-10. HEPATIC FUNCTION TESTS.[1]**

| Clinical Condition | Direct Bilirubin (mg/dL) | Indirect Bilirubin (mg/dL) | Urine Bilirubin | Serum Albumin & Total Protein (g/dL) | Alkaline Phosphatase (IU/L) | Prothrombin time (seconds) | ALT (SGPT) AST (SGOT) (IU/L) |
|---|---|---|---|---|---|---|---|
| Normal | 0.1–0.3 | 0.2–0.7 | None | Albumin, 3.4–4.7 Total protein, 6.0–8.0 | 30–115 (lab-specific) | 11–15 seconds. After vitamin K, 15% increase within 24 hours. | ALT, 5–35 AST, 5–40 (lab-specific) |
| Hepatocellular jaundice (eg, viral, alcoholic hepatitis) | ↑↑ | ↑ | ↑ | ↓ Albumin | N to ↑ | Prolonged if damage is severe. Does not respond to parenteral vitamin K. | Increased in hepatocellular damage, viral hepatitides; AST/ALT ratio often > 2:1 in alcoholic hepatitis |
| Uncomplicated obstructive jaundice (eg, common bile duct obstruction) | ↑↑ | ↑ | ↑ | N | ↑ | Prolonged if obstruction marked but responds to parenteral vitamin K. | N to minimally ↑ |
| Hemolysis | N | ↑ | None | N | N | N | N |
| Gilbert's syndrome | N | ↑ | None | N | N | N | N |
| Intrahepatic cholestasis (drug-induced) | ↑↑ | ↑ | ↑ | N | ↑↑ | N | AST N or ↑ ALT N or ↑ |
| Primary biliary cirrhosis | ↑↑ | ↑ | ↑ | N ↑ globulin | ↑↑ | N or ↑ | ↑ |

[1]Modified, with permission, from Tierney LM Jr, McPhee SJ, Papadakis MA (editors): Current Medical Diagnosis & Treatment 1996. Appleton & Lange, 1996; and Harvey AM et al (editors): The Principles and Practice of Medicine, 22nd ed. Appleton & Lange, 1988.
**AST** = aspartate aminotransferase; **ALT** = alanine aminotransferase.

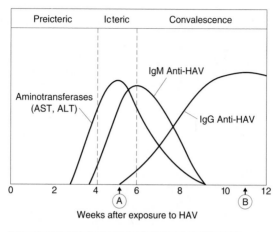

Weeks after exposure to HAV

| Patterns of Antibody Tests | | |
|---|---|---|
| | IgM Anti-HAV | IgG Anti-HAV |
| **A**  Acute HA | + | + or − |
| **B**  Convalescence (indicates previous infection) | − | + |

**Figure 8–7. HEPATITIS A:** Usual pattern of serologic changes in hepatitis A. **HA** = hepatitis A; **AST** = aspartate aminotransferase; **ALT** = alanine aminotransferase; **Anti-HAV** = hepatitis A virus antibody; **IgM** = immunoglobulin M; **IgG** = immunoglobulin G. (Reproduced, with permission, from Harvey AM et al [editors]: *The Principles and Practice of Medicine*, 22nd ed. Appleton & Lange, 1988.)

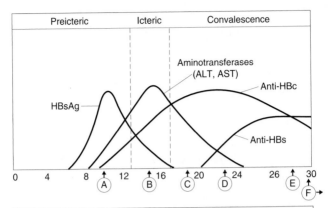

**Figure 8–8. HEPATITIS B:** Usual pattern of serologic changes in hepatitis B. **HBsAg** = hepatitis B surface antigen; **Anti-HBc** = hepatitis B core antibody; **Anti-HBs** = hepatitis B surface antibody; **AST** = aspartate aminotransferase; **ALT** = alanine aminotransferase. (Modified and reproduced, with permission, from Harvey AM et al [editors]: *The Principles and Practice of Medicine*, 22nd ed. Appleton & Lange, 1988.)

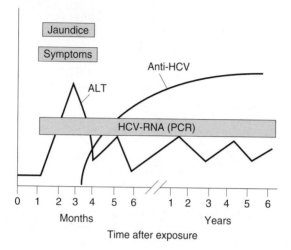

**Figure 8–9. HEPATITIS C:** The typical course of chronic hepatitis C. **ALT** = alanine aminotransferase; **Anti-HCV** = antibody to hepatitis C virus by enzyme immunoassay; **HCV RNA [PCR]** = hepatitis C viral RNA by polymerase chain reaction.) (Reproduced, with permission, from Tierney LM Jr, McPhee SJ, Papadakis MA [editors]: *Current Medical Diagnosis & Treatment 1996.* Appleton & Lange, 1996.)

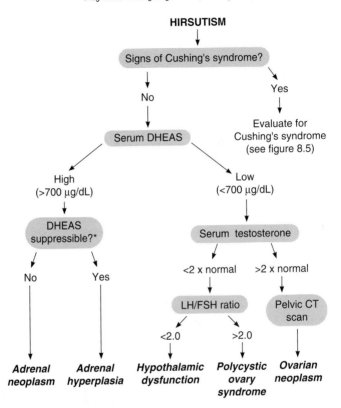

**Figure 8–10. HIRSUTISM:** Evaluation of hirsutism in females. Exceptions occur that do not fit this algorithm. **CT** = computed tomography; **DHEAS** = dehydroepiandrosterone sulfate; **FSH** = follicle-stimulating hormone; **LH** = luteinizing hormone. (*DHEAS < 170 µg/dL after dexamethasone 0.5 mg orally every 6 hours for 5 days, with DHEAS repeated on the fifth day.) (Reproduced, with permission, from Fitzgerald PA [editor]: *Handbook of Clinical Endocrinology,* 2nd ed. Appleton & Lange, 1992.)

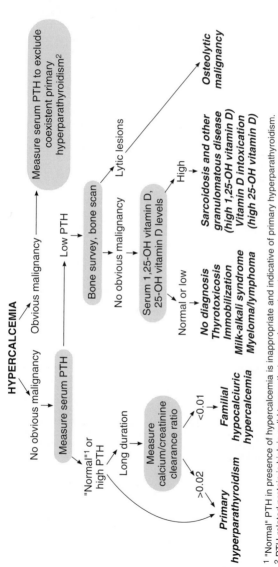

1 "Normal" PTH in presence of hypercalcemia is inappropriate and indicative of primary hyperparathyroidism.
2 PTH-related protein is high in solid tumors that cause hypercalcemia.

**Figure 8–11. HYPERCALCEMIA:** Diagnostic approach to hypercalcemia. **PTH** = parathyroid hormone. (Modified, with permission, from Harvey AM et al [editors]: *The Principles and Practice of Medicine*, 22nd ed. Appleton & Lange, 1988.)

TABLE 8–11. HYPERLIPIDEMIA: CHARACTERISTICS AND LABORATORY FINDINGS IN PRIMARY HYPERLIPIDEMIA.[1]

| Lipoprotein Disorder | Lipoprotein Abnormalities or Defect | Appearance of Serum[2] | Cholesterol (mg/dL) | Triglyceride (mg/dL) | Clinical Presentation | Comments | Risk of Atherosclerosis |
|---|---|---|---|---|---|---|---|
| None | None | Clear | < 200 | < 165 | | | Nil |
| Familial hypercholesterolemia | LDL elevated: decreased or lack of LDL receptors in liver | Clear | Usually 300–600 but may be higher; LDL cholesterol high | Normal | Xanthelasma, tendon and skin xanthomas, accelerated atherosclerosis. Detectable in childhood. | Onset at all ages. Consider hypothyroidism, nephrotic syndrome, hepatic obstruction. | ↑↑ |
| Familial combined hyperlipidemia | LDL or VLDL elevated | Turbid or clear | Usually 250–600; LDL cholesterol high | Usually 200–600 | Accelerated atherosclerosis. Associated with obesity or diabetes. | Cholesterol or triglyceride or both may be elevated—at different times and in different members of the family. | ↑↑ |
| Familial hypertriglyceridemia | VLDL elevated | Turbid | Typically normal | 200–5000 | Eruptive xanthomas. Triglycerides, if high enough, may cause pancreatitis. | Consider nephrotic syndrome, hypothyroidism, alcoholism, glycogen storage disease, oral contraceptives. | Nil |
| Hyperchylomicronemia | Chylomicrons elevated; deficiency of lipoprotein lipase or, less commonly, of C-II apolipoprotein | Creamy, separates into creamy supernate and clear infranate | Increased | Often 1000–10,000; chylomicrons | Eruptive xanthomas, lipemia retinalis, recurrent abdominal pain, hepatosplenomegaly, pancreatitis. | Onset in infancy or childhood. Aggravated by high fat intake, diabetes, alcohol. | Nil |

**TABLE 8–11 (CONTINUED).**

| Lipoprotein Disorder | Lipoprotein Abnormalities or Defect | Appearance of Serum[2] | Cholesterol (mg/dL) | Triglyceride (mg/dL) | Clinical Presentation | Comments | Risk of Athero-sclerosis |
|---|---|---|---|---|---|---|---|
| Mixed hypertriglyceridemia | VLDL and chylomicrons elevated | Creamy, separates into creamy supernate and turbid infranate | 300–1000 | Usually 500–>10,000; chylomicrons high | Recurrent abdominal pain, hepatosplenomegaly, eruptive xanthomas; glucose intolerance | Symptoms begin in adult life. Sensitive to dietary fat. Alcohol and diabetes aggravate. | Nil to ↑ |
| Dysbetalipoproteinemia (type III) | VLDL, IDL elevated; apolipoprotein E dysfunction | Turbid | 200–500 | 200–500 | Palmar xanthoma typical; other xanthoma common. | Aggravated by alcohol, estrogen. | ↑↑ |

[1]Modified, with permission, from Schroeder SA et al (editors): Current Medical Diagnosis & Treatment 1991. Appleton & Lange, 1991; from Harvey AM et al (editors): The Principles and Practice of Medicine, 22nd ed. Appleton & Lange, 1988; and from Siperstein M. 1996. The collaboration of Dr. Marvin D. Siperstein is gratefully acknowledged.

[2]Refrigerated serum overnight at 4° C.

**Key:** LDL = low-density lipoprotein, calculated as: Total cholesterol − HDL cholesterol − [Triglycerides/5]; VLDL = very low density lipoprotein; IDL = intermediate density lipoprotein.

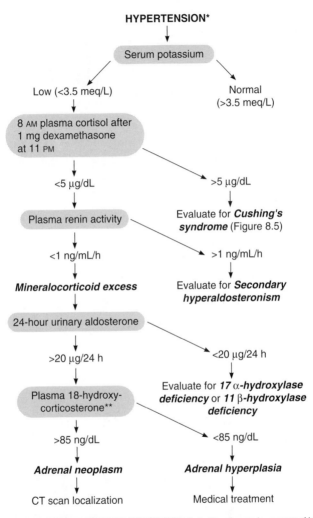

**Figure 8–12. HYPERTENSION WITH HYPOKALEMIA:** Evaluation of secondary causes of hypertension associated with hypokalemia. (*Studies are performed during a high-sodium intake [120 meq Na$^+$/d.]) (**In addition, plasma aldosterone may be measured at 8 AM supine after overnight recumbency and after 4 hours of upright posture.) (Reproduced, with permission, from Fitzgerald PA [editor]: *Handbook of Clinical Endocrinology*, 2nd ed. Appleton & Lange, 1992.)

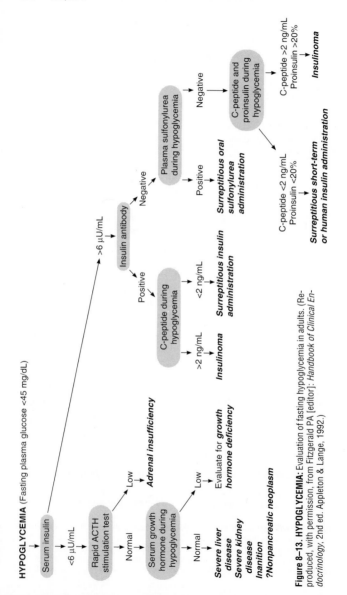

**Figure 8–13. HYPOGLYCEMIA:** Evaluation of fasting hypoglycemia in adults. (Reproduced, with permission, from Fitzgerald PA [editor]: *Handbook of Clinical Endocrinology*, 2nd ed. Appleton & Lange, 1992.)

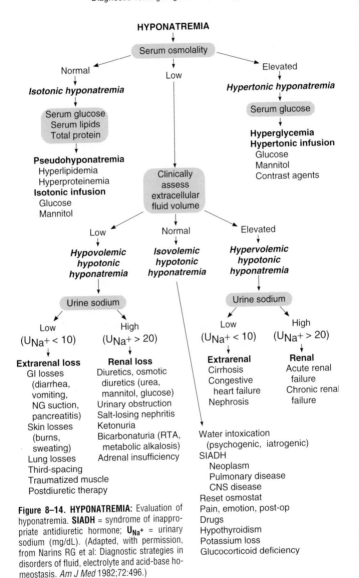

**Figure 8–14. HYPONATREMIA:** Evaluation of hyponatremia. **SIADH** = syndrome of inappropriate antidiuretic hormone; $U_{Na^+}$ = urinary sodium (mg/dL). (Adapted, with permission, from Narins RG et al: Diagnostic strategies in disorders of fluid, electrolyte and acid-base homeostasis. *Am J Med* 1982;72:496.)

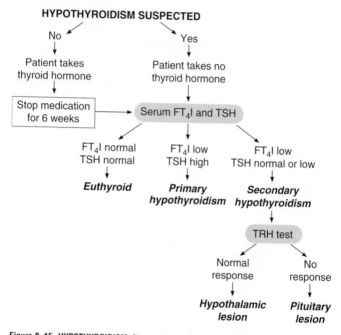

**Figure 8–15. HYPOTHYROIDISM:** Diagnostic approach to hypothyroidism. **FT₄I** = free thyroxine index; **TSH** = thyroid-stimulating hormone; **TRH** = thyroid-releasing hormone. (Modified, with permission, from Greenspan FS, Strewler GJ [editors]: *Basic and Clinical Endocrinology*, 5th ed. Appleton & Lange, 1996.)

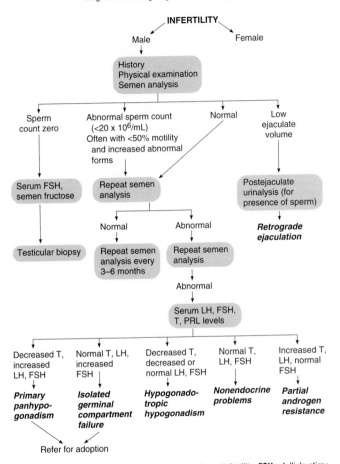

**Figure 8–16. MALE INFERTILITY:** Evaluation of male factor infertility. **FSH** = follicle-stimulating hormone; **LH** = luteinizing hormone; **PRL** = prolactin; **T** = testosterone. (Adapted, with permission, from Swerdloff RS, Boyers SM: Evaluation of the male partner of an infertile couple: An algorithmic approach. JAMA 1982;247:2418. Copyright © 1982 by American Medical Association.)

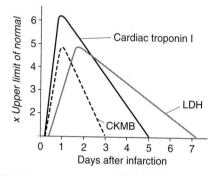

**Figure 8–17. MYOCARDIAL ENZYMES:** Time course of serum enzyme concentrations after a typical myocardial infarction. **CK-MB** = isoenzyme of CK. **LDH** = lactate dehydrogenase. (Modified, with permission, from Harvey AM et al [editors]: *The Principles and Practice of Medicine*, 22nd ed. Appleton & Lange, 1988.)

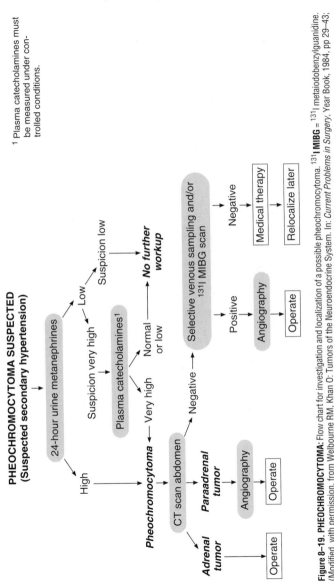

[1] Plasma catecholamines must be measured under controlled conditions.

**Figure 8–19. PHEOCHROMOCYTOMA:** Flow chart for investigation and localization of a possible pheochromocytoma. [131]I **MIBG** = [131]I metaiodobenzylguanidine. (Modified, with permission, from Welbourne RM, Khan O: Tumors of the Neuroendocrine System. In: *Current Problems in Surgery*, Year Book, 1984, pp 29–43; and Stobo JD et al [editors]: *The Principles and Practice of Medicine*, 23rd ed. Appleton & Lange, 1996.)

**TABLE 8–13. PLEURAL FLUID: PLEURAL FLUID PROFILES IN VARIOUS DISEASE STATES.[1]**

| Diagnosis | Gross Appearance | Protein (g/dL) | Glucose[2] (mg/dL) | WBC and Differential (per µL) | RBC (per µL) | Microscopic Exam | Culture | Comments |
|---|---|---|---|---|---|---|---|---|
| Normal | Clear | 1–1.5 | Equal to serum | ≤1000, mostly MN | 0 or Few | Neg | Neg | |
| **TRANSUDATES[3]** | | | | | | | | |
| Congestive heart failure | Serous | <3; sometimes ≥ 3 | Equal to serum | <1000 | <10,000 | Neg | Neg | Most common cause of pleural effusion. Effusion right-sided in 55–70% of patients. |
| Nephrotic syndrome | Serous | <3 | Equal to serum | <1000 | <1000 | Neg | Neg | Occurs in 20% of patients. Cause is low protein osmotic pressure. |
| Hepatic cirrhosis | Serous | <3 | Equal to serum | <1000 | <1000 | Neg | Neg | From movement of ascites across diaphragm. Treatment of underlying ascites usually sufficient. |
| **EXUDATES[3]** | | | | | | | | |
| Tuberculosis | Usually serous; can be bloody | 90% ≥ 3; may exceed 5 g/dL | Equal to serum; Occ <60 | 500–10,000, mostly MN | <10,000 | Concentrate Pos for AFB in <50% | May yield MTb | PPD usually positive; pleural biopsy positive; eosinophils (> 10%) or mesothelial cells (> 5%) make diagnosis unlikely. |
| Malignancy | Usually turbid, bloody; Occ serous | 90% ≥ 3 | Equal to serum; < 60 in 15% of cases | 1000–10,000 mostly MN | > 100,000 | Pos cytology in 50% | Neg | Eosinophils uncommon; fluid tends to reaccumulate after removal. |

| Condition | Appearance | Protein[3] | Glucose[2] | Cell count | RBC | AFB | MTb | Comment |
|---|---|---|---|---|---|---|---|---|
| Empyema | Turbid to purulent | ≥3 | Less than serum, often < 20 | 25,000–100,000, mostly PMN | < 5,000 | Pos | Pos | Drainage necessary; putrid odor suggests anaerobic infection. |
| Parapneumonic effusion, uncomplicated | Clear to turbid |  | Equal to serum | 5000–25,000, mostly PMN | < 5,000 | Neg | Neg | Tube thoracostomy unnecessary; associated infiltrate on chest x-ray; fluid pH ≥ 7.2. |
| Pulmonary embolism, infarction | Serous to grossly bloody | ≥3 | Equal to serum | 1000–50,000, MN or PMN | 100–> 100,000 | Neg | Neg | Variable findings; 25% are transudates. |
| Rheumatoid arthritis or other collagen-vascular disease | Turbid or yellow-green | ≥3 | Very low (< 40 in most); in RA, 5–20 mg/dL | 1000–20,000, mostly MN | < 1000 | Neg | Neg | Rapid clotting time; secondary empyema common. |
| Pancreatitis | Turbid to serosanguineous | ≥3 | Equal to serum | 1000–50,000, mostly PMN | 1000–10,000 | Neg | Neg | Effusion usually left-sided; high amylase level. |
| Esophageal rupture | Turbid to purulent; red-brown | ≥3 | Usually low | < 5000–over 50,000, mostly PMN | < 5000 | Pos | Pos | Effusion usually left-sided; high fluid amylase level (salivary); pneumothorax in 25% of cases; pH < 6.0 strongly suggests diagnosis. |

[1] Modified, with permission, from Therapy of pleural effusion. A statement by the Committee on Therapy. Am Rev Respi Dis 1968;97:479; Tierney LM Jr, McPhee SJ, Papadakis MA (editors): Current Medical Diagnosis & Treatment 1996. Appleton & Lange, 1996, and Way LW (editor): Current Surgical Diagnosis & Treatment, 10th ed. Appleton & Lange, 1994.

[2] Glucose of pleural fluid in comparison to serum glucose.

[3] Exudative pleural effusions meet at least one of the following criteria: (1) pleural fluid protein/serum protein ratio > 0.5; (2) pleural fluid LDH/serum LDH ratio > 0.6; and (3) pleural fluid LDH > 2/3 upper normal limit for serum LDH. Transudative pleural effusions meet none of these criteria. Transudative effusions also occur in myxedema and sarcoidosis.

**MN** = mononuclear cells (lymphocytes or monocytes); **PMN** = polymorphonuclear cells; **AFB** = acid-fast bacilli; **MTb** = Mycobacterium tuberculosis.

**TABLE 8–14. PRENATAL DIAGNOSTIC METHODS: AMNIOCENTESIS AND CHORIONIC VILLUS SAMPLING.[1]**

| Method | Procedure | Laboratory Analysis | Waiting Time for Results | Advantages | Disadvantages |
|---|---|---|---|---|---|
| Amniocentesis | Between the 12th and 16th weeks, and by the transabdominal approach, 10–30 mL of amniotic fluid is removed for cytologic and biochemical analysis. Preceding ultrasound locates the placenta and identifies twinning and missed abortion. | **1. Amniotic fluid:**<br>• Alpha-fetoprotein<br>• Limited biochemical analysis<br>• Virus isolation studies<br>**2. Amniotic cell culture:**<br>• Chromosomal analysis | 3–4 weeks | Over 25 years of experience. | Therapeutic abortion, if indicated, must be done in the second trimester. (RhoGam should be given to Rh-negative mothers to prevent sensitization.)<br>Risks (approximately 1%):<br>• Fetal: puncture or abortion.<br>• Maternal: infection or bleeding. |
| Chorionic villus sampling | Between the 8th and 12th week, and with constant ultrasound guidance, the trophoblastic cells of the chorionic villi are obtained by transcervical or transabdominal endoscopic needle biopsy or aspiration. | **1. Direct cell analysis:**<br>• Chromosomal studies<br>**2. Cell culture:**<br>• Limited biochemical analysis | 1–10 days | Over 5 years of investigational experience. Therapeutic abortion, if indicated, can be done in the first trimester. | Risks (approximately 3%):<br>• Fetal: abortion.<br>• Maternal: bleeding and infection (uncommon). |

[1]Modified, with permission, from Schroeder SA et al (editors): Current Medical Diagnosis & Treatment 1990. Appleton & Lange, 1990.

**PULMONARY EMBOLI SUSPECTED**

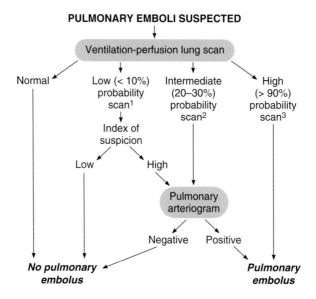

[1] Matching ventilation-perfusion defects or small subsegmental defects with mismatch.

[2] Single subsegmental defect with mismatch or multiple segmental defects with match and with mismatch.

[3] Multiple segmental or lobar defects with mismatch.

**Figure 8–20. PULMONARY EMBOLUS:** Diagnostic evaluation of possible pulmonary embolus. (Modified, with permission, from Wyngaarden JB, Smith LH [editors]: *Cecil's Textbook of Medicine,* 19th ed. Saunders, 1992.)

**TABLE 8–15. PULMONARY FUNCTION TESTS: INTERPRETATION IN OBSTRUCTIVE AND RESTRICTIVE PULMONARY DISEASE.[1]**

| Tests | Units | Definition | Obstructive Disease | Restrictive Disease |
|---|---|---|---|---|
| **SPIROMETRY** | | | | |
| Forced vital capacity (FVC) | L | The volume that can be forcefully expelled from the lungs after maximal inspiration. | N or ↓ | ↓ |
| Forced expiratory volume in one second ($FEV_1$) | L | The volume expelled in the first second of the FVC maneuver. | ↓ | N or ↓ |
| $FEV_1/FVC$ | % | | ↓ | N or ↑ |
| Forced expiratory flow from 25% to 75% of the forced vital capacity (FEF 25–75%) | L/sec | The maximal midexpiratory airflow rate. | ↓ | N or ↓ |
| Peak expiratory flow rate (PEFR) | L/sec | The maximal airflow rate achieved in the FVC maneuver. | ↓ | N or ↑ |
| Maximum voluntary ventilation (MVV) | L/min | The maximum volume that can be breathed in 1 minute (usually measured for 15 seconds and multiplied by 4). | ↓ | N or ↓ |
| **LUNG VOLUMES** | | | | |
| Slow vital capacity (SVC) | L | The volume that can be slowly exhaled after maximal inspiration. | N or ↓ | ↓ |
| Total lung capacity (TLC) | L | The volume in the lungs after a maximal inspiration. | N or ↑ | ↓ |
| Functional residual capacity (FRC) | L | The volume in the lungs at the end of a normal tidal expiration. | ↑ | N or ↑ |
| Expiratory reserve volume (ERV) | L | The volume representing the difference between functional residual capacity and residual volume. | N or ↓ | N or ↓ |
| Residual volume (RV) | L | The volume remaining in the lungs after maximal expiration. | ↑ | N or ↑ |
| RV/TLC ratio | ... | | ↑ | N or ↑ |

[1]Modified, with permission, from Tierney LM Jr, McPhee SJ, Papadakis MA (editors): Current Medical Diagnosis & Treatment 1996. Appleton & Lange, 1996.
**N** = normal; ↓ = less than predicted; ↑ = greater than predicted. Normal values vary according to subject sex, age, body size, and ethnicity.

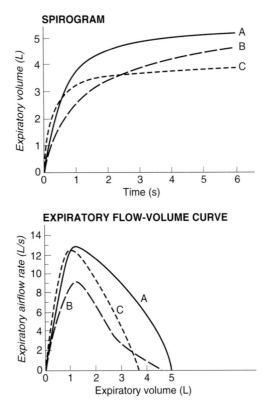

**Figure 8–21. PULMONARY FUNCTION TESTS: SPIROMETRY:** Representative spirograms (upper panel) and expiratory flow-volume curves (lower panel) for normal **(A)**, obstructive **(B)**, and restrictive **(C)** patterns. (Reproduced, with permission, from Tierney LM Jr, McPhee SJ, Papadakis MA [editors]: *Current Medical Diagnosis & Treatment 1996*. Appleton & Lange, 1996.)

## TABLE 8–16. RANSON'S CRITERIA FOR SEVERITY OF ACUTE PANCREATITIS.[1]

### Criteria present at diagnosis or admission

Age over 55 years
White blood cell count > 16,000/µL
Blood glucose > 200 mg/dL
Serum LDH > 350 IU/L (laboratory-specific)
AST (SGOT) > 250 IU/L (laboratory-specific)

### Criteria developing during first 48 hours

Hematocrit fall > 10%
BUN rise > 5 mg/dL
Serum calcium < 8 mg/dL
Arterial $P_{O_2}$ < 60 mm Hg
Base deficit > 4 meq/L
Estimated fluid sequestration > 6 L

### MORTALITY RATES CORRELATE WITH THE NUMBER OF CRITERIA PRESENT:

| Number of Criteria | Mortality |
| --- | --- |
| 0–2 | 1% |
| 3–4 | 16% |
| 5–6 | 40% |
| 7–8 | 100% |

[1]Modified from Way LW (editor): Current Surgical Diagnosis & Treatment, 10th ed. Appleton & Lange, 1994.
**LDH** = lactic dehydrogenase; **AST** = aspartate dehydrogenase; **BUN** = blood urea nitrogen.

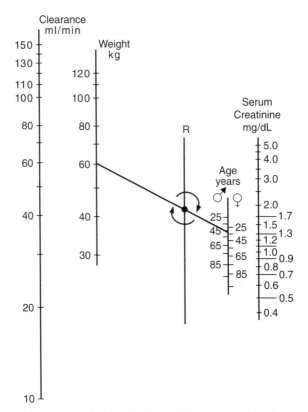

**Figure 8–22. RENAL FAILURE: ESTIMATED CREATININE CLEARANCE:** Siersback-Nielsen nomogram for estimation of creatinine clearance from serum creatinine.

1. Identify the axis point along the reference line **(R)** around which the relation between the patient's serum creatinine and creatinine clearance rotates. To do so, place a straightedge so as to connect the patient's age (in years, for male or female) with the patient's weight (in kilograms).
2. Put a dot along the reference line where the rule and line intersect.
3. Rotate the ruler to connect the patient's serum creatinine and this dot and determine where the ruler falls along the line estimating the patient's creatinine clearance.

*Note:* This nomogram is based on the assumption that an increase in weight represents an increase in lean body mass. Substantial error in the estimate occurs when a weight increase reflects obesity rather than increased lean body mass. In addition, the nomogram yields a much more accurate estimate in the presence of moderate to moderately severe renal impairment than in the presence of normal renal function. It should also not be relied upon in severe renal insufficiency (eg, serum creatinine > 5 mg/dL or creatinine clearance < 15 mL/min). (Modified, with permission, from Harvey AM et al [editors]: *The Principles and Practice of Medicine,* 22nd ed. Appleton & Lange, 1988.)

**TABLE 8–17. RENAL FAILURE: RENAL VERSUS PRERENAL AZOTEMIA.[1]**

|  | Renal | Prerenal |
|---|---|---|
| BUN (mg/dL) | > 20 | > 20 |
| Serum creatinine (mg/dL) | > 1.4 | > 1.4 |
| BUN/creatinine ratio | 10–20 | > 20 |
| Urine [Na$^+$] (meq/L) | > 40 | < 20 |
| $FE_{Na^+}$[2] | > 1% | < 1%, usually < 0.2% |
| Renal failure index[3] | > 1 | < 1 |
| Urine volume (mL/d) | Variable, often > 400 | < 400 |
| Urine osmolality (mosm/kg) | < 350 | > 500 |
| Urine specific gravity | 1.010–1.016 | > 1.040 |

[1]Modified, with permission, from Cogan MG: Fluid & Electrolytes: Physiology & Pathophysiology, Appleton & Lange, 1991; and from Tierney LM Jr, McPhee SJ, Papadakis MA (editors): Current Medical Diagnosis & Treatment 1996. Appleton & Lange, 1996.

[2] $$FE_{Na^+} = \frac{Urine\ Na^+ / Plasma\ Na^+}{Urine\ creatinine/Plasma\ creatinine} \times 100$$

[3] $$Renal\ failure\ index = \frac{Urine\ Na^+}{Urine\ creatinine/Plasma\ creatinine}$$

**TABLE 8–18. RENAL TUBULAR ACIDOSIS (RTA): LABORATORY DIAGNOSIS OF RENAL TUBULAR ACIDOSIS.[1]**

| Clinical Condition | Renal Defect | GFR | Serum [HCO3−] (meq/L) | Serum [K+] (meq/L) | Minimal Urine pH | Associated Disease States | Treatment |
|---|---|---|---|---|---|---|---|
| Normal | None | N | 24–28 | 3.5–5 | 4.8–5.2 | None | None |
| Proximal RTA (type II) | Proximal H+ secretion | N | 15–18 | ↓ | <5.5 | Drugs, Fanconi's syndrome, various genetic disorders, dysproteinemic states, secondary hyperparathyroidism, toxins (heavy metals), tubulointerstitial diseases, nephrotic syndrome, paroxysmal nocturnal hemoglobinuria. | NaHCO3 or KHCO3 (10–15 meq/kg/d), thiazides. |
| Classic distal RTA (type I) | Distal H+ secretion | N | 20–23 | ↓ | >5.5 | Various genetic disorders, autoimmune diseases, nephrocalcinosis, drugs, toxins, tubulointerstitial diseases, hepatic cirrhosis, empty sella syndrome. | NaHCO3 (1–3 meq/kg/d). |
| Buffer deficiency distal RTA (type III) | Distal NH3 delivery | ↓ | 15–18 | N | <5.5 | Chronic renal insufficiency, renal osteodystrophy, severe hypophosphatemia. | NaHCO3 (1–3 meq/kg/d). |
| Generalized distal RTA (type IV) | Distal Na+ reabsorption, K+ secretion, and H+ secretion | ↓ | 24–28 | ↑ | <5.5 | Primary mineralocorticoid deficiency (eg, Addison's disease), hyporeninemic hypoaldosteronism (diabetes mellitus, tubulointerstitial diseases, nephrosclerosis, drugs), salt-wasting mineralocorticoid-resistant hyperkalemia. | Fludrocortisone (0.1–0.5 mg/d), dietary K+ restriction, furosemide (40–160 mg/d), NaHCO3 (1–3 meq/kg/d). |

[1]Modified, with permission, from Cogan MG: Fluid & Electrolytes: Physiology & Pathophysiology. *Appleton & Lange*, 1991.
**GFR** = glomerular filtration rate.

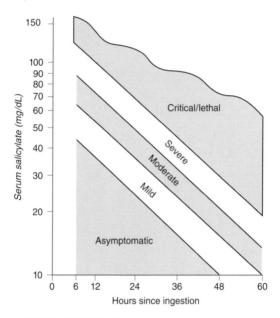

**Figure 8–23. SALICYLATE TOXICITY:** Nomogram for determining severity of salicylate intoxication. Absorption kinetics assume acute ingestion of non-enteric-coated aspirin preparation. (Modified and reproduced, with permission, from Done AK: Significance of measurements of salicylate in blood in cases of acute ingestion. Pediatrics 1960;26:800. Permission obtained also from Saunders CE, Ho MT [editors]: *Current Emergency Diagnosis & Treatment,* 4th ed. Appleton & Lange, 1992.)

**TABLE 8–19. SYNOVIAL FLUID: CLASSIFICATION OF SYNOVIAL (JOINT) FLUID.[1]**

| Type of Joint Fluid | Volume (mL) | Viscosity | Appearance | WBC (per µL) | PMNs | Gram's Stain & Culture | Glucose | Comments |
|---|---|---|---|---|---|---|---|---|
| Normal | < 3.5 | High | Clear, light yellow | < 200 | < 25% | Neg | Equal to serum | Protein 2–3.5 g/dL. |
| Non-inflammatory (Class I) | Often > 3.5 | High | Clear, light yellow | 200–2000 | < 25% | Neg | Equal to serum | Degenerative joint disease, trauma, avascular necrosis, osteochondritis dissecans; osteochondromatosis, neuropathic arthropathy, subsiding or early inflammation, hypertrophic osteoarthropathy, pigmented villonodular synovitis. |
| Inflammatory (Class II) | Often > 3.5 | Low | Cloudy to opaque, dark yellow | 3000–100,000 | ≥ 50% | Neg | > 25, but lower than serum | Protein > 3 g/dL. Rheumatoid arthritis, acute crystal-induced synovitis (gout, pseudogout), Reiter's syndrome, ankylosing spondylitis, psoriatic arthritis, sarcoidosis, arthritis accompanying ulcerative colitis and Crohn's, rheumatic fever, SLE, scleroderma; tuberculous, viral, or mycotic infections. Crystals diagnostic of gout or pseudogout: gout (urate) crystals show negative birefringence, pseudogout (calcium pyrophosphate) show positive birefringence when red compensator filter is used with polarized light microscopy. Phagocytic inclusions in PMNs suggest rheumatoid arthritis (RA cells). Phagocytosis of leukocytes by macrophages seen in Reiter's syndrome. |

**TABLE 8–19 (CONTINUED).**

| Type of Joint Fluid | Volume (mL) | Viscosity | Appearance | WBC (per μL) | PMNs | Gram's Stain & Culture | Glucose | Comments |
|---|---|---|---|---|---|---|---|---|
| Purulent (Class III) | Often > 3.5 | Low | Cloudy to opaque, dark yellow to green | Usually > 40,000, often greater than 100,000 | ≥ 75% | Usually positive | < 25, much lower than serum | Pyogenic bacterial infection (eg, *N gonorrhoeae*, *S aureus*). Bacteria on culture or Gram's-stained smear. Commonest exception: gonococci seen in only about 25% of cases. WBC count and % PMN lower with infections caused by organisms of low virulence or if antibiotic therapy already started. |
| Hemorrhagic (Class IV) | Often > 3.5 | Variable | Cloudy, pink to red | Usually > 2000 | 30% | Neg | Equal to serum | Trauma with or without fracture, hemophilia or other hemorrhagic diathesis, neuropathic arthropathy, pigmented villonodular synovitis, synovioma, hemangioma and other benign neoplasms. Many RBCs found also. Fat globules strongly suggest intra-articular fracture. |

[1]Modified, with permission, from Rodnan GP: Primer on the rheumatic diseases: Appendix III. JAMA 1973;224(5):802–803. Copyright © 1973 by American Medical Association.

**TABLE 8–20. SYPHILIS: LABORATORY DIAGNOSIS IN UNTREATED PATIENTS.[1]**

| Stage | Onset After Exposure | Persistence | Clinical Findings | Sensitivity of VDRL or RPR[2] (%) | Sensitivity of FTA - ABS[3] (%) | Sensitivity of MHA - TP[4] (%) |
|---|---|---|---|---|---|---|
| Primary | 21 days (range 10–90) | 2–12 wk | Chancre | 72 | 91 | 50–60 |
| Secondary | 6 wk–6 mo | 1–3 mo | Rash, condylomata lata, mucous patches, fever, lymphadenopathy, patchy alopecia | 100 | 100 | 100 |
| Early latent | <1 yr | Up to 1 yr | Relapses of secondary syphilis | 73 | 97 | 98 |
| Late latent | >1 yr | Lifelong unless tertiary syphilis appears | Clinically silent | 73 | 97 | 98 |
| Tertiary | 1 yr until death | Until death | Dementia, tabes dorsalis, aortitis, aortic aneurysm, gummas | 77 | 99 | 98 |

[1]Modified, with permission, from Harvey AM et al (editors): The Principles and Practice of Medicine, 22nd ed. Appleton & Lange, 1988.
[2]VDRL is a slide flocculation test for nonspecific (anticardiolipin) antibodies, used for screening, quantitation of titer, and monitoring response to treatment; RPR is an agglutination test for nonspecific antibodies, used primarily for screening.
[3]FTA - ABS is an immunofluorescence test for treponemal antibodies utilizing serum absorbed for nonpathogenic treponemes, used for confirmation of infection, not routine screening.
[4]MHA - TP is a microhemagglutination test similar to the FTA - ABS, but one which can be quantitated and automated.
**VDRL** = Venereal Disease Research Laboratories test; **RPR** = rapid plasma reagin test; **FTA-ABS** = fluorescent treponemal antibody absorption test; **MHA-TP** = microhemagglutination assay for T pallidum.

**TABLE 8–21. ALPHA-THALASSEMIA SYNDROMES.[1,2]**

| Syndrome | Alpha Globin Genes | Hematocrit | MCV (fL) |
|---|---|---|---|
| Normal | 4 | N | N |
| Silent carrier | 3 | N | N |
| Thalassemia minor | 2 | 32–40% | 60–75 |
| Hemoglobin H disease | 1 | 22–32% | 60–75 |
| Hydrops fetalis | 0 | Fetal death occurs in utero | |

[1]Modified, with permission, from Tierney LM Jr, McPhee SJ, Papadakis MA (editors): Current Medical Diagnosis & Treatment 1996. Appleton & Lange, 1996.
[2]Alpha thalassemias are due primarily to deletion in the alpha globin gene on chromosome 16.

**TABLE 8–22. BETA-THALASSEMIA SYNDROMES: FINDINGS ON HEMOGLOBIN ELECTROPHORESIS.[1,2]**

| Syndrome | Beta Globin Genes | Hb A[3] | Hb A$_2$[4] | Hb F[5] |
|---|---|---|---|---|
| Normal | Homozygous beta | 97–99% | 1–3% | < 1% |
| Thalassemia minor | Heterozygous beta$^0$ [6] | 80–95% | 4–8% | 1–5% |
| | Heterozygous beta$^+$ [7] | 80–95% | 4–8% | 1–5% |
| Thalassemia intermedia | Homozygous beta$^+$ (mild) | 0–30% | 0–10% | 6–100% |
| Thalassemia major | Homozygous beta$^0$ | 0 | 4–10% | 90–96% |
| | Homozygous beta$^+$ | | 4–10% | |

[1]Modified, with permission, from Tierney LM Jr, McPhee SJ, Papadakis MA (editors): Current Medical Diagnosis & Treatment 1996. Appleton & Lange, 1996.
[2]Beta thalassemias are usually caused by point mutations in the beta globin gene on chromosome 11 that result in premature chain terminations or defective RNA transcription, leading to reduced or absent beta globin chain synthesis.
[3]Hb A is composed of two alpha chains and two beta chains: $\alpha_2\beta_2$.
[4]Hb A$_2$ is composed of two alpha chains and two delta chains: $\alpha_2\delta_2$.
[5]Hb F is composed of two alpha chains and two gamma chains: $\alpha_2\gamma_2$.
[6]Beta$^0$ refers to defects that result in absent globin chain synthesis.
[7]Beta$^+$ refers to defects that cause reduced globin chain synthesis.

**TABLE 8-23. THYROID FUNCTION TESTS.[1]**

| | Total $T_4$ (µg/dL) | Free $T_4$ Index (ng/dL) | Total $T_3$ (ng/dL) | Sensitive Serum TSH (RIA) (µU/mL) | RAI ($^{123}$I) Uptake (at 24 hours) | Comments & Treatment |
|---|---|---|---|---|---|---|
| Normal[2] | 5.0–12 | Varies with method | 95–190 | 0.3–5 | 10–30% | |
| Hyperthyroidism | ↑ | ↑ | ↑ | ↓ | ↑ | In TRH stimulation test, TSH shows no response. Thyroid scan shows increased diffuse activity (Graves' disease) vs "hot" areas (hyperfunctioning nodules). Antithyroglobulin and antimicrosomal antibodies and thyroid-stimulating immunoglobulin elevated in Graves' disease. |
| Hypothyroidism | ↓ | ↓ | | Usually ↑ (primary[3] hypothyroidism); rarely ↓ (secondary[4] hypothyroidism) | N or ↓ | TRH stimulation test shows exaggerated response in primary hypothyroidism. In secondary hypothyroidism, TRH test helps to differentiate pituitary from hypothalamic disorders. In pituitary lesions, TSH fails to rise after TRH; in hypothalamic lesions, TSH rises but response is delayed. Antithyroglobulin and antimicrosomal antibodies elevated in Hashimoto's thyroiditis. |
| **Hypothyroidism on replacement** | | | | | | |
| $T_4$ replacement | N | N | > | N or ↓ | ↓ | TSH ↓ with 0.1–0.2 mg $T_4$ qd |
| $T_3$ replacement | ↓ | ↓ | > | N or ↓ | ↓ | TSH ↓ with 50 µg $T_3$ qd |

**TABLE 8–23 (CONTINUED).**

| | Total T$_4$ (μg/dL) | Free T$_4$ Index (ng/dL) | Total T$_3$ (ng/dL) | Sensitive Serum TSH (RIA) (μU/mL) | RAI ($^{123}$I) Uptake (at 24 hours) | Comments & Treatment |
|---|---|---|---|---|---|---|
| Euthyroid following injection of radiographic contrast dye | N | N or ↑ | N | N | ↓ | Effects may persist for 2 weeks or longer. |
| **Pregnancy** | | | | | | |
| Hyperthyroid | ↑ | ↑ | ↑ | ↓ | | Effects may persist for 6–10 weeks postpartum. RAI uptake contraindicated in pregnancy. |
| Euthyroid | ↑ | N | ↑ | N | | |
| Hypothyroid | N or ↓ | ↓ | | ↑ | | |
| Oral contraceptives, estrogens, methadone, heroin | ↑ | N | ↑ | N | N | Increased serum thyroid-binding globulin. |
| Glucocorticoids, androgens, phenytoin, L-asparaginase, salicylates (high dose) | ↓ | N | N or ↓ | N | N | Decreased serum thyroid-binding globulin. |
| Nephrotic syndrome | ↓ | N | N or ↓ | N | N | Loss of thyroid-binding globulin accounts for serum T$_4$ decrease. |
| Iodine deficiency | N | N | N | N | ↑ | Extremely rare in US. |
| Iodine ingestion | N | N | N | N | ↓ | Excess iodine may cause hypothyroidism or hyperthyroidism in susceptible individuals. |

[1] Modified, with permission, from Leeper RD: Current Concepts 1972;1:1. Courtesy of the Upjohn Co, Kalamazoo, MI.
[2] Normal values vary with laboratory.
[3] Thyroid (end-organ) failure.
[4] Pituitary or hypothalamic lesions.
**V** = variable.

**THYROID NODULE**

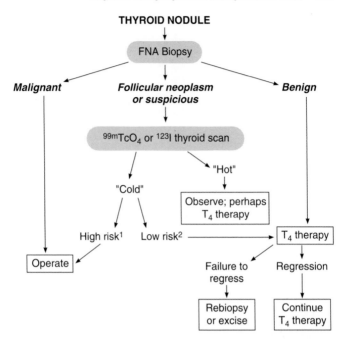

$^1$ High risk = child, young adult, male;  solitary, firm nodule;  family history of
thyroid cancer;  previous neck irradiation;  recent growth of nodule;  hoarse-
ness, dysphagia, obstruction;  vocal cord paralysis, lymphadenopathy.
$^2$ Low risk = older, female;  soft nodule;  multinodular goiter;  family history of
benign goiter;  residence in endemic goiter area.

**Figure 8–24. THYROID NODULE:** Laboratory evaluation of a thyroid nodule. **FNA** = fine-nee-
dle aspiration; **$T_4$** = thyroxine. (Modified, with permission, from Greenspan FS, Baxter JD [ed-
itors]: *Basic and Clinical Endocrinology,* 4th ed. Appleton & Lange, 1994.)

TABLE 8–24. URINE COMPOSITION: IN COMMON DISEASE STATES.[1]

| Disease | Daily Volume | Specific Gravity | Protein[2] (mg/dL) | Esterase | Nitrite | RBC | WBC | Casts | Other Microscopic Findings |
|---|---|---|---|---|---|---|---|---|---|
| Normal | 600–2500 mL | 1.003–1.030 | 0–trace (0–30) | Neg | Neg | 0 or Occ | 0 or Occ | 0 or Occ | Hyaline casts |
| Fever | ↓ | ↑ | Trace or 1+ (<30) | Neg | Neg | 0 | Occ | 0 or Occ | Hyaline casts, tubular cells |
| Congestive heart failure | ↓ | ↑ (varies) | 1–2+ (30–100) | Neg | Neg | None or 1+ | 0 | 1+ | Hyaline and granular casts |
| Eclampsia | ↓ | ↑ | 3–4+ (30–2000) | Neg | Neg | None or 1+ | 0 | 3–4+ | Hyaline casts |
| Diabetic coma | ↑ or ↓ | ↑ | 1+ (30) | Neg | Neg | 0 | 0 | 0 or 1+ | Hyaline casts |
| Acute glomerulonephritis | ↓ | ↑ | 2–4+ (100–2000) | Pos | Neg | 1–4+ | 1–4+ | 2–4+ | Blood; RBC, cellular, granular, and hyaline casts; renal tubular epithelium |
| Nephrotic syndrome | N or ↓ | N or ↑ | 4+ (>2000) | Neg | Neg | 1–2+ | 0 | 4+ | Granular, waxy, hyaline, and fatty casts; fatty tubular cells |
| Chronic renal failure | ↑ or ↓ | Low; invariable | 1–2+ (30–100) | Neg | Neg | Occ or 1+ | 0 | 1–3+ | Granular, hyaline, fatty, and broad casts |
| Collagen-vascular disease | N, ↑ or ↓ | N or ↓ | 1–4+ (30–2000) | Neg | Neg | 1–4+ | 0 or Occ | 1–4+ | Blood, cellular, granular, hyaline, waxy, fatty, and broad casts; fatty tubular cells; telescoped sediment |
| Pyelonephritis | N or ↓ | N or ↓ | 1–2+ (30–100) | Pos | Pos | 0 or 1+ | 4+ | 0 or 1+ | WBC casts and hyaline casts; many pus cells; bacteria |
| Hypertension | N of ↑ | N or ↓ | None or 1+ (<30) | Neg | Neg | 0 or Occ | 0 or Occ | 0 or 1+ | Hyaline and granular casts |

[1]Modified, with permission, from Krupp MA et al (editors): Physician's Handbook, 21st ed. Lange, 1985.
[2]Protein concentration in mg/dL is listed in parentheses.

**TABLE 8-25. VAGINAL DISCHARGE: LABORATORY EVALUATION.[1]**

| Diagnosis | pH | Odor With KOH (Positive "Whiff" Test) | Epithelial Cells | WBCs | Organisms | KOH Prep | Gram Stain | Comments |
|---|---|---|---|---|---|---|---|---|
| Normal | < 4.5 | No | N | Occ | Variable, large rods not adherent to epithelial cells | Neg | Gram-positive rods | |
| Trichomonas vaginalis vaginitis | > 4.5 | Yes | N | ↑ | Motile, flagellated organisms | Neg | Flagellated organisms | |
| Bacterial vaginosis (Gardnerella vaginalis) | > 4.5 | Yes | Clue cells[2] | Occ | Coccobacilli adherent to epithelial cells | Neg | Gram-negative coccobacilli | |
| Candida albicans vaginitis | < 4.5 | No | N | Occ slightly increased | Budding yeast or hyphae | Budding yeast or hyphae | Budding yeast or hyphae | Usually white "cottage cheese" curd |
| Mucopurulent cervicitis (N gonorrhoeae) | Variable, usually > 4.5 | No | N | ↑ | Variable | Neg | Intracellular gram-negative diplococci | |

[1]Modified, with permission, from Kelly KG: Tests on vaginal discharge. In: Walker HK et al (editors): Clinical Methods: The History, Physical and Laboratory Examinations, 3rd ed. Butterworths, 1990.

[2]Epithelial cells covered with bacteria to the extent that cells borders are obscured.

TABLE 8–26.  VALVULAR HEART DISEASE: DIAGNOSTIC EVALUATION OF CARDIAC VALVULAR DISEASE.[1]

| Diagnosis | Chest X-ray | ECG | Echocardiography | Comments |
|---|---|---|---|---|
| MITRAL STENOSIS (MS) Rheumatic disease | Straight left heart border. Large LA sharply indenting esophagus. Elevation of left main bronchus. Calcification occ seen in MV. | Broad negative phase of diphasic P in $V_1$. Tall peaked P waves, right axis deviation, or RVH appear if pulmonary hypertension is present. | **M-Mode:** Thickened, immobile MV with anterior and posterior leaflets moving together. Slow early diastolic filling slope. LA enlargement. Normal to small LV. **2D:** Maximum diastolic orifice size reduced. Reduced subvalvular apparatus. Foreshortened, variable thickening of other valves. **Doppler:** Prolonged pressure half-time across MV. Indirect evidence of pulmonary hypertension. | "Critical" MS is usually defined as a valve area $< 1.0$ cm$^2$. Balloon valvuloplasty has high initial success rates and higher patency rates than for AS. Open commissurotomy can be effective. Valve replacement is indicated when severe regurgitation is present. Catheterization can confirm echo results. |
| MITRAL REGURGITATION (MR) Myxomatous degeneration (MV prolapse) Infective endocarditis Subvalvular dysfunction Rheumatic disease | Enlarged LV and LA. | Left axis deviation or frank LVH. P waves broad, tall, or notched, with broad negative phase in $V_1$. | **M-Mode and 2D:** Thickened MV in rheumatic disease. MV prolapse; flail leaflet or vegetations may be seen. Enlarged LV. **Doppler:** Regurgitant flow mapped into LA. Indirect evidence of pulmonary hypertension. | In nonrheumatic MR, valvuloplasty without valve replacement is increasingly successful. Acute MR (endocarditis, ruptured chordae) requires emergent valve replacement. Catheterization is the best assessment of regurgitation. |
| AORTIC STENOSIS (AS) Calcific (especially in congenitally bicuspid valve) Rheumatic disease | Concentric LVH. Prominent ascending aorta, small knob. Calcified valve common. | LVH. | **M-Mode:** Dense persistent echoes of the AoV with poor leaflet excursion. LVH with preserved contractile function. **2D:** Poststenotic dilatation of the aorta with restricted opening of the leaflets. Bicuspid AoV in about 30%. **Doppler:** Increased transvalvular flow velocity, yielding calculated gradient. | "Critical" AS is usually defined as a valve area $< 0.7$ cm$^2$ or a peak systolic gradient of $> 50$ mm Hg. Catheterization is definitive diagnostic test. Prognosis without surgery is less than 50% survival at 3 yr when CHF, syncope, or angina occur. Balloon valvuloplasty has a high restenosis rate. |

| Condition / Causes | Chest X-ray | ECG | Echocardiography | Comments |
|---|---|---|---|---|
| **AORTIC REGURGITA-TION (AR)**<br>Bicuspid valves<br>Infective endocarditis<br>Hypertension<br>Rheumatic disease<br>Aorta/aortic root disease | Moderate to severe LV enlargement. Prominent aortic knob. | LVH. | **M-Mode:** Diastolic vibrations of the anterior leaflet of the MV and septum. Early closure of the valve when severe. Dilated LV with normal or decreased contractility.<br>**2D:** May show vegetations in endocarditis, bicuspid valve, or root dilatation.<br>**Doppler:** Demonstrates regurgitation. Estimates severity. | Aortography at catheterization can demonstrate AR. Acute incompetence leads to LV failure and requires AoV replacement. |
| **TRICUSPID STENOSIS (TS)**<br>Rheumatic disease | Enlarged RA only. | Tall, peaked P waves. Normal axis. | **M-Mode and 2D:** TV thickening. Decreased early diastolic filling slope of the TV. MV also usually abnormal.<br>**Doppler:** Prolonged pressure half-time across TV. | Right heart catheterization is diagnostic. Valvulotomy may lead to success, but TV replacement is usually needed. |
| **TRICUSPID REGURGI-TATION (TR)**<br>RV overload (pulmonary hypertension)<br>Inferior infarction<br>Infective endocarditis | Enlarged RA and RV. | Right axis deviation usual. | **M-Mode and 2D:** Enlarged RV. MV often abnormal and may prolapse.<br>**Doppler:** Regurgitant flow mapped into RA and venae cavae. RV systolic pressure estimated. | RA and jugular pressure tracings show a prominent V wave and rapid Y descent. Replacement of TV is rarely done. Valvuloplasty is often preferred. |

[1]Modified, with permission, from Tierney LM Jr, McPhee SJ, Papadakis MA (editors): Current Medical Diagnosis & Treatment 1996. Appleton & Lange, 1996.
**RA** = right atrium; **RV** = right ventricle; **LA** = left atrium; **LV** = left ventricle; **AoV** = aortic valve; **MV** = mitral valve; **TV** = tricuspid valve; **LVH** = left ventricular hypertrophy; **RVH** = right ventricular hypertrophy; **CHF** = congestive heart failure.

**TABLE 8–27. WHITE BLOOD CELLS: WHITE BLOOD CELL COUNT AND DIFFERENTIAL.** [1]

| Cells | Range ($10^3/\mu L$) | Increased in | Decreased in |
|---|---|---|---|
| WBC count (total) | 3.4–10.0 | Infection, hematologic malignancy. | Decreased production (aplastic anemia, folate or $B_{12}$ deficiency, drugs [eg, ethanol, chloramphenicol]); decreased survival (sepsis, hypersplenism, drugs). |
| Neutrophils | 1.8–6.8 | Infection (bacterial or early viral), acute stress, acute and chronic inflammation, tumors, drugs, diabetic ketoacidosis, leukemia (rare). | Aplastic anemia, drug-induced neutropenia (eg, chloramphenicol, phenothiazines, antithyroid drugs, sulfonamide), folate or $B_{12}$ deficiency, Chédiak-Higashi syndrome, malignant lymphoproliferative disease, physiologic (in children up to age 4 years). |
| Lymphocytes | 0.9–2.9 | Viral infection (especially infectious mononucleosis, pertussis), thyrotoxicosis, adrenal insufficiency, ALL and CLL, chronic infection, drug and allergic reactions, autoimmune diseases. | Immune deficiency syndromes. |
| Monocytes | 0.1–0.6 | Inflammation, infection, malignancy, tuberculosis, myeloproliferative disorders. | Depleted in overwhelming bacterial infection. |
| Eosinophils | 0–0.4 | Allergic states, drug sensitivity reactions, skin disorders, tissue invasion by parasites, polyarteritis nodosa, hypersensitivity response to malignancy (eg, Hodgkin's disease), pulmonary infiltrative disease, disseminated eosinophilic hypersensitivity disease. | Acute and chronic inflammation, stress, drugs (corticosteroids). |
| Basophils | 0–0.1 | Hypersensitivity reactions, drugs, myeloproliferative disorders (eg, CML), myelofibrosis. | |

[1] In the automated differential, 10,000 WBCs are classified on the basis of size and peroxidase staining as neutrophils, monocytes, or eosinophils (peroxidase-positive) and as lymphocytes or large unstained cells (LUC), which are peroxidase-negative. LUCs larger than normal lymphocytes may be atypical lymphocyte or peroxidase-negative blasts. Basophils are identified using two-angle light scattering, based on their singular resistance to lysis.
The reproducibility of 100-cell manual differentials is notoriously poor. Review of blood smears is useful to visually identify rare abnormal cells, blasts, nucleated RBCs, morphologic abnormalities (eg, hypersegmentation, toxic granulation, sickle cells, target cells, spherocytes, basophilic stippling) and to look for rouleaux (stacking of red cells due to increased globulins) and clumped platelets.
WBC differential is unlikely to be abnormal with a normal WBC count or to be changed if the total WBC count is unchanged.

# Index

NOTE: A *t* following a page number indicates tabular material and an *i* following a page number indicates an illustration. Drugs are listed under their generic names. When a drug trade name is listed, the reader is referred to the generic name.

# Recently Published Handbooks and Manuals by Appleton & Lange

**Ambulatory Medicine, 2/e**
*The Primary Care of Families*
Mark B. Mengel, MD, MPH, and L. Peter Schwiebert, MD, 1996, 672 pages (approx.), illus., paperback, ISBN 0-8385-1466-9, A1466-0

**Clinician's Pocket Reference, 8/e**
Leonard G. Gomella, MD, January 1997, 680 pp. (approx.), illus., spiral, ISBN 0-8385-1476-6, A1476-9

**Essentials of Diagnosis**
*A Pocket Guide*
Lawrence M. Tierney, Jr., MD, and Clinton E. Thompson, MD 1996, 600 pp. (approx.), paperback, ISBN 0-8385-3605-0, A3605-1

**Geriatric Medicine**
Edmund T. Lonergan, MD, 1996, 640 pp. (approx.), illus., spiral, ISBN 0-8385-1094-9, A1094-0

**Handbook of Pediatrics, 18/e**
Gerald B. Merenstein, MD, FAAP, David W. Kaplan, MD, MPH, and Adam A. Rosenberg, MD, January 1997, 1071 pp. (approx.), illus., paperback, ISBN 0-8385-3625-5, A3625-9

**HIV Manual for Health Care Professionals**
Richard D. Muma, PA-C, Barbara Ann Lyons, MA, PA-C, Richard B. Pollard, MD, and Michael J. Borucki, MD 1994, 299 pp., illus., spiral, ISBN 0-8385-0170-2, A0170-9

**HIV/AIDS Primary Care Handbook, 2/e**
Cynthia G. Carmichael, MD, J. Kevin Carmichael, MD, and Margaret A. Fischl, MD, 1996, 250 pp. (approx.), paperback, ISBN 0-8385-3777-4, A3777-8

**Internal Medicine On Call, 2/e**
Steven A. Haist, MD, John B. Robbins, MD, and Leonard Gomella, MD, 1996, 550 pages (approx.), illus., paperback, ISBN 0-8385-4056-2, A4056-6

**Neonatology, 3/e**
*Management, Procedures, On-Call Problems, Diseases and Drugs*
Tricia Lacy Gomella, MD, M. Douglas, Cunningham, MD, Fabien G. Eyal, MD, and Karin E. Zenk, PharmD, FASHP, 1995, 620 pp., illus., spiral, ISBN 0-8385-1331-X, A1331-6

**Pocket Guide to Commonly Prescribed Drugs, 2/e**
Glenn N. Levine, MD 1996, 464 pp. (approx.), paperback, ISBN 0-8385-8099-8, A8099-2

**Practical Gynecology**
Allan J. Jacobs, MD, and Michael J. Gast, MD, PhD, 1994, 538 pp., illus., spiral, ISBN 0-8385-1336-0, A1336-5

**Practical Oncology**
Robert B. Cameron 1994, 720 pp., spiral ISBN 0-8385-1326-3, A1326-6

**Poisoning & Drug Overdose, 2/e**
Kent R. Olson, MD, FACEP, 1994, 569 pp., illus., spiral, ISBN 0-8385-1108-2, A1108-8

**Surgery on Call, 2/e**
Leonard G. Gomella, MD and Alan T. Lefor, MD, 1995, 500 pp., illus., paperback, ISBN 0-8385-8746-1, A8746-8

 **To order or for more information, visit your local health science bookstore or call Appleton & Lange toll free 1-800-423-1359.**